Decoding the Digital SAT

Curvebreakers

Editor-in-Chief
Mark Hellman

Contributing Editors
Mary Kaufman, Nicholas LaPoma, Sterling Rosado, Ryan Russo

Decoding the Digital SAT

320 Old Country Road
Suite 102
Garden City, NY 11530
curvebreakerstestprep.com

ISBN:

Decoding the Digital SAT

TABLE OF CONTENTS

INTRODUCTION

Welcome to Curvebreakers' first edition of our revolutionary workbook for the new Digital SAT®!

We are thrilled to present this comprehensive guide, with hundreds of practice questions and answer explanations. It is a product of master tutors who have worked for some of the largest test preparation companies in the country. With years of experience and research, they have identified the most common mistakes students make on the SAT® and incorporated effective test-taking strategies and techniques that cannot be found anywhere else. Designed to be your ultimate companion, this book breaks down each question type into specific, concise, easy-to-follow steps, ensuring a thorough understanding of underlying concepts and the development of a systematic strategy for each question category.

The SAT® can be a stressful and overwhelming experience for many students. At Curvebreakers, we believe that every student has the potential to succeed on the SAT®, regardless of their background. With practice, our tips and techniques will help students manage their time, stay focused, and reduce test anxiety. Our goal is to provide students with confidence and preparation on test day, exceeding their expectations.

FOREWORD

What this book is and what this book isn't

<u>What this book isn't</u>

If you're looking for traditional approaches to understand and answer SAT® questions, this book isn't for you. You can find that in the explanations that the College Board provides within the answers to their practice questions. Of course, we do encourage you to do the free practice tests that the College Board makes available and read through their answers and explanations. If you understand them and can quickly apply them, that's great – go ahead and use them. However, there will almost certainly be several questions with hard-to-understand explanations. Or, even if you do understand the explanations, they may just take too long to apply. That's where we come in.

<u>What this book is</u>

The purpose of this book is to get you to the correct answer in the least amount of time. Very often, there are several approaches to answering a Reading or Writing question, and multiple ways of doing a math problem. We'll show you the strategies that most students can understand and apply quickly and successfully. It doesn't mean you have to answer using the strategies in this book. But if you don't understand a question, or a problem is taking too long to answer, these strategies can be extremely helpful. Some of them may seem weird at first, but they have been proven to work. If you practice them, we can guarantee from our years of experience in this business, you will get questions right that you would not have gotten right before reading this book.

THE STRUCTURE OF THIS BOOK

<u>This book was designed to be repetitive.</u>

Each chapter represents a separate question category and, with preparation and practice, the number of categories is quite manageable. For each category, we give specific, straightforward, step-by-step instructions and these steps are followed consistently over and over again. Often, just identifying the question category and applying the steps is half the battle to solving the question. The other half will rely on how you apply the steps. Each chapter contains a short lesson and overview, followed by examples which apply the strategies, followed by several practice questions. The practice questions will follow a loose order of difficulty: that is, the later ones will tend to be harder than the earlier ones. Repetition and practice followed by short, clear, and easy-to-understand answer explanations is the pathway to realizing your maximum score.

Some of the questions may seem quite difficult. But, oftentimes, you can eliminate one or two bad answers through Process of Elimination (POE), dramatically increasing your chance of getting to the correct answer. We'll go through how to do this in the answer explanations.

ONLINE COMPANION COURSE

DIGITAL SAT VIDEO COURSE

NICK THE TUTOR

Master the entire exam with video lessons from Nick The Tutor

New Strategies for New Digital SAT Questions

Learn how to use the in-app tools and desmos calculator

The **Digital SAT Video Course by Nick The Tutor** is the online companion course to Curvebreakers' course book, *Decoding the Digital SAT*. Follow along with Nick LaPoma, the owner and President of Curvebreakers, as he provides a full-length video course to master the entire SAT exam.

GAIN ACCESS TO THE VIDEO COURSE

nickthetutor.teachable.com

Save 20% with promo code **DECODINGSAT**

FOLLOW

youtube.com/nickthetutor

@nickthetutor

@nickthetutor

CHAPTER 1: SAT® STRUCTURE AND GENERAL STRATEGIES

Format	Reading and Writing Section	Math Section
Number of Questions	1st module: 25 questions plus 2 experimental questions; 2nd module: 25 questions plus 2 experimental questions	1st module: 20 questions plus 2 experimental questions; 2nd module: 20 questions plus 2 experimental questions
Time per stage	1st module: 32 minutes 2nd module: 32 minutes	1st module: 35 minutes 2nd module: 35 minutes
Total number of questions	54 Questions	44 Questions
Total time allotted	64 minutes	70 minutes
Average time per question	1 minute 11 seconds	1 minute 35 seconds
Question type(s) used	Four-option multiple-choice	Four-option multiple choice (≈75%); Student-Produced Response (≈25%)
Score Range	200 - 800	200 - 800

A NOTE ABOUT ADAPTIVE TESTING

Your performance on the first modules for Math and Reading/Writing determines whether you advance to the easier or harder adaptive sections. You will need to answer roughly 2/3 of the items correctly in Module 1 to advance to the more rigorous sections. If you are routed to the easier adaptive module, your final score will be capped at about 650 or so per section.

What does this mean for you? If your target score is in the 1000 - 1300 range, don't spend too much time working hard questions. For the first modules, maximize your time by making sure you get the easy questions right and as many medium questions as you can. Flag the hard questions and come back to them if you have time. If you don't have time, guess – but never leave a question blank (since you have a 25 percent chance of getting each multiple choice question right by guessing). You probably won't get the harder Module 2 but that's OK. Use the same strategy for Module 2 and you can still achieve your target score. If your target score is over 1300, you will need to move quicker to spend more time on the harder questions. But, of course, you don't want to rush too much through the easy and medium questions, to avoid careless mistakes.

SCORING

Total Score	SAT® User
1600	99+
1570	99+
1540	99
1510	99
1480	98
1450	96
1420	95
1390	93
1360	91
1330	89
1300	86
1270	83
1240	80
1210	76
1180	72
1150	67
1120	62
1090	57
1060	51
1030	46
1000	40
970	35
940	30
910	25
880	20
850	16
820	13
790	9
760	6
730	4

R/W Score	SAT® User
800	99+
780	99+
760	99
740	98
720	96
700	94
680	91
660	88
640	83
620	78
600	73
580	66
560	60
540	53
520	46
500	39
480	32
460	26
440	20
420	14
400	10
380	6
360	3
340	2
320	1

Math Score	SAT® User
800	99+
780	98
760	97
740	95
720	94
700	92
680	89
660	86
640	83
620	79
600	75
580	69
560	64
540	57
520	49
500	41
480	35
460	29
440	23
420	18
400	13
380	9
360	6
340	3
320	2

More About Scoring

- The AVERAGE SAT® score is about 1050: 530 Math and 520 Reading/Writing
- Most colleges will "superscore" your results, i.e. they will use only your highest Math and English scores from all your tests. Check with individual colleges to see their respective policies

GENERAL SAT® STRATEGIES

1. **NEVER leave a question blank.** There is no penalty for guessing.

2. **Complete easy questions first.** Spend your time wisely on the questions likely to award you points. Pick and choose which questions you can complete when time is running out.

3. **Abide by a 5-second rule (or something close to it)** If after 5 or so seconds you have no idea what to do, skip that question and return to it if time allows.

4. **Use the Digital Tools.**

    - Annotation feature allows you to highlight text and add your own notes.

    - In the Math section, you'll have access to a formula sheet.

    - Answer-Elimination feature will strike out text with a bold line and gray out the text just enough to remain legible without being a distraction.

    - The Countdown Clock is centrally placed and easy to hide. You'll get an alert when there are 5 minutes left.

    - The Mark for Review feature can help you navigate each section and quickly toggle between flagged or omitted items. The visual presentation will help eliminate carelessness and unintentionally omitted items.

    - Desmos calculator: While some students feel more comfortable with their own familiar handheld calculator, the Desmos option is right there on the screen,which can be extremely convenient for problem solving.

5. **Read every answer choice.** The exam will often include "trap" answers as distractors. Make sure you have picked the best possible answer.

6. **Use Process of Elimination (POE).** Strike out answers that are too big, too small, silly or absurd, too extreme. Being able to pinpoint these issues as grounds for elimination is crucial. You may find that eliminating three bad answer choices is how you arrive at the correct answer for a fair amount of questions.

7. **Categorize questions by topic.** Knowing the question topic helps to determine how best to tackle the problem.

8. **Use your "Letter of the Day" (A, B, C, or D) if you have no idea how to answer a question.** Using the same letter for all your guesses rather than a random letter slightly improves your odds of getting the question right.

9. **Plan to take the test more than once.** Most students will typically sit for 2 - 3 official exams (once or twice as a Junior and once as a Senior in the fall). Most schools will superscore the results, meaning they consider only the highest section scores across all test dates. A common misconception is that colleges frown upon students taking the exam several times. It is only a red flag if the results are wildly inconsistent, which can send a message that the student did not take the exam seriously.

DIGITAL TESTING TOOLS

With the new digital format of the SAT®, there are a number of helpful tools that didn't exist with the paper and pencil test.

Annotate Button: Highlight an important block of text with your cursor, then click on the button in the top right corner labeled "Annotate" topped with a picture of a highlighter. Once you do this the text will be highlighted in yellow and a box will appear at the bottom. In this box you can take notes about this chunk of text just as you would in the margin of a paper text booklet. Now every time you hover over your highlighted text, your notes will appear.

~~ABC~~ Button: Above the answer choices, you will notice a button labeled ~~ABC~~. Click this button and you will see buttons appear next to each answer choice that look like this ~~(A)~~. Click on those to cross out obvious wrong answer choices.

Question Button: At the bottom of the page you will notice a button that says Question # of #. Having trouble with a question and want to skip it for now and come back? Click this button to move onto the next question without having to select an answer.

Calculator Button: Click on the Calculator Button with the picture of a calculator and you will get, you guessed it, a calculator. Use this to do basic math all the way up through graphing.

X^2 Reference Button: Click this button to bring up a reference sheet that provides important mathematical formulas and diagrams.

⁝More Button: Clicking on the button labeled "More" will bring up a menu of useful options.

- **Shortcuts** provides a list of keyboard shortcuts that can be performed to save time.
- **Assistive Technology** details some of the technologies used by the platform to help students with additional learning needs.

CHAPTER 2: READING AND WRITING INTRODUCTION

The test starts with the Reading and Writing section, with roughly two-thirds of the questions testing Reading Comprehension and one-third testing Grammar.

Much of this section relies on your general understanding of what you are reading. This means you should have a solid understanding of vocabulary words of varying difficulty, which is difficult to teach because it relies on your memorization of definitions. When the SAT® had a separate vocab section, we used to give students a list of about 150 commonly tested words with their definitions and asked them to memorize as many as they could. It didn't always go so well. Fortunately for most students, there is no longer a specific vocab section, but there are some tough vocab words sprinkled throughout the test. The best way to improve your reading comprehension is to READ: books, newspapers, newsletters, etc., and LOOK UP words you are unfamiliar with. You can download a dictionary app on your phone or just google the word to get the definition. Eventually, these definitions will sink in. The earlier you start, the better prepared you'll be.

Aggressively use POE (Process of Elimination)! Use the Annotation Tool to cross out answer choices you know are wrong. Now go through each answer choice again that isn't crossed out and compare. You often can get rid of at least one or two. Sometimes, even if you don't know what a word means, you may sense if it implies a positive or negative meaning – use that to help you eliminate bad answers. You may be able to get to the right answer by identifying three bad answers.

For the Grammar questions, the SAT® tests the same handful of grammar rules over and over again. Knowing these rules and practicing them will get you to the correct answer. With grammar, it is equally important to understand why answer choices are wrong as well as why they are right. Do not go by *what sounds right,* go with the answer that is grammatically correct.

As stated in the introduction, the first step to answering these questions is to identify the question category. This book includes a chapter for each category with straightforward strategies that give step-by-step instructions for tackling each question type. Once you've identified the category, apply the strategy by systematically following the steps as outlined in the text examples.

The College Board tells us that the questions on the Reading and Writing section fall into four content domains:

1. Information and Ideas
2. Craft and Structure
3. Expression of Ideas
4. Standard English Conventions

When creating a study plan, this information is utterly useless. So, we've created more specific categories with headings that each question can be attributed to. This is how this book is organized – each question category represents its own chapter, with the specific strategy for tackling each one.

READING COMPREHENSION AND GRAMMAR CATEGORIES

Curvebreakers has identified 7 main categories of Reading Comprehension:

QUESTION CATEGORY	POSSIBLE # OF QUESTIONS
1. Vocabulary Word Choice	8-12
2. Main Idea	2-5
3. Support/Weaken Claim	
a. Support/Weaken Claim Without Data	3-5
b. Support/Weaken Claim With Data	3-5
4. Relevant Information From Notes	4-8
5. Text interpretation	
a. Text interpretation: Complete the Text	2-4
b. Text interpretation: Function of Sentence	1-2
c. Text interpretation: Structure of Text	1-2
d. Text interpretation: According to Text	1-3
6. Dual Passage Comparison	1-2
7. Transition Words	3-6

Curvebreakers has identified 3 main categories of Grammar:

QUESTION CATEGORY	POSSIBLE # OF QUESTIONS
1. Punctuation	
a. Punctuation: Full-Stop and Half-Stop	3-6
b. Punctuation: Comma Usage	2-6
c. Punctuation: Apostrophes	1-2
d. Punctuation: End of Sentence	0-2
2. Agreement	
a. Agreement: Subject/Verb	3-6
b. Agreement: Pronouns	1-3
3. Misplaced Modifiers	1-2

CHAPTER 3: VOCABULARY WORD CHOICE

Section: Reading and Writing
Question Subsection: Reading Comprehension
Question Category: Vocabulary Word Choice
Of the 54 Reading and Writing questions, approximately 8 - 12 may be questions from this category

EXAM QUESTION

Which choice completes the text with the most logical and precise word or phrase?

WHAT TO EXPECT

You are presented with a short paragraph that has a "______" in place of the word or phrase, and you are asked to select the correct word or phrase.

LESSON

These questions are generally the first 4 - 6 questions in the Reading and Writing section of each Module, representing the majority of Reading Comprehension. The vocabulary is generally not overly difficult, but you will need to ensure the word you select is in the correct context of the sentence. To understand the correct word in context, you will need to establish the direction of the sentence containing the blank in relation to the other sentences in the passage. Several of the passages may contain *transition words*, which are clues to help you determine this relationship. Oftentimes, you can fill in the blank with one or more of the clue words from the text, or a synonym or antonym depending on the context.

EXERCISE

Transition Word	Same or Opposite Direction?
Thus	
Rather	
Although	
Because	
However	
Consequently	
Alternatively	
Similarly	

The Curvebreakers Strategy

WRITE IN YOUR OWN WORD

1. Read the question before reading the passage to determine the Question Category.
2. Cover the answer choices by physically placing your hand over the choices.
3. Identify and highlight the "clue" word(s) or phrase(s). Every passage will contain a keyword(s) or phrase(s) that will lead you to the correct answer.
4. Based on the clue, physically write in your own word(s) for the __________.
    a. Often you can use the SAME word or a synonym of the clue word(s) if the sentence with the ________ is going in the same direction as the other sentences.
    b. Sometimes you may need to use an OPPOSITE word if the sentence with the __________ is going in an opposite direction as the other sentences.
    c. Note if the passage contains any *transition* words: this will help to determine the direction of the ___________.
5. Eliminate answer choices that don't match your selection; choose the answer choice that most closely matches your selection. Don't eliminate an answer choice because you don't know the definition of the word. If you can eliminate the other answer choices, then pick that one.

Example 1: Vocabulary Word Choice

1. While many people initially believed that the invention of the automobile would lead to a decline in urban pollution, the rapid increase in the number of cars on the road has instead ________ the problem, resulting in higher levels of smog and harmful emissions.

Which choice completes the text with the most logical and precise word or phrase?

A) exacerbated
B) diminished
C) eradicated
D) celebrated

Solution Strategy "Write in your own word"

Step 1: Read the question before reading the passage to determine the Question Category.

Which choice completes the text with the most logical and precise word or phrase?

Step 2: Cover the answer choices by physically placing your hand over the choices.

A) [redacted]
B) [redacted]
C) [redacted]
D) [redacted]

Step 3: Identify and highlight the "clue" word(s) or phrase(s). Every passage will contain a keyword(s) or phrase(s) that will lead you to the correct answer.

Step 4: Based on the clue, physically write in your own word(s) for the ________.

> While many people initially believed that the invention of the automobile would lead to a decline in urban pollution, the rapid increase in the number of cars on the road has instead ___*increased*___ the problem, resulting in higher levels of smog and harmful emissions.
>
> TIP. Use a word they give us.

Step 5: Eliminate answer choices that don't match your selection; choose the answer choice that most closely matches your selection.

✓A) exacerbated	*made worse*
B) ~~diminished~~	*lessened; decreased*
C) ~~eradicated~~	*completely destroyed*
D) ~~celebrated~~	*acknowledged an occasion with festivities*

Correct Answer: A
"Exacerbated" emphasizes the negative impact of the increased car usage on pollution.

Example 2: Vocabulary Word Choice

2. The discovery of penicillin by Alexander Fleming in 1928 marked a _______ breakthrough in the field of medicine. This accidental finding revolutionized the treatment of bacterial infections and saved countless lives. However, overuse and misuse of antibiotics have led to the emergence of antibiotic-resistant strains of bacteria, posing a significant challenge for modern healthcare.

Which choice completes the text with the most logical and precise word or phrase?

A) tumultuous
B) trivial
C) momentous
D) disheartening

Solution Strategy "Write in your own word"

Step 1: Read the question before reading the passage to determine the Question Category.

> Which choice completes the text with the most logical and precise word or phrase?

Step 2: Cover the answer choices by physically placing your hand over the choices.

> A) [redacted]
> B) [redacted]
> C) [redacted]
> D) [redacted]

Step 3: Identify and highlight the "clue" word(s) or phrase(s). Every passage will contain a keyword(s) or phrase(s) that will lead you to the correct answer.

Step 4: Based on the clue, physically write in your own word(s) for the ________.

> The discovery of penicillin by Alexander Fleming in 1928 marked a __*revolutionary*__ breakthrough in the field of medicine. This accidental finding revolutionized the treatment of bacterial infections and saved countless lives. However, overuse and misuse of antibiotics have led to the emergence of antibiotic-resistant strains of bacteria, posing a significant challenge for modern healthcare.
>
> TIP: Use a word they give us.

Step 5: Eliminate answer choices that don't match your selection; choose the answer choice that most closely matches your selection.

~~A) tumultuous~~	*chaotic*
~~B) trivial~~	*unimportant*
✓C) momentous	*significant; historic*
~~D) disheartening~~	*discouraging*

Correct Answer: C
The word "momentous" conveys the groundbreaking nature of the discovery.

Practice: Vocabulary Word Choice

1. Despite advances in technology, handwritten letters continue to hold a _______ place in people's hearts. The act of writing and receiving a personal letter conveys a sense of thoughtfulness and intimacy that electronic communication often lacks. However, the ubiquity of email and messaging apps has led to a decline in the practice of letter writing.

Which choice completes the text with the most logical and precise word or phrase?

A) sentimental
B) trivial
C) dominant
D) controversial

2. The invention of the printing press was a _______ moment in human history. Prior to its development, books were painstakingly handwritten, making them rare and expensive. However, with the printing press, books could be produced at a much faster rate, leading to increased accessibility and widespread dissemination of knowledge.

Which choice completes the text with the most logical and precise word or phrase?

A) transformative
B) insignificant
C) controversial
D) monotonous

3. Despite the prevalence of digital music streaming platforms, vinyl records have experienced a _______ resurgence in recent years. Audiophiles and music enthusiasts appreciate the warm and rich sound quality that vinyl offers, attributing it to the analog nature of the format. Additionally, the tactile experience of handling and playing vinyl records adds to the appeal for many collectors.

Which choice completes the text with the most logical and precise word or phrase?

A) euphoric
B) negligible
C) gradual
D) substantial

4. The advent of social media has had a profound impact on the way people communicate, _______ new opportunities for connection and self-expression. However, it has also raised concerns about privacy, mental health, and the spread of misinformation.

Which choice completes the text with the most logical and precise word or phrase?

A) fostering
B) restraining
C) discrediting
D) contradicting

5. The expansion of online shopping has transformed the retail industry, _______ traditional brick-and-mortar stores to rethink their strategies. With the convenience of browsing and purchasing products from the comfort of their homes, consumers are increasingly opting for online shopping experiences. Consequently, many physical stores have faced declining sales and have had to implement innovative approaches to attract customers.

Which choice completes the text with the most logical and precise word or phrase?

A) augmenting
B) prompting
C) obstructing
D) stagnating

6. The proliferation of smartphones and social media platforms has had a significant influence on interpersonal relationships, _______ new dynamics and modes of communication. In today's digital age, individuals can easily connect and interact with people from all over the world, fostering global connections and cultural exchange. However, this constant connectivity has also given rise to concerns about the quality of face-to-face interactions and the potential for online harassment and cyberbullying.

Which choice completes the text with the most logical and precise word or phrase?

A) introducing
B) impeding
C) unraveling
D) distorting

7. The Boston Tea Party, a pivotal event in early American history, was a _______ response to British taxation policies. Frustrated by the Tea Act of 1773, which granted a monopoly to the East India Company, American colonists decided to take matters into their own hands. On the night of December 16, 1773, they boarded three British ships in the Boston Harbor and dumped crates of tea into the water, symbolizing their defiance against unjust taxation.

Which choice completes the text with the most logical and precise word or phrase?

A) ephemeral
B) retaliatory
C) arbitrary
D) cooperative

8. The Louisiana Purchase of 1803 was a _______ event in United States history, expanding the nation's territory and shaping its future. Through this landmark acquisition, President Thomas Jefferson doubled the size of the country, securing control of the Mississippi River and opening up vast opportunities for westward expansion.

Which choice completes the text with the most logical and precise word or phrase?

A) monumental
B) inconsequential
C) perplexing
D) transient

9. A recent breakthrough in medical research has revealed the existence of a previously unknown hormone that plays a crucial role in regulating metabolism and weight management. This discovery may prompt scientists to ______ their current understanding of how the body controls these processes.

Which choice completes the text with the most logical and precise word or phrase?

A) abandon
B) revise
C) disregard
D) validate

10. The scientist's hypothesis regarding the effects of a certain chemical on plant growth is ______, as it does not align with the data collected from the experiments. To strengthen the hypothesis, further research and experimentation should be conducted to explore alternative explanations.

Which choice completes the text with the most logical and precise word or phrase?

A) original
B) conclusive
C) untenable
D) insightful

For answer explanations to these practice questions, go to curvebreakerstestprep.com/decoding-the-digital-sat

CHAPTER 4: MAIN IDEA

Section: Reading and Writing
Question Subsection: Reading Comprehension
Question Category: Main Idea
Of the 54 Reading and Writing questions, approximately 2 - 5 may be questions from this category.

EXAM QUESTION

Which choice best states the main idea (or purpose) of the text?

WHAT TO EXPECT

You are presented with a passage and asked to state the main purpose or main idea of the text.

LESSON

The key to answering these questions is to try to predict the main idea before reading the answer choices; that is, try to know the direction you want to go beforehand.

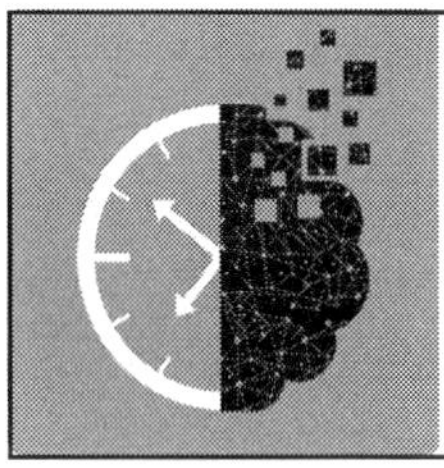

The Curvebreakers Strategy

READ AND PREDICT

1. Read the question before reading the passage to determine the Question Category.
2. Highlight key words or clauses in the passage that relate to the main idea.
3. In a few words, physically write your perception as to the main purpose of the passage.
4. Review each answer choice and choose the one that most closely matches your perception of the main idea. If there are two parts to the answer choice, separate the first and second part and evaluate each part separately. For an answer choice to be correct, both parts must be correct.

Example: Main Idea

The following text is adapted from F. Scott Fitzgerald's novel *The Great Gatsby*. The excerpt depicts a conversation between Jay Gatsby and Nick Carraway.
He smiled understandingly—much more than understandingly. It was one of those rare smiles with a quality of eternal reassurance in it, that you may come across four or five times in life. It faced, or seemed to face, the whole external world for an instant and then concentrated on you with an irresistible prejudice in your favor. It understood you just as far as you wanted to be understood, believed in you as you would like to believe in yourself, and assured you that it had precisely the impression of you that, at your best, you hoped to convey.

What is the main idea of the text?

A) Jay Gatsby's smile has an exceptional quality that makes others uneasy.
B) Jay Gatsby smiles frequently and easily understands others.
C) Jay Gatsby's smile conveys a deep sense of understanding and belief in others.
D) Jay Gatsby's smile is often misunderstood and misinterpreted by others.

Solution Strategy "Read and Predict"

Step 1: Read the question before reading the passage to determine the Question Category.

What is the main idea of the text?

Step 2: Highlight key words or clauses in the passage that relate to the main idea.

The following text is adapted from F. Scott Fitzgerald's novel *The Great Gatsby.* The excerpt depicts a conversation between Jay Gatsby and Nick Carraway.

"He smiled understandingly—much more than understandingly. It was one of those rare smiles with a quality of eternal reassurance in it, that you may come across four or five times in life. It faced, or seemed to face, the whole external world for an instant and then concentrated on you with an irresistible prejudice in your favor. It understood you just as far as you wanted to be understood, believed in you as you would like to believe in yourself, and assured you that it had precisely the impression of you that, at your best, you hoped to convey."

Step 3: In a few words, physically write your perception as to the main purpose of the passage.

This person has a rare smile that understands you. His smile is good.

Step 4: Review each answer choice and choose the one that most closely matches your perception of the main idea. If there are two parts to the answer choice, separate the first and second part and evaluate each part separately. For an answer choice to be correct, both parts must be correct.

yes *no*
A) Jay Gatsby's smile has an exceptional quality | ~~that makes others uneasy~~.
While the first part is correct, there is no indication that his smile makes others uneasy.

? *yes*
? B) Jay Gatsby smiles frequently | and easily understands others.
Don't think there was any indication of smiling frequently.

yes *yes*
✓C) Jay Gatsby's smile conveys a deep sense of understanding | and belief in others.
Both parts of this answer choice are directly supported by the text.

no *no*
~~D) Jay Gatsby's smile is often misunderstood | and misinterpreted by others.~~
Nothing in the text indicates either smile being misunderstood or misinterpreted. This contradicts his smile being good.

Correct Answer: C

Practice: Main Idea

1. Organic farming is a method of agriculture that avoids the use of synthetic chemicals such as pesticides and artificial fertilizers. Instead, organic farmers rely on natural processes and materials to grow crops, nurture soil fertility, and control pests. Advocates of organic farming argue that it is more sustainable and environmentally friendly than conventional farming methods, as it can reduce pollution and promote biodiversity.

Which choice best states the main purpose of the text?

A) To present a comprehensive guide to organic farming methods and practices.
B) To highlight the economic advantages of organic farming over conventional farming
C) To describe the environmental benefits of organic farming
D) To discuss the popularity of organic farming

2. The following text is adapted from Jane Austen's novel *Pride and Prejudice*. The excerpt portrays a conversation between Elizabeth Bennet and her close friend Charlotte Lucas.

"I am not romantic, you know. I never was. I ask only a comfortable home; and considering Mr. Collins's character, connections, and situation in life, I am convinced that my chance of happiness with him is as fair as most people can boast on entering the marriage state."

What is the main idea of the text?

A) Charlotte is expressing her desire for a romantic relationship.
B) Charlotte believes that her chance of happiness with Mr. Collins is reasonable given his circumstances.
C) Charlotte is concerned about her lack of romantic feelings for Mr. Collins.
D) Charlotte believes that her chance of happiness with Mr. Collins is superior to those of others in similar circumstances.

3. The following text is from Edgar Allan Poe's short story *The Tell-Tale Heart*. The excerpt portrays the thoughts of the narrator as he contemplates his plan to murder an old man.

"True! - nervous - very, very dreadfully nervous I had been and am; but why will you say that I am mad? The disease had sharpened my senses - not destroyed - not dulled them."

What is the main idea of the text?

A) The narrator is mildly concerned and denies any suggestion of being mentally unstable.
B) The narrator's senses have been heightened by a disease.
C) The narrator is angry at others for calling him mad.
D) The narrator's senses have been dulled by a disease.

4. The following text is adapted from William Shakespeare's play *Romeo and Juliet*. The excerpt portrays Romeo's soliloquy as he observes Juliet on the balcony.

"But, soft! What light through yonder window breaks? It is the east, and Juliet is the sun. Arise, fair sun, and kill the envious moon, Who is already sick and pale with grief, That thou, her maid, art far more fair than she."

What is the main idea of the text?

A) Romeo criticizes the moon for its envy and pale appearance compared to Juliet.
B) Romeo is puzzled by the light breaking through the window and wonders who it could be.
C) Romeo compares Juliet to the sun and expresses his admiration for her beauty.
D) Romeo is perplexed by Juliet's absence and expresses his sorrow.

5. The following text is from Ralph Waldo Emerson's essay *Self-Reliance*. The excerpt emphasizes the importance of giving credence to one's own instincts and ideas.

"Trust thyself: every heart vibrates to that iron string. Accept the place the divine Providence has found for you; the society of your contemporaries, the connection of events. Great men have always done so, and confided themselves childlike to the genius of their age, betraying their perception that the eternal was stirring at their heart, working through their hands, predominating in all their being. And we are now men, and must accept in the highest mind the same transcendent destiny; and not minors and invalids in a protected corner, not cowards fleeing before a revolution, but guides, redeemers, and benefactors, obeying the Almighty effort, and advancing on Chaos and the Dark."

What is the main idea of the text?

A) Individuals should trust their own instincts and ideas, embracing their unique place in society and the guidance of the eternal.
B) Great men have always recognized the importance of following societal conventions and relying on the ideas of others.
C) Society expects individuals to conform and be submissive, suppressing their own instincts and ideas.
D) Individuals should be fearful and cautious, and obey the Almighty.

6.The following text is adapted from Henry David Thoreau's essay *Civil Disobedience*.
"It is not desirable to cultivate a respect for the law, so much as for the right. The only obligation which I have a right to assume is to do at any time what I think right. Law never made men a whit more just; and, by means of their respect for it, even the well-disposed are daily made the agents of injustice."

Which choice best states the main purpose of the text?

A) To argue that the well-disposed are the primary perpetrators of injustice.
B) To convey that Individuals should always comply with the law to maintain social order.
C) To call attention to laws that are inherently unjust and should be disobeyed by all.
D) To suggest that the cultivation of respect for the right is more important than respect for the law.

7. The following text is adapted from Charles Darwin's book *On the Origin of Species*. The excerpt explores the concept of natural selection and its role in species adaptation.

"It is interesting to contemplate a tangled bank, clothed with many plants of many kinds, with birds singing in the bushes, with various insects flitting about, and with worms crawling through the damp earth, and to reflect that these elaborately constructed forms, so different from each other, and dependent on each other in so complex a manner, have all been produced by laws acting around us."

What is the main idea of the text?

A) The interdependence and complexity of life forms on Earth have resulted from the action of natural laws.
B) The diverse forms of life on a tangled bank are a result of human intervention and cultivation.
C) The intricate structures of plants and animals are the product of random chance and not subject to laws.
D) Natural selection is solely responsible for the creation of different species on Earth.

For answer explanations to these practice questions, go to curvebreakerstestprep.com/decoding-the-digital-sat

CHAPTER 5: SUPPORT OR WEAKEN CLAIM

Section: Reading and Writing
Question Subsection: Reading Comprehension
Question Category: Support or Weaken Claim
Question Subcategories: Support or Weaken Claim (Without Data) and Support or Weaken Claim (With Data)
Of the 54 Reading and Writing questions, approximately 6 - 10 may be questions from this category.

These questions can be presented with or without data. We will look at each type separately.

A. Question Subcategory: Support/Weaken Claim (without Data)

Approximately half the questions will not show data.

EXAM QUESTION (Examples)

Which finding, if true, would most strongly support the claim?
Which quotation most effectively illustrates the claim?
Which finding, if true, would most directly undermine (weaken) the hypothesis?

WHAT TO EXPECT

You are presented with text and asked to select the answer choice that would support or weaken the claim.

LESSON

The key to answering these questions is to first identify and understand the specific claim. Often you can find the claim by locating the phrase, *The [scientist, student, author, etc] claims that…..*and highlighting the part of the sentence that immediately follows. If the specific word, "claim" is not used in the passage, look for similar words to identify the claim, such as:

showed....	posited....	argued...	asserts....	suggested....
concludes...	hypothesized...	portrays....	found....	According to....

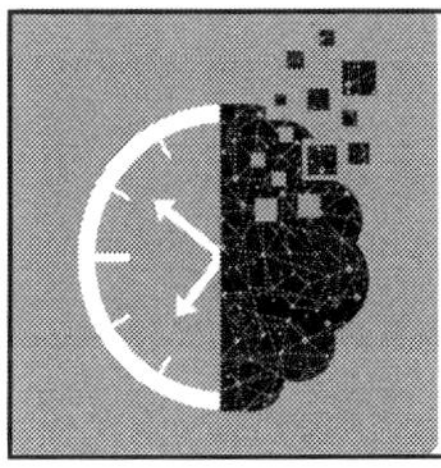

The Curvebreakers Strategy

SUMMARIZE THE CLAIM

1. Read the question before reading the passage to determine the Question Category.
2. Highlight the specific claim, usually the part of the sentence located directly following words such as *claim, hypothesize, found, argue*, etc. This is the key information needed to answer the question.
3. Try to summarize the claim in a few words and write that summary down.
4. Select the answer choice that most closely matches your summary if it is in *support* of the claim; select the answer choice that opposes your summary if asked to *weaken* the claim.

Example: Support or Weaken Claim (without data)

In the field of psychology, the nature-nurture debate has long been a topic of interest and discussion. This debate centers around the relative influence of genetics (nature) and environmental factors (nurture) in shaping human behavior and development. Some researchers argue that genetic factors play a dominant role in determining individual differences, while others emphasize the impact of environmental influences.

Which finding, if true, would most directly support the nurture perspective?

A) Studies examining the impact of socio-economic status on academic achievement consistently find that children from disadvantaged backgrounds tend to have lower educational outcomes compared to children from privileged backgrounds.
B) Research conducted with adoptive children reveals that they often exhibit more similarities in personality and cognitive abilities with their biological families than with their adoptive families.
C) Twin studies consistently show that identical twins, who share the same genetic makeup, often display differences in personality traits and behavior when raised in different environments.
D) Recent advances in neuroscience have uncovered the existence of specific genes linked to certain psychological disorders, indicating a strong genetic component in the development of these conditions.

Solution Strategy: Summarize the Claim

Step 1: Read the question before reading the passage to determine the Question Category.

Which finding, if true, would most directly support the nurture perspective?

Step 2: Highlight the specific claim, usually the part of the sentence located directly following words such as claim, hypothesize, found, argue, etc. This is the key information needed to answer the question.

In the field of psychology, the nature-nurture debate has long been a topic of interest and discussion. This debate centers around the relative influence of genetics (nature) and environmental factors (nurture) in shaping human behavior and development. Some researchers argue that genetic factors play a dominant role in determining individual differences, while others emphasize the impact of environmental influences.

Step 3: Try to summarize the claim in a few words and write that summary down.

Nurture: environmental influences most important

Step 4: Select the answer choice that most closely matches your summary if it is in support of the claim; select the answer choice that opposes your summary if asked to weaken the claim.

✓A) Studies examining the impact of socio-economic status on academic achievement consistently find that children from disadvantaged backgrounds tend to have lower educational outcomes compared to children from privileged backgrounds.
Supports the nurture perspective by highlighting the impact of environmental factors on educational achievement.

~~B) Research conducted with adoptive children reveals that they often exhibit more similarities in personality and cognitive abilities with their biological families than with their adoptive families.~~
Supports the nature perspective by emphasizing the genetic influences from biological families.

✓C) Twin studies consistently show that identical twins, who share the same genetic makeup, often display differences in personality traits and behavior when raised in different environments.
Supports the nurture perspective as it suggests that environmental factors play a significant role in shaping individual differences.

~~D) Recent advances in neuroscience have uncovered the existence of specific genes linked to certain psychological disorders, indicating a strong genetic component in the development of these conditions.~~
Supports the nature perspective as it indicates the existence of specific genes linked to psychological disorders.

Correct Answer: C
Choice C is the best answer because it directly supports the nurture perspective by indicating that environmental factors have a significant impact on individual differences. It demonstrates that differences in behavior and personality traits can be attributed to the varying environments in which identical twins are raised. While Choice A also supports the nurture perspective, it limits the narrative to education.

Practice: Support or Weaken Claim (without data)

1. The painter Georgia O'Keeffe was known for her unique style and contributions to American modernism. A scholar suggests that one of O'Keeffe's likely goals during her career was to redefine gender norms and empower women artists.

Which finding, if true, would most strongly support the scholar's claim?

A) O'Keeffe's paintings often featured strong and independent female subjects, reimagining traditional representations of women in art.
B) Female artists who were active during the same period as O'Keeffe were frequently inspired by her work and credited her as a major influence.
C) O'Keeffe's later paintings, created in the 1950s and 1960s, received more recognition and critical acclaim than her earlier works.
D) Artworks that were created in collaboration with O'Keeffe displayed distinct stylistic elements that set them apart from works created by other artists.

2. In his influential book *The Republic*, Plato explores various aspects of an ideal society and presents his theory of the philosopher-kings. One of Plato's central claims is that a just society can only be achieved through the rule of philosopher-kings: ________.

Which quotation from *The Republic* most effectively illustrates this claim?

A) "The city whose prospective rulers are least eager to rule must be the most free from faction and civil war."
B) "Until philosophers are kings, or the kings and princes of this world have the spirit and power of philosophy, and political greatness and wisdom meet in one, and those commoner natures who pursue either to the exclusion of the other are compelled to stand aside, cities will never have rest from their evils."
C) "Justice in the life and conduct of the state is possible only as first it resides in the hearts and souls of its citizens."
D) "The punishment which the wise suffer who refuse to take part in the government, is to live under the government of worse men."

3. The discovery of exoplanets, planets that orbit stars outside our solar system, has opened up new possibilities for the existence of habitable worlds beyond Earth. Scientists have identified various factors that contribute to a planet's potential habitability, including its distance from its host star, the presence of water, and the stability of its atmosphere. One hypothesis suggests that the prevalence of Earth-like exoplanets in the habitable zone is relatively high.

Which finding, if true, would most directly challenge this hypothesis?

A) Recent advancements in observational techniques have allowed scientists to detect smaller, Earth-sized exoplanets more easily, increasing the number of potentially habitable candidates
B) Astronomers have observed several exoplanets in the habitable zone that possess atmospheres with a composition similar to Earth's, including the presence of oxygen.
C) Further analysis of exoplanet data has indicated that planets within the habitable zone tend to have stable climates and consistent surface temperatures.
D) Recent studies have revealed that a significant number of exoplanets discovered so far are classified as gas giants, resembling Jupiter and Saturn rather than Earth-like planets.

4. In the play *Hamlet* by William Shakespeare, the character Hamlet is known for his introspection and philosophical contemplation. One of the central themes explored in the play is the nature of human existence and the complexities of human emotions. Throughout the play, Hamlet struggles with his own thoughts and emotions, expressing the idea that humans are often caught between conflicting impulses and desires.

Which quotation from *Hamlet* most effectively illustrates this idea?

A) "To be, or not to be: that is the question."
B) "I could be bounded in a nutshell and count myself a king of infinite space, were it not that I have bad dreams."
C) "This above all: to thine own self be true."
D) "Though this be madness, yet there is method in 't."

B. Question Subcategory: Support/Weaken Claim (with Data)

Approximately half the questions will show data.

EXAM QUESTION (Examples)

Which choice most effectively uses data from the graph to illustrate the claim?
Which choice best describes data from the table to complete the statement?
Which choice most effectively describes data from the graph to weaken the conclusion?

WHAT TO EXPECT

You are presented with a table or graph which is followed by text relating to the table or graph. You are then asked to select the answer choice that would support or weaken the claim.

LESSON

Just as with the *without data* passages, the key to answering these questions is to first identify and understand the specific claim. Often you can find the claim by locating the phrase, *The [scientist, student, author, etc] claims that*.....and highlighting the part of the sentence that immediately follows. If the specific word, "claim' is not used in the passage, look for similar words to identify the claim.

showed....	posited....	argued...	asserts....	suggested....
concludes...	hypothesized...	portrays....	found....	According to....

These questions have the further element of a table or graph before the passage text. Some questions can be answered without referencing the data; for others you will need specific information from the table or graph.

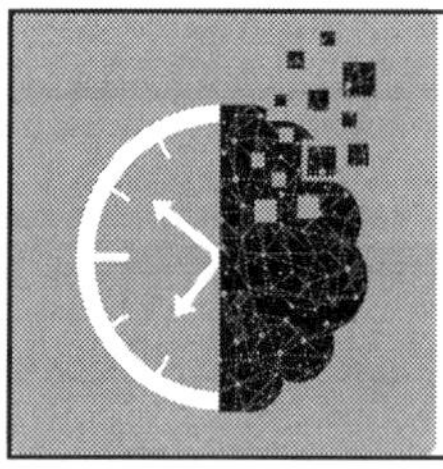

The Curvebreakers Strategy

SUMMARIZE THE CLAIM; USE DATA WHEN NECESSARY

1. Read the question before reading the passage to determine the Question Category.
2. Highlight the specific claim, usually the part of the sentence located directly following words such as *claim, hypothesize, found, argue*, etc. This is the key information needed to answer the question
3. Try to summarize the claim in a few words and write that summary down. Don't go directly to the table or graph – if you can understand and summarize the claim, you may be able to answer the question without even referring to the table or graph.
4. If more than one answer choice matches your summary, then check the data to see which one corresponds to the data given and eliminate answer choices that do not correspond to the data.
5. If you do not understand the claim, you may be able to eliminate answer choices that do not conform to the graph or table. Check the data in the graph or table and eliminate answer choices that conflict with the given data.

Example: Support or Weaken Claim (with data)

Number of Electric Cars Sold by Top Manufacturers (in thousands)

Year	Tesla	Nissan	BMW	Chevrolet
2015	50.6	43.4	24.1	15.4
2016	76.2	54.2	62.2	24.7
2017	103.0	67.0	103.0	43.9
2018	245.2	85.7	142.6	61.0
2019	367.5	104.3	153.0	68.6

An automotive analyst is studying the electric car market and claims that Tesla has significantly increased its electric car sales between 2015 and 2019, making it the top-selling electric car manufacturer during this period.

Which choice most effectively uses data from the table to support the analyst's claim?

A) Tesla sold over 840,000 electric cars between 2015 and 2019.
B) BMW sold 153.0 thousand electric cars in 2019, which is less than Tesla's sales of 367.5 thousand that year.
C) Tesla's electric car sales tripled from 2015 to 2019.
D) Between the period from 2015 to 2019, Tesla's electric car sales went from 50,600 to 367,500.

Solution Strategy: Summarize the Claim; Use Data When Necessary

Step 1: Read the question before reading the passage to determine the Question Category.

Which choice most effectively uses data from the table to support the analyst's claim?

Step 2: Highlight the specific claim, usually the part of the sentence located directly following words such as claim, hypothesize, found, argue, etc. This is the key information needed to answer the question

An automotive analyst is studying the electric car market and claims that Tesla has significantly increased its electric car sales between 2015 and 2019, making it the top-selling electric car manufacturer during this period.

Step 3: Try to summarize the claim in a few words and write that summary down. Don't go directly to the table or graph – if you can understand and summarize the claim, you may be able to answer the question without even referring to the table or graph.

Tesla sales went up between 2015 and 2019.

Step 4: If more than one answer choice matches your summary, then check the data to see which one corresponds to the data given and eliminate answer choices that do not correspond to the data.

~~A) Tesla sold over 840,000 electric cars between 2015 and 2019.~~
Only gives total sales – does not indicate that sales are increasing.

~~B) BMW sold 153.0 thousand electric cars in 2019, which is less than Tesla's sales of 367.5 thousand that year.~~
Does not indicate that sales are increasing.

✓C) Tesla's electric car sales tripled from 2015 to 2019.
Indicates that sales are increasing from 2015 to 2019.

✓D) Between the period from 2015 to 2019, Tesla's electric car sales went from 50,600 to 367,500.
Indicates that sales are increasing from 2015 to 2019.

Correct Answer: D
While both Choices C and D support the claim that Tesla sales have increased between 2015 and 2019, Answer Choice C incorrectly says sales "tripled." If sales tripled from the 2015 amount of 50,600, the 2019 amount would be 50,600 x 3 = 151,800. Since the table shows sales increasing from 50,600 to 367,500, the answer must be D.

Practice: Support or Weaken Claim (with data)

1.

Table: Examples of Classical Music Influence in Contemporary Popular Songs

Artist	Year	Pop Song Title	Melody Sample from Classical Music	Composition Sample from Classical Music
John Smith	2019	"Symphony of Dreams"	Yes	No
Emily Johnson	2020	"Classical Rhapsody"	Yes	Yes
Michael Brown	2018	"Modern Sonata"	No	No
Sarah Thompson	2021	"Orchestral Pop"	Yes	Yes

In the field of music, the influence of various genres and styles on contemporary artists has been a subject of study. One particular area of interest is the impact of classical music on popular music. Classical music has a rich history and distinctive characteristics, and many argue that its influence on popular music is substantial compared to other genres.

Which statement, if true, most effectively uses data from the table to support the claim that classical music has had a significant influence on popular music?

A) Many contemporary popular songs sample melodies and compositions from classical music.
B) Classical music compositions are rarely performed or studied in music schools and conservatories.
C) Pop music charts occasionally feature songs that are influenced by classical music, but the majority of popular songs draw from other genres.
D) Classical music instruments and orchestral arrangements are rarely used in popular music productions.

2.

Blood Pressure Levels of Participants Before and After the Study Period

	Group A - Initial BP	Group A - Final BP	Group B - Initial BP	Group B - Final BP
Person 1	130	120	135	132
Person 2	140	132	138	136
Person 3	125	118	132	130
Person 4	132	125	130	126
Person 5	136	130	140	138

A team of researchers conducted a study to investigate the effects of exercise on cardiovascular health. They divided the participants into two groups: Group A, which engaged in regular aerobic exercise, and Group B, which did not engage in any exercise. The researchers measured the participants' blood pressure levels before and after the study period to assess any changes. The researchers concluded that regular aerobic exercise has a positive impact on cardiovascular health, noting that ________.

Which choice most effectively uses data from the table to support the research team's conclusion?

A) the participants in both groups saw declines of 50-60% in average blood pressure levels after the study period compared to their initial levels.
B) the participants in Group A and Group B had similar average blood pressure levels after the study period.
C) the participants in Group A had significantly lower average blood pressure levels after the study period compared to their initial levels, while the averages remained relatively unchanged in Group B.
D) the participants in both groups had lower average blood pressure levels after the study period compared to their initial levels.

3.

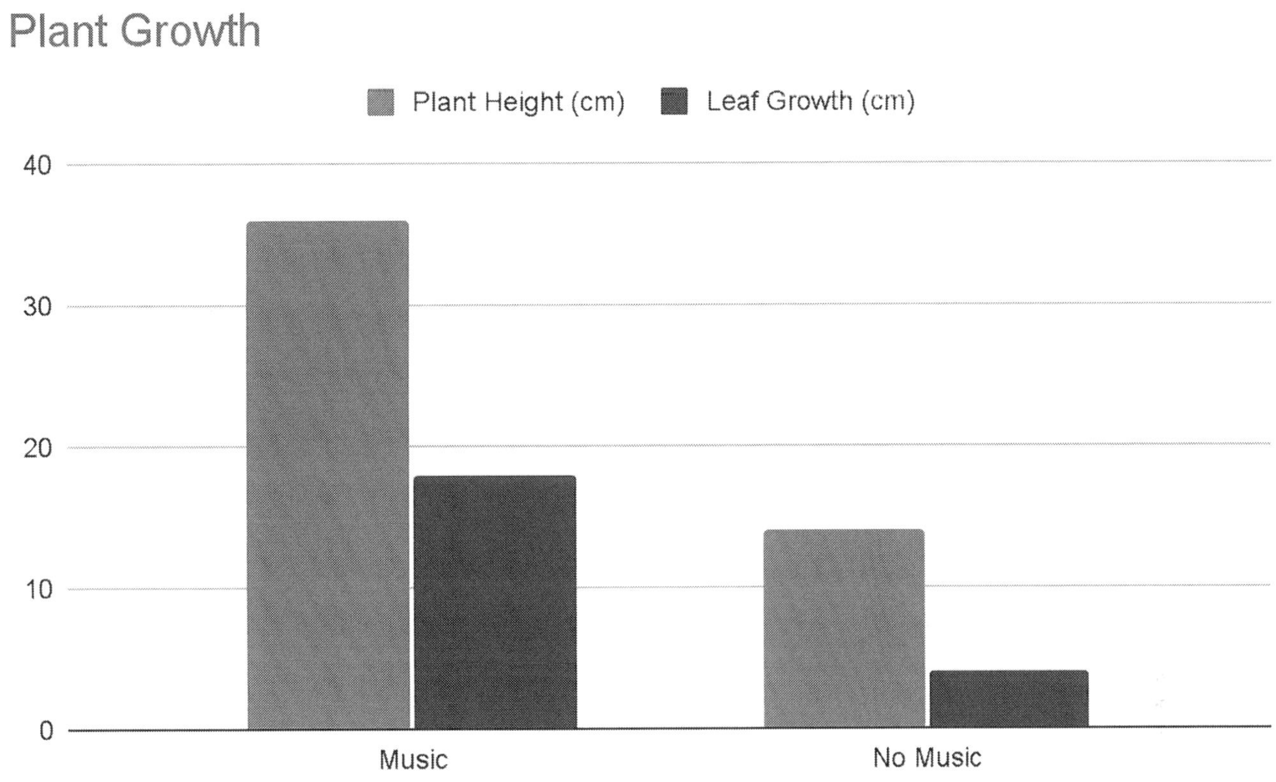

In a study investigating the effects of music on plant growth, a group of researchers exposed one set of plants to classical music for several hours each day, while another set of plants received no music exposure. The researchers measured the height and leaf growth of the plants over a period of four weeks. At the end of the study, the researchers concluded that the plants exposed to classical music exhibited significantly greater growth compared to the plants without music exposure.

Which choice, if true, would most effectively weaken the researchers' conclusion?

A) The plants in both groups were initially of the same height and had similar leaf growth.
B) The plants exposed to classical music received the same amount of sunlight as the plants without music exposure.
C) The greatest increase in plant growth occurred within the first week of the study.
D) The plants without music exposure experienced adverse environmental conditions during the study.

4.

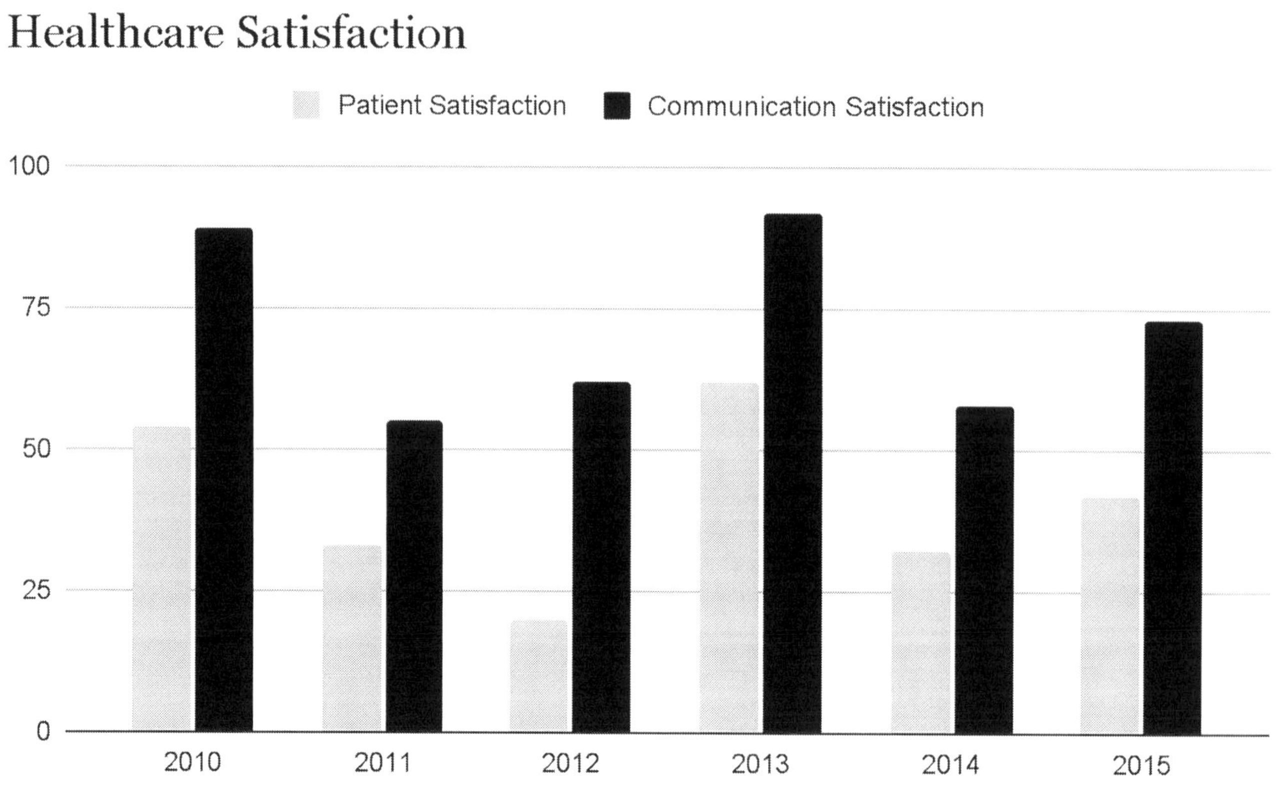

In the field of healthcare, understanding patient satisfaction and its associated factors is crucial for improving the quality of care. Researchers have conducted studies to assess patient satisfaction levels and identify specific aspects of care that contribute to patient experiences. Recent research by Dr. Emily Sullivan aimed to explore patient satisfaction not only as a general measure but also in relation to specific areas of care, such as communication with healthcare providers or wait times. Dr. Sullivan's findings revealed that a general measure of patient satisfaction may not fully capture the nuances of satisfaction in specific areas of care. For instance, in a study conducted in a hospital setting, general patient satisfaction _______

Which choice most effectively uses data from the study to illustrate the claim?

A) aligned closely with satisfaction regarding communication with healthcare providers in 2010 but differed from satisfaction regarding communication by a large amount in 2015.
B) was substantially lower than satisfaction regarding communication with healthcare providers each year from 2010 to 2015.
C) reached its highest level between 2010 and 2015 in the same year that satisfaction regarding wait times reached their lowest levels.
D) was substantially lower than satisfaction regarding wait times in 2010 and substantially higher than satisfaction regarding wait times in 2015.

For answer explanations to these practice questions, go to <u>**curvebreakerstestprep.com/decoding-the-digital-sat**</u>

CHAPTER 6: RELEVANT INFORMATION FROM NOTES

Section: Reading and Writing
Question Subsection: Reading Comprehension
Question Category: Relevant Information from Notes
Of the 54 Reading and Writing questions, approximately 4 - 8 may be questions from this category.

EXAM QUESTION

The student wants to [*text will say what the student wants to do*]. Which choice most effectively uses relevant information from the notes to accomplish this goal?

WHAT TO EXPECT

You are presented with a series of bullets that represent notes taken by a student researching a particular topic. You are told what the student wants to do and asked to select the answer choice that uses relevant information from the notes to accomplish this goal.

LESSON

These questions are the last set of Reading and Writing questions.
The key to answering these questions are the words that immediately follow the phrase "*The student wants to….*" – what is being presented, introduced, or emphasized. Oftentimes the question can be answered by just matching these words with synonymous words in the answer choices; the notes may not even be necessary. Generally, better answers are ones that are most specific.

EXERCISE

Choose Answer A) or B) in each numbered row.

#	GOAL	ANSWER A)	ANSWER B)
1	The student wants to provide an explanation and example of "cryptocurrency."	Cryptocurrency is a digital or virtual form of currency that uses cryptography for secure financial transactions and controls the creation of additional units, such as Bitcoin and Ethereum.	In the field of computer science, cryptocurrency refers to the practice of securing data with encryption algorithms to prevent unauthorized access and ensure data privacy.
2	The student wants to make a generalization about the impact of Einstein's theory of relativity	The theory of relativity, formulated by Albert Einstein, revolutionized our understanding of space, time, and gravity	Albert Einstein's theory of relativity encompasses both special and general relativity, explaining the behavior of objects in motion and the effects of gravity.
3	The student wants to compare the capacities of the two stadiums.	Stadium X can accommodate more than 80,000 spectators, making it one of the largest stadiums in the country.	Stadium Y has a seating capacity of approximately 60,000, whereas Stadium Z has a slightly smaller capacity of around 55,000.
4	The student wants to describe the concept of "nanotechnology" to an audience unfamiliar with advanced materials.	Nanotechnology is a term used in architecture to describe the design and construction of buildings that are inspired by nature.	Nanotechnology is a field of science and engineering that deals with materials and devices on an incredibly small scale.

The Curvebreakers Strategy

FOCUS ON THE GOAL

1. Read the question before reading the passage to determine the Question Category.
2. Determine exactly what the student wants to do by highlighting the part of the sentence following the words, "*The student wants to….*".
3. Skim each bullet from the notes and write "*yes*" next to each bullet that pertains to the goal of the student, and write "*no*" next to each bullet that does not pertain to the goal of the student. Highlight information from the notes that directly pertains to the student's goal.
4. Focus on the student's specific goal. Eliminate answer choices that may be true but don't accomplish the goal. For example, if the student wants to emphasize the *aim* of a research study, eliminate answer choices that pertain to the study's *methodology*. Similarly, if a student wants to explain *how* something is done, eliminate answer choices that explain *why* something is done. (Oftentimes the notes may not be needed at all to answer the question).
5. Choose an answer choice that restates SPECIFIC facts from the notes that you have marked as "yes." Avoid generalizations.

Example: Relevant Information From Notes

While researching a topic, a student has taken the following notes:

- The Hubble Telescope was named after American astronomer Edwin P. Hubble (1889-1953).
- The Hubble Space Telescope was launched in 1990.
- Hubble has observed distant galaxies and captured stunning images of celestial bodies, such as planets, nebulae, and star clusters,providing evidence for the expansion of the universe.
- Hubble has also contributed to the discovery of dark energy, a mysterious force driving the universe's expansion.
- Hubble took 12 years to build; it was originally scheduled for launch in 1983 but was delayed.

The student wants to present the achievements of the Hubble Space Telescope. Which choice most effectively uses relevant information from the notes to accomplish this goal?

A) Since its launch in 1990, the Hubble Space Telescope has been instrumental in observing the universe.
B) The Hubble Space Telescope, named after American astronomer Edwin P. Hubble, took 12 years to build and was launched in 1990.
C) The Hubble Space Telescope has made significant contributions to our understanding of the universe, including observing distant galaxies and capturing stunning images of celestial bodies.
D) The Hubble Space Telescope has observed distant galaxies, providing evidence for the expansion of the universe and contributing to the discovery of dark energy.

Solution Strategy: Focus On The Goal

Step 1: Read the question before reading the passage to determine the Question Category.

Which choice most effectively uses relevant information from the notes to accomplish this goal?

Step 2: Determine exactly what the student wants to do by highlighting the part of the sentence following the words, "The student wants to…."..

The student wants to present the achievements of the Hubble Space Telescope

Step 3: Skim each bullet from the notes and write "yes" next to each bullet that pertains to the goal of the student, and write "no" next to each bullet that does not pertain to the goal of the student.

- ***No*** • The Hubble Telescope was named after American astronomer Edwin P. Hubble (1889-1953).
- ***No*** • The Hubble Space Telescope was launched in 1990.
- ***Yes*** • Hubble has observed distant galaxies and captured stunning images of celestial bodies, such as planets, nebulae, and star clusters, providing evidence for the expansion of the universe.
- ***Yes*** • Hubble has also contributed to the discovery of dark energy, a mysterious force driving the universe's expansion.
- ***No*** • Hubble took 12 years to build; it was originally scheduled for launch in 1983 but was delayed.

Step 4: Focus on the student's specific goal. Eliminate answer choices that may be true but don't accomplish the goal.

Goal is to present Hubble achievements

~~A) Since its launch in 1990, the Hubble Space Telescope has been instrumental in observing the universe.~~
Not a specific achievement

~~B) The Hubble Space Telescope, named after American astronomer Edwin P. Hubble, took 12 years to build and was launched in 1990.~~
Not a specific achievement

✓C) The Hubble Space Telescope has made significant contributions to our understanding of the universe, including observing distant galaxies and capturing stunning images of celestial bodies.
Does talk about achievements

✓D) The Hubble Space Telescope has observed distant galaxies, providing evidence for the expansion of the universe and contributing to the discovery of dark energy.
Does talk about achievements; includes more specific language- "providing evidence"; also mentions dark energy which is consistent with notes.

Step 5: Choose an answer choice that restates SPECIFIC facts from the notes that you have marked as "yes." Avoid generalizations.

Correct Answer: D
While both answer choices C and D are "achievements," Choice D is more specific and also includes info about the discovery of dark energy, which is not mentioned in Choice C and is supported by the notes.

Practice: Relevant Information From Notes

1. While conducting research on renewable energy sources, a student has gathered the following information:

- Solar power is derived from harnessing the energy of the sun and converting it into electricity.
- Wind power is generated by capturing the kinetic energy of the wind and transforming it into electrical energy.
- Solar power is considered a clean energy source with no harmful emissions.
- Wind power is also an environmentally friendly energy source, producing no greenhouse gas emissions.
- Solar power installations typically involve the use of solar panels or photovoltaic cells.
- Wind power installations consist of wind turbines that capture wind energy and convert it into electricity.

The student wants to compare solar power and wind power as renewable energy sources. Which choice most effectively uses the relevant information from the notes to accomplish this goal?

A) Solar power is derived from the sun and converted into electricity, unlike wind power.
B) Solar power installations involve the use of solar panels or photovoltaic cells, whereas wind power installations consist of wind turbines.
C) Renewable energy sources, such as solar and wind, are necessary to reduce the effects of climate change.
D) While solar power is derived from the sun and converted into electricity using solar panels or photovoltaic cells, wind power is generated by capturing the kinetic energy of the wind through the use of wind turbines.

2. While researching a topic, a student has taken the following notes:

- The Impressionist movement originated in France in the 19th century.
- Impressionist artists sought to capture the fleeting effects of light and atmosphere in their paintings.
- They used loose brushwork, vibrant colors, and quick, spontaneous brushstrokes.
- One notable Impressionist painter is Claude Monet, known for his series of paintings depicting water lilies.

The student wants to provide an explanation and example of the Impressionist movement. Which choice most effectively uses relevant information from the notes to accomplish this goal?

A) The Impressionist movement, which originated in France in the 19th century, was characterized by artists' efforts to capture the fleeting effects of light and atmosphere through loose brushwork and vibrant colors. Claude Monet, a notable Impressionist painter, exemplified this style in his famous water lily series.
B) Claude Monet, a French painter, was a key figure in the Impressionist movement, which began in the 19th century. This artistic movement aimed to depict the transient qualities of light and atmosphere through the use of loose brushwork and vibrant colors.
C) The Impressionist movement, started by Claude Monet and other artists in France during the 19th century, focused on portraying the ephemeral nature of light and atmosphere. Monet is still viewed as one of the greatest impressionist painters to have ever lived.
D) Artists of the Impressionist movement, such as Claude Monet, were inspired by the changing effects of light and atmosphere. They utilized loose brushwork, vibrant colors, and spontaneous brushstrokes to capture these fleeting moments in their paintings.

3. While researching a topic, a student has taken the following notes:

- The impact of climate change on coral reefs is a growing concern for marine scientists.
- Dr. Emily Turner conducted a study to investigate the effects of rising ocean temperatures on coral bleaching.
- She collected water samples from various reef locations and monitored coral health over several months.
- The study aimed to determine the correlation between temperature increases and the occurrence of coral bleaching.
- Findings showed a clear relationship between rising ocean temperatures and increased instances of coral bleaching.

The student wants to present the aim of Dr. Emily Turner's research study. Which choice most effectively uses relevant information from the notes to accomplish this goal?

A) Dr. Emily Turner's study revealed a correlation between rising ocean temperatures and coral bleaching.
B) Coral bleaching is a growing concern for marine scientists due to the impact of climate change.
C) Investigating the effects of rising ocean temperatures on coral bleaching was the primary focus of Dr. Emily Turner's study.
D) Dr. Emily Turner collected water samples and monitored coral health to understand the impact of climate change on coral reefs.

4. While researching a topic, a student has taken the following notes:

- In the early 20th century, Marie Curie became the first woman to win a Nobel Prize.
- She won Nobel Prizes in both Physics and Chemistry for her groundbreaking research on radioactivity.
- Curie's discoveries revolutionized the field of science and paved the way for numerous advancements.
- Her work laid the foundation for modern applications such as radiation therapy in medicine.
- To this day, Marie Curie remains the only person to have received Nobel Prizes in two different scientific fields.

The student wants to emphasize the uniqueness of Marie Curie's achievement. Which choice most effectively uses relevant information from the notes to accomplish this goal?

A) Marie Curie's discoveries revolutionized the field of science and paved the way for numerous advancements.
B) Curie won Nobel Prizes in both Physics and Chemistry, making her the first woman to achieve such a remarkable feat.
C) Marie Curie's work laid the foundation for modern applications in medicine, particularly in the field of radiation therapy.
D) To this day, Marie Curie remains a prominent figure in scientific history due to her groundbreaking research on radioactivity.

5.While researching a topic, a student has compiled the following notes:

- Dogs belong to the Canidae family, while cats belong to the Felidae family.
- Dogs are known for their loyalty and social nature, while cats are often characterized as more independent.
- Dogs are generally larger in size compared to cats, which are typically smaller and more agile.
- Dogs are descendants of wolves, whereas cats have evolved from smaller wildcat ancestors.

The student wants to emphasize a key behavioral distinction between dogs and cats. Which choice effectively highlights this difference?

A) Dogs are known for their loyalty and social nature, setting them apart from cats.
B) Dogs belong to the Canidae family, while cats belong to the Felidae family.
C) Dogs are generally larger in size compared to cats.
D) Dogs are descendants of wolves, whereas cats have evolved from smaller wildcat ancestors.

6. While researching a topic, a student has taken the following notes:

- In the past decade, the use of social media platforms has skyrocketed, with billions of people now actively engaging in social networking.
- Social media has transformed the way people communicate, allowing for instant connection and sharing of information.
- The rise of social media has also given individuals and businesses new opportunities for self-expression, branding, and marketing.
- Social media platforms offer a wide range of features and tools, including messaging, photo sharing, and live video streaming.

The global reach of social media has connected people from different parts of the world, facilitating cross-cultural interactions and collaborations. The student wants to emphasize the rise in worldwide interconnectedness brought about by social media platforms. Which choice effectively highlights this increase?

A) Social media platforms offer a wide range of features and tools, including messaging, photo sharing, and live video streaming.
B) The use of social media platforms has skyrocketed in the past decade, transforming the way people communicate and allowing for instant sharing of information.
C) In the past decade, billions of people have actively engaged in social networking, leading to a significant increase in global connectivity.
D) Social media has given individuals and businesses new opportunities for self-expression, branding, and marketing, fostering cross-cultural interactions and collaborations.

7. While researching a topic, a student has taken the following notes:

- Psychological experiments often rely on participants from the general population.
- Researchers use various sampling methods to select participants for their studies.
- Simple random sampling involves randomly selecting individuals from the target population.
- Stratified random sampling divides the target population into distinct groups and randomly selects participants from each group.
- Convenience sampling involves selecting participants based on their accessibility and availability.

The student wants to explain stratified random sampling to an audience unfamiliar with sampling techniques. Which choice most effectively uses relevant information from the notes to accomplish this goal?

A) Stratified random sampling is a commonly used method in psychological research, involving the random selection of individuals from the general population.
B) Stratified random sampling is a sampling technique in psychological research that involves selecting participants based on their accessibility and availability.
C) Due to its randomness, stratified random sampling is a superior sampling technique in comparison to convenience sampling.
D) Stratified random sampling is a sampling method in psychological research where the target population is divided into distinct groups, and participants are randomly selected from each group.

8. While researching a topic, a student has taken the following notes:

- The Gullah are a group of African Americans who have lived in parts of the southeastern United States since the 18th century.
- Gullah culture is influenced by West African and Central African traditions.
- Louise Miller Cohen is a Gullah historian, storyteller, and preservationist.
- She founded the Gullah Museum of Hilton Head Island, South Carolina, in 2003.
- Vermelle Rodrigues is a Gullah historian, artist, and preservationist.
- She founded the Gullah Museum of Georgetown, South Carolina, in 2003.

The student wants to explain the duration and purpose of Cohen's and Rodrigues's work to an audience unfamiliar with these historians. Which choice most effectively uses relevant information from the notes to accomplish this goal?

A) The Gullah Museum of Hilton Head Island, founded by Louise Miller Cohen in 2003, showcases the rich cultural heritage of the Gullah people who have lived in the southeastern United States for centuries.
B) Louise Miller Cohen and Vermelle Rodrigues are Gullah historians, artists, and preservationists who have dedicated their work to preserving the Gullah culture, which has thrived in the southeastern United States since the 18th century.
C) Since 2003, Louise Miller Cohen and Vermelle Rodrigues have been actively involved in preserving the Gullah culture through their respective Gullah Museums in Hilton Head Island and Georgetown, South Carolina.
D) The Gullah people, whose roots date back to the 18th century, have found dedicated advocates in Louise Miller Cohen and Vermelle Rodrigues, who established the Gullah Museums in Hilton Head Island and Georgetown, South Carolina, respectively.

9. While researching a topic, a student has taken the following notes:

- Photosynthesis is the process by which plants convert sunlight into energy.
- Chlorophyll, a pigment found in plant cells, absorbs light energy and drives the photosynthesis process.
- During photosynthesis, plants take in carbon dioxide from the air and release oxygen as a byproduct.
- The energy absorbed from sunlight is used to convert carbon dioxide and water into glucose, a form of stored energy.
- Glucose produced during photosynthesis serves as the primary source of energy for plant growth and development.

The student wants to emphasize how photosynthesis contributes to plant growth. Which choice most effectively uses relevant information from the notes to accomplish this goal?

A) Chlorophyll, a pigment found in plant cells, is responsible for absorbing light energy during photosynthesis.
B) Photosynthesis is the process by which plants convert sunlight, carbon dioxide, and water into glucose, which serves as their primary source of energy for growth and development.
C) During photosynthesis, plants take in carbon dioxide and release oxygen as a byproduct, contributing to oxygen levels in the atmosphere.
D) The process by which energy is absorbed from sunlight, converting carbon dioxide and water into glucose, and releasing oxygen, is known as photosynthesis.

For answer explanations to these practice questions, go to curvebreakerstestprep.com/decoding-the-digital-sat

CHAPTER 7: TEXT INTERPRETATION

Section: Reading and Writing
Question Subsection: Reading Comprehension
Question Category: Text Interpretation
Of the 54 Reading and Writing questions, approximately 7 - 11 may be questions from this category.

These questions test your understanding of text. They can generally be separated into 4 subcategories. We will look at each type separately. While the strategies are similar for each question type, there are some differences to be aware of.

A. Complete the Text
B. Function of Sentence
C. Structure of Text
D. According to the Text

A. Question Subcategory: Text Interpretation – Complete the Text

Of the 54 Reading and Writing questions, approximately 2 - 4 may be questions from this subcategory.

EXAM QUESTION

Which choice most logically completes the text?

WHAT TO EXPECT

You are presented with a passage containing various facts and the last sentence ends with a "__________". You need to select the answer choice that best completes this sentence.

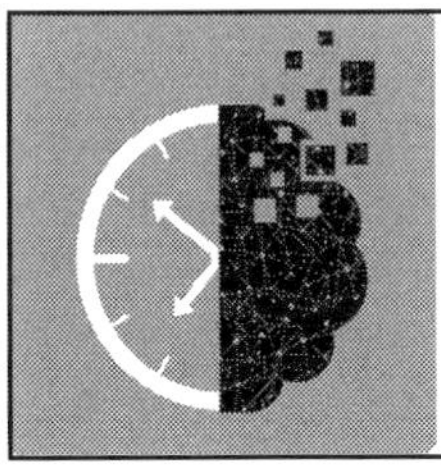

The Curvebreakers Strategy

READ AND PREDICT

1. Read the question before reading the passage to determine the Question Category.
2. Highlight key words or phrases.
3. Based on your understanding of the text, fill in the blank with your own prediction of what should complete the text. Do not read the answer choices until after you've noted your prediction
4. Select the answer choice that most closely matches your prediction. If there are two parts to the answer choice, separate the first and second part and evaluate each part separately. For an answer choice to be correct, both parts must be correct.

Example: Text Interpretation – Complete the Text

Many historians argue that the printing press, invented by Johannes Gutenberg in the mid-15th century, played a critical role in the spread of knowledge and ideas throughout Europe. As printed books became more accessible and affordable, ________

Which choice most logically completes the text?

A) the printing press was soon replaced by more advanced technologies.
B) people's literacy rates increased, enabling them to read and engage with new ideas.
C) the oral tradition of storytelling continued to flourish alongside printed books.
D) the price of handwritten manuscripts increased dramatically.

Solution Strategy: Read and Predict

Step 1: Read the question before reading the passage to determine the Question Category.

Which choice most logically completes the text?

Step 2: Highlight key words or phrases.

Step 3: Based on your understanding of the text, fill in the blank with your own prediction of what should complete the text. Do not read the answer choices until after you've noted your prediction.

Many historians argue that the printing press, invented by Johannes Gutenberg in the mid-15th century, played a critical role in the **spread of knowledge and ideas throughout Europe**. As printed books became more accessible and affordable, *knowledge / ideas spread through Europe.*

Step 4: Select the answer choice that most closely matches your prediction. If there are two parts to the answer choice, separate the first and second part and evaluate each part separately. For an answer choice to be correct, both parts must be correct.

no *no*
~~A) the printing press was soon replaced | by more advanced technologies.~~
No indication of this nor does this choice mention the spread of knowledge/ideas

? *yes*
✓B) people's literacy rates increased, | enabling them to read and engage with new ideas.
Possible answer – consistent with spread of knowledge/ideas

no *no*
C) the oral tradition of storytelling continued to flourish | alongside printed books.
No indication of this nor does this choice mention the spread of knowledge/ideas

D) the price of handwritten manuscripts increased dramatically.
No indication of this nor does this choice mention the spread of knowledge/ideas

Correct Answer: B
Consistent with the printing press's role in the spread of knowledge and ideas.

Practice: Text Interpretation – Complete the Text

1. The conquest of the Inca Empire by Spanish conquistadors in the 16th century marked a pivotal moment in South American history, shaping the region's indigenous civilizations and laying the foundation for colonial rule. The encounter between the Spanish and the Inca brought forth profound changes in social, cultural, and political structures. The impact of Spanish colonization resulted in the imposition of a new socio-economic system, the spread of Christianity, and the exploitation of natural resources. Despite the significant disruptions caused by colonization, elements of indigenous cultures and traditions endured, merging with European influences to create a distinct mestizo identity. Today, the legacy of Spanish colonization continues to shape the cultural landscape of South America ________.

Which choice most logically completes the text?

A) as contemporary societies grapple with the negative consequences of colonial rule.
B) by influencing various aspects of South American society, including language, religion, and governance.
C) with debates revolving around historical justice and efforts to preserve indigenous languages.
D) indicating a harmonious coexistence between colonizers and indigenous peoples.

2. Studies on primate behavior have revealed that social grooming serves various functions within a group, including strengthening bonds between individuals, reducing tension, and promoting social cohesion. Researchers conducted an experiment to investigate whether similar behaviors exist among elephants, highly social animals known for their complex social structures. The findings indicated that elephants engage in reciprocal tactile interactions, using their trunks to touch and caress each other. These interactions not only strengthen social bonds but also serve as a means of _________.

Which choice most logically completes the text?

A) fostering cooperation, trust, and coordination within the elephant group.
B) establishing a hierarchy and maintaining order in the elephant social structure.
C) competing for resources and asserting dominance among individual elephants.
D) facilitating reproductive behaviors and ensuring the survival of the elephant species.

3. The Trail of Tears was a tragic chapter in Native American history, as numerous tribes, including the Cherokee, Creek, and Choctaw, were forcibly removed from their ancestral lands in the southeastern United States. This forced relocation, carried out under the Indian Removal Act of 1830, resulted in immense suffering, death, and the loss of traditional lands and ways of life. Thousands of Native Americans endured a treacherous journey to unfamiliar territories in present-day Oklahoma, facing disease, starvation, and harsh conditions along the way. The Trail of Tears remains a somber reminder of the impact of _________.

Which choice most logically completes the text?

A) the peaceful coexistence and cultural exchange between Native American tribes and European settlers, leading to a harmonious blending of traditions.
B) the trauma on Native American communities, with most tribes continuing to experience harsh conditions to this day.
C) colonization and the dispossession of Native American lands and resources, fundamentally altering their societies and livelihoods.
D) the intergenerational effects on Native American societies and individuals, shaping their collective memory and resilience in the face of adversity.

4. The exploration of space has been a testament to human curiosity and ingenuity, as scientists and astronauts have embarked on groundbreaking missions to unravel the mysteries of the universe. From the first manned moon landing to the deployment of space telescopes, these endeavors have provided invaluable insights into celestial bodies and expanded our understanding of the cosmos. However, space exploration is not without its challenges. Astronauts face prolonged periods of weightlessness, cosmic radiation, and isolation, necessitating the use of advanced technologies and rigorous training to ensure their safety and mission success. These challenges underscore the importance of _________.

Which choice most logically completes the text?

A) robust communication networks for seamless data transmission and real-time monitoring capabilities.
B) continuous advancements in space vehicle propulsion systems and spacecraft engineering designs.
C) comprehensive mission planning, risk management strategies, and meticulous execution of protocols.
D) international collaboration and cooperation in space exploration endeavors, fostering shared knowledge and resources.

5. In the realm of astronomy, the discovery of exoplanets has revolutionized our understanding of the universe and the possibility of extraterrestrial life. Over the past few decades, astronomers have identified thousands of planets orbiting stars beyond our solar system. The existence of these exoplanets raises intriguing questions about _________.

Which choice most directly addresses the question raised in the passage?

A) the potential habitability of these exoplanets and the conditions required for life to thrive.
B) the technological advancements in telescopes used to detect and study exoplanets.
C) the history of space exploration and the discoveries made within our own solar system.
D) the mathematical models and simulations used to predict the existence of exoplanets.

6. A group of researchers led by Dr. Maria Rodriguez and Dr. Jonathan Chen conducted a study to investigate the effects of a specific gene mutation on the growth of fruit flies (Drosophila melanogaster). They introduced a mutation in the gene responsible for wing development and compared the wing sizes of mutated flies to those of normal flies. The results revealed that the mutated flies exhibited significantly smaller wings compared to the normal flies. These findings suggest that ________.

Which choice most logically completes the text?

A) the wing size of fruit flies is primarily determined by external factors.
B) the gene mutation affects the normal development of wing size in fruit flies.
C) other genes unrelated to wing development play a role in fruit fly growth.
D) the mutation only affects the size of male fruit fly wings, not females.

7. A team of scientists led by Dr. Emily Johnson and Dr. Daniel Lee conducted an experiment to examine the effect of different soil compositions on plant growth. They grew two groups of tomato plants, one in soil enriched with organic matter and the other in soil without any additives. After several weeks of monitoring, the plants in the enriched soil group exhibited significantly greater height and more abundant foliage compared to the plants in the unenriched soil group. These findings suggest that ________.

Which choice most logically completes the text?

A) the presence of additives in soil can hinder plant growth and development.
B) enriched soil always results in significantly greater plant height and foliage .
C) external factors like temperature and light intensity also contribute to plant growth.
D) organic matter in the soil positively influences plant growth and development.

B. Question Subcategory: Text Interpretation – Function of Sentence

Of the 54 Reading and Writing questions, approximately 1 - 2 may be questions from this subcategory.

EXAM QUESTION

Which choice best describes the function of the underlined sentence in the text as a whole?

WHAT TO EXPECT

You are presented with a passage containing a sentence that is underlined. You are asked to state the function of this sentence in the overall structure of the text.

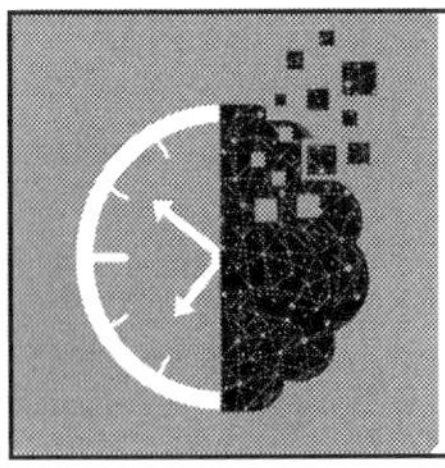

The Curvebreakers Strategy

READ AND PREDICT

1. Read the question before reading the passage to determine the Question Category.
2. Highlight key words or phrases.
3. Try to summarize your interpretation of the underlined text and write that summary down.
4. Select an answer choice that is consistent with your summary. If there are two parts to the answer choice, separate the first and second part and evaluate each part separately. For an answer choice to be correct, both parts must be correct. Avoid overly broad answer choices; correct answers will usually relate to something specific.

Example: Text Interpretation – Function of Sentence

Archaeologists have discovered a new cave painting in a remote region, providing valuable insights into the ancient civilization that inhabited the area. The painting depicts a hunting scene with several figures and animals, offering clues about the society's hunting practices and the types of animals they encountered. Experts believe that this discovery will contribute to a better understanding of the daily life and cultural traditions of this civilization. Additionally, analysis of the painting's pigments suggests the use of natural dyes sourced from local plants, indicating the civilization's connection to the surrounding environment.

Which choice best describes the function of the third sentence in the overall structure of the text?

A) It introduces the experts' belief about the impact of the discovery on modern civilization.
B) It provides a detailed description of the cave painting and its subject matter.
C) It explains why the cave painting is significant for archaeologists studying the ancient civilization.
D) It reveals the location of the cave painting and the region where the ancient civilization lived.

Solution Strategy: Read and Predict

Step 1: Read the question before reading the passage to determine the Question Category.

Which choice best describes the function of the third sentence in the overall structure of the text?

Step 2: Highlight key words or phrases.

Archaeologists have discovered a new cave painting in a remote region, providing valuable insights into the ancient civilization that inhabited the area. The painting depicts a hunting scene with several figures and animals, offering clues about the society's hunting practices and the types of animals they encountered. Experts believe that this discovery will contribute to a better understanding of the daily life and cultural traditions of this civilization. Additionally, analysis of the painting's pigments suggests the use of natural dyes sourced from local plants, indicating the civilization's connection to the surrounding environment.

Step 3: Try to summarize your interpretation of the underlined text and write that summary down.

Discovery of cave paintings contributes to better understanding of ancient civilization.

Step 4: Select an answer choice that is consistent with your summary. If there are two parts to the answer choice, separate the first and second part and evaluate each part separately. For an answer choice to be correct, both parts must be correct. Avoid overly broad answer choices; correct answers will usually relate to something specific.

yes | *no*
A) It introduces the experts' belief | ~~about the impact of the discovery on modern civilization.~~
The text specifically says "ancient civilization." There is no inference about modern civilization.

~~B) It provides a detailed description of the cave painting and its subject matter.~~
" a hunting scene with several figures and animals" is not a detailed description. Nor does the underlined sentence have anything to do with the subject matter.

? | *yes*
?C) It explains why the cave painting is significant | for archaeologists studying the ancient civilization.
Possible answer – not sure if passage "explains" why painting is significant, though.

no | *no*
~~D) It reveals the location of the cave painting | and the region where the ancient civilization lived.~~
The underlined sentence has nothing to do with location, nor is the painting's location revealed.

Correct Answer: C
While it may not be clear what the sentence is "explaining," Choice C is better than any other answer choice.

Practice: Text Interpretation – Function of Sentence

1. The following text is from Charles Dickens' 1859 novel *A Tale of Two Cities*. The narrator describes the French aristocracy's attitude towards the common people.

"The leprosy of unreality disfigured every human creature in attendance upon Monseigneur. In the outermost room were half a dozen exceptional people who had had, for a few years, some vague misgiving in them that things in general were going rather wrong. <u>As a promising way of setting them right, half of the half-dozen had become members of a fantastic sect of Convulsionists, and were even then considering within themselves whether they should foam, rage, roar, and turn cataleptic on the spot."</u>

Which choice best states the function of the underlined sentence in the overall structure of the text?

A) To provide a solution for the problems faced by the French aristocracy
B) To criticize the futile attempts of the aristocracy to address societal issues
C) To describe the daily activities of the people in attendance upon Monseigneur
D) To introduce a new group of characters that will play a significant role in the story

2. The Sahara Desert is one of the driest and hottest regions on Earth, with extreme temperatures and scarce water resources. Despite these challenging conditions, a unique group of plants, known as xerophytes, have adapted to survive in this harsh environment. <u>Xerophytes possess specific features that enable them to thrive in arid conditions, such as reduced leaf surface area, deep root systems, and mechanisms to minimize water loss</u>. These adaptations allow xerophytes to conserve water and efficiently utilize the limited resources available.

Which choice best describes the function of the underlined sentence in the text as a whole?

A) It introduces the concept of xerophytes and their adaptations to the Sahara Desert.
B) It provides a contrast between the Sahara Desert and other regions with abundant water resources.
C) It explains why the Sahara Desert has extreme temperatures and scarce water resources.
D) It emphasizes the importance of xerophytes in maintaining the ecological balance of the Sahara Desert.

3. The discovery of antibiotics revolutionized the field of medicine by providing effective treatments for bacterial infections. One key challenge in the use of antibiotics is the development of antibiotic resistance, where bacteria evolve and become resistant to the drugs. <u>To address this issue, researchers have been studying alternative approaches, such as bacteriophages, which are viruses that can target and kill specific bacteria</u>. These viruses have been found to be highly effective against certain bacterial strains.

Which choice best describes the function of the third sentence in the overall structure of the text?

A) It explains the process by which bacteriophages develop antibiotic resistance.
B) It introduces the concept of bacteriophages as essential components of antibiotics.
C) It highlights the significance of bacteriophages in combating antibiotic resistance.
D) It emphasizes the limitations of bacteriophages as alternatives to antibiotics.

C. Question Subcategory: Text Interpretation – Structure of Text

Of the 54 Reading and Writing questions, approximately 1 - 2 may be questions from this subcategory.

EXAM QUESTION

Which choice best describes the overall structure of the text?

WHAT TO EXPECT

You are presented with a passage and asked to describe the overall structure of the text.

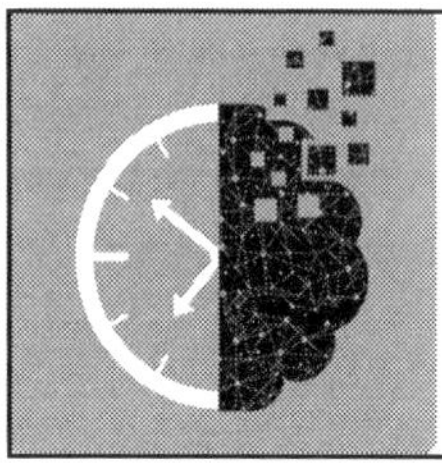

The Curvebreakers Strategy

SUMMARIZE AND USE P.O.E. (PROCESS OF ELIMINATION)

1. Read the question before reading the passage to determine the Question Category.
2. Highlight key words or phrases.
3. Try to summarize your interpretation of what the text is conveying and write that summary down.
4. Most of these answer choices can be separated into two parts: evaluate each part separately. For an answer choice to be correct, both parts must be correct.

Example: Text Interpretation – Structure of Text

The following passage is from Emily Dickinson's poem *Hope is the Thing with Feathers*:

Hope is the thing with feathers
That perches in the soul,
And sings the tune without the words,
And never stops at all.

Which choice best describes the overall structure of the text?

A) The speaker expresses a longing for a particular quality, then reflects on the consequences of its absence.
B) The speaker introduces a metaphorical concept, then provides details about its nature and behavior.
C) The speaker acknowledges a common belief, then presents a contrasting viewpoint.
D) The speaker observes a natural phenomenon, then draws a parallel to a human experience.

Solution Strategy: Summarize and Use POE

Step 1: Read the question before reading the passage to determine the Question Category.

Which choice best describes the overall structure of the text?

Step 2: Highlight key words or phrases.

Hope is the thing with feathers
That perches in the soul,
And sings the tune without the words,
And never stops at all.

Step 3: Try to summarize your interpretation of what the text is conveying and write that summary down.

Hope has feathers, it sings, and never stops.

Step 4: Most of these answer choices can be separated into two parts: evaluate each part separately. For an answer choice to be correct, both parts must be correct.

? no
A) The speaker expresses a longing for a particular quality,| ~~then reflects on the consequences of its absence.~~

yes ?
? B) The speaker introduces a metaphorical concept,| then provides details about its nature and behavior.
Hope has feathers is a metaphor.

no no
C) ~~The speaker acknowledges a common belief~~,| ~~then presents a contrasting viewpoint~~.

no yes
D) ~~The speaker observes a natural phenomenon~~,| then draws a parallel to a human experience.

Correct Answer: B
Process of Elimination.

Practice: Text Interpretation – Structure of Text

1.The following text is from William Wordsworth's poem *I Wandered Lonely as a Cloud*.

I wandered lonely as a cloud
That floats on high o'er vales and hills,
When all at once I saw a crowd,
A host, of golden daffodils;
Beside the lake, beneath the trees,
Fluttering and dancing in the breeze.

Which choice best describes the overall structure of the text?

A) The speaker expresses his state of solitude, then describes a sudden encounter with a group of daffodils.
B) The speaker reflects on the beauty of nature, then depicts a serene scene by a lake.
C) The speaker expresses his joyous discovery, then vividly describes the movement of daffodils in the wind.
D) The speaker emphasizes his sense of isolation, then reflects on the vastness of the landscape.

2. The Beatles' album *Sgt. Pepper's Lonely Hearts Club Band* (1967) is considered a groundbreaking work in the history of popular music. The album's cover art, featuring a colorful collage of various figures and icons, reflects the band's artistic experimentation and departure from their earlier image. The cover's intricate design and inclusion of notable individuals from different fields symbolize the album's theme of celebrating creativity and the power of music. The innovative and eclectic musical compositions within the album further reinforce the band's departure from conventional pop music, incorporating elements of psychedelia, orchestral arrangements, and diverse musical styles. Through the combination of the album's cover art and its musical content, *Sgt. Pepper's* stands as a testament to the Beatles' artistic evolution and influence on popular music.

Which choice best describes the overall structure of the text?

A) It introduces the Beatles' album *Sgt. Pepper's Lonely Hearts Club Band*, then discusses its cover art and the band's departure from their earlier image.
B) It describes the album cover's intricate design and inclusion of notable figures, then criticizes the way in which they symbolize the album's theme.
C) It outlines the innovative musical compositions on the album, then analyzes how they reflect the band's departure from conventional pop music.
D) It highlights the Beatles' artistic evolution and influence on popular music, then provides examples from the album *Sgt. Pepper's* to support this claim.

D. Question Subcategory: Text Interpretation – According to Text

Of the 54 Reading and Writing questions, approximately 1 - 3 may be questions from this subcategory.

EXAM QUESTION (Examples)

Based on the text, in what way is the ....?
According to the text, how did the researchers determine.......?
According to the text, what is true about.......?

WHAT TO EXPECT

These are catch-all text interpretation questions not identified in one of the previous categories. You are presented with a passage and then asked a question testing your understanding of what you've just read.

The Curvebreakers Strategy

USE P.O.E. (PROCESS OF ELIMINATION)

1. Read the question before reading the passage to determine the Question Category. Highlight the specific clause in the question that specifies what you should be looking for.
2. Highlight key words or phrases.
3. Try to predict the direction that the answer should follow and write that prediction down.
4. For answer choices that can be separated into two parts, evaluate each part separately. For an answer choice to be correct, both parts must be correct.
5. Select the best answer choice based on the key words or phrases. Beware of answer choices with language that is too extreme or definitive, such as "best," "only," "every," "all."

Example: Text Interpretation – According to Text

In the following text adapted from Emily Bronte's 1847 novel *Wuthering Heights*, Mr. Lockwood describes his first impressions of Wuthering Heights, the home of his landlord, Mr. Heathcliff.

Wuthering Heights is the name of Mr. Heathcliff's dwelling. 'Wuthering' being a significant provincial adjective, descriptive of the atmospheric tumult to which its station is exposed in stormy weather. Pure, bracing ventilation they must have up there at all times, indeed: one may guess the power of the north wind blowing over the edge, by the excessive slant of a few stunted firs at the end of the house; and by a range of gaunt thorns all stretching their limbs one way, as if craving alms of the sun.

According to the text, what is true about Wuthering Heights?

A) It never experiences fair weather.
B) It is a dwelling with a peaceful and calm atmosphere.
C) It is a place exposed to harsh weather and strong winds.
D) It is surrounded by lush vegetation and tall trees.

Solution Strategy: Use POE

Step 1: Read the question before reading the passage to determine the Question Category. Highlight the specific clause in the question that specifies what you should be looking for.

According to the text, what is true about Wuthering Heights?

Step 2: Highlight key words or phrases.

Wuthering Heights is the name of Mr. Heathcliff's dwelling. 'Wuthering' being a significant provincial adjective, descriptive of the atmospheric tumult to which its station is exposed in stormy weather. Pure, bracing ventilation they must have up there at all times, indeed: one may guess the power of the north wind blowing over the edge, by the excessive slant of a few stunted firs at the end of the house; and by a range of gaunt thorns all stretching their limbs one way, as if craving alms of the sun.

Step 3: Try to predict the direction that the answer should follow and write that prediction down.

Something to do with bad weather

Step 4: For answer choices that can be separated into two parts, evaluate each part separately. For an answer choice to be correct, both parts must be correct.

Step 5: Select the best answer choice based on the key words or phrases. Beware of answer choices with language that is too extreme or definitive, such as "best," "only," "every," "all."

? A) It never experiences fair weather.
This is consistent with bad weather but "never" seems too extreme.

~~B) It is a dwelling with a peaceful and calm atmosphere.~~
Contradicts text.

✓C) It is a place exposed to harsh weather and strong winds.
Consistent with bad weather.

~~D) It is surrounded by lush vegetation and tall trees.~~
Contradicts "stunted" firs.

Correct Answer: C
Choice C is best. While Choice A is going in the right direction in terms of bad weather, the use of the word "never" is extreme – this would mean that the home never, ever, ever, had one decent day of weather, and this isn't supported by the text.

Practice: Text Interpretation – According to Text

1. The following text is from Robert Frost's poem *The Road Not Taken* (1916):

Two roads diverged in a yellow wood,
And sorry I could not travel both
And be one traveler, long I stood
And looked down one as far as I could
To where it bent in the undergrowth;

Then took the other, as just as fair,
And having perhaps the better claim,
Because it was grassy and wanted wear;
Though as for that the passing there
Had worn them really about the same,

And both that morning equally lay
In leaves no step had trodden black.
Oh, I kept the first for another day!
Yet knowing how way leads on to way,
I doubted if I should ever come back.

Based on the text, what is the speaker's attitude towards the two diverging roads?

A) The speaker confidently chooses the road less traveled and expresses no regret for not being able to explore both paths.
B) The speaker carefully considers the advantages of each road before making a choice.
C) The speaker is uncertain and hesitant about choosing one road over the other, and is unable to choose either road.
D) The speaker is confident in his decision to take the less worn road.

2. The following text is from Fyodor Dostoevsky's 1866 novel *Crime and Punishment*. The passage focuses on the protagonist, Raskolnikov, who is contemplating the consequences of his actions.

He had become so completely absorbed in himself, and isolated from his fellows that he dreaded meeting, not only his landlady, but anyone at all. He was crushed by poverty, but the anxieties of his position had of late ceased to weigh upon him. He had given up attending to matters of practical importance; he had lost all desire to do so. Nothing that any landlady could do had a real terror for him. But to be stopped on the stairs, to be forced to listen to her trivial, irrelevant gossip, to pestering demands for payment, threats and complaints, and to rack his brains for excuses, to prevaricate, to lie—no, rather than that, he would creep down the stairs like a cat and slip out unseen."

According to the text, what can be inferred about Raskolnikov's state of mind?

A) Raskolnikov is devastated by financial problems and fears confronting his landlady.
B) Raskolnikov is confident in his ability to manage his financial situation and deal with his landlady's demands.
C) Raskolnikov has become indifferent to his financial difficulties and the interactions with his landlady.
D) Raskolnikov is fearful of leaving his apartment and interacting with others in the building.

3. The Great Barrier Reef, located off the coast of Australia, is one of the most diverse and important ecosystems in the world. It is home to thousands of species of marine life and provides numerous ecological and economic benefits. However, in recent years, the reef has been facing various threats, including coral bleaching, pollution, and ocean acidification. Scientists are deeply concerned about the future of the Great Barrier Reef and its ability to recover from these challenges.

According to the text, why are scientists concerned about the Great Barrier Reef?

A) The reef is experiencing significant population declines among marine species.
B) The reef is no longer a popular tourist attraction due to its deteriorating condition.
C) Scientists believe that the reef has lost its ecological importance and should be left to natural processes.
D) The reef is facing multiple threats that are jeopardizing its health and recovery.

4. In the field of paleontology, the discovery of new fossil specimens can often shed light on the evolutionary history of different species. Recently, researchers unearthed a well-preserved fossil of an ancient bird species, named Avioraptor longus, in a remote region of South America. This discovery is particularly significant because it provides evidence of an early avian lineage in the southern hemisphere, challenging the previous assumption that such lineages were exclusively found in the northern hemisphere.

According to the passage, why is the discovery of Avioraptor longus significant?

A) It confirms the previous assumption about avian lineages being exclusively found in the northern hemisphere.
B) It reveals new insights into the evolutionary history of ancient bird species.
C) It disproves the theory of avian lineages originating in the southern hemisphere.
D) It provides evidence of a well-preserved fossil of an ancient bird species.

For answer explanations to these practice questions, go to curvebreakerstestprep.com/decoding-the-digital-sat

CHAPTER 8: DUAL PASSAGES

Section: Reading and Writing
Question Subsection: Reading Comprehension
Question Category: Dual Passages
Of the 54 Reading and Writing questions, approximately 1 - 2 may be questions from this category.

EXAM QUESTION

Based on the texts, how would [the person mentioned in Text 1] respond to the [conclusion, conventional wisdom, etc.] discussed in Text 2?

WHAT TO EXPECT

You are presented with two consecutive passages and asked what the author of one text would say about the information presented in the other text.

LESSON

The Dual Passages will present two viewpoints. Often, you can get to the correct answer choice by understanding the relationship between the passages – that is, do they agree or disagree? There will be words in the answer choices that are clues to this relationship.

Examples of Agreement Words in Answer Choices	Examples of Disagreement Words in Answer Choices
Concede	Dispute
Acknowledge	Challenge
Reasonable	Unexpected
Justifiable	Questionable

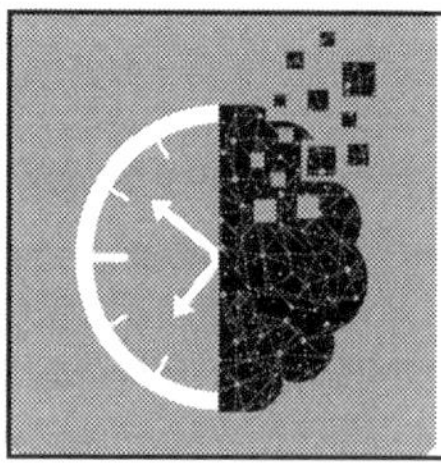

The Curvebreakers Strategy

SUMMARIZE AND USE P.O.E. (PROCESS OF ELIMINATION)

1. Read the question before reading the passage to determine the Question Category.
2. Read Text 1 and highlight key words or phrases.
3. Try to summarize the findings in Text 1 and write that summary down.
4. Read Text 2 and highlight key words or phrases.
5. Try to summarize the findings in Text 2 and write that summary down.
6. Determine whether or not the two texts have conflicting viewpoints or similar viewpoints.
7. Based on the language in the answer choices, determine which choices present conflicting viewpoints and which present similar viewpoints. Select the answer choice based on this determination.
8. If there are two parts to the answer choice, evaluate each part separately. For an answer choice to be correct, both parts must be correct.

Example: Dual Passages

Text 1:

Researchers have long studied the effects of exercise on mental health. Regular physical activity has been shown to have a positive impact on mood, reduce symptoms of anxiety and depression, and improve overall well-being. The mechanisms behind these effects are still being explored, but increased blood flow to the brain, the release of endorphins, and the reduction of stress hormones are believed to play a role.

Text 2:

In a recent study, Dr. Johnson and her team investigated the relationship between exercise and mental health in older adults. They found that even a moderate level of physical activity, such as walking or gardening, was associated with improved mental well-being. The participants who engaged in regular exercise reported lower levels of stress, increased feelings of happiness, and improved cognitive function compared to those who were more sedentary.

Based on the texts, how would Dr. Johnson and her team (Text 2) most likely respond to the findings discussed in Text 1?

A) By supporting and further emphasizing the positive impact of exercise on mental health based on their own study's results.
B) By questioning the validity of the mechanisms proposed in Text 1 and suggesting alternative explanations.
C) By dismissing the effects of exercise on mental health in older adults and focusing on other factors.
D) By recommending further research to determine the long-term effects of exercise on mental health.

Solution Strategy: Summarize and Use POE

Step 1: *Read the question before reading the passage to determine the Question Category.*

Based on the texts, how would Dr. Johnson and her team (Text 2) most likely respond to the findings discussed in Text 1?

Step 2: *Read Text 1 and highlight key words or phrases.*

Researchers have long studied the effects of exercise on mental health. Regular physical activity has been shown to have a positive impact on mood, reduce symptoms of anxiety and depression, and improve overall well-being. The mechanisms behind these effects are still being explored, but increased blood flow to the brain, the release of endorphins, and the reduction of stress hormones are believed to play a role.

Step 3: *Try to summarize the findings in Text 1 and write that summary down.*

Exercise is good.

Step 4: *Read Text 2 and highlight key words or phrases.*

In a recent study, Dr. Johnson and her team investigated the relationship between exercise and mental health in older adults. They found that even a moderate level of physical activity, such as walking or gardening, was associated with improved mental well-being. The participants who engaged in regular exercise reported lower levels of stress, increased feelings of happiness, and improved cognitive function compared to those who were more sedentary.

Step 5: *Try to summarize the findings in Text 2 and write that summary down.*

Exercise is good for older adults.

Step 6: *Determine whether or not the two texts have conflicting viewpoints or similar viewpoints.*

Both agree exercise is good.

Step 7: Based on the language in the answer choices, determine which choices present conflicting viewpoints and which present similar viewpoints. Select the answer choice based on this determination.

yes *yes*
✓A) By supporting and further emphasizing | the positive impact of exercise on mental health based on their own study's results.
"Support" is agreement.

no *no*
~~B) By questioning the validity~~ | of the mechanisms proposed in Text 1 and suggesting alternative explanations.
"Questioning the validity" conflicts with agreement.

no *no*
C) ~~By dismissing~~ | the effects of exercise on mental health in older adults and focusing on other factors.
"Dismissing" conflicts with agreement.

? *?*
? D) By recommending further research | to determine the long-term effects of exercise on mental health.
Only Text 1 gives any indication of further research, "still being explored". Text 2 gives no indication of further research.

Correct Answer: A.
Text 2 states that even a moderate level of physical activity was associated with improved mental well-being in older adults. This aligns with the positive impact of exercise on mood, anxiety, depression, and overall well-being mentioned in Text 1. Therefore, Dr. Johnson and her team would likely support and reinforce the findings from Text 1 based on their own study's results.

Practice: Dual Passages

1.

Text 1:

Studies have shown a correlation between regular meditation practice and improved stress management. Meditation techniques, such as mindfulness and deep breathing, can help individuals reduce stress levels, enhance relaxation, and promote overall well-being. The practice of focusing on the present moment and cultivating a non-judgmental attitude can have significant benefits for mental and emotional health.

Text 2:

Dr. Patel and her team conducted a study on the effects of meditation on stress reduction in college students. They found that participants who engaged in a mindfulness meditation program experienced a significant decrease in perceived stress levels compared to those who did not participate. The participants reported feeling more calm, focused, and better equipped to manage daily challenges after the meditation program.

Based on the texts, how would Dr. Patel and her team (Text 2) most likely respond to the findings discussed in Text 1?

A) By highlighting the limitations of meditation as a stress management technique and proposing other approaches.
B) By disputing the correlation between meditation and stress reduction and suggesting alternative factors.
C) By affirming and providing additional evidence for the positive effects of regular meditation on stress management.
D) By recommending further research to examine the long-term effects of meditation on stress management.

2.

Text 1:

Scientists have long been intrigued by the ability of certain bird species to migrate long distances. Research has shown that birds possess a combination of innate abilities and learned behaviors that enable them to navigate across vast distances using celestial cues, landmarks, and magnetic fields. However, the precise mechanisms and strategies employed by migratory birds are still being investigated.

Text 2:

In a recent study, Dr. Lopez and her team examined the migratory patterns of a specific bird species known for its impressive long-distance migration. They found that these birds rely on a combination of genetic factors and environmental cues to guide their journeys. The study revealed that specific genes associated with navigation and orientation play a crucial role in the birds' ability to migrate accurately. Additionally, the birds' exposure to certain environmental cues during early developmental stages further enhances their navigational skills.

Based on the texts, how would Dr. Lopez and her team (Text 2) most likely respond to the findings discussed in Text 1?

A) By corroborating the understanding of the mechanisms and strategies employed by migratory birds based on their own study's results.
B) By challenging the existing research on bird migration and proposing alternative explanations.
C) By suggesting that migratory birds rely solely on innate abilities and genetic factors for navigation.
D) By recommending further research to explore the impact of human activity on bird migration patterns.

3.

Text 1:

For many years, it was believed that the diversity of plant and animal species in tropical rainforests was primarily driven by high levels of rainfall and temperature. The theory suggested that the abundance of resources in these regions supported a wide range of species. However, recent research has challenged this notion by highlighting the importance of ecological interactions, such as competition, predation, and mutualism, in shaping species diversity.

Text 2:

In a groundbreaking study, Dr. Rodriguez and her team investigated the factors influencing species diversity in tropical rainforests. They found that while rainfall and temperature play a role in determining species distribution, ecological interactions are crucial drivers of species diversity. Their study revealed that competitive interactions among species, predator-prey relationships, and mutually beneficial interactions all contribute to the rich biodiversity observed in tropical rainforest ecosystems.

Based on the texts, how would Dr. Rodriguez and her team (Text 2) most likely respond to the beliefs presented in Text 1 about the drivers of species diversity in tropical rainforests?

A) By supporting and providing evidence for the importance of ecological interactions in shaping species diversity.
B) By questioning the validity of the theory and proposing alternative factors as the primary drivers of species diversity.
C) By dismissing the significance of rainfall and temperature and focusing only on ecological interactions.
D) By recommending further research to explore the influence of other environmental factors on species diversity.

4.

Text 1:

Research conducted by Dr. Anderson and her team suggests that exposure to nature has numerous benefits for mental health. Their study found that spending time in natural environments, such as parks or forests, can reduce stress levels, improve mood, and enhance cognitive function. These findings support the idea that nature-based interventions can play a significant role in promoting mental well-being.

Text 2:

In a critical review of existing research, Dr. Roberts argues that while nature exposure may have some positive effects on mental health, the evidence is not as conclusive as widely portrayed. He notes that many studies suffer from methodological limitations and biases, making it difficult to draw firm conclusions. Dr. Roberts suggests that further rigorous research is needed to better understand the complex relationship between nature exposure and mental health outcomes.

Based on the texts, how would Dr. Roberts (Text 2) most likely respond to the findings presented in Text 1 about the benefits of nature exposure for mental health?

A) By supporting the findings and emphasizing the importance of nature-based interventions in mental well-being.
B) By disputing the conclusiveness of the findings and highlighting methodological limitations in existing research.
C) By proposing alternative explanations for the observed benefits of nature exposure on mental health.
D) By recommending the expansion of nature-based interventions without further research or scrutiny.

For answer explanations to these practice questions, go to curvebreakerstestprep.com/decoding-the-digital-sat

CHAPTER 9: TRANSITION WORDS

Section: Reading and Writing
Question Subsection: Reading Comprehension
Question Category: Transition Words
Of the 54 Reading and Writing questions, approximately 3 - 6 may be questions from this category.

EXAM QUESTION

Which choice completes the text with the most logical transition?

WHAT TO EXPECT

You are presented with a short paragraph that has a "________" in place of the words and you are asked to complete the text with the correct transition word(s).

LESSON

Transition words help to emphasize some sort of relationship between two thoughts (often between a sentence and the sentence before or after). To select the proper transition word(s), we need to determine this relationship. There are a number of reasons to use transitions, but the most commonly tested are:

- **Same Direction**: when the second statement is a result of the first statement or it illustrates or emphasizes the first statement, use a *same-direction* word(s).
- **Contrast**: when the second statement represents a contrast from the first statement, use a *contrasting* word(s).
- **Addition**: when new information is presented to reinforce the first idea, use an *addition* word(s).

Exercise:

Choose the direction of the Transition Words

	Same Direction?	Contrast?	Addition?
Therefore			
Consequently			
But			
Moreover			
However			
In other words			
Nevertheless			
Similarly			
Accordingly			
Furthermore			
For example			
In contrast			
Likewise			

The Curvebreakers Strategy

WRITE IN YOUR OWN WORD

1. Read the question before reading the passage to determine the Question Category.
2. Cover the answer choices by physically placing your hand over the choices.
3. Identify and highlight the "clue" word(s) or phrase(s). Every passage will contain a keyword(s) or phrase(s) that will lead you to the correct answer.
4. Reread the sentence with the ________ as well as the immediate sentence before and after the ________ and try to determine the relationship between the sentence with the ________ and the other two sentences. Write that relationship down: same/different/addition.
5. Write your own transition word in the ________ based on your understanding of the relationship.
6. Eliminate answer choices that don't match your selection; choose the answer choice that most closely matches your selection.

Example 1: Transition Words

1. Geoscientists have long considered Hawaii's Mauna Loa volcano to be Earth's largest shield volcano by volume, measuring approximately 74,000 cubic kilometers. ________ according to a 2020 study by local geoscientist Michael Garcia, Hawaii's Pūhāhonu shield volcano is significantly larger, boasting a volume of about 148,000 cubic kilometers.

Which choice completes the text with the most logical transition?

A) Secondly,
B) Consequently,
C) Moreover,
D) However,

Solution Strategy: Write in Your Own Word

Step 1: Read the question before reading the passage to determine the Question Category.

Which choice completes the text with the most logical transition?

Step 2: Cover the answer choices by physically placing your hand over the choices.

A) [redacted]
B) [redacted]
C) [redacted]
D) [redacted]

Step 3: Identify and highlight the "clue" word(s) or phrase(s). Every passage will contain a keyword(s) or phrase(s) that will lead you to the correct answer.

Geoscientists have long considered Hawaii's Mauna Loa volcano to be Earth's largest shield volcano by volume, measuring approximately 74,000 cubic kilometers. ________ according to a 2020 study by local geoscientist Michael Garcia, Hawaii's Pūhāhonu shield volcano is significantly larger, boasting a volume of about 148,000 cubic kilometers.

Step 4: Reread the sentence with the ________ as well as the immediate sentence before and after the ________ and try to determine the relationship between the sentence with the ________ and the other two sentences. Write that relationship down: same/contrast/addition.

Loa volcano is large <u>but</u> Puhahonu volcano is larger. Contrast.

Step 5: Write your own transition word in the _______ based on your understanding of the relationship.

Geoscientists have long considered Hawaii's Mauna Loa volcano to be Earth's largest shield volcano by volume, measuring approximately 74,000 cubic kilometers. ***but*** according to a 2020 study by local geoscientist Michael Garcia, Hawaii's Pūhāhonu shield volcano is significantly larger, boasting a volume of about 148,000 cubic kilometers.

Step 6: Eliminate answer choices that don't match your selection; choose the answer choice that most closely matches your selection.

~~A) Secondly,~~
Same direction. Implies a listing or sequence, but there's no first point made.

~~B) Consequently,~~
Same direction. Suggests a result or effect.

~~C) Moreover,~~
Addition. Adds extra information or emphasizes a point.

✓D) However,
Contrast.

Correct Answer: D
"However" is used to introduce a statement that contrasts with or seems to contradict something that has been said previously. In this case, the previously mentioned fact was that Mauna Loa was considered the largest shield volcano by volume. The statement that follows introduces a contradicting point: that the Pūhāhonu shield volcano is actually larger.

Example 2: Transition Words

2. Before California's 1911 election to approve a proposition granting women the right to vote, activists across the state sold tea to promote the cause of suffrage. In San Francisco, the Woman's Suffrage Party sold Equality Tea at local fairs. _______ in Los Angeles, activist Nancy Tuttle Craig, who ran one of California's largest grocery store firms, distributed Votes for Women Tea.

Which choice completes the text with the most logical transition?

A) For example,
B) However,
C) Similarly,
D) Alternatively,

Solution Strategy: Write in Your Own Word

Step 1: Read the question before reading the passage to determine the Question Category.

Which choice completes the text with the most logical transition?

Step 2: Cover the answer choices by physically placing your hand over the choices.

A) [redacted]
B) [redacted]
C) [redacted]
D) [redacted]

Step 3: Identify and highlight the "clue" word(s) or phrase(s). Every passage will contain a keyword(s) or phrase(s) that will lead you to the correct answer.

Before California's 1911 election to approve a proposition granting women the right to vote, activists across the state sold tea to promote the cause of suffrage. In San Francisco, the Woman's Suffrage Party sold Equality Tea at local fairs. _______ in Los Angeles, activist Nancy Tuttle Craig, who ran one of California's largest grocery store firms, distributed Votes for Women Tea.

Step 4: *Reread the sentence with the ______ as well as the immediate sentence before and after the ______ and try to determine the relationship between the sentence with the ______ and the other two sentences. Write that relationship down: same/contrast/addition.*

Sold tea in SF and LA to promote suffrage. Same direction.

Step 5: *Write your own transition word in the ______ based on your understanding of the relationship.*

Before California's 1911 election to approve a proposition granting women the right to vote, activists across the state sold tea to promote the cause of suffrage. In San Francisco, the Woman's Suffrage Party sold Equality Tea at local fairs. ___*Also*___ in Los Angeles, activist Nancy Tuttle Craig, who ran one of California's largest grocery store firms, distributed Votes for Women Tea.

Step 6: *Eliminate answer choices that don't match your selection; choose the answer choice that most closely matches your selection.*

? A) For example,
Same direction.

~~B) However,~~
Contrast

✓C) Similarly,
Same direction.

~~D) Alternatively,~~
Contrast

Correct Answer: C
Of the two same-direction answer choices, "Similarly" works better because it is used to draw a parallel or make a comparison between two related ideas or actions.

Practice: Transition Words

1. Solar energy is a renewable and environmentally friendly source of power. Solar panels capture sunlight and convert it into electricity that can be used to power homes, businesses, and other facilities. ______ the initial cost of installing solar panels can be high, the long-term savings on energy bills often outweigh the upfront investment.

Which choice completes the text with the most logical transition?

A) In contrast,
B) As a result,
C) For instance,
D) Although

2. In November 1934, Amrita Sher-Gil was living in what must have seemed like the ideal city for a young artist: Paris. She was studying firsthand the color-saturated style of France's modernist masters and beginning to make a name for herself as a painter. ______ Sher-Gil longed to return to her childhood home of India; only there, she believed, could her art truly flourish.

Which choice completes the text with the most logical transition?

A) Still,
B) Therefore,
C) Indeed,
D) Furthermore,

3. The invention of the printing press by Johannes Gutenberg in the 15th century revolutionized the dissemination of knowledge and paved the way for the mass production of books. ________ this technological advancement, books were laboriously handwritten and limited to a select few. The printing press allowed for faster and more efficient production of books, making them accessible to a wider audience.

Which choice completes the text with the most logical transition?

A) Prior to
B) In addition to
C) As a result of
D) In contrast to

4. In a revolutionary scientific experiment, researchers conducted a series of tests on a newly developed compound and observed its effects on cancer cells. ________ the experiments, the researchers discovered that the compound effectively inhibited the growth and proliferation of cancer cells, offering promising potential for future cancer treatments. This breakthrough has brought new hope to the field of oncology.

Which choice completes the text with the most logical transition?

A) Despite
B) In addition to
C) As a result of
D) Prior to

5. Although novels and poems are considered distinct literary forms, many authors have created hybrid works that incorporate elements of both. Bernardine Evaristo's *The Emperor's Babe*, ________ is a verse novel, a book-length narrative complete with characters and a plot but conveyed in short, crisp lines of poetry rather than prose.

Which choice completes the text with the most logical transition?

A) by contrast,
B) consequently,
C) secondly,
D) for example,

6. The Great Barrier Reef is one of the world's most spectacular natural wonders, stretching over 2,300 kilometers off the coast of Australia. It is home to a staggering diversity of marine life, including over 1,500 species of fish. ________ the reef faces numerous challenges, such as coral bleaching and ocean acidification, which threaten its delicate ecosystem and biodiversity.

Which choice completes the text with the most logical transition?

A) For instance,
B) Nevertheless,
C) Meanwhile,
D) In addition,

7. Archaeologist Sue Brunning explains why the seventh-century ship burial site at Sutton Hoo in England was likely the tomb of a king. First, the gold artifacts inside the ship suggest that the person buried with them was a wealthy and respected leader. ________ the massive effort required to bury the ship would likely only have been undertaken for a king.

Which choice completes the text with the most logical transition?

A) For instance,
B) Nevertheless,
C) Meanwhile,
D) In addition,

8. In the history of tennis, the rivalry between Roger Federer and Rafael Nadal is widely regarded as one of the greatest in the sport. They have faced each other numerous times in high-stakes matches, producing thrilling encounters and showcasing their exceptional skills. ________ their contrasting playing styles have captivated fans and analysts alike.

Which choice completes the text with the most logical transition?

A) Regardless,
B) Nevertheless,
C) Furthermore,
D) Afterward,

For answer explanations to these practice questions, go to curvebreakerstestprep.com/decoding-the-digital-sat

CHAPTER 10: PUNCTUATION – FULL-STOP AND HALF-STOP

Section: Reading and Writing
Question Subsection: Grammar
Question Category: Full-Stop and Half-Stop Punctuation
Of the 54 Reading and Writing questions, approximately 3 - 6 may be questions from this category.

EXAM QUESTION

Which choice completes the text so that it conforms to the conventions of Standard English?

WHAT TO EXPECT

You are presented with a short paragraph that has a "______" in place of the words and you are asked to complete the text with the correct answer choice. These questions can be identified by noticing that Full-Stop or Half-Stop Punctuation is changing among any of the 4 answer choices.

LESSON

Rather than going into the weeds with proper grammar terminology, let's keep it simple:

A COMPLETE idea can STAND ALONE
For example, 'John eats" is complete. It contains a subject and a verb and expresses a complete thought.

An INCOMPLETE idea is MISSING SOMETHING
For example, "Although John eats" is incomplete. Even though it contains a subject and verb, it does not express a complete thought.

Determining *Complete* versus *Incomplete* ideas will determine the type of punctuation needed to link the 2 ideas.

Full-Stop and Half-Stop Punctuation

FULL-STOP: LINKS 2 COMPLETE IDEAS	HALF-STOP: NEED COMPLETE IDEA TO THE LEFT
Period (.)	Colon (:)
Semicolon (;)	Long Dash (—)
Comma + FANBOYS* (, FANBOYS)	
Question/Exclamation Mark (?/!)	

*FANBOYS = For, And, Nor, But, Or, Yet, So

The Rules:
- Full-Stop Punctuation can link ONLY 2 complete ideas.
- Half-Stop Punctuation must have a complete idea to the LEFT (the right can be either Complete or Incomplete).

TIP: Don't use punctuation if you don't need punctuation. Watch out for over-punctuation.

Exercise: Complete or Incomplete Idea?

	Complete?	Incomplete?
It smells		
To read a book		
Why does she look so sad		
When he goes to school		
Counting from one to ten		
They were too noisy		

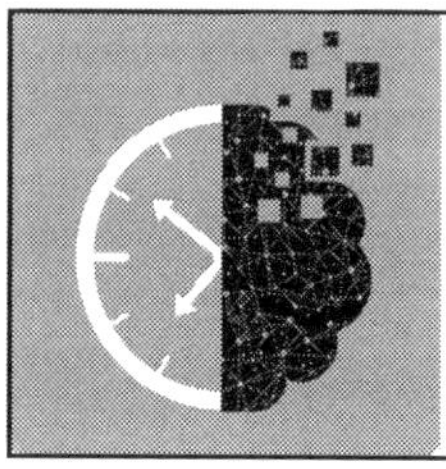

The Curvebreakers Strategy

VERTICAL LINE TEST

1. Read the question before reading the passage to determine the Question Category.
2. If Full-Stop or Half-Stop punctuation is included in any of the answer choices, draw a vertical line after the proposed punctuation in each answer choice. (Draw the vertical line through the FANBOYS if FANBOYS is tested).
3. Read to the left of the vertical line and mark it *Complete* or *Incomplete*.
4. Read to the right of the vertical line and mark it *Complete or Incomplete*.
5. Select the proper punctuation based on the rules for Full-Stop/ Half-Stop punctuation.

Example 1: Full-Stop and Half-Stop Punctuation

1. The professor made an important announcement during ______ there will be an upcoming field trip to the local museum, which will enhance our understanding of the historical artifacts we have been studying.

Which choice completes the text so that it conforms to the conventions of Standard English?

A) class
B) class:
C) class,
D) class, at which

Solution Strategy: Vertical Line Test

Step 1: Read the question before reading the passage to determine the Question Category.

Which choice completes the text so that it conforms to the conventions of Standard English?

Step 2: If Full-Stop or Half-Stop punctuation is included in any of the answer choices, draw a vertical line after the proposed punctuation in each answer choice. (Draw the vertical line through the FANBOYS if FANBOYS is tested).

The professor made an important announcement during ______ | there will be an upcoming field trip to the local museum, which will enhance our understanding of the historical artifacts we have been studying.

Step 3: *Read to the left of the vertical line and mark it "Complete" or "Incomplete."*

C
Ex: A) class |

Step 4: *Read to the right of the vertical line and mark it ""Complete" or "Incomplete."*

C C
Ex: A) class |

Step 5: *Select the proper punctuation based on the rules for Full-Stop/Half Stop punctuation.*

C C
~~A)~~ class |
The left side is Complete: *The professor made an important announcement during class*
The right side is Complete: *there will be an upcoming field trip to the local museum, which will enhance our understanding of the historical artifacts we have been studying.*

This answer choice has no punctuation. Since we have two complete ideas, we need to have Full-Stop or Half-Stop punctuation.

C C
✓B) class: |
This answer choice has a colon, which is Half-Stop Punctuation. With Half-Stop we need a complete idea to the left, which we have.

C C
? C) class, |
This answer choice has a comma and falls under the rules of commas, discussed in the next chapter.

I C
~~D)~~ class, at which |
The left side is now Incomplete because of the words "at which": *The professor made an important announcement during class, at which*
The right side is Complete: *there will be an upcoming field trip to the local museum, which will enhance our understanding of the historical artifacts we have been studying.*
This answer choice can be eliminated based on the unnecessary words *"at which."*

Correct Answer: B
Answer Choice B is better than Choice C because it has Half-Stop punctuation with a complete idea to the left. The comma in Choice C falls under the rules of commas discussed in the next chapter.

Example 2: Full-Stop and Half-Stop Punctuation

2. A study published by Rice University geoscientist Ming Tang in 2019 offers a new explanation for the origin of Earth's _______ structures called arcs form when a dense oceanic plate subducts under a less dense continental plate, melts in the mantle below, and then rises and bursts through the continental crust above.

Which choice completes the text so that it conforms to the conventions of Standard English?

A) continents geological
B) continents': geological
C) continent's; geological
D) continents. Geological

Solution Strategy: Vertical Line Test

Step 1: Read the question before reading the passage to determine the Question Category.

Which choice completes the text so that it conforms to the conventions of Standard English?

Step 2: If Full-Stop or Half-Stop punctuation is included in any of the answer choices, draw a vertical line after the proposed punctuation in each answer choice. (Draw the vertical line through the FANBOYS if FANBOYS is tested).

A study published by Rice University geoscientist Ming Tang in 2019 offers a new explanation for the origin of Earth's ________ | structures called arcs form when a dense oceanic plate subducts under a less dense continental plate, melts in the mantle below, and then rises and bursts through the continental crust above.

Step 3: Read to the left of the vertical line and mark it "Complete" or "Incomplete."

Step 4: Read to the right of the vertical line and mark it '"Complete" or "Incomplete."

Step 5: Select the proper punctuation based on the rules for Full-Stop/ Half-Stop punctuation.

C *C*
~~A)~~ continents | geological
The left side is Complete: *A study published by Rice University geoscientist Ming Tang in 2019 offers a new explanation for the origin of Earth's continents*
The right side is Complete: *geological structures called arcs form when a dense oceanic plate subducts under a less dense continental plate, melts in the mantle below, and then rises and bursts through the continental crust above.*
This answer choice has no punctuation. Since we have two complete ideas, we need Full-Stop or Half-Stop punctuation.

C *C*
~~B)~~ continents': | geological
This answer choice has a colon, which is Half-Stop Punctuation. Based on the Vertical Line test, this choice would work because with Half-Stop, we need a complete idea to the left – and we have that. But this choice is incorrect because there is no reason to put an apostrophe after *continents* since there is no possession.

C *C*
~~C)~~ continent's; | geological
This answer choice has a semicolon, which is Full-Stop Punctuation. Based on the Vertical Line test, this choice would work because with Full-Stop, we need two complete ideas – and we have that. But this choice is incorrect because there is no reason to put an apostrophe after *continents* since there is no possession.

C *C*
✓D) continents. | Geological
This answer choice has a period, which is Full-Stop Punctuation. This choice works because with Full-Stop, we need two complete ideas – and we have that.

Correct Answer: D

Practice: Full-Stop and Half-Stop Punctuation

1. In the world of literature, William Shakespeare is revered as one of the greatest playwrights of all time. His works, such as *Romeo and Juliet*, *Hamlet*, and *Macbeth*, continue to be celebrated for their timeless themes and ________________ Shakespeare's mastery of language and his ability to capture the complexities of human nature exerted a profound influence on subsequent generations of writers, shaping the course of English literature.

Which choice completes the text so that it conforms to the conventions of Standard English?

A) compelling characters,
B) compelling, characters.
C) compelling characters.
D) compelling, characters,

2. In the world of classical music, two composers stand out as exceptional ________________________ Their contributions to music encompassed a wide range of genres, from symphonies and concertos to choral works and chamber music, leaving an indelible mark on the history of Western classical music.

Which choice completes the text so that it conforms to the conventions of Standard English?

A) figures: Johann Sebastian Bach and Wolfgang Amadeus Mozart.
B) figures—Johann Sebastian Bach— and Wolfgang Amadeus Mozart.
C) figures, Johann Sebastian Bach and Wolfgang Amadeus Mozart.
D) figures Johann Sebastian Bach and Wolfgang Amadeus Mozart.

3. Fibonacci numbers, a sequence of integers named after Italian mathematician Leonardo of Pisa, also known as Fibonacci, have fascinating mathematical properties. In this sequence, each number is the sum of the two preceding ones, starting with 0 and 1. As the sequence progresses, the ratio between consecutive Fibonacci numbers approaches a ____________ known as the golden ratio. This ratio, approximately equal to 1.618, exhibits intriguing mathematical and aesthetic properties.

Which choice completes the text so that it conforms to the conventions of Standard English?

A) threshold;
B) threshold:
C) threshold
D) threshold, to be

4. In the nineteenth century, the American landscape painter Thomas Cole founded the Hudson River School, an artistic movement that celebrated the natural beauty of the United States. The movement was characterized by its detailed, realistic depictions of the American wilderness. It primarily focused on the Hudson River Valley and surrounding ____________ the artists believed symbolized "a divine presence in nature."

Which choice completes the text so that it conforms to the conventions of Standard English?

A) regions: which
B) regions; which
C) regions – which
D) regions, which

5. The students had one goal in mind as they entered the debate ____________ to present compelling arguments and persuasive evidence that would sway the judges in their favor.

Which choice completes the text so that it conforms to the conventions of Standard English?

A) competition –
B) competition;
C) competition
D) competition.

6. During the Renaissance period, a humanist was an advocate of human potential and the study of humanities. Humanists believed in the importance of education and the _______ that individuals could achieve great heights through intellectual and artistic pursuits. They emphasized the value of critical thinking, cultural appreciation, and the exploration of diverse ideas.

Which choice completes the text so that it conforms to the conventions of Standard English?

A) enlightenment—asserting
B) enlightenment; asserting
C) enlightenment asserting
D) enlightenment. Asserting

7. During her expedition through the dense rainforest, biologist Dr. Elena Martinez stumbled upon a hidden waterfall glistening in the _______________ by its beauty, Dr. Martinez stood in awe, captivated by the sheer power and serenity of nature's masterpiece.

Which choice completes the text so that it conforms to the conventions of Standard English?

A) sunlight mesmerized
B) sunlight mesmerized,
C) sunlight. Mesmerized
D) sunlight, mesmerized

8. The team of scientists embarked on an ambitious expedition to the unexplored depths of the _____________ with state-of-the-art research vessels, cutting-edge technology, and a wealth of scientific knowledge, they aimed to uncover the mysteries that lie beneath the surface and expand our understanding of marine ecosystems.

Which choice completes the text so that it conforms to the conventions of Standard English?

A) ocean; equipped
B) ocean, equipped
C) ocean, equipped,
D) ocean equipped:

9. The Alvarez theory, developed in 1980 by physicist Luis Walter Alvarez and his geologist son Walter Alvarez, maintained that the secondary effects of an asteroid impact caused many dinosaurs and other animals to die _______ it left unexplored the question of whether unrelated volcanic activity might have also contributed to the mass extinctions.

Which choice completes the text so that it conforms to the conventions of Standard English?

A) out but
B) out, but
C) out
D) out,

10. The concept of evolution, as proposed by Charles Darwin in his seminal work *On the Origin of Species*, suggests that species gradually change over time in response to their environment and the process of natural selection. Darwin's theory revolutionized our understanding of life on Earth, demonstrating how organisms adapt and evolve to ensure their ___________________ it sparked considerable debate and controversy among scientists and religious communities.

Which choice completes the text so that it conforms to the conventions of Standard English?

A) survival, and,
B) survival. However,
C) survival, and
D) survival and: however,

For answer explanations to these practice questions, go to curvebreakerstestprep.com/decoding-the-digital-sat

CHAPTER 11: PUNCTUATION – COMMA USAGE

Section: Reading and Writing
Question Subsection: Grammar
Question Category: Punctuation – Comma Usage
Of the 54 Reading and Writing questions, approximately 2 - 6 may be questions from this category.

EXAM QUESTION

Which choice completes the text so that it conforms to the conventions of Standard English?

WHAT TO EXPECT

You are presented with a short paragraph that has a " ______ " in place of the words and you are asked to complete the text with the correct answer choice. These questions can be identified by noticing that the use of commas is changing in the answer choices.

LESSON

While there are many reasons to use commas, the SAT® traditionally focuses on three.

3 MAIN REASONS TO USE A COMMA	
After every item in a list*	Use commas to separate words and word groups in a list of three or more items (including the last item that comes before "and" or "or"). Use a comma to separate two adjectives when the order of the adjectives is interchangeable.
Before and after non-essential information**	Non-essential Information is a word, phrase, or clause that is not essential to the meaning of the sentence. When a nonessential clause is removed from the sentence, the sentence still makes sense without it. Think of nonessential information as a bonus; it provides extra, although unnecessary, information to the sentence.
After an Introductory word, phrase, or clause	Use commas after introductory clauses, phrases, or transition words that come before the main clause, or before quotations.

* Semicolons are sometimes used in complex lists in place of commas. Although semicolons are most often used as Full-Stop punctuation to link 2 complete ideas, they can also be used to separate elements in a list if the elements themselves contain commas.

** In addition to using commas before and after non-essential information, long dashes or parentheses can also be used. In the instances long dashes are used, they are used in place of commas and are not considered Half-Stop punctuation. But they need to be used consistently in the sentence – for example, you cannot use a long dash and a comma before and after nonessential information. It has to be either two long dashes or two commas.

The Curvebreakers Strategy

KNOW THE 3 MAIN REASONS TO USE A COMMA

1. Read the question before reading the passage to determine the Question Category.
2. If commas are changing in any of the answer choices, review the 3 main reasons to use a comma (in addition to Full-Stop punctuation with a FANBOYS):

    a. **After every item in a list**
    b. **Before and after non-essential information**
    c. **After an Introductory word, phrase, or clause**

3. Select the answer choice that uses the comma properly. If punctuation is not needed, do not use punctuation.

Example 1: Comma Usage

1. The Great Barrier Reef, located off the coast of Queensland, Australia, is the largest coral reef system in the world. It is home to a diverse range of marine life, including more than 1,500 species of fish, 411 species of hard coral, and 134 species of sharks and rays. The reef is also a popular tourist destination, attracting millions of visitors each year. However, the Great Barrier Reef has been facing significant threats __________________ pollution, and overfishing, which have led to widespread coral bleaching and the decline of many species. In response, conservation organizations are working tirelessly to restore and protect this unique and fragile ecosystem.

Which choice completes the text so that it conforms to the conventions of Standard English?

A) such as, climate change,
B) such as climate change,
C) such as, climate, change,
D) such as climate change

Solution Strategy: Know the 3 main reason to use a comma

Step 1: Read the question before reading the passage to determine the Question Category.

Which choice completes the text so that it conforms to the conventions of Standard English?

Step 2: If commas are changing in any of the answer choices*, review the 3 main reasons to use a comma (in addition to Full-Stop punctuation with a FANBOYS):*

1. After every item in a list
2. Before and after non-essential information
3. After an Introductory word, phrase, or clause

Step 3: Select the answer choice *that uses the comma properly. If punctuation is not needed, do not use punctuation.*

After every item in a list

~~A) such as, climate change,~~
There is no reason to place a comma after as. This would mean that the clause "climate change" is non-essential, which is incorrect.

✓B) such as climate change,
The placement of the comma here correctly identifies that "climate change" is part of a list which includes pollution and overfishing.

~~C) such as, climate, change,~~
There is no reason to place a comma after either "as" or "climate." Beware of too many commas in the answer choices.

~~D) such as climate change~~
The comma is required after "climate change" because it represents the first of a list.

Correct Answer: B
Comma Rule: After every item in a list

Example 2: Comma Usage

2. The Giant's Causeway, a natural wonder located on the coast of Northern ________ is composed of over 40,000 basalt columns that were formed by volcanic activity millions of years ago. According to local legend, the causeway was built by the giant Finn MacCool as a way to reach Scotland, where he intended to confront his Scottish rival. Geologists, however, have determined that the unique structure was created by the rapid cooling of lava, which caused the basalt to fracture into the distinctive hexagonal columns that can be seen today.

Which choice completes the text so that it conforms to the conventions of Standard English?

A) Ireland
B) Ireland,
C) Ireland:
D) Ireland;

Solution Strategy: Know the 3 main reason to use a comma

Step 1: Read the question before reading the passage to determine the Question Category.

Which choice completes the text so that it conforms to the conventions of Standard English?

Step 2: If commas are changing in any of the answer choices, *review the 3 main reasons to use a comma (in addition to Full-Stop punctuation with a FANBOYS):*

1. After every item in a list
2. Before and after non-essential information
3. After an Introductory word, phrase, or clause

Step 3: Select the answer choice *that uses the comma properly. If punctuation is not needed, do not use punctuation.*

Before and after non-essential information

~~A) Ireland~~
The comma rule is "Before and After Nonessential Information." Therefore a comma is needed both before and after "*a natural wonder located on the coast of Northern Ireland*" because it is nonessential – it can be removed and the sentence would not lose essential information.

✓B) Ireland,
The comma rule is "Before and After Nonessential Information." The comma is correctly used because a comma is needed both before and after "*a natural wonder located on the coast of Northern Ireland*" because it is nonessential – it can be removed and the sentence would not lose essential information.

/ /
~~C) Ireland:~~ |
Since we are testing Half-Stop punctuation (colon), let's do the Vertical Line Test. Half-Stop requires a Complete Idea to the left of the punctuation. "*The Giant's Causeway, a natural wonder located on the coast of Northern Ireland*" is an Incomplete idea.

/ /
~~D) Ireland;~~ |
Since we are testing Full-Stop punctuation (semicolon), let's do the Vertical Line Test. Full-Stop can only connect 2 Complete Ideas. "*The Giant's Causeway, a natural wonder located on the coast of Northern Ireland*" is an Incomplete idea.

Correct Answer: B
Comma Rule: Before and after non-essential information

Example 3: Comma Usage

3. In the world of literature, Jane Austen is celebrated for her insightful novels and compelling characters. Her novel *Pride and Prejudice*, published in 1813, is a timeless classic that continues to captivate readers with its witty social commentary and romantic plot. The story revolves around the spirited Elizabeth Bennet and her tumultuous relationship with the proud Mr. Darcy. Through a series of _______ Austen masterfully explores themes of love, class, and personal growth.

Which choice completes the text so that it conforms to the conventions of Standard English?

A) miscommunications later,
B) miscommunications;
C) miscommunications,
D) miscommunications, later,

Solution Strategy: Know the 3 main reason to use a comma

Step 1: Read the question before reading the passage to determine the Question Category.

Which choice completes the text so that it conforms to the conventions of Standard English?

Step 2: If commas are changing in any of the answer choices, *review the 3 main reasons to use a comma (in addition to Full-Stop punctuation with a FANBOYS):*

1. After every item in a list
2. Before and after non-essential information
3. After an Introductory word, phrase, or clause

Step 3: Select the answer choice *that uses the comma properly. If punctuation is not needed, do not use punctuation.*

After an Introductory word, phrase, or clause

~~A) miscommunications later,~~
There should be no comma after* "later" *as it does not follow a list, is not an intro, and is not before/after nonessential information. Nor is the word* "later" *necessary to this sentence. Answer choices should be concise – don't include words that are redundant or not needed.

I *C*
~~B) miscommunications;~~ |
Since we are testing Full-Stop punctuation (semicolon), let's do the Vertical Line Test. Full-Stop can only connect 2 Complete Ideas.* "Through a series of miscommunications" *is Incomplete.

✓C) miscommunications,
The comma is correctly used to separate the introductory phrase "Through a series of miscommunications" from the clause that follows.

~~D) miscommunications, later,~~
***Even though the word* later *has commas before and after, indicating it is nonessential, the insertion of this word is not needed and makes the sentence awkward. Answer choices should be concise – don't include words that are redundant or not needed*.**

Correct Answer: C,
Comma Rule: After an Introductory word, phrase, or clause

Practice: Comma Usage

1. In the field of genetics, researchers analyze various DNA sequences to understand the complexity of life. They examine the genetic code, its structure, and its functions. DNA, a molecule consisting of ________________ carries vital information that determines the traits and characteristics of organisms. By studying the patterns and interactions within DNA, scientists gain insights into the mechanisms of inheritance, evolution, and disease development.

Which choice completes the text so that it conforms to the conventions of Standard English?

A) nucleotide bases:
B) nucleotide bases,
C) nucleotide bases
D) nucleotide, bases

2. In African culture, storytelling plays a central role in preserving traditions and conveying ancestral wisdom. Through oral traditions, tales of bravery, love, and resilience are passed down from generation to generation. These narratives reflect the diverse heritage and rich history of the continent, providing insights into cultural practices, ________________ and societal values.

Which choice completes the text so that it conforms to the conventions of Standard English?

A) spiritual beliefs,
B) spiritual, beliefs,
C) spiritual, beliefs
D) spiritual beliefs;

3. During the height of the Roman Empire, gladiatorial games were a popular form of entertainment. These spectacles took place in grand amphitheaters, where skilled fighters, known as gladiators, engaged in combat. These ________________ displayed the power and dominance of the Roman Empire, captivating audiences with their fierce displays of strength and skill.

Which choice completes the text so that it conforms to the conventions of Standard English?

A) battles; often to the death;
B) battles often to the death,
C) battles:, often to the death,
D) battles, often to the death,

4. In the realm of art history, the Renaissance period stands as a pivotal era of artistic and cultural rebirth. During this time, artists sought to revive the classical traditions of ancient Greece and Rome, embracing humanism and depicting the beauty of the natural world. This movement _______ a shift in artistic techniques, leading to the development of perspective, anatomical accuracy, and the mastery of light and shadow.

Which choice completes the text so that it conforms to the conventions of Standard English?

A) prompted
B) having prompted,
C) prompted,
D) prompting

5. During the Enlightenment, a period marked by intellectual and philosophical advancements, one name stands out — Voltaire. Known for his wit, satire, and outspoken views, ________________ was a prolific writer whose works challenged established norms and advocated for freedom of thought and expression.

Which choice completes the text so that it conforms to the conventions of Standard English?

A) Voltaire, a key figure in shaping the philosophical landscape of the 18th century—
B) Voltaire—a key figure in shaping the philosophical landscape of the 18th century—
C) Voltaire, a key figure in shaping the philosophical landscape of the 18th century
D) Voltaire—a key figure in shaping the philosophical landscape of the 18th century,

6. In her groundbreaking research, scientist Marie Curie made significant contributions to the field of radioactivity. Through her experiments, Curie _______ the properties and behavior of radioactive elements. Her discoveries not only expanded our understanding of atomic physics but also paved the way for advancements in medical treatments and nuclear technology. Curie's relentless pursuit of knowledge and her unwavering dedication to scientific exploration continue to inspire generations of scientists.

Which choice completes the text so that it conforms to the conventions of Standard English?

A) investigated
B) investigated,
C) investigated—
D) investigated:

7. A study conducted by South American archaeologist Carmen González in 2020 sheds light on the ancient civilizations of the people known as the Tiwanaku and Wari. Through extensive excavation and analysis of _________ González uncovered evidence of advanced urban planning, intricate artwork, and sophisticated agricultural practices. Her findings contribute to our understanding of the cultural and technological achievements of these pre-Columbian societies.

Which choice completes the text so that it conforms to the conventions of Standard English?

A) artifacts
B) artifacts,
C) artifacts;
D) artifacts:

8. The art gallery showcased a diverse range of artworks — including paintings, sculptures, and ____________ created by contemporary artists from around the world; each piece reflected the artists' unique perspectives, exploring themes such as identity, social justice, and environmental issues.

Which choice completes the text so that it conforms to the conventions of Standard English?

A) installations:
B) installations;
C) installations,
D) installations —

9.The chef prepared an exquisite feast for the guests: a delectable appetizer of smoked salmon bruschetta with a tangy lemon dill sauce; followed by a velvety roasted butternut squash soup garnished with toasted pumpkin seeds and a drizzle of truffle oil; then came the main course, a succulent herb-crusted rack of lamb accompanied by a medley of roasted root vegetables and a ____________ and finally, for dessert, a decadent chocolate lava cake served with a scoop of Madagascar vanilla bean ice cream and a sprinkle of crushed pistachios.

Which choice completes the text so that it conforms to the conventions of Standard English?

A) savory herb-infused jus,
B) savory herb-infused jus;
C) savory herb-infused jus –
D) savory, herb-infused jus,

10. The garden was adorned with vibrant flowers: blooming tulips in various shades of red, pink, and __________ fragrant lavender bushes emitting a soothing aroma; and delicate daisies swaying gently in the breeze.

Which choice completes the text so that it conforms to the conventions of Standard English?

A) yellow
B) yellow,
C) yellow:
D) yellow;

11. In her analysis of Edith Wharton's *The House of Mirth* (1905), scholar Candace Waid observes that the novel depicts the upper classes of New York society as "consumed by the appetite of a soulless ____________ an apt assessment given that *The House of Mirth* is set during the Gilded Age, a period marked by rapid industrialization, economic greed, and widening wealth disparities.

Which choice completes the text so that it conforms to the conventions of Standard English?

A) emptiness";
B) emptiness,";
C) emptiness",
D) emptiness,"

For answer explanations to these practice questions, go to curvebreakerstestprep.com/decoding-the-digital-sat

CHAPTER 12: PUNCTUATION – APOSTROPHES

Section: Reading and Writing
Question Subsection: Grammar
Question Category: Punctuation – Apostrophes
Of the 54 Reading and Writing questions, approximately 1 - 2 may be questions from this category.

EXAM QUESTION

Which choice completes the text so that it conforms to the conventions of Standard English?

WHAT TO EXPECT

You are presented with a short paragraph that has a "______" in place of the words and you are asked to complete the text with the correct answer choice. These questions can be identified by noticing that apostrophes are changing in the answer choices.

If there are multi-sentence passages, most of the time you can just focus on the sentence with the ___________ to determine if and where we need an apostrophe.

LESSON

Apostrophes are used for two reasons:

1. For Possession (with Nouns)
2. For Contraction (with Pronouns)

When there is possession, put the apostrophe after the thing doing the possessing. Be aware that most plural words end in "*s*" but many do not end in "*s*".

EXERCISE

Do we have possession? If so, where does the apostrophe go?

	Possession Yes/No?	Where does the apostrophe go?
My mammas house		
The movies theme		
The queen of hearts		
The birds nests		
The chocolate bunnies		
The childrens toys		
My grandfathers books		
One weeks work		
Two weeks work		
Charles umbrella		

Pronouns do NOT generally take apostrophes for possession. Pronouns only take apostrophes for contractions.

PRONOUN CONTRACTIONS (use apostrophe):
They're.....They are
It's.....It is
I'm.....I am
He's.....He is
She's.....She is
Who's.....Who is/Who has
We're.....We are

PRONOUN POSSESSION (do NOT use apostrophe):
Its
Their
His
Hers
Ours
Whose

The Curvebreakers Strategy

PUT APOSTROPHE FOR POSSESSION AFTER THE THING DOING THE POSSESSING

1. Read the question before reading the passage to determine the Question Category.
2. If apostrophes are changing in any of the answer choices, review the 2 main reasons to use apostrophes.
   a. For Possession (with Nouns): Put the apostrophe after the thing doing the possessing.
   b. For Contraction (with Pronouns): Pronouns do not take apostrophes for possession.
3. Select the answer choice that uses the apostrophes properly. If punctuation is not needed, do not use punctuation

Example 1: Apostrophes

1. In 1943, Swiss chemist Albert Hofmann accidentally discovered the hallucinogenic effects of lysergic acid diethylamide, more commonly known as LSD. While working in his laboratory, Hofmann unintentionally absorbed a small amount of the substance through his skin, experiencing its potent psychedelic properties. Over the following decades, LSD gained popularity for its ability to induce altered states of consciousness and was widely used for both recreational and therapeutic purposes. However, due to concerns about the drug's potential for abuse and negative side effects, LSD was eventually classified as a Schedule I controlled substance, making it illegal in most countries. Researchers are now reevaluating the ______ potential therapeutic applications.

Which choice completes the text so that it conforms to the conventions of Standard English?

A) drugs
B) drug's
C) drugs'
D) drugs's

Solution Strategy: Put apostrophe for possession after the thing doing the possessing

Step 1: Read the question before reading the passage to determine the Question Category.

Which choice completes the text so that it conforms to the conventions of Standard English?

Step 2: If apostrophes are changing in any of the answer choices, review the 2 main reasons to use apostrophes.

1. For Possession (with Nouns): Put the apostrophe after the thing doing the possessing.
2. For Contraction (with Pronouns): Pronouns do not take apostrophes for possession.

There is possession: the therapeutic applications of/belonging to the drug.

Step 3: Select the answer choice *that uses the apostrophes properly. If punctuation is not needed, do not use punctuation*

The thing being tested is the singular drug LSD. Put the apostrophe after the thing doing the possessing. Since "the drug" is doing the possessing, put the apostrophe after the "g" in drug.

~~A) drugs~~
No possession is indicated, which is required in this context.

✓B) drug's
The apostrophe followed by "s" indicates possession, showing that the potential therapeutic applications belong to the drug (LSD).

~~C) drugs'~~
The apostrophe after "s" indicates possession for a plural noun, but "drug" should be singular in this case referring to LSD.

~~D) drugs's~~
The apostrophe after the "s'" is grammatically incorrect.

Correct Answer: B
Put the apostrophe after the thing doing the possessing (drug).

Example 2: Apostrophes

2. Despite ___________ reputation for being lazy, the sloth is actually quite busy during the nighttime hours.

A) it's
B) their
C) its
D) its'

Solution Strategy: Pronouns do not take apostrophes for possession.

Step 1: Read the question before reading the passage to determine the Question Category.

Which choice completes the text so that it conforms to the conventions of Standard English?

Step 2: If apostrophes are changing in any of the answer choices, review the 2 main reasons to use apostrophes.

1. For Possession (with Nouns): Put the apostrophe after the thing doing the possessing.
2. For Contraction (with Pronouns): Pronouns do not take apostrophes for possession.

There is possession: the reputation of/belonging to the sloth.

Step 3: Select the answer choice that uses the apostrophes properly. If punctuation is not needed, do not use punctuation

The thing being tested is the singular sloth. The answer choices all have pronouns and pronouns do NOT take apostrophes for possession.

~~A) it's~~
it's is a contraction of "it is" or "it has," which wouldn't fit in this context.

~~B) their~~
their is plural and "sloth" is singular.

✓C) its
its is the possessive pronoun that shows that the reputation belongs to the sloth

~~D) its'~~
its' is not a valid word in English grammar.

Correct Answer: C
Pronouns do not take apostrophes for possession.

Practice: Apostrophes

1. The ________________ report highlighted its impressive financial growth over the past year, with revenue increasing by 20% and the number of satisfied customers reaching an all-time high. The report also emphasized the importance of the employees' dedication and hard work in achieving these remarkable results.

Which choice completes the text so that it conforms to the conventions of Standard English?

A) companies' annual report
B) companys' annual report
C) companys annual report
D) company's annual report

2. My ________________ broke down on the way to the airport, causing her to miss her flight.

Which choice completes the text so that it conforms to the conventions of Standard English?

A) sister's friends car
B) sisters friends' car
C) sister's friend's car
D) sisters' friends' car

3.Throughout history, musicians have drawn inspiration from a variety of sources, including nature, emotions, and personal experiences. Many composers have created masterpieces that evoke a range of feelings, from joy and exhilaration to sadness and contemplation. These compositions are a testament to the ________________ ability to capture the essence of human existence and translate it into the language of music

Which choice completes the text so that it conforms to the conventions of Standard English?

A) composers'
B) composers
C) composer's
D) composers's

4. Statistical analysts estimate that a significant portion of research papers published in scientific journals are the collaborative efforts of multiple researchers. These papers often represent the culmination of extensive investigations and experiments conducted by teams of scientists from different disciplines. The collaborative nature of scientific research ensures that a wide range of expertise is brought together to tackle complex _______.

Which choice completes the text so that it conforms to the conventions of Standard English?

A) problems'
B) problems
C) problem's
D) problems's

5. During archaeological excavations, researchers carefully uncover artifacts and analyze their features to gain insights into ancient civilizations. By studying pottery, tools, and other objects, archaeologists can determine the cultural practices, technological advancements, and daily life of the people who lived in the area centuries ago. These discoveries contribute to our understanding of the region's rich _______.

Which choice completes the text so that it conforms to the conventions of Standard English?

A) region's rich history's
B) regions rich history's
C) regions' rich histories.
D) region's rich history.

6. When studying ancient civilizations, historians analyze primary sources such as texts, inscriptions, and artifacts to piece together the narratives of the past. These sources provide firsthand accounts and material evidence that shed light on the political structures, social dynamics, and ____________________ By examining these sources, historians gain a deeper understanding of the complexities and intricacies of the past.

Which choice completes the text so that it conforms to the conventions of Standard English?

A) cultural practice's of ancient societies.
B) cultural practices of ancient societies.
C) cultural practices of ancient societies'.
D) cultural practices' of ancient societies.

7. The scientist's groundbreaking research focused on understanding the behavior of dolphins in their natural habitat. By studying their communication patterns and social interactions, the scientist aimed to unravel the mysteries of these highly intelligent creatures. Through careful observation and data analysis, the scientist discovered that _______________ play a crucial role in their complex social structure.

Which choice completes the text so that it conforms to the conventions of Standard English?

A) dolphins communications
B) dolphins' communications
C) dolphin's communications
D) dolphins' communications'

8. The photographer's keen eye for detail allowed him to capture the essence of the ________ vibrant streets. His photographs showcased the unique architecture, bustling crowds, and the myriad of sights that define the urban landscape.

Which choice completes the text so that it conforms to the conventions of Standard English?

A) cities
B) cities'
C) city's
D) citys'

9. The author's eloquent prose and vivid descriptions transported readers to a world of enchantment. Her novels were filled with captivating characters, intricate plotlines, and the exploration of __________.

Which choice completes the text so that it conforms to the conventions of Standard English?

A) human's psyche
B) humans' psyche
C) human's psyches
D) humans' psyches

10. The domestic cat is well known for __________ independent nature and selective sociability.

Which choice completes the text so that it conforms to the conventions of Standard English?

A) it's
B) their
C) its
D) its'

11. After the heavy storm, the birds quickly returned to ________ nests to check on their eggs.

Which choice completes the text so that it conforms to the conventions of Standard English?

A) there
B) they're
C) their
D) theirs'

For answer explanations to these practice questions, go to curvebreakerstestprep.com/decoding-the-digital-sat

CHAPTER 13: ENDING PUNCTUATION

Section: Reading and Writing
Question Subsection: Grammar
Question Category: End of Sentence Punctuation
Of the 54 Reading and Writing questions, approximately 0-1 may be questions from this category.

EXAM QUESTION

Which choice completes the text so that it conforms to the conventions of Standard English?

WHAT TO EXPECT

You are presented with a short paragraph that has a "______' in place of the words and you are asked to complete the text with the correct answer choice. These questions can be identified by noticing that ending punctuation is changing in the answer choices.

LESSON

3 OPTIONS FOR END-OF-SENTENCE PUNCTUATION	
Period	A period marks the end of a declarative sentence: a statement of fact or to give a command. They are by far the most common ending punctuation mark.
Question Mark	A question mark indicates a direct question, request, or plea for more information.
Exclamation Point	An exclamation point is used to show excitement or emphasis. Exclamation points are often overused.

EXERCISE

Choose the correct End-Of-Sentence Punctuation

	Period (.)	Question Mark (?)	Exclamation Point (!)
Why is this so complicated			
The teacher yelled at her students to "walk, don't run"			
He graduated with an M.B.A.			
My favorite quote is "to be or not to be; that is the question"			
School starts at 7 a.m.			
I hate that school starts so early			
Can you believe it			

The Curvebreakers Strategy

KNOW THE 3 OPTIONS FOR END OF SENTENCE PUNCTUATION

1. Read the question before reading the passage to determine the Question Category.
2. If end-of-sentence punctuation is changing in any of the answer choices, review the 3 punctuation options

   a. Period (.): to indicate the end of a sentence
   b. Question Mark (?): to indicate a question
   c. Exclamation Point (!): to indicate strong emotion, surprise, or emphasis

3. Select the answer choice that uses the correct punctuation, usually based on the text immediately preceding the __________

Example: End of Sentence Punctuation

After months of hard work and dedication, the team finally completed the project ________________

Which choice completes the text so that it conforms to the conventions of Standard English?

A) on time, and within budget.
B) on time and within budget!
C) on time and within budget?
D) on time; and within budget.

Solution Strategy: Kow the 3 options for end of sentence punctuation

Step 1: Read the question before reading the passage to determine the Question Category.

Which choice completes the text so that it conforms to the conventions of Standard English?

Step 2: If end-of-sentence punctuation is changing in any of the answer choices, review the 3 punctuation options

1. Period (.): to indicate the end of a sentence
2. Question Mark (?): to indicate a question
3. Exclamation Point (!): to indicate strong emotion, surprise, or emphasis

Step 3: Select the answer choice that uses the correct punctuation, usually based on the text immediately preceding the ________

C   I
~~A) on time, an|d within budget.~~
Since we are testing Full-Stop punctuation (comma+FANBOYS), let's do the Vertical Line Test by putting the vertical line through the FANBOYS (and). Full-Stop can only connect 2 Complete Ideas, which we don't have ("*within budget*" is not complete).

✓B) on time and within budget!
The exclamation mark adds emphasis and conveys a sense of excitement or satisfaction about the team's accomplishment. The sentence describes the completion of a project after months of hard work and dedication, and the exclamation mark helps to highlight the achievement and celebratory tone of the statement

~~C) on time and within budget?~~
The statement is not a question.

C   I
D) on time;| and within budget.
Since we are testing Full-Stop punctuation (semicolon), let's do the Vertical Line Test by putting the vertical line through the FANBOYS (*and*). Full-Stop can only connect 2 Complete Ideas, which we don't have ("*and within budget*" is not complete).

Correct answer: B) on time and within budget!

Practice: End of Sentence Punctuation

1. The guests were delighted by the chef's culinary skills, ________

Which choice completes the text so that it conforms to the conventions of Standard English?

A) weren't they?
B) wasn't he?
C) weren't they!
D) weren't they.

2. The scientists conducted extensive experiments to validate their hypothesis ________

Which choice completes the text so that it conforms to the conventions of Standard English?

A) and their findings were consistent with their predictions.
B) and their findings were consistent with their predictions!
C) and their findings were consistent with their predictions?
D) and their findings were consistent, with their predictions.

3. Can you believe that, after all the hours we spent studying for the exam, the teacher decided to postpone it until ________

Which choice completes the text so that it conforms to the conventions of Standard English?

A) next week!
B) next week.
C) next week?
D) next week;

For answer explanations to these practice questions, go to curvebreakerstestprep.com/decoding-the-digital-sat

CHAPTER 14: SUBJECT/VERB AGREEMENT

Section: Reading and Writing
Question Subsection: Grammar
Question Category: Subject/Verb Agreement
Of the 54 Reading and Writing questions, approximately 3 - 6 may be questions from this category.

EXAM QUESTION

Which choice completes the text so that it conforms to the conventions of Standard English?

WHAT TO EXPECT

You are presented with a short paragraph that has a "______" in place of the words and you are asked to complete the text with the correct answer choice. These questions can be identified by noticing that the answers contain different verbs or different versions of the same verb.

LESSON

What is Subject/Verb Consistency?
Verbs must agree with subjects in number (singular vs. plural), in person or thing (he/she/it), and in tense (past vs. present).

EXERCISE

Circle the Correct Verb

Michael and Nico (play, plays, playing) the clarinet.
Last night, the Board (vote, votes, voted) on the proposal.
Nancy (was, is, are) currently at the movies.
The President and Vice-President (greets, greet, greeting) the voters.
(Is, Are, Were) the News on at 6pm today?
The dog (is going, will go, has gone) to the vet tomorrow.
The United States (have, has, having) a large population..

What is a Prepositional Phrase?
A Prepositional Phrase is a short phrase that begins with a Preposition. A preposition is a word to show direction, time, or place. The insertion of a prepositional phrase in a sentence will often make it difficult to determine the subject of the sentence.

TIP: Think of a Preposition as any of the short directional words that can fill the ______ in the phrase:

"______________ the box"

Examples of Prepositions:

Examples of Prepositions				
In	Of	For	On	Above
At	Under	Inside	Near	Next to
With	Between	By	Across	Below

EXERCISE

Trim the Fat by crossing out the prepositional phrase; Circle the Correct Verb

Every one of those stories (seem/seems) fictitious.
The meaning of your words (is/are) quite clear.
The samples on the trays in the lab (need/needs) testing.
The damage from these last two storms (seem/seems) worse than the prior two storms.
Everyone within these walls (has/have) heard the story.
Historians of the period (identifies, identify) five eras.

The Curvebreakers Strategy

BE CONSISTENT WITH SUBJECT AND TRIM THE FAT

1. Read the question before reading the passage to determine the Question Category.
2. Trim the Fat by crossing out the non-essential information between commas, or any prepositional phrase.
3. Identify and highlight the Subject pertaining to the Verb. The Subject is a noun or pronoun; the Verb is the action performed by the Subject.
4. Eliminate answer choices that are not consistent with the identified subject. Generally, singular verbs end in "s" and plural verbs don't end in "s".

TIP: The words "having" or 'being" will usually not be part of the correct answer choices.
Beware of awkward-sounding verbs that end in "ing." Before selecting an answer choice with an "ing" ending, make sure it is consistent with the Subject.

TIP: Be careful with collective nouns (such as everyone, team, family, government, jury, etc.) which refer to a group or collection of individuals but are treated as a single entity. Despite representing multiple individuals, these nouns are considered singular in grammatical terms.

Example 1: Subject/Verb Agreement

1. The development of renewable energy technologies, such as solar, wind, and hydroelectric power, ________ the potential to reduce our reliance on fossil fuels and mitigate the effects of climate change.

Which choice completes the text so that it conforms to the conventions of Standard English?

A) have
B) has
C) had
D) having

Solution Strategy: Be consistent with subject and trim the fat

Step 1: Read the question before reading the passage to determine the Question Category.

Which choice completes the text so that it conforms to the conventions of Standard English?

Step 2: Trim the Fat by crossing out the non-essential information between commas, or any prepositional phrase.

The development ~~of renewable energy technologies, such as solar, wind, and hydroelectric power,~~ ________ the potential to reduce our reliance on fossil fuels and mitigate the effects of climate change.

"Of" is a preposition; "of renewable energy technologies" is a prepositional phrase so cross it out. There are commas before and after "such as solar, wind, and hydroelectric power" indicating that this phrase is non-essential, so cross it out as well.

Step 3: Identify and highlight the subject pertaining to the verb. The subject is a noun or pronoun; the verb is the action performed by the subject.

The subject is "development" which is singular. Therefore, the verb must be singular.

Step 4: Eliminate answer choices that are not consistent with the identified subject. Generally, singular verbs end in "s" and plural verbs don't end in "s".

~~A) have~~
The plural verb form does not agree with the singular subject "The development"

✓B) has
This singular verb form agrees with the singular subject "The development"

~~C) had~~
The past tense is not consistent within the context of the sentence. We know we're not in the past tense because of the present tense words "reduce" and "mitigate."

~~D) having~~
The present participle form does not fit the context of the sentence. And avoid "having" in most instances.

Correct Answer: B
The development.....has

Example 2: Subject/Verb Agreement

2. In the field of neuroscience, researchers are investigating the relationship between brain activity and human behavior. Through various imaging techniques, they can observe how specific regions of the brain ________ during certain cognitive tasks.

Which choice completes the text so that it conforms to the conventions of Standard English?

A) activates
B) activate
C) activated
D) have activated

Solution Strategy: Be consistent with subject and trim the fat

Step 1: Read the question before reading the passage to determine the Question Category.

Which choice completes the text so that it conforms to the conventions of Standard English?

Step 2: Trim the Fat by crossing out the non-essential information between commas, or any prepositional phrase.

Through various imaging techniques, they can observe how specific regions of the brain _______ during certain cognitive tasks.

"Of" is a preposition; "of the brain" is a prepositional phrase so cross it out.

Step 3: Identify and highlight the subject pertaining to the verb. The subject is a noun or pronoun; the verb is the action performed by the subject.

The subject is "regions" which is plural. Therefore, the verb must be plural.

Step 4: Eliminate answer choices that are not consistent with the identified subject. Generally, singular verbs end in "s" and plural verbs don't end in "s".

~~A) activates~~
The singular verb form does not agree with the plural "regions."

✓B) activate
This plural verb form agrees with the plural "regions."

~~C) activated~~
The past tense is not consistent within the context of the sentence. We know we're not in the past tense because of the word "observe" which is present tense.

~~D) have activated~~
The past tense is not consistent within the context of the sentence. We know we're not in the past tense because of the word "observe" which is present tense.

Correct Answer: B
specific regions....activate

Practice: Subject/Verb Agreement

1. In his groundbreaking study on language acquisition, Professor Johnson investigates how children _______ new vocabulary and grammatical structures at a rapid pace.

Which choice completes the text so that it conforms to the conventions of Standard English?

A) learn
B) learns
C) learned
D) learning

2. The group of students _______ for their field trip to the museum.

Which choice completes the text so that it conforms to the conventions of Standard English?

A) is preparing
B) are preparing
C) prepare
D) were preparing

3. During the 19th century, author Jane Austen penned several novels that _______ enduring classics of English literature.

Which choice completes the text so that it conforms to the conventions of Standard English?

A) become
B) becomes
C) became
D) have become

4. In the field of astronomy, black holes _______ some of the most fascinating objects in the universe.

Which choice completes the text so that it conforms to the conventions of Standard English?

A) are
B) have
C) were
D) is

5. The team of scientists _______ the new species of orchid deep in the rainforest.

Which choice completes the text so that it conforms to the conventions of Standard English?

A) have discovered
B) has discovered
C) is discovering
D) having discovered

6. The ancient ruins in the valley _______ evidence of a thriving civilization.

Which choice completes the text so that it conforms to the conventions of Standard English?

A) provide
B) is providing
C) provides
D) providing

7. In today's digital age, information is readily accessible with just a few clicks. The internet has revolutionized the way we obtain knowledge and _________ with others.

Which choice completes the text so that it conforms to the conventions of Standard English?

A) connected
B) connect
C) are connecting
D) are being connected

8. The collection of books _______ a wide range of topics.

Which choice completes the text so that it conforms to the conventions of Standard English?

A) covering
B) cover
C) have covered
D) covers

9. Her internship that summer made her realize that politics and the law ____________ .

Which choice completes the text so that it conforms to the conventions of Standard English?

A) was a living thing
B) was a thing that was alive
C) were living things
D) were things that were living

10. Biomedical engineers combine the problem solving skills and design approaches used in engineering and medical knowledge in order _______________ healthcare.

Which choice completes the text so that it conforms to the conventions of Standard English?

A) for advancing
B) for the advancement of
C) of advancing
D) to advance

For answer explanations to these practice questions, go to curvebreakerstestprep.com/decoding-the-digital-sat

CHAPTER 15: PRONOUN AGREEMENT

Section: Reading and Writing
Question Subsection: Grammar
Question Category: Pronoun Agreement
Of the 54 Reading and Writing questions, approximately 0 - 1 may be questions from this category.

EXAM QUESTION

Which choice completes the text so that it conforms to the conventions of Standard English?

WHAT TO EXPECT

You are presented with a short paragraph that has a "______" in place of the words and you are asked to complete the text with the correct answer choice. These questions can be identified by noticing that pronouns are changing among the answer choices.

LESSON

A Pronoun is a word that we use in place of a noun or phrase

What is Pronoun Consistency?
Pronouns must agree with the subject the pronoun is referring to: singular with singular, plural with plural.

EXERCISE

Highlight the Subject and Circle the Correct Pronoun

Kristina and Ella completed (her/ their/ our) assignment.
Nick's company will have (its/ their/ his) annual picnic next week.
If a student wants to do well, (they/ he or she/ we) must do all the homework.
President Kennedy delivered (his/ their/ its) inaugural address in 1961.
Each dog and cat played with (their/ its/ her) own chew toys.
The teachers began (their/ his or her/ its) lessons.
Everyone seems to be out for (himself/ themself/ themselves)

The Curvebreakers Strategy

BE CONSISTENT WITH SUBJECT

1. Read the question before reading the passage to determine the Question Category.
2. Identify and highlight the subject pertaining to the pronoun. The subject will be a noun or pronoun.
3. Eliminate answer choices that are not consistent with the identified subject.

TIP: Be careful with collective nouns (such as everyone, team, family, government, jury, etc.) which refer to a group or collection of individuals but are treated as a single entity. Despite representing multiple individuals, these nouns are considered singular in grammatical terms

Example 1: Pronoun Agreement

1. Some companies offer employees flexible work arrangements, such as telecommuting or flexible hours, to improve work-life balance. Employees who take advantage of these options may find that _______ overall job satisfaction increases.

Which choice completes the text so that it conforms to the conventions of Standard English?

A) their
B) his or her
C) its
D) one's

Solution Strategy: Be consistent with subject

Step 1: Read the question before reading the passage to determine the Question Category.

Which choice completes the text so that it conforms to the conventions of Standard English?

Step 2: Identify and highlight the subject pertaining to the pronoun. The subject will be a noun or pronoun.

Some companies offer employees flexible work arrangements, such as telecommuting or flexible hours, to improve work-life balance. Employees who take advantage of these options may find that _______ overall job satisfaction increases.

The subject of the sentence is "Employees."

Step 3: Eliminate answer choices that are not consistent with the identified subject.

The subject "Employees" is plural. Therefore, the verbs and pronouns must be plural.

✓A) their
The plural pronoun their agrees with the plural subject Employees.

~~B) his or her~~
His and Her are singular pronouns and do not agree with the plural subject Employees.

~~C) its~~
Its is a singular pronoun and does not agree with the plural subject Employees. Also its refers to a thing and not a person.

~~***D) one's***~~
One's is singular and does not agree with the plural subject Employees.

Correct Answer: A
Employees.....their

Example 2: Pronoun Agreement

2. Everyone within these walls had been convicted of a crime and was now paying _______ debt to society.

Which choice completes the text so that it conforms to the conventions of Standard English?

A) their
B) his or her
C) they're
D) its

Solution Strategy: Be consistent with subject

Step 1: Read the question before reading the passage to determine the Question Category.

Which choice completes the text so that it conforms to the conventions of Standard English?

Step 2: Identify and highlight the subject pertaining to the pronoun. The subject will be a noun or pronoun.

Everyone ~~within these walls~~ had been convicted of a crime and was now paying _______________ debt to society.

The subject of the sentence is "Everyone."

Step 3: Eliminate answer choices that are not consistent with the identified subject.

The subject "Everyone" is singular (collective pronoun). Therefore, the verbs and pronouns must be singular.

✓A) their
Even though this choice seems correct, the plural pronoun "their" actually does not agree with the singular subject "Everyone." While the use of "their" is common in casual language for singular subjects, it is not technically grammatically correct.

✓B) his or her
His and Her are singular pronouns and agree with the singular subject Everyone.

~~C) they're~~
The contraction for "they are" does not fit within the context of this sentence.

~~D) its~~
"its" refers to a thing and not a person.

Correct Answer: B
Everyone......his or her

Practice: Pronoun Agreement

1. Urban farming initiatives, such as community gardens and rooftop greenhouses, provide city dwellers with access to fresh, locally-grown produce. These initiatives not only help to reduce the carbon footprint of food transportation, but also enable people to reconnect with _______ food sources.

Which choice completes the text so that it conforms to the conventions of Standard English?

A) their
B) Its
C) his or her
D) one's

2. Mental well-being is one of the most important aspects of our health, and one that is often overlooked by patients and doctors alike. But it is important to examine a ______________ state as well as his or her physical state.

Which choice completes the text so that it conforms to the conventions of Standard English?

A) a persons mental state
B) a person's mental state
C) the mental state of a person
D) people's mental states

3. Maya and her friends decided to go on a road trip together. ___________________ bags, filled the car with fuel, and set off on an exciting adventure.

Which choice completes the text so that it conforms to the conventions of Standard English?

A) She packed her
B) They packed their
C) They packed they're
D) She packed they're

4. The ancient civilization of Egypt has fascinated historians and archaeologists for centuries. _______________ at the grandeur of the pyramids, the intricate hieroglyphs adorning temple walls, and the mysteries surrounding the lives of pharaohs.

Which choice completes the text so that it conforms to the conventions of Standard English?

A) They are marveling
B) We marvel
C) It marvels
D) They marvel

5. The Revolutionary War tested the resolve and unity of the American people, but ______________ victorious, securing their sovereignty and establishing the United States of America. This pivotal moment in history laid the foundation for the democratic principles and values that continue to shape the nation to this day.

Which choice completes the text so that it conforms to the conventions of Standard English?

A) having emerged
B) they emerged
C) emerging
D) it emerged

6. The Philippines is known for its rich cultural heritage and natural beauty. ______________ stunning landscapes, including pristine beaches, lush rainforests, and breathtaking mountains.

Which choice completes the text so that it conforms to the conventions of Standard English?

A) It boasts
B) They boast
C) They boast of
D) They boasted of

For answer explanations to these practice questions, go to curvebreakerstestprep.com/decoding-the-digital-sat

CHAPTER 16: MISPLACED MODIFIERS

Section: Reading and Writing
Question Subsection: Grammar
Question Category: Misplaced Modifiers
Of the 54 Reading and Writing questions, approximately 1 - 2 may be questions from this category.

EXAM QUESTION

Which choice completes the text so that it conforms to the conventions of Standard English?

WHAT TO EXPECT

You are presented with a short paragraph that has a " ______" in place of the words and you are asked to complete the text with the correct sentence clause. These questions can be identified by noticing that the difference in the answer choices is the order of the language.

LESSON

A Modifier is a word or phrase that describes a noun or action in a sentence. The Modifier should be placed as close to the thing it is describing as possible.

Modifiers very often open the sentence in the form of a dependent clause which is followed by a comma (comma rule: after intro). The word (or group of words) after this comma must reasonably apply to whatever subject is found immediately after the comma.

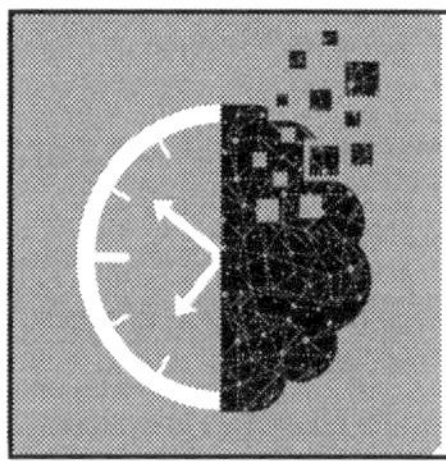

The Curvebreakers Strategy

Highlight the Modifier and draw an arrow next to the closest word or phrase to determine if the modifier is misplaced

1. Read the question before reading the passage to determine the Question Category.
2. Highlight the Modifier (usually the opening phrase of the sentence followed by a comma).
3. Draw an arrow from the highlighted text to the next the closest word (or group of words). If the word (or group of words) with the arrow does not directly apply to the highlighted text, the modifier is misplaced.
4. Select the answer choice where the word (or group of words) directly applies to the highlighted text.

EXERCISE

Circle the Modifier; Draw an arrow next to the closest word (or group of words).	Is the Modifier Misplaced? Y/N
Walking home from school, the scenery and pleasant weather was the perfect way for Rebecca to decompress.	
Walking home from school, Rebecca felt the scenery and pleasant weather was the perfect way to decompress.	
Combining these findings with climate-change predictions for the next decade, the scientists suggest that the changes will come earlier to the coasts.	
Combining these findings with climate-change predictions for the next decade, the coasts are more likely to experience the changes earlier.	
Particularly listening to new music, these songs all have that modern sound.	
Particularly listening to new music, you've surely noticed the modern sound.	

Example 1: Misplaced Modifiers

1. Although they can be quite expensive, _______ because of their smooth, velvety texture and rich flavor.

Which choice completes the text so that it conforms to the conventions of Standard English?

A) many people enjoy truffles
B) truffles are enjoyed by many people
C) the enjoyment of truffles is
D) people enjoy truffles

Solution Strategy: Highlight the Modifier and draw an arrow

Step 1: *Read the question before reading the passage to determine the Question Category.*

Which choice completes the text so that it conforms to the conventions of Standard English?

Step 2: *Highlight the Modifier (usually the opening phrase of the sentence followed by a comma).*

Step 3: *Draw an arrow from the highlighted text to the next the closest word (or group of words). If the word (or group of words) with the arrow do not directly apply to the highlighted text, the modifier is misplaced.*

Although they can be quite expensive, _______ *because of their smooth, velvety texture and rich flavor.*

The** ______ **should refer to things that are "quite expensive."

Step 4: *Select the answer choice where the word (or group of words) directly applies to the highlighted text.*

~~A) many people~~ enjoy truffles
The modifier* "Although they can be quite expensive" *does not properly connect with the subject* "many people," *causing an awkward sentence structure.* ("many people" *are not* "quite expensive"*).

✓B) truffles are enjoyed by many people
This choice correctly places the modifier* "Although they can be quite expensive" *next to* "truffles" *and maintains a clear sentence structure. (*"truffles" *are* "quite expensive"*).

~~C) the enjoyment~~ of truffles is
The modifier* "Although they can be quite expensive" *does not properly connect with the subject* "the enjoyment," *causing an awkward sentence structure.(*"the enjoyment" *is not* "quite expensive"*).

~~D) people~~ enjoy truffles
The modifier "Although they can be quite expensive" *does not properly connect with the subject* "people," *causing an awkward sentence structure.(*"people" *are not* "quite expensive").

Correct Answer: B
Ask "what is quite expensive?" Answer; *"truffles"*

Example 2: Misplaced Modifiers

2. Despite being compact and portable, ______________________ .

Which choice completes the text so that it conforms to the conventions of Standard English?

A) USB flash drives have become a popular choice because they can store large amounts of data
B) users have found that flash drives can store large amounts of data
C) large amounts of data can also be stored, making flash drives a popular choice
D) it is also convenient to store large amounts data on flash drives

Solution Strategy: Highlight the Modifier and draw an arrow

Step 1: Read the question before reading the passage to determine the Question Category.

Which choice completes the text so that it conforms to the conventions of Standard English?

Step 2: Highlight the Modifier (usually the opening phrase of the sentence followed by a comma).

Step 3: Draw an arrow from the highlighted text to the next the closest word (or group of words). If the word (or group of words) with the arrow do not directly apply to the highlighted text, the modifier is misplaced.

Despite being compact and portable, ____________

The ______ should refer to something that is compact and portable.

Step 4: Select the answer choice where the word (or group of words) directly applies to the highlighted text.

✓A) USB flash drives have become a popular choice because they can store large amounts of data
This choice correctly places the modifier "Despite being compact and portable" next to "USB flash drives" and maintains a clear sentence structure. (USB drives are compact and portable).

~~B) users~~ have found that flash drives can store large amounts of data
The modifier "Despite being compact and portable" does not properly connect with the subject "users," causing an awkward sentence structure. (users are not compact and portable).

~~C) large amounts~~ of data can also be stored, making flash drives a popular choice
The modifier "Despite being compact and portable" does not properly connect with the subject "large amounts of data," causing an awkward sentence structure. (large amounts of data are not compact and portable).

~~D) it~~ is also convenient to store large amounts data on flash drives
The modifier "Despite being compact and portable" does not properly connect with the subject "it," causing an awkward sentence structure. (it is not compact and portable).

Correct answer: A
Ask "what is compact and portable?" Answer; "USB flash drives"

Practice: Misplaced Modifiers

1. Walking through the park, ____________

Which choice completes the text so that it conforms to the conventions of Standard English?

A) the flowers bloomed with vibrant colors and filled the air with a sweet fragrance.
B) the beauty of the flowers delighted the visitors.
C) visitors were delighted by the beauty of the flowers.
D) the flowers' beauty delighted the visitors.

2. With their vibrant colors and intricate patterns, _______ to decorate homes and add a touch of elegance.

Which choice completes the text so that it conforms to the conventions of Standard English?

A) popular choices have become area rugs
B) the popular choices for homes are area rugs
C) homes find popular choices in area rugs
D) area rugs have become popular choices

3. Recognized for their durability and timeless style, _______ for both casual and formal occasions.

Which choice completes the text so that it conforms to the conventions of Standard English?

A) leather jackets are wardrobe staples
B) wardrobe staples are leather jackets
C) many wardrobes include leather jackets
D) many people own leather jackets

4. Driving through the city, ___________________________. The bustling streets were crowded with cars, and the sounds of honking horns filled the air. People hurried along the sidewalks, their faces masked by a sense of urgency. Amidst the urban chaos, the beauty of the city's architecture still managed to captivate.

Which choice completes the text so that it conforms to the conventions of Standard English?

A) the towering skyscrapers filled the view
B) you could see the towering skyscrapers filling the view
C) the view was filled with towering skyscrapers
D) the towering skyscrapers could be seen filling the view

5. Renowned theoretical physicist Albert Einstein was also a brilliant mathematician. Named as one of the greatest discoveries in the 20th century, _______ revolutionized our understanding of space, time, and gravity.

Which choice completes the text so that it conforms to the conventions of Standard English?

A) Einstein developed the theory of relativity which
B) the impact of Einstein's theory of relativity
C) Einstein's theory of relativity
D) the transformative nature of Einstein's theory of relativity

For answer explanations to these practice questions, go to curvebreakerstestprep.com/decoding-the-digital-sat

CHAPTER 17: MATH INTRODUCTION AND GENERAL STRATEGIES

There are often several ways to solve a math problem. You don't have to solve it the way the SAT® wants you to. Since our purpose is to get you to the correct answer in the quickest amount of time, we'll walk you through the strategies, techniques, tips, etc., that our students find extremely helpful. A number of these strategies may seem unfamiliar. However, they have been proven to work and, with practice, they can work for you too.

The College Board tells us that the questions on the Math section fall into four content domains:

1. Algebra
2. Advanced Math
3. Problem-Solving and Data Analysis
4. Geometry and Trigonometry

We've identified the specific categories most commonly tested within these headings, with each question category representing its own chapter, with the specific strategy for tackling each one.

MATH GENERAL STRATEGIES

1. **NEVER leave a question blank.** There is no penalty for guessing.

2. **Complete easy questions first.** Questions follow a loose order of difficulty, meaning they tend to get harder as you go. Spend your time wisely on the questions likely to award you points. Pick and choose which questions you can complete when time is running out.

3. **Abide by a 5-second rule (or something close to it).** If after 5 or so seconds you have no idea what to do, skip that question and return to it if time allows.

5. **BALLPARK:** You may be able to get an answer in the ballpark, even if you don't know how to fully solve a problem.

6. **BITE-SIZE:** Break the question down into manageable Bite-sized steps when you get to a stopping point after each step.

7. **Use your CALCULATOR wisely.** Don't trust it unquestioningly; you should always be mentally checking to see if what it's spitting out makes sense.

8. **Know when to walk away!** Beware time-sucker problems. Take a guess and move on.

9. **F**or EVERY math question, ask if the question would be easier if I **Plugged In** for the Variable or Plugged in the Answer.

CHAPTER 18: PLUGGING IN FOR THE VARIABLE

LESSON

"Plugging In" means that you're replacing a variable with an actual number.

Plugging In is often a very effective strategy, especially if you're not sure how to solve a problem algebraically. Even if you know how to solve the problem algebraically, Plugging In can often get you to the answer choice more quickly. It can also make difficult problems much more manageable. You should be able to use this strategy on several math problems.

The Curvebreakers Strategy

PLUG IN FOR THE VARIABLE

1. **If the question contains the words "in terms of.....," cross it out – it is meant to confuse you. Highlight what the question is asking.**
2. **Identify a variable(s) to plug in.** Usually, it's best to plug in for the variable that shows up the most or the variable that appears in the answer choices. Don't plug in for the *Lonely Variable*: the one by itself.
3. **Plug in a number for the variable(s).** Pick a number that makes the math easy (2,3,10,etc.).. If the problem contains a graph, chart, or table, see if you can use numbers (or coordinates) given in the graph, chart, or table to plug in. Avoid using 0; use 1 sparingly (to avoid situations in which more than one answer choice works).
4. **Work the steps of the problem.**
5. **Put a TV around the Target Value.**
6. **Check each answer choice to find your Target Value.** If more than one works, plug in a different number.

Example 1: PLUG IN FOR THE VARIABLE

1. Which expression is equivalent to $\frac{3}{a^2} + \frac{1}{2a} + \frac{2}{a}$?

A) $\frac{6}{a^2+3a}$

B) $\frac{2a+3}{a^3}$

C) $\frac{5a+6}{2a^2}$

D) $6a^2$

Solution Using the Strategy: Plug in for the Variable

Step 1: Identify a variable(s) to plug in.

The variable in both the question and answer choices is a. Let's try $a = 2$

Step 2: Work the steps of the problem.

Plug In $a = 2$

$$\frac{3}{(2)^2} + \frac{1}{2(2)} + \frac{2}{(2)} = \quad \frac{3}{4} + \frac{1}{4} + \frac{2}{2} = 2$$

Step 3: Put a box around the Target Value.

$\boxed{2}$

Target Value (TV)

Step 4: Check each answer choice to find your Target Value.

When we plug in $a = 2$, we need a TV of 2.

A) $\frac{6}{a^2+3a}$ $\frac{6}{(2)^2+3(2)} = \frac{6}{10}$ ***No***

B) $\frac{2a+3}{a^3}$ $\frac{2(2)+3}{(2)^3} = \frac{7}{8}$ ***No***

C) $\frac{5a+6}{2a^2}$ $\frac{5(2)+6}{2(2)^2} = \frac{16}{8} = 2$ ***Yes***

D) $6a^2$ $6(2)^2 = 24$ ***No***

Correct Answer: C

Example 2: PLUG IN FOR THE VARIABLE

2. If $\frac{x}{6} = \frac{y+1}{3}$, what is the value of *y* in terms of x?

A) $\frac{3x-1}{6}$

B) $\frac{x-6}{2}$

C) $\frac{x-2}{2}$

D) $2x = 1$

Solution Using the Strategy: Plug in for the Variable

Step 1: If the question contains the words "in terms of.....," cross it out – it is meant to confuse you. Highlight what the question is asking.

If $\frac{x}{6} = \frac{y+1}{3}$, what is the value of y ~~in terms of x~~?

Step 2: Identify a variable(s) to plug in.

Let's plug in for x since it shows up the most and appears in the answer choices. Let's try $x = 2$

Step 3: Work the steps of the problem.

Step 4: Put a box around the Target Value.

Plug In $x = 2$

$$\frac{2}{6} = \frac{y+1}{3}$$

Cross multiply to get: $6(y+1) = 6$
Distribute: $6y + 6 = 6$
Subtract 6 from both sides to get $6y = 0$
Divide both sides by 6 to get

$$\boxed{y = 0}$$

Target Value (TV)

Step 5: Check each answer choice to find your Target Value.

When we plug in $x = 2$, we need a TV of 0.

A) $\frac{3x-1}{6}$ $\frac{3(2)-1}{6} = \frac{5}{6}$ *No*

B) $\frac{x-6}{2}$ $\frac{(2)-6}{2} = \frac{-4}{2}$ *No*

C) $\frac{x-2}{2}$ $\frac{(2)-2}{2} = 0$ *Yes*

D) $2x - 1$ $2(2) - 1 = 3$ *No*

Correct Answer: C

Practice: PLUG IN FOR THE VARIABLE

1. If $x - y = 3$ and $z = 4x - 5 - 4y$, what is the value of z?

A) -2
B) 2
C) -7
D) 7

$$a = \frac{b - c}{c}$$

2. In the equation above, if b is positive and c is negative, which of the following must be true?

A) $a = 1$
B) $a > 1$
C) $a = -1$
D) $a < -1$

3. Which of the following expressions is equivalent to $\sqrt{2x^{\frac{1}{2}}}$?

A) $\sqrt{2}x^{\frac{1}{4}}$
B) $\sqrt{2}x$
C) $2x^{\frac{1}{4}}$
D) $2x$

4. The cost to buy a certain number of pencils from a stationery shop is $12 when buying 20 pencils. With a purchase of 30 pencils, the cost is $16. If the cost increases at a constant rate as the number of pencils bought increases, which of the following linear models best describes the cost c in dollars to buy n pencils?

A) $c = 0.4n + 4$
B) $c = 0.5n + 9$
C) $c = 0.75n + 6$
D) $c = 0.75n + 9$

$$x^3 - x^2 - 32x + 60$$

5. If the expression above can be written in the equivalent form $y(x - 2)$, which equation represents the value of y?

A) $x^2 - x + 28$
B) $x^2 + x - 30$
C) $x^2 - x + 30$
D) $x^2 + x + 28$

6. If the lengths of the sides of a rectangular swimming pool with an area of 60 square meters are tripled, what is the new area of the pool in square meters?

A) 180
B) 360
C) 540
D) 720

7. The volume of a cylinder is given by the formula $V = \pi r^2 h$. If the height of a cylinder is doubled, what is the ratio of the new volume to the old volume?

A) 1:2
B) 1:4
C) 2:1
D) 4:1

8. Every element in a data set is multiplied by 5, and each resulting product is then decreased by 2. If y is the mean of the final data set, which of the following expressions gives the mean of the original set in terms of y?

A) $\frac{y+2}{5}$
B) $\frac{y-2}{5}$
C) $5y+2$
D) $5y-2$

For answer explanations to these practice questions, go to curvebreakerstestprep.com/decoding-the-digital-sat

CHAPTER 19: PLUG IN THE ANSWER

LESSON

Plugging in the Answer (sometimes referred to as PITA or Backsolving) is often the quickest way to get to the correct answer. See if you can use this strategy when there are only numbers in the answer choices and not variables.

Basic Rule of Thumb: PITA vs Plugging In
Plug in for the variable when there are variables in the answer choices.
Try PITA when there are no variables in the answer choices but numbers only.

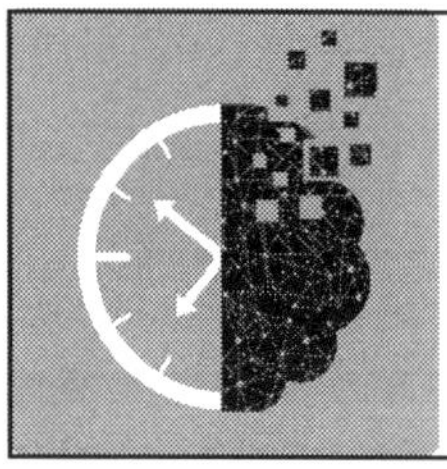

The Curvebreakers Strategy

PLUG IN THE ANSWER

1. **Start with Answer Choice B or C by drawing an arrow to the left of the answer choice (except if the question asks for the greatest or smallest value – then start there).** Sometimes, when starting with one of the middle answer choices, you will know whether to go higher or lower if that answer choice doesn't work.
2. **Put a Label over the answer choices.** Write in exactly what it is you're looking to solve for directly over the answer choices.
3. **Label each additional column as necessary.** Create a table with columns when there are several steps needed to solve the problem.
4. **Work the steps of the problem.**
5. **When one answer works, STOP.** Since you're working with numbers only, you do not have to check every answer choice.

Example 1: PLUG IN THE ANSWER

1. If $\frac{20}{x-1} - \frac{18}{x+1} = 2$, what is the value of x?

A) 3
B) 4
C) 5
D) 6

Solution Strategy: Plug in the Answer

Step 1: Start with Answer Choice B or C by drawing an arrow to the left of the answer choice (except if the question asks for the greatest or smallest value – then start there).

Step 2: Put a Label over the answer choices..

Step 3: Label each additional column as necessary.

Step 4: Work the steps of the problem.

x	$\frac{20}{x-1}-\frac{18}{x+1}$		= 2?
A) 3			
➘ B) 4	$\frac{20}{4-1}-\frac{18}{4+1}$	$=\frac{20}{3}-\frac{18}{5}$	= 2 *No*
C) 5	$\frac{20}{5-1}-\frac{18}{5+1}$	$=\frac{20}{4}-\frac{18}{6}$	= 2 *Yes*
D) 6			

Step 5: When one answer works, STOP.

When Answer Choice C (5) is plugged in for x, we get 2.

Correct Answer: C

Example 2: PLUG IN THE ANSWER

2. At a bookstore, the owner sells paperback novels for $10 each and hardcover novels for $25 each. Altogether, she sold 120 novels for $2,250. How many paperback novels did she sell?

A) 50
B) 60
C) 70
D) 80

Solution Strategy: Plug in the Answer

Step 1: Bite-size

At a bookstore, the owner sells paperback novels for $10 each / and hardcover novels for $25 each. / Altogether, she sold 120 novels / for $2,250 /. How many paperback novels did she sell?

Step 2: Start with Answer Choice B or C by drawing an arrow to the left of the answer choice (except if the question asks for the greatest or smallest value – then start there).

Step 3: Put a Label over the answer choices.

Step 4: Label each additional column as necessary.

Step 5: Work the steps of the problem.

# paperback	# hardcover (120 minus paper)	$ paperback ($10)	$hardcover ($25)	Total = 2,250?
A) 50	70	$500	$1750	$2250 **Yes**
↘ B) 60	60	$600	$1500	$2100 **No**
C) 70	50	$700	$1250	$1950 **No**
D) 80				

- For Choice B. 2nd column: # hardcovers. Since total novels = 120, then if Answer Choice B were correct, the number of hardcovers would be 120 - 60 = 60.
- For Choice B. 3rd and 4th columns: cost of paperbacks and cost of hardcovers. Use the prices given in the question to calculate $600 as the cost for paperbacks and $1500 as the cost for hardcovers.
- For Choice B. Last column: Total Cost. Does it add to $2250? $1500 + $600 = $2100. Since that doesn't add to $2500, Answer Choice B is incorrect. Move on to Answer Choice A or C.
- For Choice C. If we now try Answer Choice C, we calculate the total cost as $1950.
- Since we now know that we're going in the wrong direction (we needed a higher cost than $2100 from Answer Choice B, not a lower cost), the answer choice must be A.

Step 5: When one answer works, STOP.

When Answer Choice A (50) is plugged in for the number of paperbacks, we get a total cost of $2,250.

Correct Answer: A

Practice: PLUG IN THE ANSWER

1. If $x > 0$, which of the following is a solution to the equation $(x - 4)^2 - 121 = 0$?

A) 7
B) 11
C) 15
D) 16

$$\frac{3}{a} - 13 = 10a$$

2. What is the value of a in the given equation?

A) 0.2
B) 0.3
C) 1.2
D) 1.3

3. A company charges a flat rate of $30 plus $0.50 per mile driven for their delivery service. If your budget for a delivery is $150, what is the farthest distance, to the nearest mile, that the company can deliver your package?

A) 240 miles
B) 270 miles
C) 280 miles
D) 290 miles

4. What is the solution to the equation $7 + 6(5x)^{\frac{1}{3}} = 37$?

A) 13
B) 25
C) 31
D) 49

5. In a marathon, the first half of the race is 3 kilometers shorter than the second half. If the total length of the marathon is 42 kilometers, how long is the first half of the race?

A) 18 km
B) 19.5 km
C) 20 km
D) 21 km

6. If the expression $4x^2 - 3x - 7 = 0$, then which of the following is the least value of x?

A) -1

B) $\frac{1}{2}$

C) $\frac{3}{2}$

D) 2

7. The length of a rectangle is 3 meters longer than twice its width. If the perimeter of the rectangle is 30 meters, what is the length of the rectangle?

A) 8 m
B) 9 m
C) 10 m
D) 11 m

$$6x - 12ax = 18$$

8. In the given equation, a is a constant. The equation has no solution. What is the value of a?

A) 0

B) $\frac{1}{2}$

C) $\frac{3}{2}$

D) 2

For answer explanations to these practice questions, go to curvebreakerstestprep.com/decoding-the-digital-sat

CHAPTER 20: BASIC ALGEBRA

Section: Math
Question Subsection: Algebra and Functions
Question Category: Basic Algebra
Of the 44 Math questions, approximately 6 - 10 may be questions from this category.

While Plugging In and Plugging In The Answer are very useful techniques, you will still need to know how to do basic algebra.

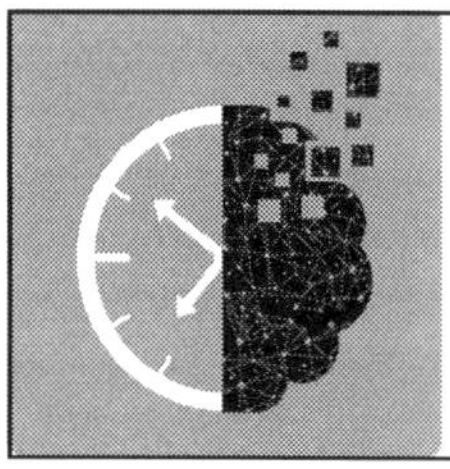

The Curvebreakers Strategy

ISOLATE THE VARIABLE

1. Isolate the Variable
2. Use PEMDAS for the order of operations (Parentheses, Exponents, Multiplication, Division, Addition, Subtraction)
3. Combine Like Terms
4. Perform the same operation on both sides of the equation
5. Know how to Cross Multiply

Example 1: Basic Algebra

1. What is the solution to the equation: $x = \frac{x+6}{3}$?

A) 0.5
B) 1
C) 1.3
D) 3

Solution Strategy: Isolate the Variable

Step 1: *Isolate the variable. First, multiply both sides by the reciprocal 3, or get the equation into a format where we can cross multiply:*

$$\frac{x}{1} = \frac{x+6}{3}$$

$$3x = x + 6$$

Step 2: *Isolate the x by first subtracting x from both sides and then dividing by 3:*

$$3x = x + 6$$
$$\underline{-x \quad -x}$$
$$2x = 6$$
$$x = 3$$

Correct Answer: D

Example 2: Basic Algebra

2. If $z = xy + 4$, then what is the value of x, in terms of y and z?

A) $\frac{y}{z-4}$

B) $\frac{y}{z+4}$

C) $\frac{z-4}{y}$

D) $\frac{z+4}{y}$

Solution Strategy: Isolate the Variable

Step 1: Cross out "in terms of." Underline what it is we're looking for (x).

If $x = xy + 4$. What is the value <u>of x,</u> ~~in terms of y and z~~?

Step 2: First isolate the x by subtracting 4 from both sides:

$$
\begin{array}{l}
z = xy + 4 \\
\underline{-4 \qquad\quad -4} \\
z - 4 = xy
\end{array}
$$

Step 3: Next divide both sides by y to get x by itself:

$$\frac{z - 4}{y} = \frac{xy}{y}$$

$$\frac{z - 4}{y} = x$$

Correct Answer: C

Practice: Basic Algebra

1. What is the value of x if $\frac{5(x-1)}{4} - 1 = 0$?

A) $\frac{4}{9}$

B) $\frac{5}{9}$

C) $\frac{9}{5}$

D) $\frac{9}{4}$

2. If $\frac{3}{2x} - \frac{1}{4} = 2$ then $x = ?$

A) $\frac{1}{2}$

B) $\frac{2}{3}$

C) 2

D) 3

3. Mara bought 6 identical backpacks for her family trip. She used a coupon for $72 off the entire purchase. The cost for the entire purchase after using the coupon was $168. What was the original price, in dollars, for 1 backpack?

[ ]

4. If $AB = \frac{1}{2}xy^2$, which of the following gives the value of y, in terms of AB and x?

A) $y = \sqrt{\frac{x}{2AB}}$

B) $y = \sqrt{\frac{AB}{2x}}$

C) $y = \sqrt{\frac{2AB}{x}}$

D) $y = \frac{2AB}{x}$

5. The formula for converting degrees Celsius (C) to degrees Fahrenheit $F = \frac{9}{5}C + 32$. Which of the following expressions gives the value of C in terms of F?

A) $\frac{5}{9}(F - 32)$

B) $\frac{9}{5}F - 32$

C) $\frac{9}{5}F + 32$

D) $\frac{F - 32}{5}$

6. What is the <u>least</u> value of $x + 11$ if $|2x - 3| = 19$.

[ ]

For answer explanations to these practice questions, go to curvebreakerstestprep.com/decoding-the-digital-sat

CHAPTER 21: SLOPE INTERCEPT FORM OF A LINE

Section: Math
Question Subsection: Algebra and Functions
Question Category: Slope Intercept Form of a Line
Of the 44 Math questions, approximately 3 - 6 may be questions from this category.

LESSON

The 2 basic things you need to know in order to solve Linear Equations:

1. The Equation of a Straight Line:

$$y = mx + b$$

Where m = **the slope** and b = **the y-intercept**
The slope (m) represents how quickly the line is changing.
The y-intercept *(b)* is the point where the line crosses the y-axis, i.e. when the value of $x = 0$.
When asked to find the slope or y-intercept, you must first get the equation into the $y = mx + \mathrm{b}$ format by isolating the y.

2. To calculate the Slope:

$$\frac{y_2 - y_1}{x_2 - x_1}$$

Slope is often also referred to as $\frac{rise}{run}$ or $\frac{change\ in\ y}{change\ in\ x}$.

It does not matter which value you use as y_2 first as long as you make sure to match it with x_2.

Meaning of Parallel and Perpendicular Lines
Parallel lines never touch and therefore have the same slope and no solutions;
Perpendicular lines have negative reciprocal slopes and one solution.

Linear Word Problems
Many Word problems are often just different ways of presenting a Linear Equation.
Slope will be represented by words like “increase/decrease,” “per,” “each,” “every,” “additional.” Y-intercept will be represented by words like “initial,” “beginning,” “starting,” or “zero” as the independent variable.

TIP: On the test, linear equations will often use different variables than x and y. In these instances, determine which value is acting as your y and which one is acting as your x. The y, which is your dependent variable, is typically alone on one side of the equation.

The Curvebreakers Strategy

WRITE OUT THE FORMULAS REQUIRED

1. Write out the equation of a straight line
2. Write out the slope formula

Example 1: Slope Intercept Form of a Line

1. In the standard (x,y) coordinate plane, what is the slope of a line that is perpendicular to a line passing through the points (-3,5) and (1,-1)?

A) $-\frac{3}{2}$

B) $-\frac{1}{3}$

C) $\frac{2}{3}$

D) 3

Strategy: Write out the slope formula

Step 1: Write out the slope formula:

$$\frac{y_2 - y_1}{x_2 - x_1}$$

Step 2: Calculate the slope:

We're given the points (-3,5), (1,-1)

$$\frac{(-1)-(5)}{(1)-(-3)} = \frac{-6}{1+3} = \frac{-6}{4} = \frac{-3}{2}$$

Step 3: Since we're looking for the slope of a line PERPENDICULAR to this line, the slope is the negative reciprocal.

$$= \frac{2}{3}$$

Correct Answer: C

Example 2: Slope Intercept Form of a Line

2. The function $p(t) = 5t + 10$ models the number of people who visit a museum over time. Which of the following best describes the meaning of the number 5 in the equation?

A) The number of people who visited the museum on the first day it opened
B) The average number of people who visit the museum each week
C) The total number of people who have visited the museum since it opened
D) The approximate increase in the number of people who visit the museum each day

Strategy: Write out the equation of a straight line

Step 1: Recognize that the function is a linear equation:

Think of	$p(t) = 5t + 10$
As	$y = mx + b$

Therefore, the slope is 5 and the y-intercept is 10, and we are asked the meaning of the slope. The slope represents the approximate increase in the number of people who visit the museum each day.

Correct Answer: D

Practice: Slope Intercept Form of a Line

1. Which of the following is the equation of a line parallel to the line with equation $y = -3x + 2$?

A) $y = 3x + 2$

B) $y = -3x - 4$

C) $y = -2x + 4$

D) $y = \frac{1}{3}x + 2$

2. If $f(x)$ is a linear function such that $f(-2) = 8$ and $f(4) = -2$, what is the slope of the graph of $y = f(x)$?

A) $-\frac{1}{4}$

B) $-\frac{5}{3}$

C) $\frac{1}{4}$

D) 6

3. Which of the following is the equation of a line perpendicular to the line with equation $2x + 5y = 10$?

A) $5x - 2y = 5$
B) $2x - 5y = 10$
C) $-2x - 5y = 10$
D) $5x + 2y = 4$

4. A company's costs can be modeled by the equation P(x) = 20 + 3.5x, where x represents the number of units produced. Which of the following best describes the meaning of the number 20 in the equation?

A) The revenue generated by selling 3.5 units
B) The cost of producing one unit
C) The fixed costs incurred by the company
D) The increase in cost for each 3.5 units produced

5. Which of the following could be the graph of the linear equation $\frac{3}{2}y - 6x = -3$?

A)

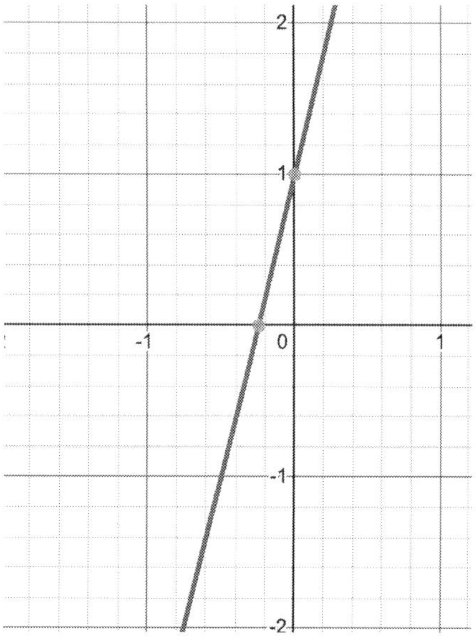

B)

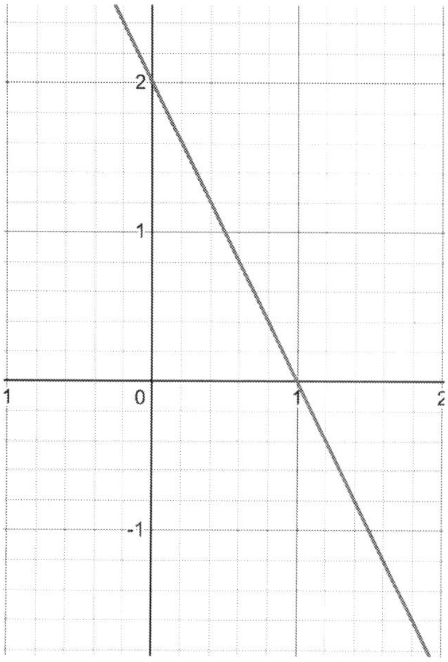

C)

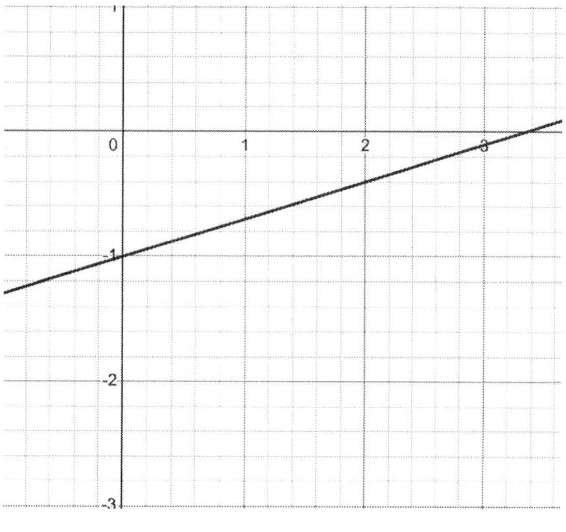

D)

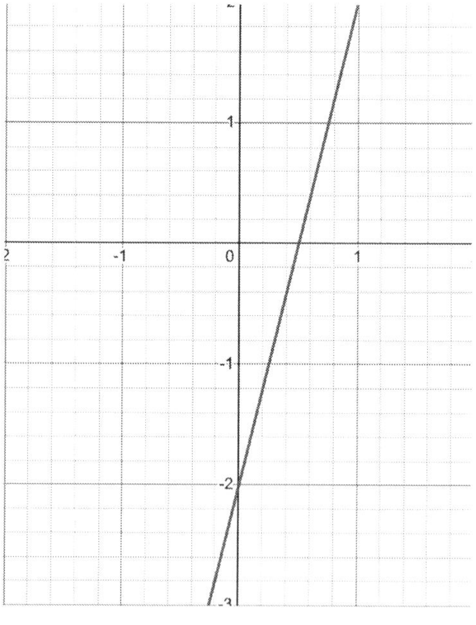

6. If m is a constant less than 0, which of the following could be the graph of $y = 2m(x+y)$?

A) 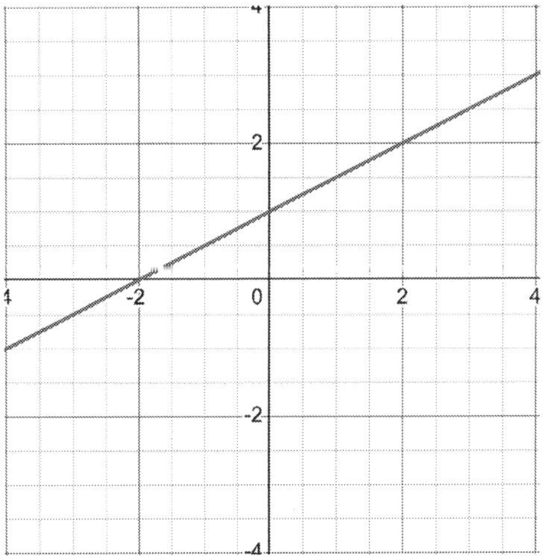

B) 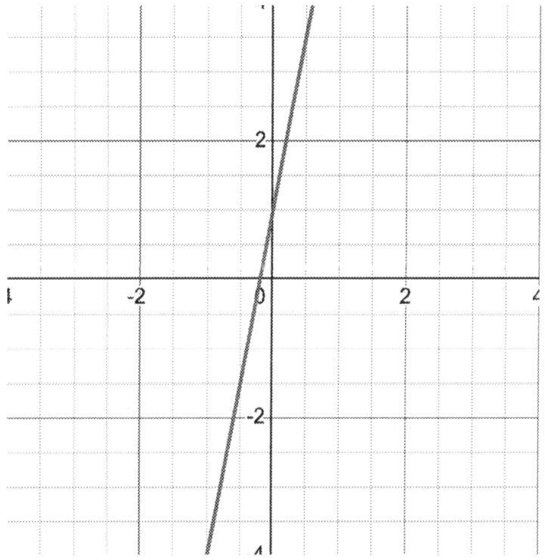

C) 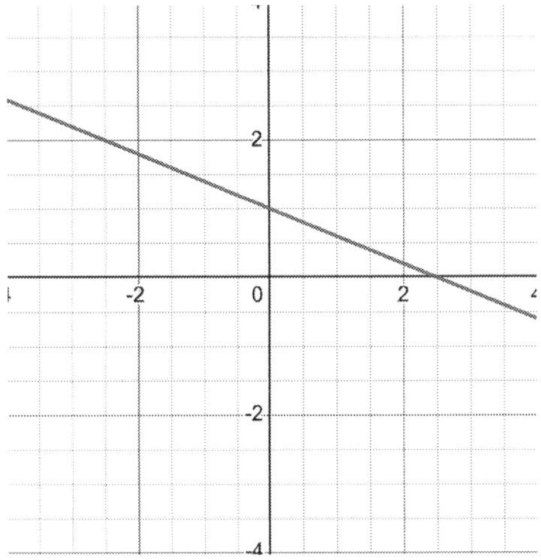

D) 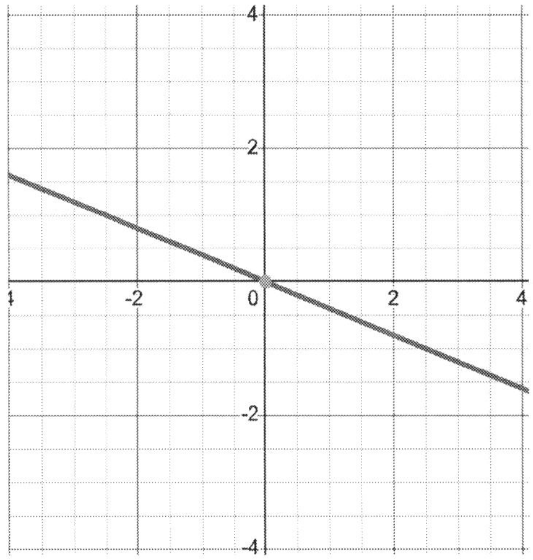

For answer explanations to these practice questions, go to curvebreakerstestprep.com/decoding-the-digital-sat

CHAPTER 22: PROPORTIONS

Section: Math
Question Subsection: Numbers and Operations
Question Category: Proportions
Of the 44 Math questions, approximately 2 - 5 may be questions from this category.

LESSON

When two ratios or fractions are equal in value, they are said to be in proportion.

Set up a proportion when given one complete relationship between two variables and one incomplete relationship between two variables of the same kind. Ratios can be written several ways. For example, a one to two ratio can be written as:

$\frac{1}{2}$, 1:2, or 1 to 2.

Proportions can pop up in a number of scenarios. They can be part of a word problem (recipes and surveys are common) or part of a geometry problem (like questions involving similar triangles or scale drawings). The key to solving proportion questions is to always keep things consistent and properly arranged by physically writing the units, both top and bottom.

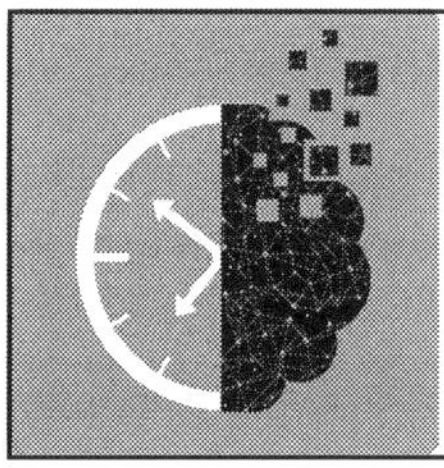

The Curvebreakers Strategy

WRITE OUT BOTH TOP AND BOTTOM UNITS

1. Separate the text into bite-sized pieces.
2. When you are given one complete relationship and one incomplete relationship, set up a proportion. Write the units for both the numerator and denominator to ensure you're comparing apples to apples.
3. Cross multiply.

Example 1: Proportions

1. If 5 pens cost $3, how many pens can be bought for $12?

A) 20
B) 15
C) 10
D) 5

Strategy: Write out both top and bottom units

Step 1: Separate the text into bite-sized pieces.

If 5 pens cost \$3, / how many pens can be bought for \$12?

Step 2: When you are given one complete relationship and one incomplete relationship, set up a proportion. Write the units for both the numerator and denominator to ensure you're comparing apples to apples.

$$\frac{5\ pens}{\$3} = \frac{x\ pens}{\$12}$$

Step 3: Cross multiply.

$3x = 60$ pens
$x = 20$

Correct Answer: A

Example 2: Proportions

2. If Jayden walks 14.5 inches in one step, approximately how many feet will he walk in 100 steps?

A) 12
B) 15
C) 121
D) 1,450

Strategy: Write out both top and bottom units

Step 1: Separate the text into bite-sized pieces.

If Jayden walks 14.5 inches in one step / , approximately how many feet will he walk in 100 steps?

Step 2: When you are given one complete relationship and one incomplete relationship, set up a proportion. Write the units for both the numerator and denominator to ensure you're comparing apples to apples.

$$\frac{14.5\ inches}{1\ step} = \frac{x\ inches}{100\ steps}$$

Step 3: Cross multiply.

$x = 1{,}450$ inches

Step 4: Since we are asked for feet and not inches, we can set up another proportion to convert inches to feet:

$$\frac{12\ inches}{1\ foot} = \frac{1{,}450\ inches}{x\ feet}$$

Cross multiply to get $12x = 1{,}450$ inches.
Divide both sides by 12 to get $x = 120.8$ feet

Correct Answer: C

Practice: Proportions

1. A container holds 2 liters of liquid. If 3/4 of the container is filled with liquid, how many liters of liquid are in the container?

A) 1.5 liters
B) 1.8 liters
C) 2.25 liters
D) 2.67 liters

2. A car is traveling at a constant rate of 60 feet per second. How long will it take the car to travel 1/4 mile at this rate? (Note: 1 mile = 5,280 feet)

A) 6 seconds
B) 11 seconds
C) 22 seconds
D) 44 seconds

3. If the ratio of 6a to 4b is 1 to 5, what is the ratio of 2a to b?

A) 1 to 5
B) 3 to 5
C) 4 to 15
D) 12 to 1

For answer explanations to these practice questions, go to curvebreakerstestprep.com/decoding-the-digital-sat

CHAPTER 23: FUNCTIONS

Section: Math
Question Subsection: Algebra and Functions
Question Category: Functions
Of the 44 Math questions, approximately 3 - 5 may be questions from this category.

LESSON

A function is a relationship between inputs where each input is related to exactly one output. It is a way to produce an ordered pair: an x value and a y value. For example, f(2) = 10 produces the coordinates (2,10); when you input 2 into the function, you get an output of 10. If functions seem confusing to you, think of the function f(x) as y.

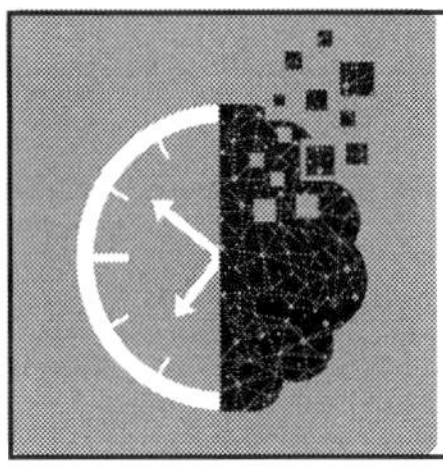

The Curvebreakers Strategy

THINK OF f(x) AS y

1. Think of f(x) as the value of y when you input x into the equation.
2. Determine the x and y values of both coordinates, and fill in the equation.

Example 1: Functions

1. The function g is defined by $g(x) = 5x - 3$ for all values of x. What is the value of $g(2) + g(7)$?

A) 9
B) 28
C) 39
D) 41

Solution Strategy: "THINK OF f(x) as y"

Step 1: Think of $g(x)$ as the value of y when you input x into the equation.

$g(x) = 5x - 3$
$y = 5x - 3$

Step 2: Calculate $g(2)$

When we input x = 2 into the equation, what is the value of y?

$y = 5x - 3$
$y = 5(2) - 3 = 7$
Therefore $g(2) = 7$

Step 3: Calculate $g(7)$

When we input x = 7 into the equation, what is the value of y?

$y = 5x - 3$
$y = 5(7) - 3 = 32$
Therefore $g(7) = 32$

Step 3: Calculate $g(2) + g(7)$

(7) + (32) = 39

Correct Answer: C

Example 2: Functions

2. In the linear function f, $f(2) = 7$ and $f(4) = 9$, which equation defines f?

A) $f(x) = 2x + 3$
B) $f(x) = x + 5$
C) $f(x) = 3x + 1$
D) $f(x) = 5x + 1$

Solution

Step 1: Determine the ordered pairs: the x and y values

$f(2)$ = 7 is (2,7)
$f(4)$ = 9 is (4,9)

Step 2: Write out the equation of a straight line

$y = mx + b$

Step 3: Write out the slope formula

$$\frac{y_2 - y_1}{x_2 - x_1}$$

Step 4: Calculate the slope

$$\frac{(9) - (7)}{(4) - (2)} = \frac{2}{2} = 1$$

The only answer choice with a slope of 1 is Answer Choice B.
No additional work is necessary.

Correct answer: B

Practice: Functions

1. If $g(x) = 3x - 5$, then $g(4) =$?

A) 7
B) 9
C) 11
D) 13

2. If $f(x) = 3x + 1$, what is one possible value of *x* for which $6 < f(x) < 22$?

A) 3
B) 7
C) 9
D) 10

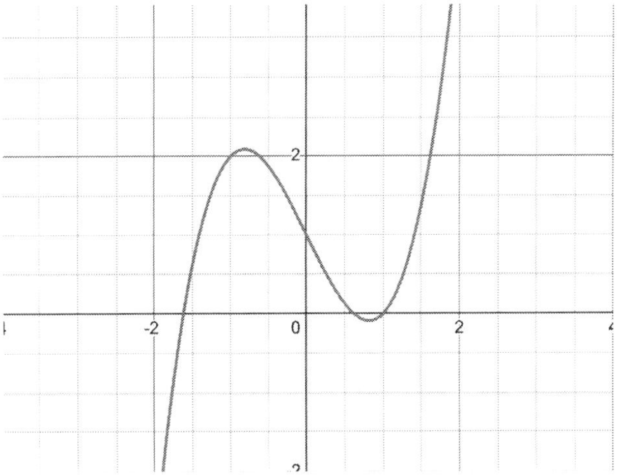

3. The graph of $h(x)$ is shown above. What must be true about $h(x)$?

A) $h(0)$ is negative.
B) $h(0)$ has two values.
C) $h(x)$ has three solutions for which $h(x) = 0$.
D) $h(2)$ is zero.

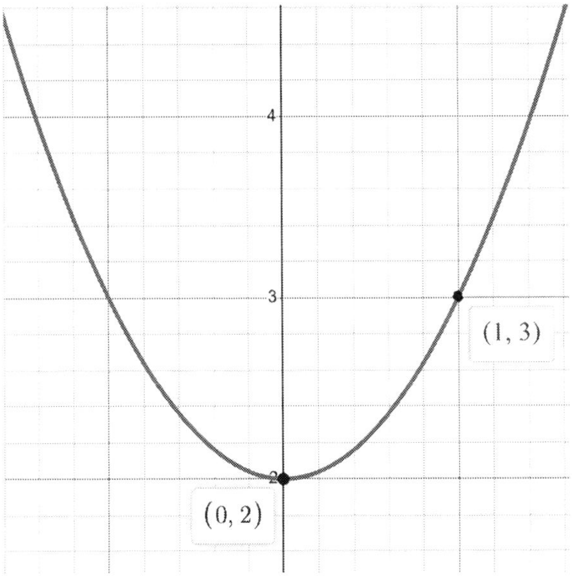

4. If the figure above is the graph of $y = f(x)$, which of the following could be the equation of $f(x)$?

A) $f(x) = (x + 2)^2$
B) $f(x) = (x - 2)^2$
C) $f(x) = (x + 4)^2$
D) $f(x) = x^2 + 2$

5. If g is a function and $g(4) = 9$, which of the following CANNOT be the definition of g?

A) $g(x) = x^2 - 7x + 12$
B) $g(x) = 3x - 3$
C) $g(x) = -4x + 25$
D) $g(x) = x + 6$

x	f(x)
-2	4
-1	0
0	-2
1	-2
2	0

6. A function is plotted in the xy-plane. The function passes through the points in the table above. Which of these equations could represent the function?

A) $f(x) = 2x + 8$
B) $f(x) = 2x^2 - 2$
C) $f(x) = (x - 2)(x - 1)$
D) $f(x) = x^2 - 3x + 2$

7. The function $h(x) = 1000(1.05)^x$ models the value, in dollars, of a certain investment account over time, where x is the number of years since the initial investment. Which of the following is the best interpretation of "$h(8)$ is approximately equal to 1,478" in this context?

A) The value of the investment account is estimated to be approximately $1,478 in 8 years.
B) The value of the investment account is estimated to be approximately $8,780 in 8 years.
C) The investment account is estimated to increase in value by approximately $1,478 every year.
D) The investment account is estimated to increase in value by approximately 47.8% after 8 years.

For answer explanations to these practice questions, go to curvebreakerstestprep.com/decoding-the-digital-sat

CHAPTER 24: SYSTEMS OF EQUATIONS

Section: Math
Question Subsection: Algebra and Functions
Question Category: Systems of Equations
Of the 44 Math questions, approximately 3 - 6 may be questions from this category.

LESSON

Systems of Equations are two or more equations with two or more variables. On the test, you will mostly encounter linear systems: 2 lines with 2 variables and neither variable will be raised to a larger power than 1.

Before we discuss the methods for solving, let's first discuss the possible outcomes for a linear system:

1. **One Solution**: 2 distinct lines with the solution being the point at which the lines intersect.
2. **No Solutions**: these lines never intersect; therefore, they are parallel and have the same slope.
3. **Infinite Solutions**: these lines are identical – they may not appear identical at first glance, but if they were to be simplified or rearranged, they would be equivalent.

While there are several ways to solve a system, we will discuss the 3 main ways:

A. **Substitution**

Replace one variable with an expression that contains the other variable.

B. **Stack and Solve**

Place one equation on top of the other, in the same format, and add the equations together to cancel one of the variables. You may have to manipulate one or both equations to get them in a format that, when added, one of the variables will add to 0. Once you solve for one variable, plug it back into one of the equations to solve for the second variable.

C. **Graphing the Intersection**

Any function that relates two variables can be graphed on your calculator. First, rewrite the equations in the standard $y=mx+b$ format. You can then graph the equations as functions and find the intersection. After graphing the lines, use either the "intersection" or "table" function to find the intersection (or solution).

The Curvebreakers Strategy

SUBSTITUTE, STACK, OR GRAPH

1. With Substitution, replace one variable with an expression that contains the other variable.
2. With Stack & Solve, add the equations together to cancel out one of the variables.
3. With Graphing, graph the lines and find the intersection.

Example 1: Substitute

1. If $a = 2b + 3$ and $b = 5a + 1$, what is the value of a?

A) $-\frac{5}{9}$

B) $-\frac{2}{9}$

C) $\frac{2}{9}$

D) $\frac{5}{9}$

Solution Strategy: Substitute

Step 1: With Substitution, replace one variable with an expression that contains the other variable.

Whenever we see the variable b, replace it with $5a + 1$.

$$\begin{aligned} a &= 2(5a+1)+3 \\ a &= 10a+2+3 \\ a &= 10a+5 \\ -10a & \quad -10a \\ \hline -9a &= 5 \\ a &= -\frac{5}{9} \end{aligned}$$

Correct Answer: A

Example 2: Stack and Solve

$9x + 5y = 22$
$7x - 5y = 10$

2. For the solution (x,y) to the system of equations above, what is the value of $x - y$?

A) $-\frac{5}{14}$

B) $\frac{6}{5}$

C) $\frac{14}{5}$

D) 14

Solution Strategy: Stack and Solve

Step 1: With Stack & Solve, add the equations together to cancel out one of the variables.

$$\begin{aligned} 9x + 5y &= 22 \\ \underline{7x - 5y} &\underline{= 10} \\ 16x &= 32 \\ x &= 2 \end{aligned}$$

Step 2: Substitute $x = 2$ into one of the equations to find the value of y.

$$\begin{aligned} 9(2) + 5y &= 22 \\ 18 + 5y &= 22 \\ -18 \quad & \quad -18 \\ 5y &= 4 \\ y &= \frac{4}{5} \end{aligned}$$

Step 3: Solve $x - y$

$$(2) - (\frac{4}{5}) = \frac{10}{5} - \frac{4}{5} = \frac{6}{5}$$

Correct Answer: B

Practice: Systems of Equations

1. If $2x + y = 5$ and $y = 3x - 2$, what is the value of x?

A) -1

B) $-\frac{2}{5}$

C) $\frac{1}{5}$

D) $\frac{7}{5}$

$$2b = 1 - 3a$$
$$-5 - a = 2b$$

2. Based on the system of equations above, what is the value of ab?

A) -12
B) -1
C) -7
D) 7

$$2x + 3y = 12$$
$$-y + 4x = 10$$

3. The solution to the given system of equations is (x,y). What is the value of $y - x$?

$$4x - 3y = 12$$
$$8x - 6y = 24$$

4. How many solutions does the above system of equations have?

A) 0
B) 1
C) 2
D) Infinitely many solutions

5. A convenience store sells bags of chips and bottles of soda. On Monday, Aroze bought 10 bags of chips and 12 bottles of soda for \$22.50, and on Tuesday he bought 6 bags of chips and 9 bottles of soda for \$14.25. If the cost of a bag of chips and a bottle of soda is the same for all purchases, what is the cost of 16 bags of chips and 21 bottles of soda?

A) \$36.75
B) \$46.25
C) \$59.25
D) \$61.50

For answer explanations to these practice questions, go to curvebreakerstestprep.com/decoding-the-digital-sat

CHAPTER 25: INEQUALITIES

Section: Math
Question Subsection: Numbers & Operations
Question Category: Inequalities
Of the 44 Math questions, approximately 1 - 2 may be questions from this category.

LESSON

Treat an inequality like a regular equation with an = sign; the process for isolating the variable is the same as a standard equation.

Greater Than	$>$
Greater Than or Equal To	$\geq$
Less Than	$<$
Less Than or Equal To	$\leq$

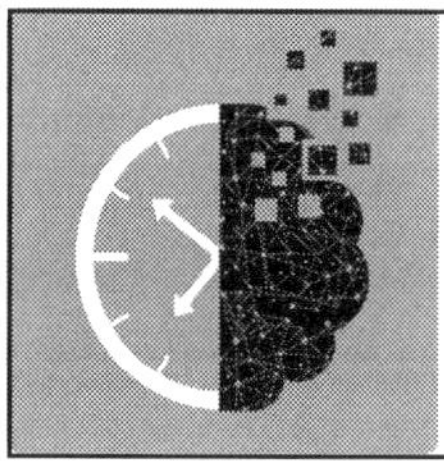

The Curvebreakers Strategy

REMEMBER TO FLIP THE SIGN

Just remember to FLIP THE SIGN when multiplying or dividing by a negative number.

Example: Inequalities

If $-3y + 7 > 19$, which of the following describes all possible values of y?

A) $y < 4$
B) $y < -5$
C) $4 > y$
D) $-4 > y$

Solution Strategy: Remember to Flip the Sign

Step 1: Subtract 7 from both sides.

$$\begin{array}{l} -3y + 7 > 19 \\ \underline{\quad\;\; -7 \;\; -7} \\ -3y \qquad > 12 \end{array}$$

Step 2: Divide both sides by -3. Remember to flip the direction of the inequality since we're dividing by a negative number.

$$\frac{-3y}{-3} > \frac{12}{-3}$$

$y < -4$

which can be rewritten as:
$-4 > y$

Correct Answer: D

Practice: Inequalities

1. If $6x + 2 < 26$, then which of the following is a possible value for x?

A) 3.5
B) 4
C) 4.5
D) 5

2. What is the greatest value of y for which $|y + 3| \le 2$?

A) -1
B) -2
C) -3
D) -5

3. If $x > 9$, which of the following is the smallest?

A) $\frac{3}{x}$

B) $\frac{x}{3}$

C) $\frac{x}{9}$

D) $\frac{10-x}{x}$

For answer explanations to these practice questions, go to curvebreakerstestprep.com/decoding-the-digital-sat

CHAPTER 26: QUADRATICS

Section: Math
Question Subsection: Numbers and Operations
Question Category: Quadratics
Of the 44 Math questions, approximately 2 - 4 may be questions from this category.

LESSON

1. A **quadratic** equation is an equation of the second degree, meaning it contains at least one term that is squared. A quadratic function's graph looks like a parabola, and its equation has the form:

$$y = ax^2 + bx + c$$

with a, b, and c being constants, or numerical coefficients, and x is an unknown variable.

If a is positive: parabola opens upward

If a is negative: parabola opens downward

2. Know how to factor a quadratic using the **FOIL** method (First, Outer, Inner, Last). Set the function equal to zero and solve. When the leading coefficient is equal to 1, find two integers that multiply to c and add to b. Don't get confused by the wording in the question: zeros, roots, solutions, x-intercepts all mean the same thing.

$$(a + b)(c + d) = ac + ad + bc + bd$$

3. If a quadratic is difficult to factor using the FOIL method, the formula is:

$$x = \frac{-b \pm \sqrt{b^2 - 4ac}}{2a}$$

- The **discriminant** is the part of the quadratic formula underneath the square root symbol: $b^2 - 4ac$. The discriminant tells us whether there are two solutions, one solution, or no solutions.

$b^2 - 4ac < 0$	The equation has 0 real solutions. The graph does not cross the x-axis.
$b^2 - 4ac = 0$	The equation has 1 real solution. The graph crosses the x-axis at 1 point.
$b^2 - 4ac > 0$	The equation has 2 real solutions. The graph crosses the x-axis at 2 points.

4. There are 2 ways to find the **vertex** of the parabola (the vertex of a parabola is the minimum or maximum point of the equation).

A. To find the vertex of a parabola from the General Form $y = ax^2 + bx + c$, use the formula

$$x = \frac{-b}{2a}$$

Then, once you find the x-coordinate of the vertex, plug it into the General Form to find the y-coordinate.

B. Or use the Standard Form of a parabola to find the vertex. The Standard form is:

$$y = a(x - h)^2 + k$$

where a is a constant and (h,k) is the vertex of the parabola.

The Curvebreakers Strategy

KNOW THE BASIC EQUATIONS

1. General Form: $y = ax^2 + bx + c$
2. FOIL method: $(a + b)(c + d) = ac + ad + bc + bd$
3. Standard Form: $y = a(x - h)^2 + k$
4. Discriminant: $b^2 - 4ac$
5. x-coordinate of Vertex: $x = \frac{-b}{2a}$

Example 1: Quadratics

1. What is the sum of the distinct possible values of x for the equation $x^2 - x - 12 = 0$?

A) –4
B) –3
C) 4
D) 1

Solution Strategy: FOIL

Step 1: Understand the question. Since we are asked to find the sum of the distinct possible values of x, we need to find both solutions and add them together.

Step 2: Use the FOIL method to find 2 numbers that multiply to -12 and add to -1. The numbers that work are -4 and +3 as follows:

$(x - 4)(x + 3) = 0$

Step 3: Set both equations equal to 0 to solve for x:

$(x - 4) = 0$; $(x + 3) = 0$
Therefore $x = 4$; $x = -3$

Adding the two solutions together gives us: $4 + (-3) = 1$

Correct Answer: D

Example 2: Quadratics

$$4x^2 + 8x + c = 0$$

2. In the given equation, c is a constant. The equation has exactly one solution. What is the value of c?

A) -2
B) -1
C) 2
D) 4

Solution Strategy: Know the discriminant rules

Step 1: To determine the value of c, we can use the discriminant:

$b^2 - 4ac$

where a, b, and c are the coefficients of the quadratic equation $a^2 + bx + c = 0$.

Step 2: Substitute known values into the discriminant formula.

For the given equation, $a = 4$, $b = 8$, *and* $c = c$.
Substituting these values into the discriminant formula, we have:
$(8)^2 - 4(4)(c)$

$64 - 16c$

Step 3: Set the discriminant formula to zero (one solution).

$$\begin{aligned} 64 - 16c &= 0 \\ +16c \quad & +16c \\ \hline 64 &= 16c \\ 4 &= c \end{aligned}$$

Correct Answer: D

Practice: Quadratics

1. What is the product of the distinct possible values of y for the equation $y^2 + 6y + 5 = 0$?

A) –6
B) –1
C) 5
D) 6

2. If $\sqrt{x^2 - 11x + 34} = 4$, then what are the roots of the equation?

A) $x = 2; x = -4$
B) $x = -2; x = 9$
C) $x = 2; x = -9$
D) $x = 2; x = 9$

3. One of the factors of $2x^3 + 6x^2 - 20x$ is $x + k$ where k is a positive constant. What is the value of k?

A) -5
B) 2
C) 3
D) 5

$$3x^2 - 5x + 7 = 0$$

4. How many distinct real solutions does the given equation have?

A) Exactly one
B) Exactly two
C) Infinitely many
D) Zero

5. The equation $x^2 - 20x + c = 0$ has no real solutions if $c > n$. What is a possible value of n?

A) 99
B) 101
C) 103
D) 104

6. The function $g(x) = (x - 7)(x + 4)$ is defined by the given equation. For what value of x does $g(x)$ reach its minimum?

A) $-\frac{7}{4}$

B) $-\frac{4}{7}$

C) $\frac{3}{2}$

D) 4

7. The equation $f(x) = 2x^2 - 12x + 18$ defines the function f. For what value of x does $f(x)$ reach its minimum?

For answer explanations to these practice questions, go to curvebreakerstestprep.com/decoding-the-digital-sat

CHAPTER 27: GRAPHS

Section: Math
Question Subsection: Data, Statistics, & Probability
Question Category: Graphs
Of the 44 Math questions, approximately 2 - 5 may be questions from this category.

LESSON

There are often several ways to solve graphing problems. Choose the method that will get you to the answer in the least amount of time.

1. **Observation**: Oftentimes you can answer graph questions by simply viewing the trends or the data points in the graph.
2. **Know the Transformation Rules**: Just knowing the main transformation rules can get you to the correct answer choice without requiring calculations (see below).
3. **Use your Graphing Calculator:** Plug the values into your calculator and match the graph generated with the graph in the question.
4. **Process of Elimination:** For example, if you are presented with a parabola, eliminate answer choices related to linear equations.
5. **Plug In:** You may be given data points that you can use to plug into equations in the answer choices to find the correct answer.

TRANSFORMATION OF GRAPHS

In relation to $f(x)$:

- $f(x) + c$ is shifted upward c units in the xy-plane
- $f(x) - c$ is shifted downward c units in the xy-plane
- $f(x + c)$ is shifted to the left c units in the xy-plane
- $f(x - c)$ is shifted to the right c units in the xy-plane
- $-f(x)$ is flipped upside down over the x-axis
- $f(-x)$ is flipped left-right over the y-axis
- $|f(x)|$ the result of flipping upward all the parts of the graph that appear below the x-axis
- $a \cdot f(x)$ widens the graph if $|a| < 1$ and narrows the graph if $|a| > 1$

The Curvebreakers Strategy

SELECT THE QUICKEST OPTION TO SOLVE

1. Observation
2. Know the Transformation Rules
3. Use your Graphing Calculator
4. POE
5. Plug In

Example 1: Graphs

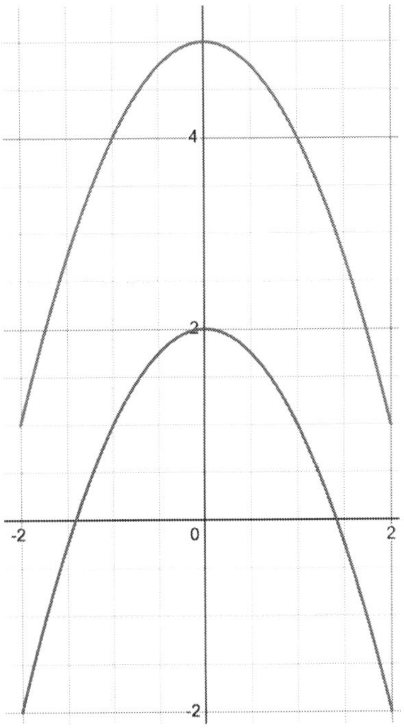

1. The graphs of the functions m (top) and n (bottom) are shown in the xy-plane above. Which of the following could be equal to $n(x)$?

A) $m(x+3)$
B) $m(x-3)$
C) $(x)+5$
D) $m(x)-3$

Solution Strategy: Use the Transformation Rules

Step 1: Identify the quickest way to solve: Know the transformation rules.

Equations that represent the transformation of graphs that apply to this question are:

- $f(x)+c$ is shifted upward c units in the xy-plane
- $f(x)-c$ is shifted downward c units in the xy-plane
- $f(x+c)$ is shifted to the left c units in the xy-plane
- $f(x-c)$ is shifted to the right c units in the xy-plane

Step 2: Identify the relevant equation from the transformation rules.

Since $n(x)$ is shifting <u>down</u> what appears to be 5 units in relation to $m(x)$, the relevant equation is:

- $f(x)-c$ is shifted downward c units in the xy-plane

Correct Answer: D

Example 2: Graphs

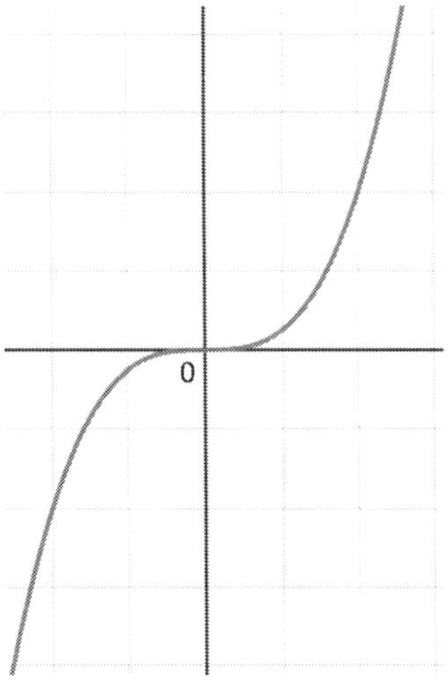

2. Which of the following equations is depicted in the graph above?

A) $y = \frac{3x}{x^3} + 5$

B) $y = \frac{x^3}{4}$

C) $y = 2x + 4$

D) $y = (3x - 8)(3x + 1)$

Solution Strategy: Plug In

Step 1: Identify the quickest way to solve: POE and Plug In

Step 2: Use POE to eliminate an answer choice(s).

Answer Choice C is a linear equation and would be graphed as a line. This answer choice can be eliminated.

~~C) $y = 2x + 4$~~

Answer Choice D is a quadratic equation and would be graphed as a parabola. This answer choice can be eliminated.

~~D) $y = (3x - 8)(3x + 1)$~~

Step 3: Plug In

For the 2 remaining answer choices, we can just plug in values from the graph. Let's start with the easiest to visualize (0,0) where $x = 0$ and $y = 0$.

Only Answer Choice B works: $y = \frac{x^3}{5}$ $\quad (0) = \frac{(0)^3}{5}$

Correct Answer: B

Practice: Graphs

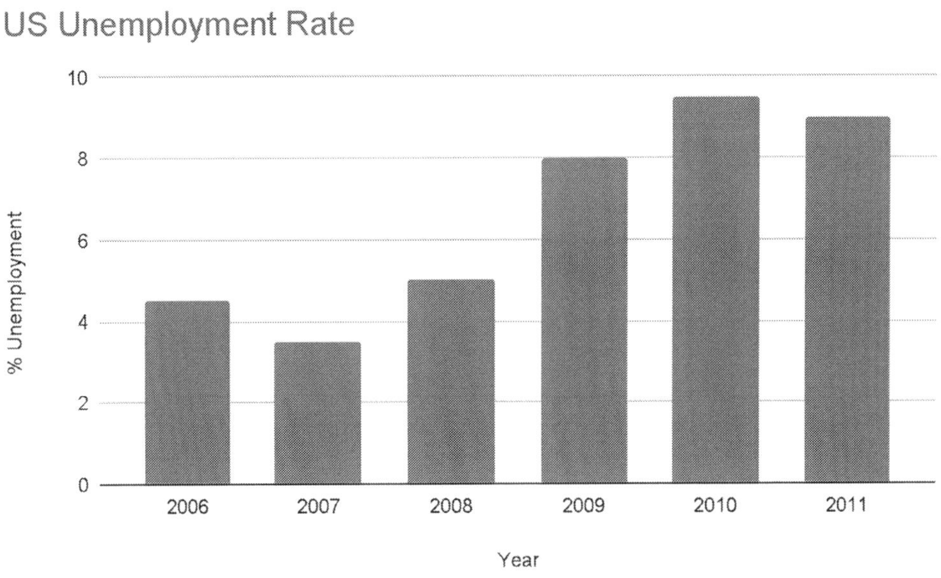

1. The bar graph above shows the U.S. unemployment rate from 2006 to 2011. Based on the data presented in the graph, which of the following statements is accurate?

A) The unemployment rate in 2006 was approximately double the unemployment rate in 2008.
B) The unemployment rate in 2006 was approximately one-third the unemployment rate in 2009.
C) The unemployment rate declined in 2011 as compared to 2008.
D) The unemployment rate in 2010 was higher than that of any other year listed.

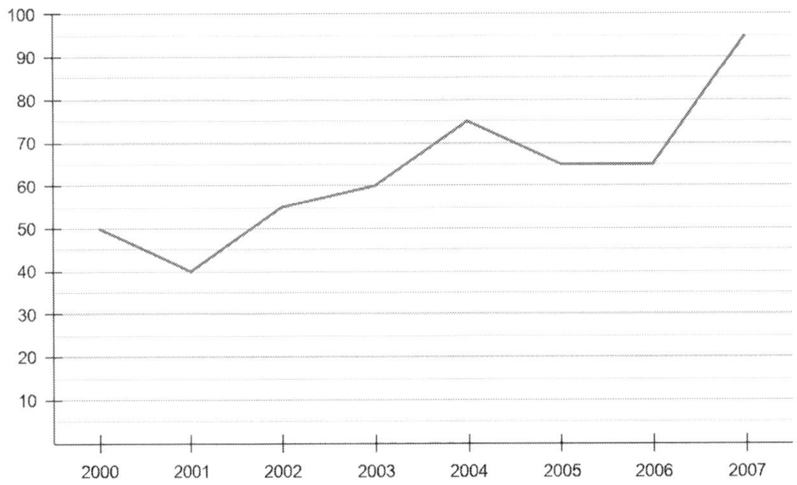

2. The line graph above shows the annual snowfall amounts (in inches) in a particular city from 2000 to 2007. According to the graph, what was the greatest change (in absolute value) in the annual snowfall amounts between two consecutive years?

A) 30 inches
B) 45 inches
C) 55 inches
D) 95 inches

3. A certain function has 4 distinct zeros. Which of the graphs below could represent the function in the *xy*-plane?

A)

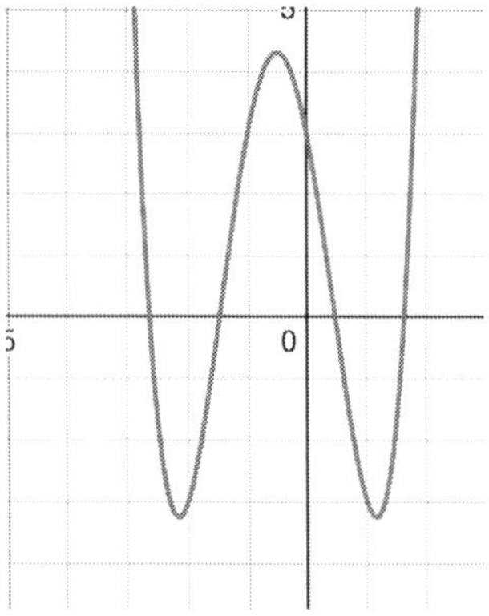

B)

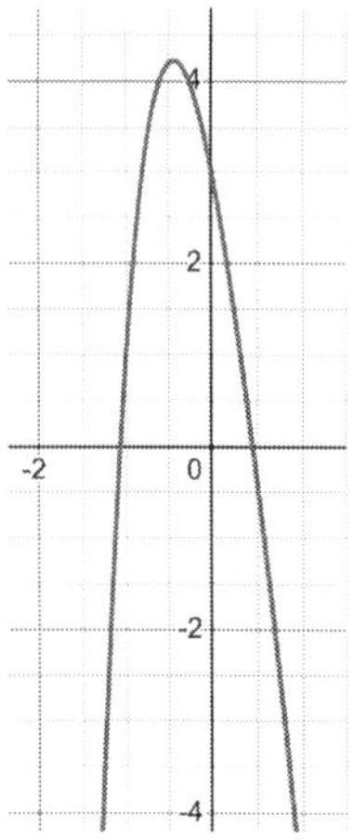

C)

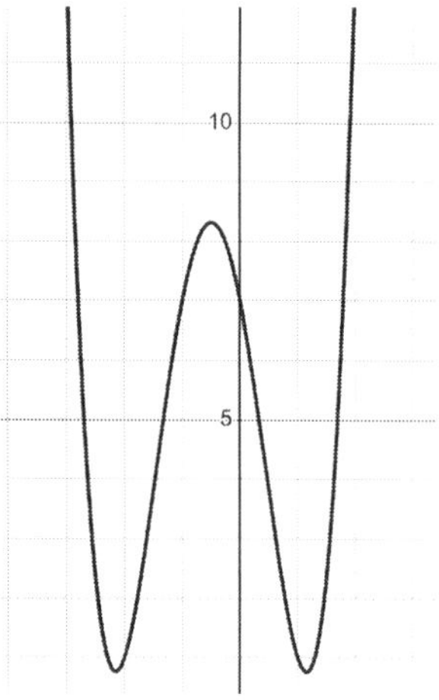

D)

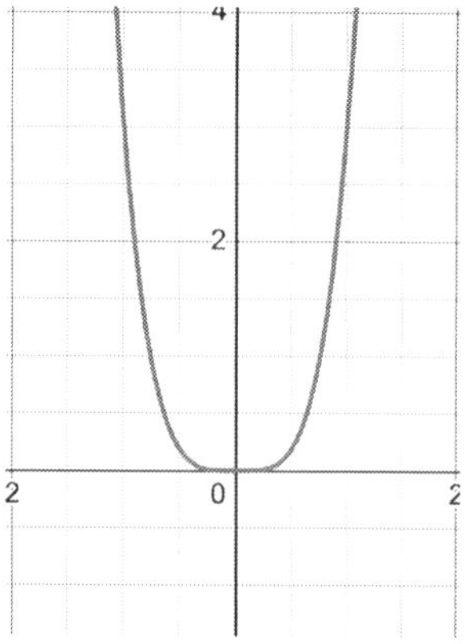

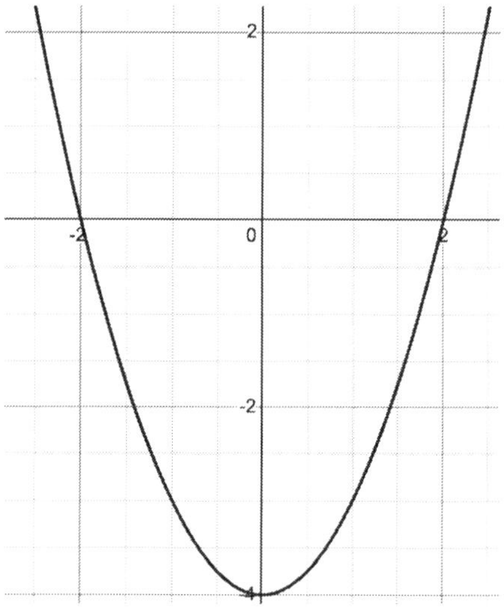

4. Which of the following equations best describes the graph above?

A) $f(x) = -x^2+4$
B) $f(x)\ x^2 - 2x$
C) $f(x)\ x^2 + 4$
D) $f(x)\ x^2 - 4$

For answer explanations to these practice questions, go to curvebreakerstestprep.com/decoding-the-digital-sat

CHAPTER 28: PERCENTS

Section: Math
Question Subsection: Numbers and Operations
Question Category: Percents
Of the 44 Math questions, approximately 2 - 5 may be questions from this category.

LESSON

Percents are used to indicate portions of a whole.
To solve questions with percents, translate the text into a mathematical equation. Replace the words from the left of the table with the elements in an equation from the right of the table.

Rewrite the text as an equation:

TEXT	EQUATION
PERCENT	/100 (over 100)
OF	. (multiply)
IS	= (equals)
WHAT, HOW MUCH, HOW MANY, ETC.	x (variable)

Exponential Growth Formula: $A = I(1 \pm r)^t$

I represents Initial Value, r represents Rate, t represents Time, and A represents the final value of growth.

The Curvebreakers Strategy

TRANSLATE THE TEXT INTO A MATH EQUATION

1. Whenever you see the word “percent” in the question, it means to put it over 100.
2. Whenever you see the word “of” in the question, it means to multiply.
3. Whenever you see the word “is” in the question, it means equals.
4. Whenever you see the words “what, how much, how many, etc.” in the question, this is the variable.

Example 1: Percents

1. 12 is approximately what percent of 8?

A) 67%
B) 140%
C) 150%
D) 167%

Solution Strategy: Translate

Step 1: Translate the text into a math equation.

English: 12 is approximately what percent of 8?
Math: 12 = $x/100 \cdot 8$

Step 2: Now we have a simple equation we can solve:

$$12 = (\frac{x}{100})(\frac{8}{1})$$

Let's put it into a format where we can cross multiply:

$$\frac{12}{1} = \frac{8x}{100}$$

$8x = 1200$, divide both sides by 8 to solve for x

$x = 150$

Correct Answer: C

Example 2: Percents

2. Ashanti earns $8.50 per hour as a cashier. She works 30 hours each week and has 20% of her total pay deducted for taxes. What is her weekly take-home pay?

A) $51.00
B) $204.00
C) $255.00
D) $315.25

Solution Strategy: Translate

Step 1: Separate the text into bite-sized pieces.

Ashanti earns $8.50 per hour / as a cashier. She works 30 hours each week / and has 20% of her total pay deducted / for taxes. What is her <u>weekly take-home pay</u>?

A) $51.00
B) $204.00
C) $255.00
D) $315.25

Step 2: Translate into a math equation.

$8.50 per hour x 30 hours = $255 earned per week

Calculate 20% of total pay to find how much is deducted. Translate the text to a math equation:

$\frac{20}{100} \cdot total\ pay = \frac{20}{100} \cdot \$255 = \$51$ deducted for taxes

Subtract taxes from total earned:

$255 - 51 = 204$

Correct Answer: B

Practice: Percents

1. If Camryn uses a 30% off coupon for a dress that originally cost \$80, how much will the dress be before tax and shipping fees?

A) \$24.00
B) \$50.00
C) \$56.00
D) \$104.00

2. If 30 percent of a number P is 90, what is 0.5 percent of P?

A) 0.15
B) 1.5
C) 15
D) 45.0

3. The number x is 120% greater than the number y. The number y is 80% less than 60. What is the value of x?

A) 2.2
B) 12.0
C) 26.4
D) 48.0

	Men	**Women**
Prefer Tea	23	19
Prefer Coffee	169	192
Total	192	211

4. The table above shows the number of individuals who prefer tea or coffee by gender in a certain cafe. What percent of all individuals in this cafe, rounded to the nearest percent, are male coffee drinkers?

A) 12
B) 42
C) 80
D) 88

5. 900 is r % greater than 200. What is the value of r?

A) 350
B) 400
C) 500
D) 700

6. Aliyah has \$5,000 in her savings account. Each month, she gains 0.8% in interest. After 2 months, she deposits \$1,200 into her account. Which is closest to the amount of money in Aliyah's savings account after two months?

A) \$5,040.00
B) \$5,080.32
C) \$6,280.32
D) \$7,032.00

For answer explanations to these practice questions, go to curvebreakerstestprep.com/decoding-the-digital-sat

CHAPTER 29: EXPONENTS AND RADICALS

Section: Math
Question Subsection: Numbers and Operations
Question Category: Exponents and Radicals
Of the 44 Math questions, approximately 2 - 5 may be questions from this category.

LESSON

Remember this acronym for the most commonly tested rules for exponents:

MADSPM

When the bases are the same:
MULTIPLY/ADD DIVIDE/SUBTRACT POWER/MULTIPLY

MULTIPLY/ADD $a^x a^y = a^{x+y}$

DIVIDE/SUBTRACT $\frac{a^x}{a^y} = a^{x-y}$

POWER/MULTIPLY $(a^x)^y = a^{xy}$

Other Exponent and Radical Rules to Remember:

$$1^{396} = 1$$

$$15^0 = 1$$

$$2^{-2} = \frac{1}{2^2}$$

$$16^{\frac{1}{2}} = \sqrt{16}$$

$$9^{\frac{3}{4}} = \sqrt[4]{9^3}$$

Factoring with a Greatest Common Factor (GCF):

Use a number that divides into all of the terms' coefficients.

Example:

$4x^5 - 16x^2$ can be factored as $4x^2\,(x^3 - 4)$

The Curvebreakers Strategy

MADSPM for Exponents

1. Identify the bases and make sure they are the same.
2. Multiply/Add
3. Divide/Subtract
4. Power/Multiply

Example 1 : Exponents and Radicals

1. What is the solution to the expression $\frac{\left(x^{\frac{1}{3}}\right)^2}{x^{\frac{1}{6}}}$?

A) $x^{\frac{1}{9}}$

B) $x^{\frac{1}{2}}$

C) $x^{\frac{2}{3}}$

D) x

Solution Strategy: MADSPM

Step 1: MADS<u>PM</u> tells us to multiply the exponents because the numerator is to a power.

The numerator $(x^{\frac{1}{3}})^2$ becomes $x^{\frac{2}{3}}$

Step 2: Because the second step is to divide, MA<u>DS</u>PM tells us to subtract the exponents:

$\frac{x^{\frac{2}{3}}}{x^{\frac{1}{6}}}$ Subtract the exponents: $\frac{2}{3}-\frac{1}{6}=\frac{4}{6}-\frac{1}{6}=\frac{3}{6}=\frac{1}{2}$

Therefore the answer is $x^{\frac{1}{2}}$

Correct answer: B

Example 2: Exponents and Radicals

2. What is the solution to the equation $\sqrt[3]{x+3} = 2$?

A) -5
B) -2
C) 2
D) 5

Solution

Step 1: Raise both sides of the equation to the 3rd power to cancel out the cube root:

$$\left(\sqrt[3]{x+3}\right)^3 = 2^3$$

This expression equals: $x + 3 = 2^3$

Step 2: Now solve for x

$$x + 3 = 8$$
$$x = 5$$

Correct Answer: D

Practice: Exponents and Radicals

1. If $\sqrt{x+7} + x = 13$, what is x?

A) -3
B) 2
C) 9
D) 18

2. Which of the following is equivalent to $(5x^2y^3)^{\frac{1}{2}}$?

A) $\frac{1}{5x^4y^6}$
B) $\frac{1}{10}xy^{\frac{1}{2}}$
C) $\sqrt{5}xy^{\frac{3}{2}}$
D) $5x^4y^6$

3. The expression $\frac{1}{x^2}$ is equal to all the following EXCEPT?

A) $(x^{-10})\,(x^{-4})^{-2}$
B) $\frac{x^{-4}}{x^{-2}}$
C) $(x^2)^{-1}$
D) $\left(\frac{1}{x^{-1}}\right)^2$

4. Two variables m and n are related such that for each increase of 1 in the value of m, the value of n decreases by a factor of 3. When $m = 0$, $n = 120$. Which equation represents this relationship?

A) $n = 3m^{120}$
B) $n = (120)3^m$
C) $n = 0.1(3)^{120m}$
D) $n = (120/3)^m$

5. The function $h(t) = 5000(2)^{\frac{t}{5}}$ represents the population of a city t years after an initial observation. How much time, in years, does it take for the population of the city to double?

For answer explanations to these practice questions, go to curvebreakerstestprep.com/decoding-the-digital-sat

CHAPTER 30: MEAN, MEDIAN, MODE, and RANGE

Section: Math
Question Subsection: Data, Statistics, & Probability
Question Category: Mean/Median/Mode/Range
Of the 44 Math questions, approximately 1 - 3 may be questions from this category.

LESSON

MEAN = Average

Mean = Sum of all numbers / Number of elements

MEDIAN = Middle

Arrange the numbers in ascending order from smallest to largest. If the set has an odd number of elements, the median is the middle number. If the set has an even number of elements, the median is the average of the two middle numbers.

MODE = Most

Identify the number(s) with the highest frequency. If there is more than one number with the same highest frequency, the set is considered multimodal (having multiple modes). If all numbers have the same frequency, the set is uniform and has no mode.

RANGE = the difference between the highest and lowest values.

The spread or difference between the smallest and largest values in the dataset.

TIP: Most of the questions from this category involve the Mean.

The Curvebreakers Strategy

USE THE "AVERAGE PIE" FOR MEAN QUESTIONS

To organize information for average (mean) questions, draw an Average Pie.

Whenever you can fill in the pie with 2 knowns, you can calculate the unknown as follows:

# of Things x Average = Total

Draw as many Average Pies as you need to answer the question.

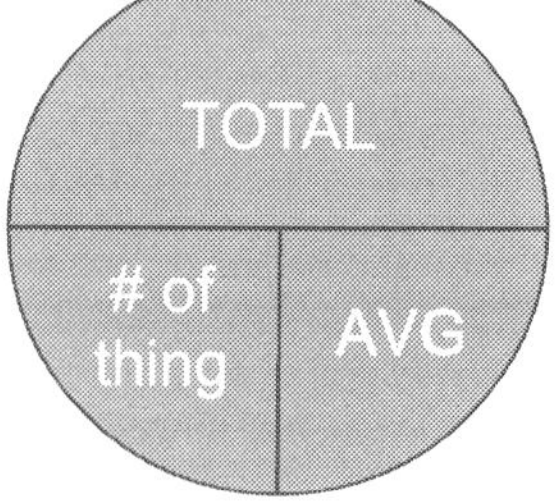

Example: Mean/Median/Mode/Range

In a bowling tournament, Amir has an average score of 180 for his first five games. If Amir's scores for the first three games were 200, 180, and 160 respectively, what was his average score for the last two games?

A) 180
B) 170
C) 165
D) 160

Solution Strategy: Average Pie

Step 1: Separate the text into bite-sized pieces.

In a bowling tournament, Amir has an average score of 180 for his first five games /. If Amir's scores for the first three games were 200, 180, and 160 respectively, / what was his average score for the last two games?

Let's draw as many Average Pies as we need to in order to solve the problem:

Step 2: Draw Average Pie #1 for the five games.

1. The average is 180.
2. The number of things is 5.
3. The total is 180 x 5 = 900.

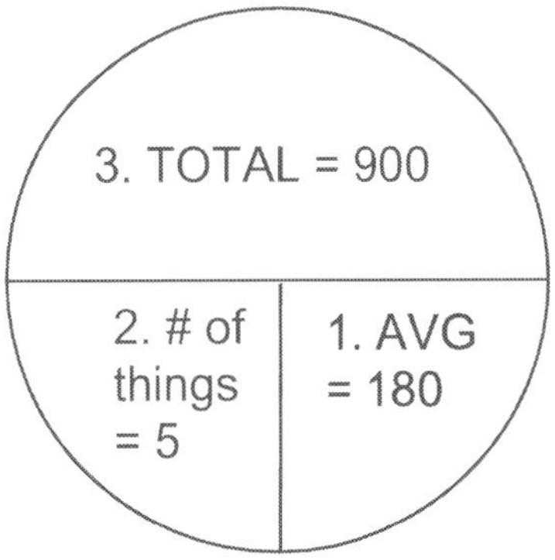

Step 3: Draw Average Pie #2 for the first three games

1. The number of things is 3.
2. The total is 200 + 180 + 160 = 540.
3. Finding the average for the first three games isn't necessarily needed to solve the problem. What's important is the total of the three games so that the total of the last two games can be determined.

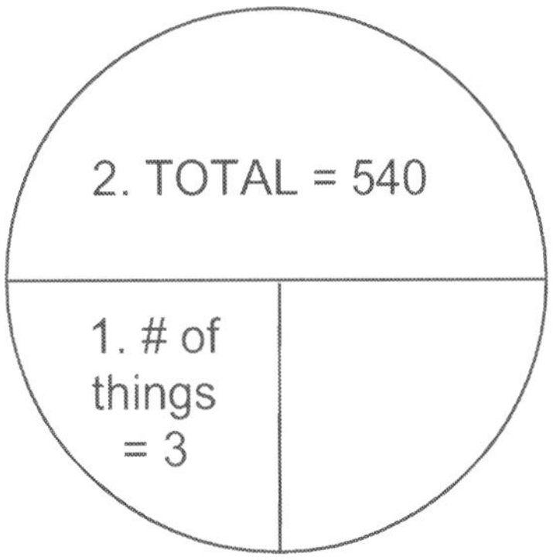

Step 4: Draw Average Pie #3 for the last two games.

1. The number of things is 2.
2. The total of the last two games is the five-game total minus the three-game total (refer to totals in Avg Pies #1 and #2). 900 - 540 = 360.
3. The average is 360 / 2 = 180.

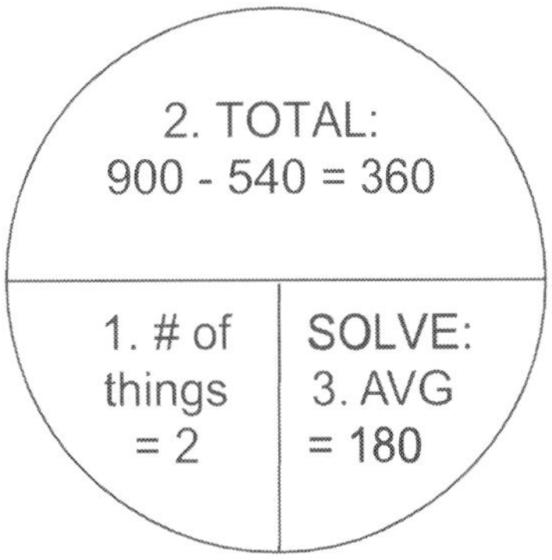

Correct Answer: A

Practice: Mean, Median, Mode, and Range

Data set A: 6, 7, 8, 9
Data set B: 1, 2, 2, 2, 100

1. The lists give the values in data sets A and B. Which statement is correct?

A) The mean of data set A is greater than the median of data set A.
B) The range of data set B is less than the mean of data set B.
C) The mode of data set B is equal to the median of data set B.
D) The mean of data set A is greater than the mean of data set B.

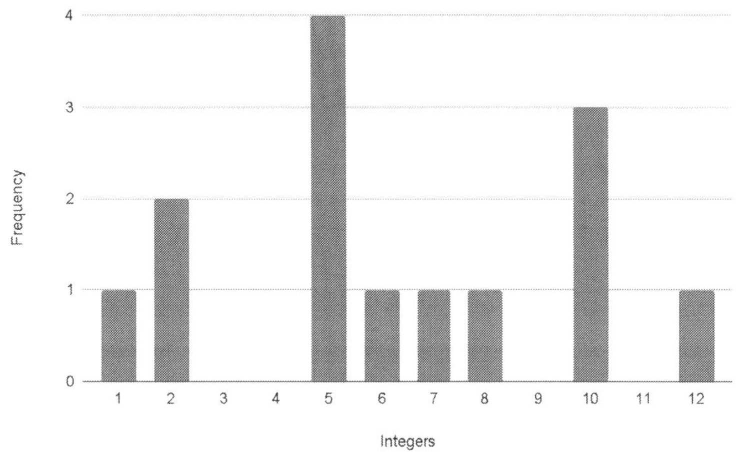

2. The bar graph above shows the distribution of randomly selected integers from 1 to 12. What is the mean, median, and mode of the list of numbers?

A) mean = 7.3; median = 5.5; mode =5
B) mean = 5.25; median = 6; mode = 5
C) mean = 1.5; median = 5.5; mode = 8
D) mean = 6.3; median = 5.5; mode = 8

3. Sara purchases 2 books for \$10 each, 3 pens for \$2 each, and 4 notebooks for \$5 each. What is the average price of all the items she bought?

A) \$1.89
B) \$4.50
C) \$5.11
D) \$5.63

4. The average age of 6 friends in a group is 25 years. If the youngest person leaves the group, the average age of the remaining 5 friends becomes 27 years. What is the age of the youngest person?

A) 13 years
B) 15 years
C) 17 years
D) 21 years

218, 226, 227, 228,120, 122, 125, 130, 190, 211

5. To the nearest tenth, what is the value when the range of this set of numbers is subtracted from the median of this set of numbers?

For answer explanations to these practice questions, go to curvebreakerstestprep.com/decoding-the-digital-sat

CHAPTER 31: PROBABILITY

Section: Math
Question Subsection: Data, Statistics, & Probability
Question Category: Probability
Of the 44 Math questions, approximately 1 - 2 may be questions from this category.

LESSON

Probability is the likelihood that something will happen. It is calculated by creating a ratio of the desired outcomes to the total outcomes. Probability ranges between 0 and 1, inclusive, or between 0% and 100%.

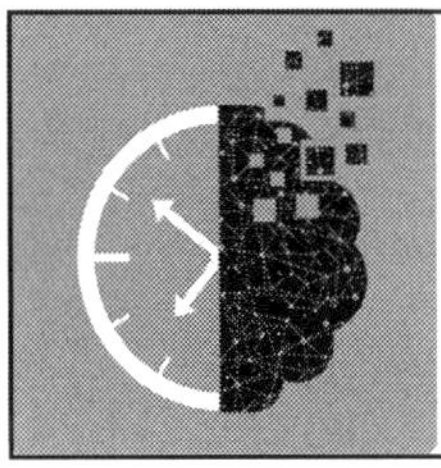

The Curvebreakers Strategy

USE THE FORMULA FOR PROBABILITY

$$\text{PROBABILITY} = \frac{SUCCESS}{TOTAL}$$

Examples of Probability

Questions 1 and 2 refer to the table below.

The table below classifies 120 students from a high school who participate in different extracurricular activities: sports, music, or art. Each student is further categorized as either a sophomore, junior, or senior.

	Sophomore	**Junior**	**Senior**	**Total**
Sports	4	17	24	45
Music	24	19	16	59
Art	12	4	0	16
Total	40	40	40	120

1. What is the probability that a randomly selected student from this high school does NOT participate in sports?

A) .375
B) .491
C) .500
D) .625

Solution Strategy: Use the Formula for Probability

Step 1: Since this is a probability question, let's write the formula:

$$\text{PROBABILITY} = \frac{SUCCESS}{TOTAL}$$

Step 2: Determine the total.

The total will be any of the randomly selected students. According to the table, there are a total of 120 students.

Step 3: Determine the success.

In this case, success is defined as a student who does *not* participate in sports. The fastest way to find the number of students not involved in sports is to subtract the number of sports students from the total:

120 – 45 = 75

Step 4: Plug in the numbers for Success and Total into the probability formula and solve.

$$P = \frac{S}{T} = \frac{75}{120} = .625$$

Correct Answer: D

2. If a senior is selected at random, what is the probability that the student will participate in sports?

A) $\frac{1}{3}$
B) $\frac{2}{3}$
C) $\frac{1}{5}$
D) $\frac{3}{5}$

Solution Strategy: Use the Formula for Probability

Step 1: Since this is a probability question, let's write the formula:

PROBABILITY = $\frac{SUCCESS}{TOTAL}$

Step 2: Determine the total.

Since we're told that a senior is selected at random, the total will be any of the randomly selected seniors = 40

Step 3: Determine the success.

Success will be a senior who participates in sports = 24.

Step 4: Plug in the numbers for Success and Total into the probability formula and solve.

$$P = \frac{S}{T} = \frac{24}{40} = \frac{3}{5}$$

Correct Answer: D

Practice: Probability

	Round	Square
Vanilla	**13**	**9**
Chocolate	**21**	**7**

1. A bakery offers a selection of vanilla and chocolate cakes. The cakes are categorized as either round or square in shape. If a cake is chosen at random and is known to be square, what is the likelihood that it is a chocolate-flavored cake?

A) $\frac{7}{16}$

B) $\frac{9}{16}$

C) $\frac{7}{50}$

D) $\frac{16}{50}$

2. A 6-sided die, with sides 1, 2, 3, 4, 5, and 6, is thrown. What is the probability that the die lands on a prime-numbered face?

A) $\frac{1}{3}$

B) $\frac{1}{2}$

C) $\frac{2}{3}$

D) $\frac{5}{6}$

POSITION	**NUMBER OF PLAYERS**
Shortstop	4
Pitcher	2
Catcher	6
Outfield	8

3. Ella will draft 1 player at random from a list of 20 players for her fantasy baseball team. Each player in the list plays only 1 position. The number of players who play a particular position is given in the table above. What is the probability that the player Ella drafts will play shortstop or outfield?

A) $\frac{1}{5}$

B) $\frac{2}{5}$

C) $\frac{1}{2}$

D) $\frac{3}{5}$

CARD	NUMBER
Clubs	10
Spades	8
Hearts	6
Diamonds	4
Jokers	2

4. Camryn will use a deck of 30 playing cards for a game in which each player randomly draws cards from the deck. The distribution of the cards by suit (plus the Jokers) is shown above. Camryn will randomly draw 2 cards from the deck, one after the other, without replacing the first card. What is the probability that Camryn will draw a Hearts first and a Joker second?

A) $\frac{1}{75}$
B) $\frac{2}{145}$
C) $\frac{4}{15}$
D) $\frac{39}{145}$

5. In Nico's wallet, he has 8 5-dollar bills, 9 10-dollar bills, and 7 20-dollar bills. How many additional 5-dollar bills does he need to add to his wallet so that the probability of randomly taking out a 5-dollar bill from his wallet is 0.6?

A) 12
B) 16
C) 20
D) 24

For answer explanations to these practice questions, go to curvebreakerstestprep.com/decoding-the-digital-sat

CHAPTER 32: REPRESENTS SITUATION

Section: Math
Question Subsection: Algebra and Functions
Question Category: Represents Situation
Of the 44 Math questions, approximately 1 - 4 may be questions from this question category.

EXAM QUESTION

You are given data and variables and are asked, *Which of the following equations represents this situation?*

LESSON

Most of these questions can be answered by using POE (Process of Elimination).

The Curvebreakers Strategy

BITE-SIZE AND POE

1. Separate the text into bite-sized pieces.
2. Note what the variables represent.
3. In each answer choice, highlight what works and eliminate what doesn't.
4. If you can't solve it in this manner, try Plugging In numbers for the variables.

Example 1: Represents Situation

1. A container holds red and blue liquids. The total volume of the liquids is 60. The volume of the red liquid is 20 liters more than twice the volume of blue liquid. Which system of equations represents this situation, where y represents the volume (in liters) of blue liquid and x represents the the volume (in liters) of red liquid?

A) $x + y = 60$
$x = 2y + 20$

B) $x + y = 20$
$2y = 60 - x$

C) $x + y = 20$
$2x = 60 - y$

D) $x + y = 60$
$y = 2x + 20$

Solution Strategy: Bite-size and POE

Step 1: Separate the text into bite-sized pieces.

A container holds red and blue liquids. The total volume of the liquids is 60. / The volume of the red liquid is 20 liters more than twice the volume of blue liquid. / Which system of equations represents this situation, where y represents the volume (in liters) of blue liquid and x represents the the volume (in liters) of red liquid?

Step 2: Note what the variables represent.

y = blue liquid; x = red liquid

Step 3: In each answer choice, highlight what works and eliminate what doesn't

Since the total volume of liquid = 60, highlight any answer choices that show x and y adding to 60 and eliminate any answer choices that don't. (POE B and C)

A) $x + y = 60$
$x = 2y + 20$

B) ~~$x + y = 20$~~
$2y = 60 - x$

C) ~~$x + y = 20$~~
$2x = 60 - y$

D) $x + y = 60$
$y = 2x + 20$

Since we're told that the number of red liquid (*x*) is 20 more than twice the number of blue liquid (*y*), select Answer Choice A. (POE D)

A) $x + y = 60$
$x = 2y + 20$

Correct Answer: A

Example 2: Represents Situation

2. A coffee shop sells two sizes of coffee cups: small for \$2.50 and large for \$3.50. If the shop makes at least \$135 per day in sales, which inequality represents this situation, where s represents the number of small cups sold and l represents the number of large cups sold?

A) $2.50l + 3.50s \geq 135$
B) $2.50s + 3.50l \geq 135$
C) $2.50s + 3.50l \leq 135$
D) $2.50s + 3.50l > 135$

Solution Strategy: Bite-size and POE

Step 1: Separate the text into bite-sized pieces.

A coffee shop sells two sizes of coffee cups: small for \$2.50 / and large for \$3.50 / . If the shop makes at least \$135 per day / in sales, which inequality represents this situation, where s represents the number of small cups sold and l represents the number of large cups sold?

Step 2: Note what the variables represent.

s = small cups; l = large cups

Step 3: In each answer choice, highlight what works and eliminate what doesn't

Since small cups are $2.50(s)$ and large are $3.50(l)$, highlight any answer choices that contain $2.50s$ and $.3.50l$ and eliminate any answer choices that don't.

~~A) $2.50l + 3.50s \geq 135$~~
B) $2.50s + 3.50l \geq 135$
C) $2.50s + 3.50l \leq 135$
D) $2.50s + 3.50l > 135$

Since we're told that the coffee shop makes at least $135 in sales, highlight anything in the answer choices that show $135 or more and eliminate anything that does not. (POE C and D)

~~A) $2.50l + 3.50s \geq 135$~~
B) $2.50s + 3.50l \geq 135$
~~C) $2.50s + 3.50l \leq 135$~~
~~D) $2.50s + 3.50l > 135$~~

Correct Answer: B

Practice: Represents Situation

1. A company charges a flat fee of $25 plus $5 per hour for computer repair services. If the total cost of the service is $90, how many hours did the repair take?

A) $5h + 25 = 90$
B) $25h + 5 = 90$
C) $5h + 90 = 25$
D) $90h + 5 = 25$

2. A school is holding a fundraiser where students can sell chocolate bars for $2 each and raffle tickets for $5 each. The school wants to raise a total of $500. Which equation represents this situation, where x represents the number of chocolate bars sold and y represents the number of raffle tickets sold?

A) $5x + 2y = 500$
B) $x + y = 500 / 7$
C) $7x + 5y = 500$
D) $2x + 5y = 500$

3. A vending machine dispenses candy bars for $1.25 each and bags of chips for $0.75 each. If the vending machine made $62.50 in one day, which equation represents this situation, where x represents the number of candy bars sold and y represents the number of bags of chips sold?

A) $1.25x + 0.75y = 62.50$
B) $1.25x + 0.75y = 75$
C) $1.25(x + y) = 62.50$
D) $0.75(x + y) = 62.50$

For answer explanations to these practice questions, go to curvebreakerstestprep.com/decoding-the-digital-sat

CHAPTER 33: GEOMETRY FACTS

Section: Math
Question Subsection: Geometry and Measurement
Of the 44 Math questions, approximately 6 - 10 may be questions from this category.

LESSON

The SAT® gives us basic reference information so you will not need to memorize the formulas. However, if you do memorize at least the most commonly used formulas, it will **save you time**.

Lessons on geometry will be divided into the following chapters to reflect the types of questions most asked on the test:

1. Angles
2. Triangles
3. Quadrilaterals
4. Circles
5. Radians
6. Volume
7. Trigonometry

SAT® REFERENCE TABLE

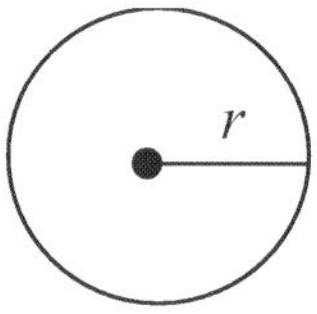

$A = \pi r^2$
$C = 2\pi r$

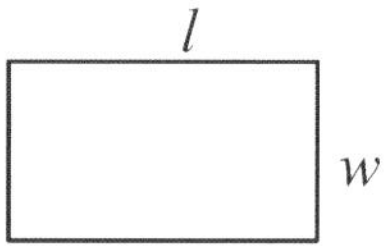

$A = l \cdot w$

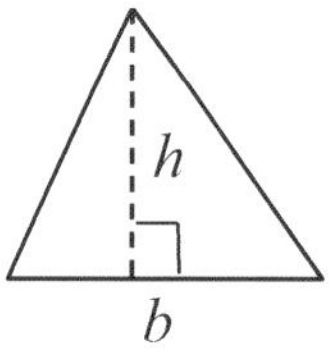

$A = \frac{1}{2}bh$

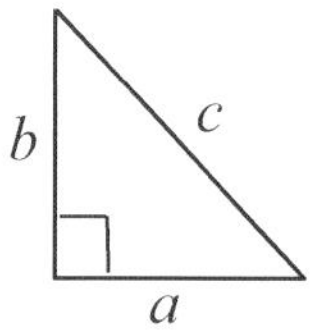

$c^2 = a^2 + b^2$

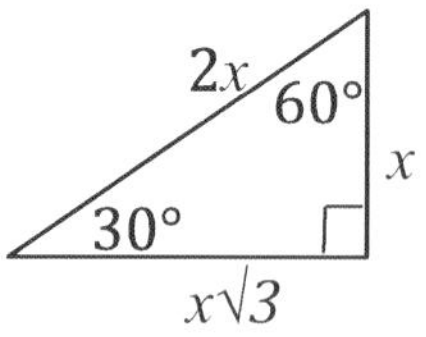

Special Right Triangle

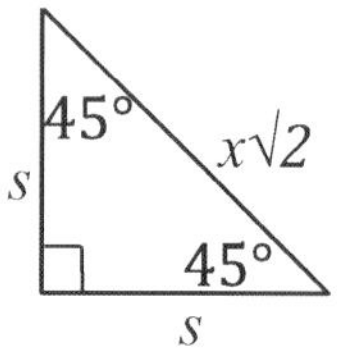

Special Right Triangle

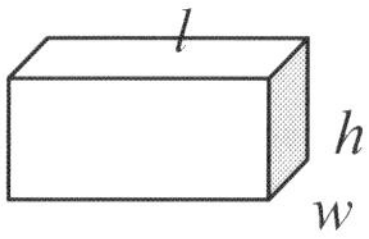

$V = lwh$

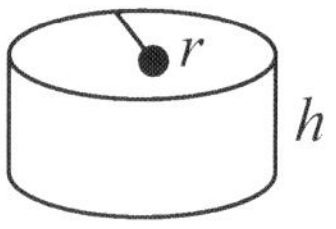

$V = \pi r^2 h$

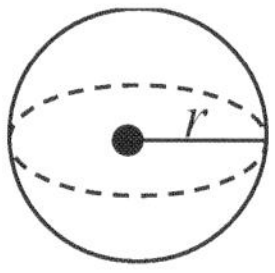

$V = \frac{4}{3}\pi r^3$

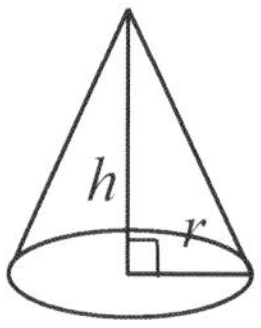

$V = \frac{1}{3}\pi r^2 h$

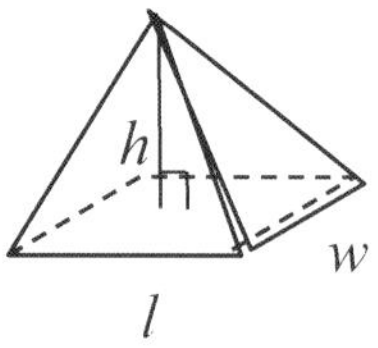

$V = \frac{1}{3}lwh$

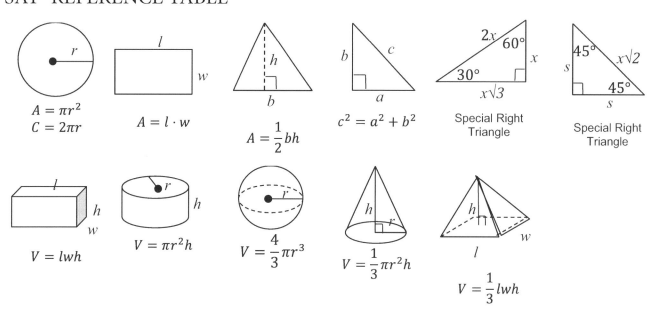

The number of degrees of arc in a circle is 360
The number of radians of arc in a circle is 2π
The sum of the measures in degrees of the angles of a triangle is 180

There are also some basic geometry facts you should know:

ANGLE FACTS

- There are 90 degrees in a right angle.
- When two lines intersect, the opposite angles are equal.
- There are 180 degrees in a triangle.
- Two lines are called perpendicular when they meet at a 90 degree angle.
- The sign for perpendicular is $\perp$
- There are 180 degrees in a straight line.
- Bisect means to cut exactly in half.
- The angles of any four-sided figure add up to 360 degrees.

FOUR-SIDED FACTS

In a square:

- All four sides are equal.
- Each of the 4 angles is 90 degrees.
- Area = s^2
- Perimeter = 4s

In a rectangle:

- Opposite sides are equal.
- Each of the 4 angles is 90 degrees.
- Area = lw
- Perimeter = 2l + 2w

In a parallelogram:

- Opposite sides are parallel and equal.
- Area = bh

In a quadrilateral:

- Angles add up to 360 degrees.

TRIANGLE FACTS

In any triangle:

- The largest side or hypotenuse is opposite the largest angle.
- The smallest side is opposite the smallest angle.
- Equal sides are opposite equal angles.
- Angles add up to 180 degrees.
- $A = \frac{1}{2}bh$
- The height is perpendicular to the base.
- Perimeter is the sum of the sides.
- Any side of the triangle must be greater than the difference but less than the sum of the other two sides.

In an Isosceles triangle:

- Two angles and sides are equal.
- Angles opposite the equal sides are equal.

In an Equilateral triangle:

- All sides are equal.
- All angles each equal 60 degrees.

CIRCLE FACTS

In any circle

- There are 360 degrees in a circle.
- The equation of a circle with center (h,k) and radius r is $(x - h)^2 + (y - k)^2 = r^2$

Radius

- A radius is the distance from the center to any point on the edge of the circle.
- All radii in a circle are equal.

Diameter

- A diameter is the straight line distance from one point on the circle to another, passing through the center.
- It is the longest line or chord in the circle.
- It equals twice the radius.

Chord

- A chord is any line segment from one point on the circle to another.
- The diameter is the longest chord.

Circumference

- The circumference is the distance around the outside of the circle.
- The formula for circumference is $\pi d \; or \; 2\pi r$

Arc

- An arc is part of the circumference.
- Arc measure is proportional to the size of the interior angle.

Area

- The area of a circle is the amount of space inside the circumference of the circle.
- The formula for area is πr^2

LINE FACTS

Line Segment

- The degree measure of a line segment is 180 degrees.

Tangent

- A tangent line is always perpendicular to the radius.

Perpendicular

- Two lines that intersect in a 90 degree angle are perpendicular and their slopes are negative reciprocals.

TRANSFORMATION FACTS

Rotation

- Rotation means turning an object around a point, which is called the center of rotation.

Reflection

- To reflect an object means to create its mirror image across a line of reflection.
- Lines reflected across the *x*-axis have slopes that are negatives of each other and also *y*-intercepts that are negatives of each other.
- Lines reflected across the *y*-axis have the same *y*-intercept and slopes that are negatives of each other.

Symmetry

- A figure has reflective symmetry if it looks the same after a reflection.
- A figure has rotational symmetry if it can be rotated and still look the same.

TRIGONOMETRY FACTS

- SOHCAHTOA: The 3 basic trig ratios to calculate sides in a Right triangle:

  sin = $\frac{OPP}{HYP}$ cos = $\frac{ADJ}{HYP}$ tan = $\frac{OPP}{ADJ}$

- When two angles are complementary (meaning they add to 90 degrees), the sine of one angle equals the cosine of the other.

The Curvebreakers Strategy

DRAW, LABEL, FORMULAS, CARVE

1. Draw the shape if no shape is given
2. Label all relevant information
3. Write out all complete formulas or geometry facts needed to solve
4. See if you can carve up complex shapes into the SAT®'s favorite shapes: right triangles and rectangles.

For answer explanations to these practice questions, go to curvebreakerstestprep.com/decoding-the-digital-sat

Chapter 34: ANGLES

Section: Math
Question Category: Angles
Expect at least one angle question.

LESSON

- There are 90 degrees in a right angle.
- When two lines intersect, the opposite angles are equal.
- There are 180 degrees in a triangle.
- Two lines are called perpendicular when they meet at a 90 degree angle.
- The sign for perpendicular is $\perp$
- There are 180 degrees in a straight line.
- Bisect means to cut exactly in half.
- The angles of any four-sided figure add up to 360 degrees.

When parallel lines are intersected by a straight line, two kinds of angles are created: BIG angles and SMALL angles. All BIG angles are equal. All SMALL angles are equal. BIG + SMALL = 180 degrees.

Example 1: ANGLES

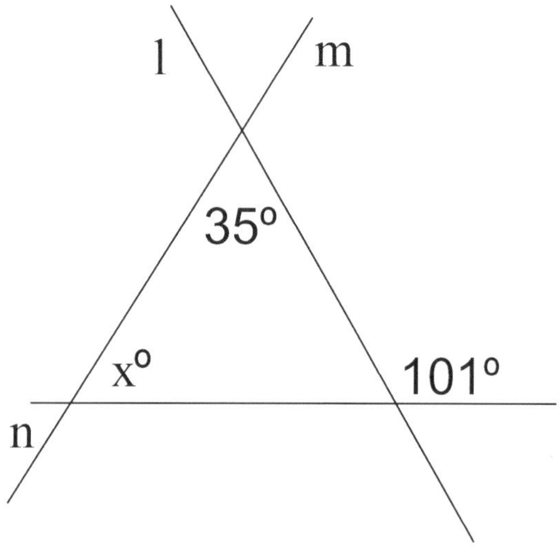

1. Intersecting lines l, m, and n are shown above. What is the value of x in degrees?

A) 35
B) 61
C) 66
D) 79

Solution Strategy: Draw, Label, Formulas, Carve

Step 1: Label

Since we know the measure of a line is 180°, this means that the angle directly to the left of 101° is 79° (180 - 101 = 79)

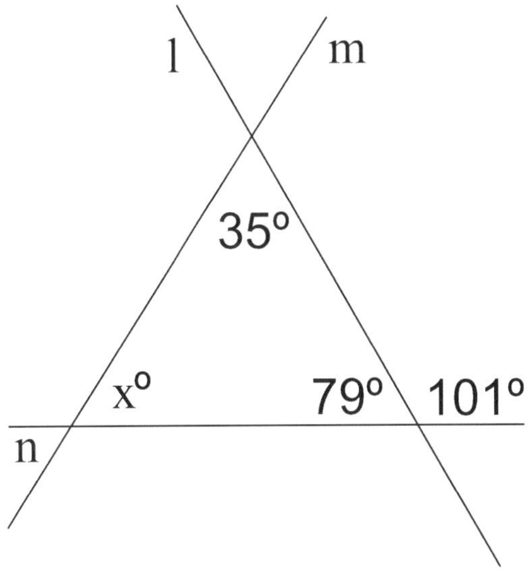

Step 2: Carve out the triangle.

Since we know the angles of a triangle add up to 180°, we can calculate *x* by subtracting the other 2 angles from 180 (180 - 79 - 35 = 66)

Correct Answer: C

Example 2: ANGLES

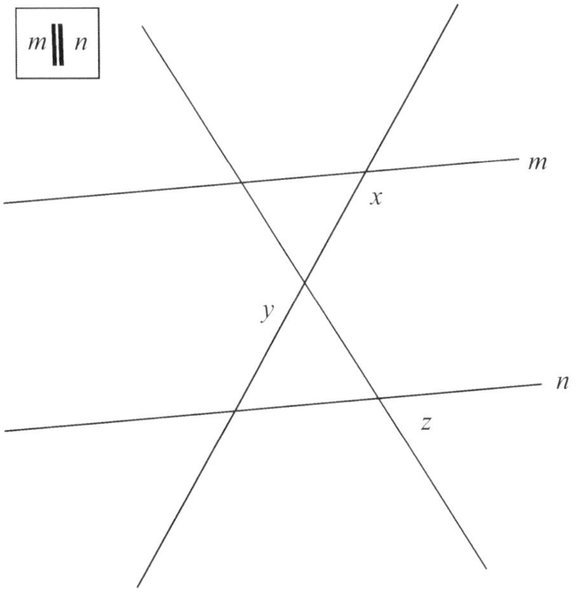

2. If the figure above, $m \parallel n$ and $x = 110°$ and $y = 130°$. What is the measure of z, in degrees?

A) 50
B) 60
C) 70
D) 110

Solution Strategy: Draw, Label, Formulas, Carve

Step 1: Label

We are given x = 110 and y = 130.
Since we know the measure of a line is 180º, this means that the angle directly to the left of x = 70º and the angle to the right and below y = 50º

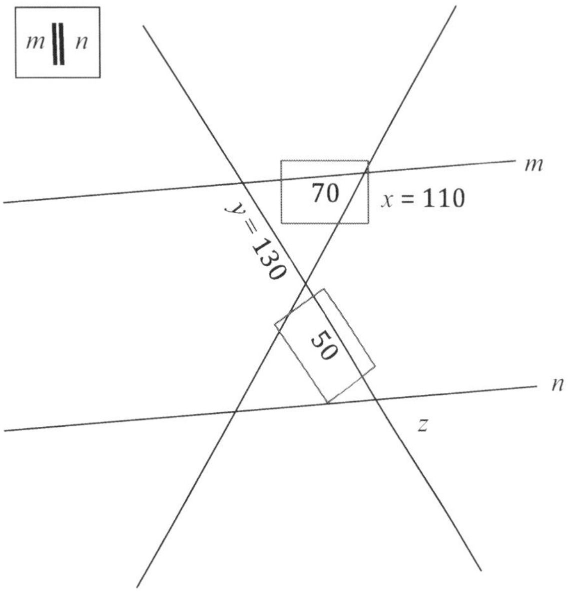

Step 2: Keep labeling: Since m and n are parallel, when a straight line intersects 2 parallel lines, the big angles are equal to the big angles and the small angles are equal to the small angles. So we can label 110 as the big bottom angle and 70 as the small bottom angel.

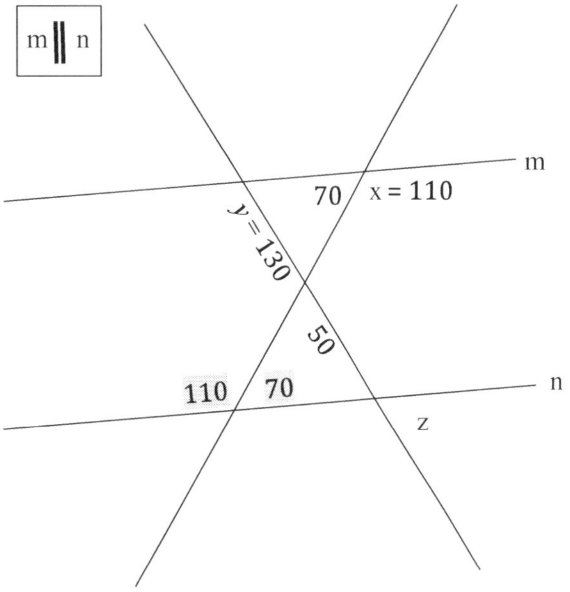

Step 3: Carve out the triangle

Recognizing that the bottom figure is a triangle, and a triangle has 180°, the third angle of the triangle must be 180 - 70 - 50 = 60°. And since z is a vertical angle directly opposite, so it must be 60° as well.

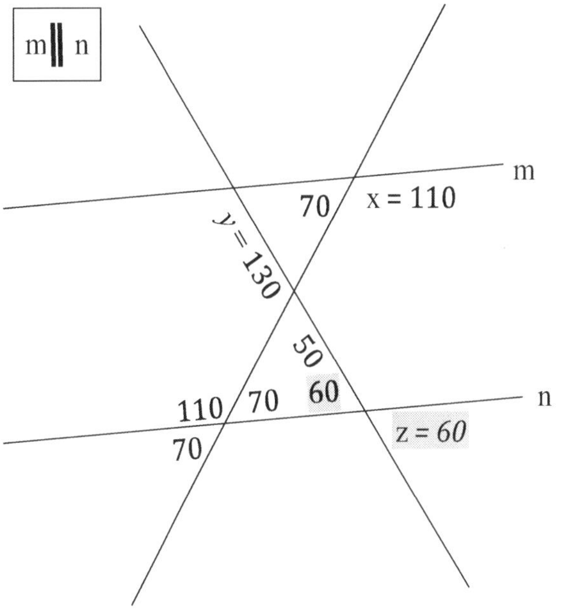

Correct Answer: B

Practice: ANGLES

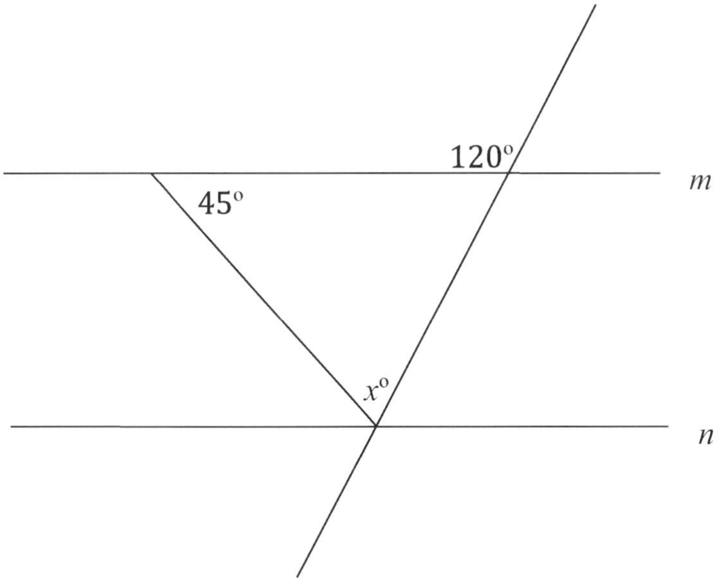

1. In the figure above, if line m is parallel to line n, what is the value of x?

A) 115°
B) 75°
C) 65°
D) 45

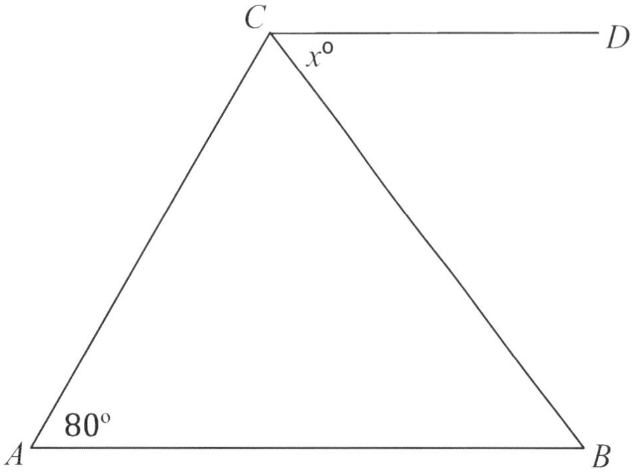

2. In the figure above, $\overline{AB} \simeq \overline{AC}$ and $\overline{AB} \parallel \overline{CD}$. What is the value of x in degrees?

A) 30
B) 40
C) 50
D) 80

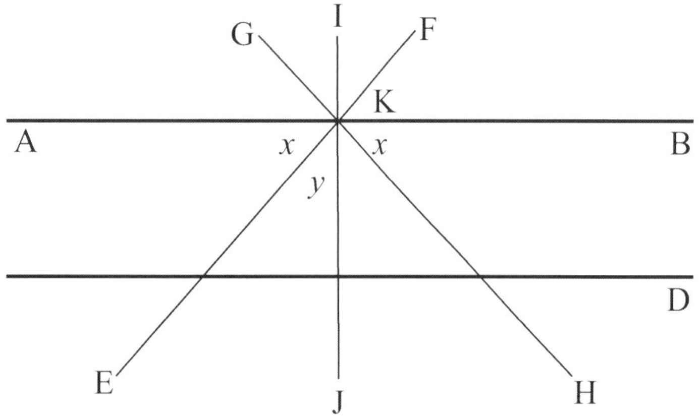

3. In the figure above, $\overline{AB} \parallel \overline{CD}$ and $\overline{IJ}$ bisects ∠EKH. Which of the following is equal to $4y$ in terms of x?

A) $360 - 4x$
B) $180 - 3x$
C) $360 + 4x$
D) $180 + 2x$

For answer explanations to these practice questions, go to curvebreakerstestprep.com/decoding-the-digital-sat

Chapter 35: TRIANGLES

Section: Math
Question Category: TRIANGLES
Expect about three triangle questions, one of which will be related to similar triangles.

LESSON

The SAT® will often ask triangle questions involving special right triangles, and triangles with the Pythagorean triples of 3:4:5; 6:8:10; or 5:12:13. Knowing these may save you time on the test by not having to do the Pythagorean Theorem. The reference table tells us how to calculate the sides of special right triangles and is shown below:

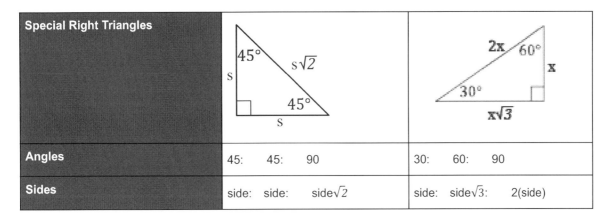

Special Right Triangles	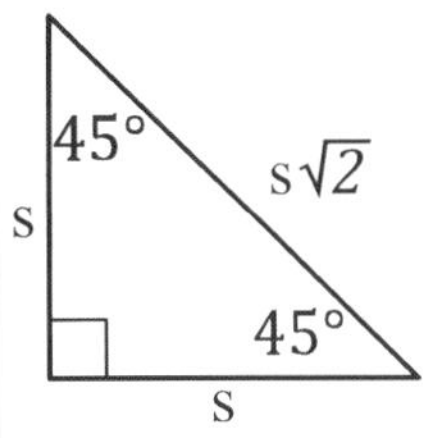	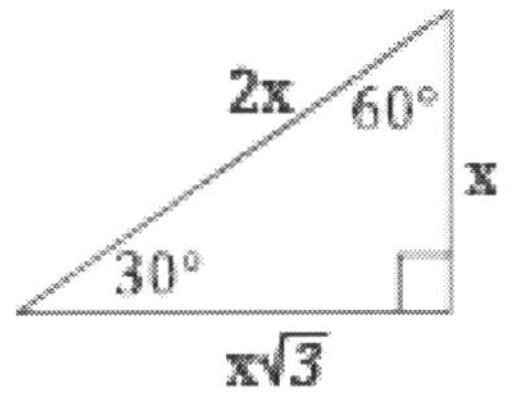
Angles	45: 45: 90	30: 60: 90
Sides	side: side: side$\sqrt{2}$	side: side$\sqrt{3}$: 2(side)

Similar Triangles

- ✦ Similar triangles have the same angle measurements.
- ✦ The corresponding sides of similar triangles are PROPORTIONAL.

In any triangle:

- The largest side or hypotenuse is opposite the largest angle.
- The smallest side is opposite the smallest angle.
- Equal sides are opposite equal angles.
- Angles add up to 180 degrees.
- $A = \frac{1}{2}bh$
- The height is perpendicular to the base.
- Perimeter is the sum of the sides.
- Any side of the triangle must be greater than the difference but less than the sum of the other two sides.

In an isosceles triangle:

- Two angles and sides are equal.
- Angles opposite the equal sides are equal.

Example 1: TRIANGLES

1. In a right triangle, the two shorter sides are 7 cm and 11 cm long. What is the length of the longest side, in cm?

A) $\sqrt{18}$
B) $\sqrt{72}$
C) $\sqrt{77}$
D) $\sqrt{170}$

Solution Strategy: Draw, Label, Formulas, Carve

Step 1: Draw the triangle and label the sides.

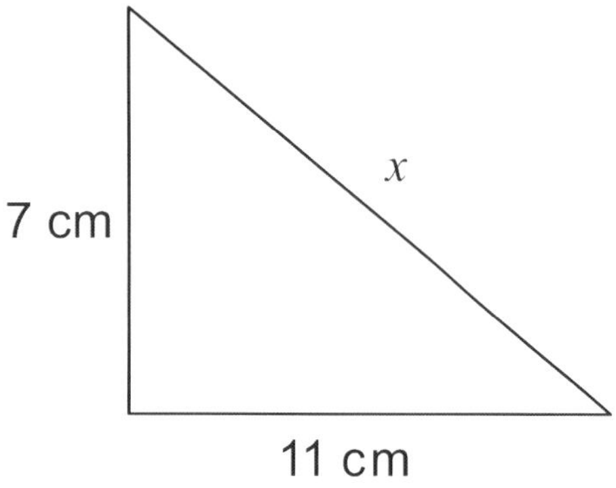

Step 2: Use the Pythagorean Theorem to find the 3rd side.

$$a^2 + b^2 = c^2 \rightarrow 7^2 + 11^2 = c^2$$
$$49 + 121 = c^2$$
$$170 = c^2$$
$$c = \sqrt{170}$$

Correct Answer: D

Example 2: TRIANGLES

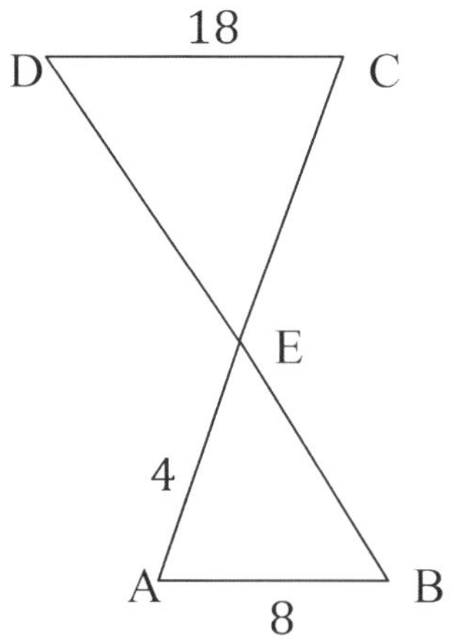

Note: Figure not drawn to scale

2. In the figure above, $\overline{AB} \parallel (\overline{DC})$. What is the length of $\overline{AC}$?

A) 13
B) 16
C) 20
D) 24

Solution Strategy: Draw, Label, Formulas, Carve

Step 1: Recognize that we have 2 similar triangles since all angles are equal.

Step 2: Redraw the triangles to visualize the correct proportion to set up.

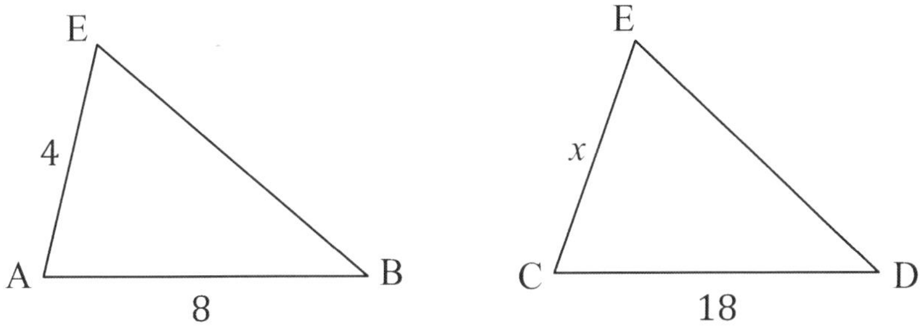

Step 3: Set up a proportion to find the length of $\overline{EC}$, since similar triangles are proportional.

In order to find the length of $\overline{AC}$ we need to first find the length of $\overline{EC}$. Set up a proportion with side $\overline{AE}$ over side $\overline{CE}$ and set that equal to sides $\overline{AB}$ over side $\overline{CD}$. We will cross multiply and then solve for x.

$$\frac{4}{x} = \frac{8}{18}$$

$72 = 8x$

$x = 9$

Step 4: The question asked for the length of $\overline{AC}$ so we have to add the lengths of $\overline{AE}$ and $\overline{CE}$ together to find the correct answer.

$4 + 9 = 13$

Correct Answer: A

Practice: TRIANGLES

1. A right triangle (not shown) has a hypotenuse with a length of 13 and a leg with the length of 5. What is the length of the other leg?

A) 5
B) 8
C) 12
D) 13

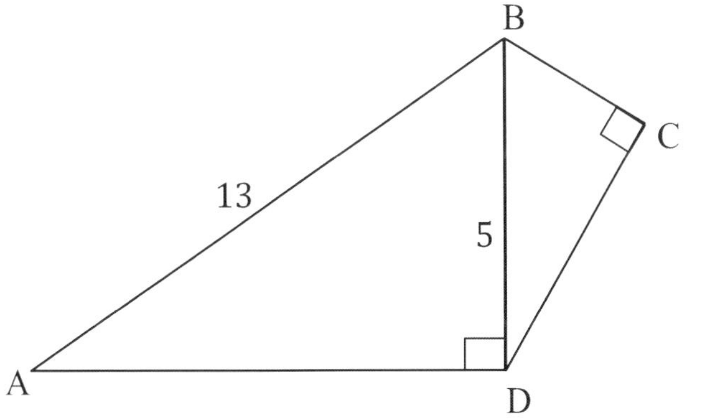

2. In the figure above, $\overline{CD} = \frac{1}{3}\overline{AD}$. What is the perimeter of quadrilateral $ABCD$?

A) 32
B) 37
C) 63
D) 72

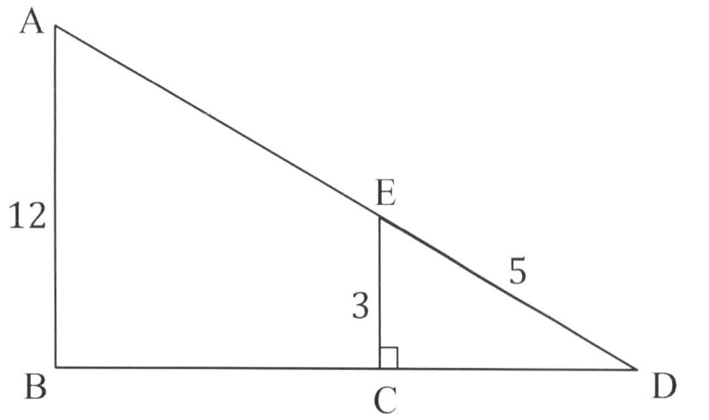

3. In the figure above, $\overline{BA}$ is parallel to $\overline{EC}$. What is the length of $\overline{BD}$?

A) 16
B) 18
C) 20
D) 24

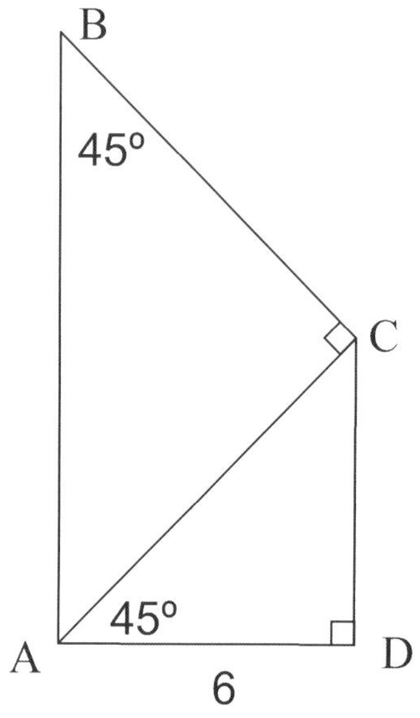

4. In quadrilateral ABCD above, what is the length of $\overline{AB}$?

A) 12
B) $6\sqrt{3}$
C) $6\sqrt{2}$
D) 6

5. What is the area of an equilateral triangle with a perimeter of 24?

A) 24
B) $16\sqrt{3}$
C) 32
D) $32\sqrt{3}$

For answer explanations to these practice questions, go to curvebreakerstestprep.com/decoding-the-digital-sat

Chapter 36: QUADRILATERALS

Section: Math
Question Category: QUADRILATERALS
Expect about one quadrilateral question.

LESSON

In a square:

- All four sides are equal.
- Each of the 4 angles is 90 degrees.
- Area = s^2
- Perimeter = $4s$

In a rectangle:

- Opposite sides are equal.
- Each of the 4 angles is 90 degrees.
- Area = $l \cdot w$
- Perimeter = $2l + 2w$

In a parallelogram:

- Opposite sides are parallel and equal.
- Area = $b \cdot h$

In any quadrilateral:

- Angles add up to 360 degrees.

Example 1: QUADRILATERALS

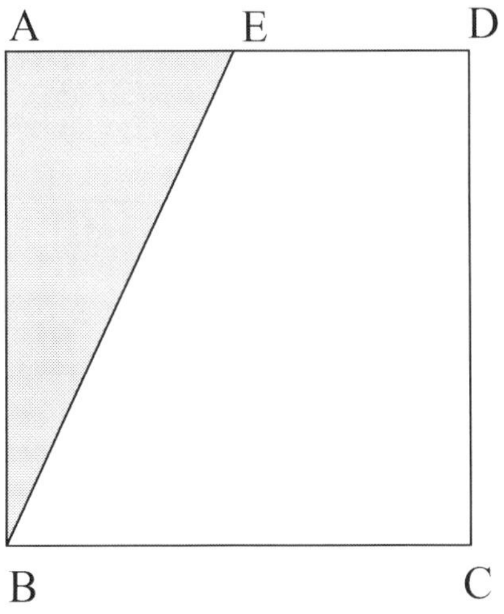

1. In the figure above, ABCD is a square with side length 18 centimeters. The midpoint of AD is E. What is the area, in square centimeters, of the shaded region?

A) 50
B) 81
C) 243
D) 324

Solution Strategy: Draw, Label, Formulas, Carve

Step 1: Label

Since we know that each side of the square is 18, and we're told that E is the midpoint of AD, then AE is equal to 9.

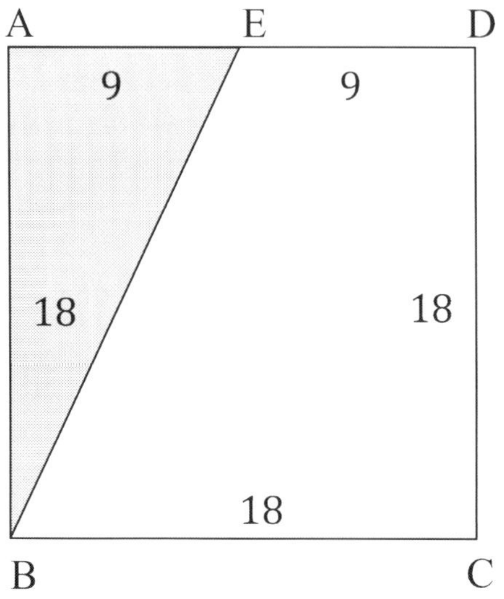

Step 2: Formula

The shaded region is a triangle, and we know the base and height, so we can calculate the area:

$$A = \frac{1}{2}bh$$

$$A = \frac{1}{2}(9)(18) = 81$$

Correct Answer: B

Example 2: QUADRILATERALS

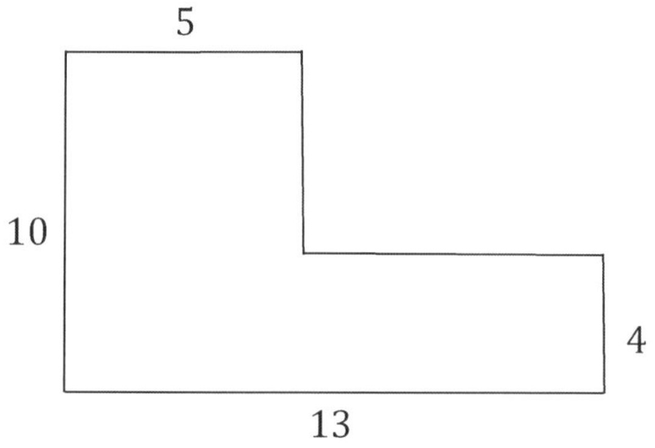

2. In the figure above, all angles are right angles, and the side lengths given are in centimeters. What is the area, in square centimeters, of the figure?

A) 75
B) 82
C) 86
D) 92

Solution Strategy: Draw, Label, Formulas, Carve

Step 1: Carve the figure up into two rectangles and figure out the length of the smaller rectangle.

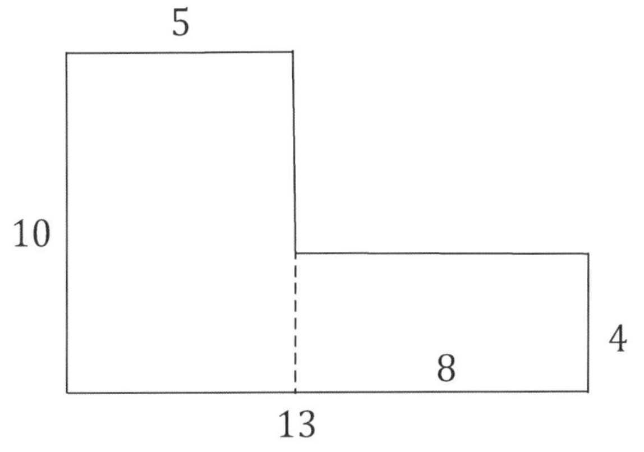

Length of the small rectangle:
$13 - 5 = 8$

Step 2: Now we can find the area of both rectangles and add them together to get the total area.

The larger rectangle has a width of 5 and a length of 10.
$A = l \cdot w = (5) \cdot (10) = 50$

The second, smaller rectangle has a width of 4 and a length of 8.
$A = l \cdot w = (8) \cdot (4) = 32$

Step 3: Add the two numbers together to get the total area.
$50 + 32 = 82$

Correct Answer: B

Practice: QUADRILATERALS

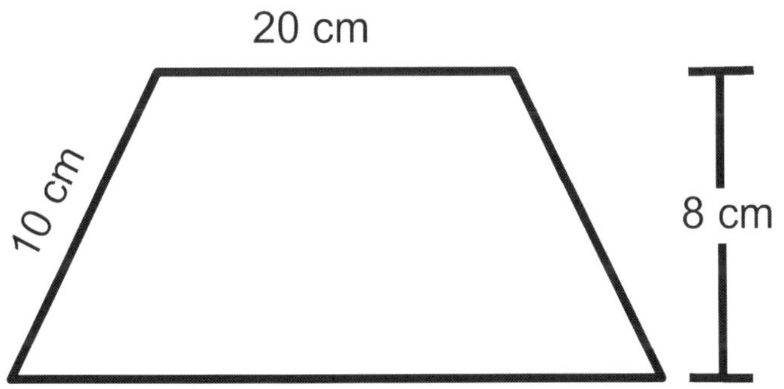

Note: Figure not drawn to scale

1. What is the area of the trapezoid shown above, in square centimeters?

A) 120
B) 180
C) 210
D) 240

2. Kamal is painting the ceiling in his local community center. The ceiling is 60 feet wide and 80 feet long. If 1 can of paint can cover exactly 250 square feet, what is the minimum number of cans of paint he will need in order to cover the ceiling with 1 coat of paint?

A) 9
B) 10
C) 19
D) 20

For answer explanations to these practice questions, go to curvebreakerstestprep.com/decoding-the-digital-sat

Chapter 37: CIRCLES AND RADIANS

Question Category: CIRCLES
Expect about two circle questions.

LESSON ON CIRCLES

All Circles

- There are 360 degrees in a circle.
- The equation of a circle with center (h,k) and radius r is $(x - h)^2 + (y - k)2 = r^2$

Radius

- A radius is the distance from the center to any point on the edge of the circle.
- All radii in a circle are equal.

Diameter

- A diameter is the straight line distance from one point on the circle to another, passing through the center.
- It is the longest line or chord in the circle.
- The diameter equals twice the radius.

Chord

- A chord is any line segment from one point on the circle to another.
- The diameter is the longest chord.

Circumference

- The circumference is the distance around the outside of the circle.
- The formula for circumference is πd or $2\pi r$

Arc

- An arc is part of the circumference.
- Arc measure is proportional to the size of the central angle.

Area

- The area of a circle is the amount of space inside the circumference of the circle.
- The formula for area is πr^2
- A sector is part of the area.
- The measure of the sector is proportional to the size of the central angle.

Example 1: CIRCLES

1. In a circle, the measure of arc XY is 75 degrees. Point O is the center of the circle. What is the measure, in degrees, of its associated angle XOY?

A) 30
B) 65
C) 75
D) 105

Solution:

Step 1: *Recognize that arcs and sectors are proportional to the central angle.*

Step 2: *Draw and label*

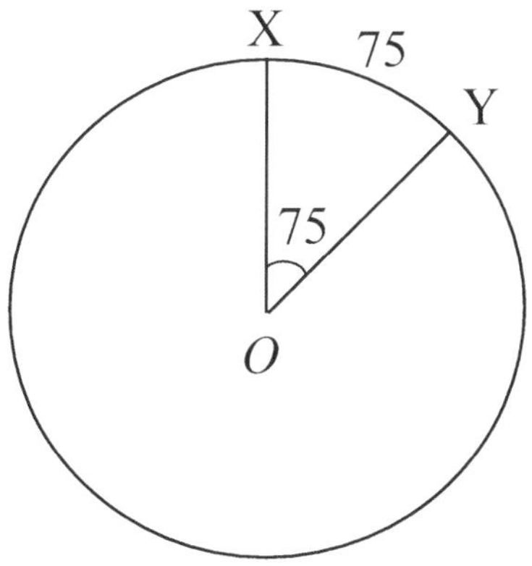

In a circle, the measure of an arc is equal to the measure of its associated central angle. Therefore, if the measure of the arc is 75 degrees, the measure of the associated angle will also be 75 degrees.

Correct Answer: C

Example 2: CIRCLES

2. Consider the circle with the equation $(x-5)^2+(y+3)^2=36$ in the xy-plane. This circle is translated so that its center moves to the origin (0, 0), resulting in a new circle.

What is the equation of this new circle?

A) $x^2+y^2=36$
B) $(x-5)^2+(y+3)^2=0$
C) $x^2+y^2=6$
D) $(x-5)^2+(y+3)^2=6^2$

Solution:

Step 1: *Recognize that the equation of a circle is: $(x-h)^2+(y-k)^2=r^2$ with center (h,k) and radius r to be able to find the center.*

We can find the center by looking at the number with the opposite sign in each of the parentheses of the equation. Therefore we see that the *h* value is equal to 5 and the *k* value is equal to -3.

Step 2: *The radius would not change if we translated the circle. This means:*

Our equation would still be equal to 36.

Step 3: *Since the point (0,0) now replaces (5,-3) we know that the answer has to be A since those terms would disappear.*

Correct Answer: A

Practice: CIRCLES

$$(x-2)^2+(y+1)^2=25$$

1. A certain circle is defined by the equation above. What is the diameter of this circle?

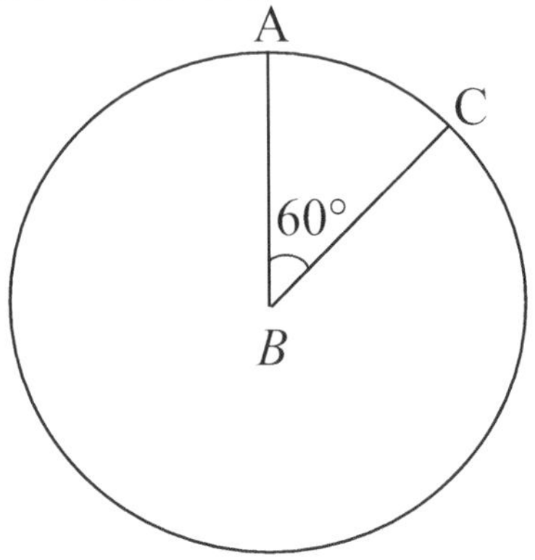

2. The circle above with center B has an area of 48, What is the area of sector AC?

A) 48
B) 16
C) 12
D) 8

3. A circle in the xy-plane has a diameter with endpoints (3, -2) and (9, -2). An equation of this circle is $(x-6)^2+(y+2)^2=r^2$, where r is a positive constant. What is the value of r?

A) 1
B) 2
C) 3
D) 6

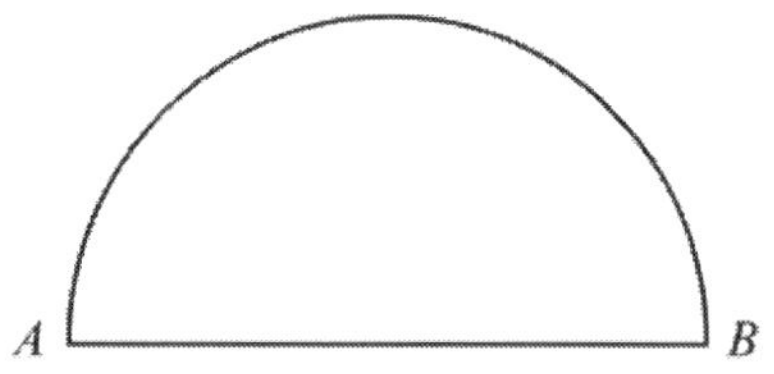

4. The semicircle shown in the figure above has an area of 50π. What is the measure of arc AB?

A) $5\pi\sqrt{2}$
B) 10π
C) $10\pi\sqrt{2}$
D) 20π

LESSON ON RADIANS

Section: Math
Question Category: Radians
Expect about 0-1 Radian questions.

A radian is an angle whose corresponding arc in a circle is equal to the radius of the circle.

A circle has 360 degrees or 2π radians, which means one radian is about $360/(2\pi)$ or 57.3 degrees.

π radians = 180°
1 radian = $180°/\pi$

Example: Radians

An angle in standard position measures $\frac{7\pi}{6}$ radians. What is the degree measure of this angle?

A) 60
B) 120
C) 210
D) 300

Solution:

Step 1: Since π radians = 180°, we can set up the proportion:

$$\frac{\pi\, radians}{180\ degrees} = \frac{\frac{7}{6}\pi\ radians}{x\ degrees}$$

Step 2: Cross multiply

$$\pi x = 180\left(\frac{7\pi}{6}\right)$$
$$\pi x = 210\pi$$
$$x = 210$$

Correct Answer: C

Practice: Radians

1. What is the degree measure of an angle that measures $\frac{3\pi}{4}$ radians?

A) 45
B) 90
C) 135
D) 180

For answer explanations to these practice questions, go to curvebreakerstestprep.com/decoding-the-digital-sat

Chapter 38: VOLUME

Section: Math
Question Category: Volume
Expect about one volume question.

LESSON

Generally, you can answer volume questions by getting the formula from the Reference Table (or memorizing it) and plugging in the numbers they give you.

Example 1: Volume

1. A cylinder has a height of 12 meters and a radius of 5 meters. What is the volume, in cubic meters, of the cylinder?

A) 24π
B) 60π
C) 144π
D) 300π

Solution:

Step 1: Refer to the Reference Table for the formula for volume of a cylinder:

$$V = \pi r^2 h$$

Step 2: Plug the numbers given into the equation:

$$V = \pi(5)^2 \cdot (12)$$

$$V = 300\pi$$

Correct Answer: D

Example 2: Volume

2. What is the volume of a sphere with a diameter of 4?

A) $\frac{3}{4}\pi$
B) $\frac{4}{3}\pi$
C) $\frac{16}{3}\pi$
D) $\frac{32}{3}\pi$

Solution:

Step 1: Refer to the Reference Table for the formula for volume of a sphere:

$$V = \frac{4}{3}\pi r^3$$

Step 2: Plug the numbers given into the equation. The radius is half the diameter:

$$V = \frac{4}{3}\pi(2)^3$$
$$V = \frac{4}{3}\pi(8)$$
$$V = \frac{32}{3}\pi$$

Correct Answer: D

Practice 1: Volume

1. A cube has an edge length of 8 centimeters. What is the volume, in cubic centimeters, of the cube?

A) 24
B) 48
C) 64
D) 512

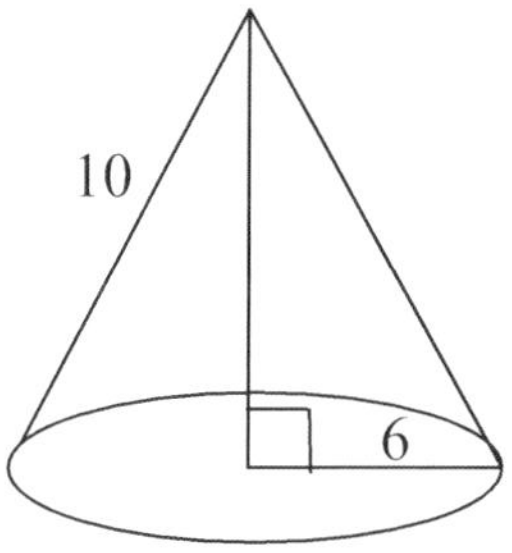

2. In the cone shown above, the radius of the base is 6 and the slant height is 10. What is the approximate volume of the cone?

A) 62.8
B) 226.2
C) 301.5
D) 377

For answer explanations to these practice questions, go to curvebreakerstestprep.com/decoding-the-digital-sat

Chapter 39: TRIGONOMETRY

Section: Math
Question Category: Trigonometry
Expect about one trig question.

LESSON

Most trigonometry questions test your knowledge of SOHCAHTOA

SOHCAHTOA: The 3 basic trig ratios to calculate sides in a right triangle:

$$sin = \frac{OPP}{HYP}$$

$$cos = \frac{ADJ}{HYP}$$

$$tan = \frac{OPP}{ADJ}$$

When two angles are complementary (meaning they add to 90 degrees), the sine of one angle equals the cosine of the other.

Example 1: Trigonometry

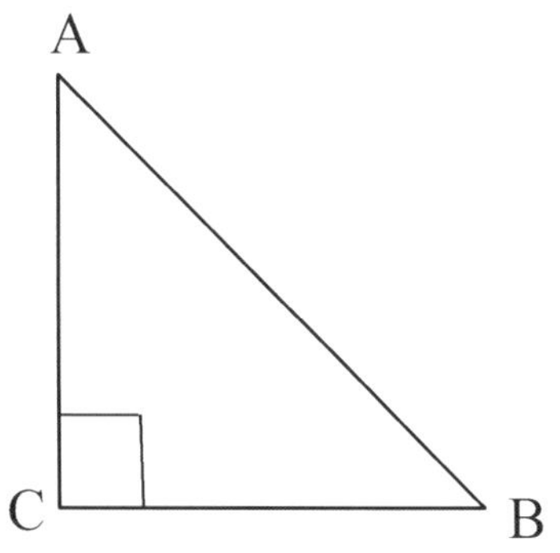

1. In triangle ABC above, the measure of cos A is $\frac{1}{2}$. What is the measure of sin A?

A) $\frac{1}{2}$
B) $\frac{\sqrt{3}}{2}$
C) $\frac{\sqrt{3}}{3}$
D) 2

Solution Strategy: SOHCAHTOA

Step 1: SOHCAHTOA

Since we know cos A is $\frac{1}{2}$, CAH tells us that side $\overline{AC}$ (Adjacent) is equal to 1 and side $\overline{AB}$ (hypotenuse) is equal to 2.

Step 2: Now we can use the Pythagorean Theorem to solve for the missing side length $\overline{BC}$.

$$a^2 + b^2 = c^2$$
$$a^2 + (1)^2 = (2)^2$$
$$a^2 = 3$$
$$a = \sqrt{3}$$

This means that $\overline{BC} = \sqrt{3}$

Step 3: Now that we know all 3 sides of the triangle we can find sin A which is the opposite side $\overline{BC}$ over the hypotenuse $\overline{BC}$.

$$sin = \frac{OPP}{HYP}$$

$$sin\ A = \frac{\sqrt{3}}{2}$$

Correct Answer: B

Example 2: Trigonometry

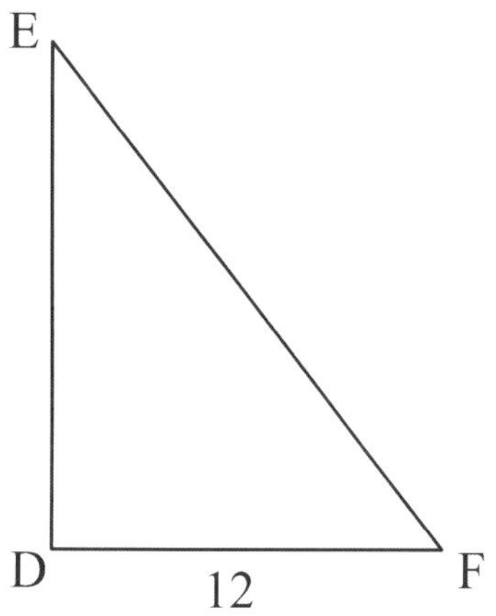

2. In right triangle DEF above, the measure of sin E is $\frac{3}{5}$. What is the length of side EF?

A) 13
B) 20
C) 24
D) 25

Solution Strategy: SOHCAHTOA

Step 1: Draw another triangle that has the ratios of the sides so that we can then see the actual side lengths of the triangle given to us.

$$sin = \frac{OPP}{HYP}$$

Since sin E is $\frac{3}{5}$, side DF (opposite) is 3, and side EF is 5 (hypotenuse).

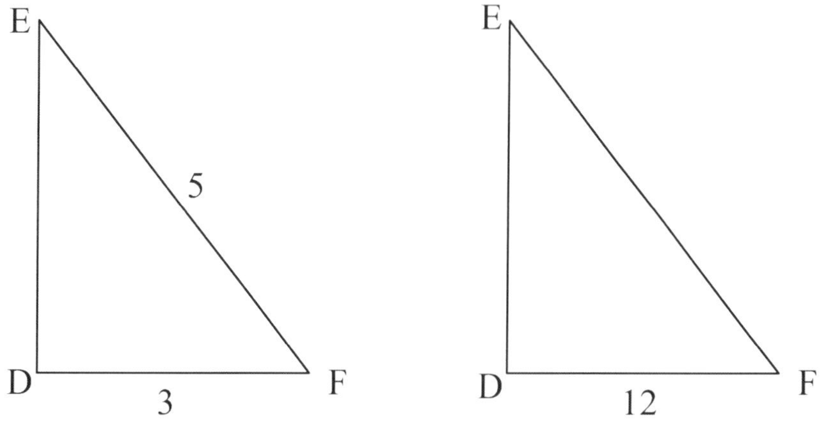

Step 2: Once we have both triangles we see that there is a scale factor of 4 getting us to our original triangle. We can set up a proportion with x as side EF:

$$\frac{3}{12} = \frac{5}{x}$$

Step 3: Cross multiply

$3x = 60$
$x = 20$

Correct Answer: B

Practice: Trigonometry

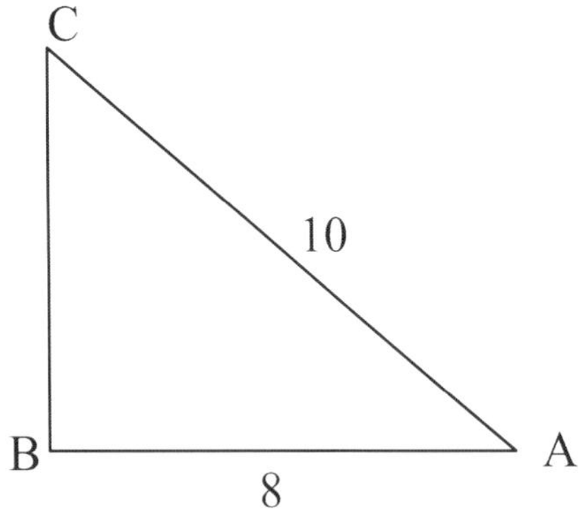

1. In right triangle ABC above, the measure of side AB is 8 and the measure of side AC is 10. What is the value of tan A?

A) $\frac{3}{4}$
B) $\frac{3}{5}$
C) $\frac{4}{5}$
D) $\frac{1}{2}$

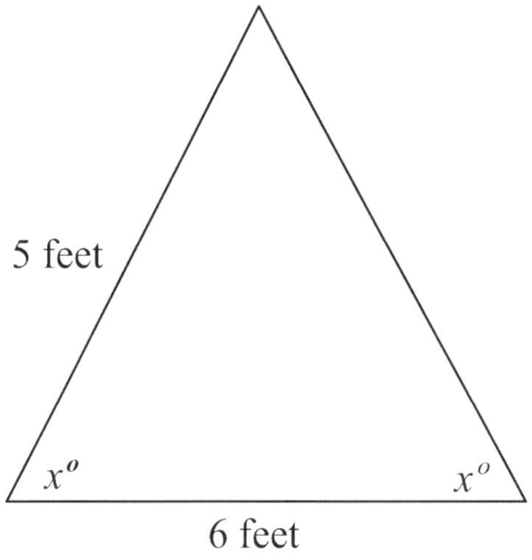

2. Jaya sketches out the above diagram for the sail of a boat she is building. What is the value of sin x?

A) $\frac{3}{8}$
B) $\frac{2}{5}$
C) $\frac{3}{5}$
D) $\frac{4}{5}$

For answer explanations to these practice questions, go to curvebreakerstestprep.com/decoding-the-digital-sat

CHAPTER 40: STATISTICS & SURVEY DESIGN

Section: Math
Question Subsection: Data, Statistics, & Probability
Question Category: Statistics & Survey Design
Of the 44 math questions, approximately 0 - 1 may be questions from this category.

LESSON

The purpose of statistics is to apply the findings of a small group to a much larger scale. Statistics is not an exact science, so avoid definitive language in the answer choices such as “all” or “most,” and look for words such as “plausible,” “likely,” “roughly,” “about.”

✦ **Margin of Error**: usually a small amount that is allowed for in case of miscalculation.
✦ **Standard Deviation**: measures the amount of variability from the mean.

To reduce the error rate of a survey, the sample should be as **large** as possible and as **random** as possible.

The Curvebreakers Strategy

1. **If required, calculate the Lower and Upper Bounds.**
2. **Avoid Definitive Language in the Answer Choices.**
3. **The best survey designs have LARGE and RANDOM samples.**

Example 1: Statistics & Survey Design

1. To estimate the average score of students in a class, a random sample of scores was taken. Based on the sample, it is estimated that the average score is 75, with an associated margin of error of 4. Based on this estimate and margin of error, which of the following is the most appropriate conclusion about the average score of students in the class?

A) It is plausible that the average score is between 71 and 79.

B) It is plausible that the average score is less than 71.

C) The average score is exactly 75.

D) It is plausible that the average score is greater than 79.

Solution:

Step 1: Calculate the lower bound:

75 - 4 = 71

Step 2: Calculate the upper bound:

75 + 4 = 79

Therefore, based on this estimate and margin of error, the most appropriate conclusion about the average score of students in the class is that it is plausible that the average score is between 71 and 79.

Correct Answer: A

Example 2: Statistics & Survey Design

2. A customer satisfaction survey conducted by a restaurant chain reveals that 92% of surveyed customers rated their dining experience as excellent. Which of the following conclusions is most valid based on this survey?

A) The restaurant chain provides the best food among all competitors.
B) This restaurant chain has the highest customer satisfaction rating among all competitors.
C) 8% of customers had a poor dining experience at the restaurant.
D) Approximately 92% of all customers who have dined at the restaurant rated their experience as excellent.

Solution:

Step 1: Avoid definitive language in answer choices

A) The restaurant chain provides the ~~best food~~ among ~~all~~ competitors.
~~B~~) This restaurant chain has the ~~highest~~ customer satisfaction rating among ~~all~~ competitors.
? C) 8% of customers had a poor dining experience at the restaurant.
✓D) Approximately 92% of all customers who have dined at the restaurant rated their experience as excellent.

Correct Answer: D

Look for words like "approximately" when answering questions about survey design. The survey states that 92% of surveyed customers rated their dining experience as excellent. Therefore, the conclusion that approximately 92% of all customers who have dined at the restaurant rated their experience as excellent is a direct interpretation of the information provided.

Practice: Statistics & Survey Design

1. If the mean of a data set is 50 and the standard deviation is 3, which of the following contains the interval one standard deviation from the mean?

A) 40-56
B) 44-56
C) 47-53
D) 54-62

2. A national survey was conducted to estimate the proportion of adults who own a smartphone. Out of a random sample of 2,000 adults, 1,500 indicated that they own a smartphone. If the survey has a margin of error of 2%, which of the following represents the approximate range for the percentage of adults nationwide who likely own a smartphone?

A) 71-75%
B) 73-77%
C) 75-79%
D) 78-82%

3. A survey was conducted to estimate the proportion of voters supporting a particular referendum. Out of a random sample of 1,500 voters, 55% indicated support for the referendum. The survey had a margin of error of 2.5%. On election day, the referendum passed with 57% of the votes. Based on this information, which of the following conclusions is most supported by the data?

A) The survey accurately predicted the outcome of the referendum.
B) The survey results were too close to make an accurate prediction about the outcome of the referendum.
C) The survey results incorrectly predicted the outcome of the referendum.
D) No conclusions can be made using the survey results.

4. A company wants to survey its employees to gather feedback on workplace satisfaction. The company has 10 departments with a total of 5,000 employees. Which of the following surveying methods would result in the most accurate representation of the employees' opinions?

A) Survey all 1,000 employees who have been with the company for more than 10 years.
B) Randomly select 50 employees from each department to send surveys to.
C) Survey the first 500 employees who arrive at work on a specific day.
D) Survey only the employees who work on the ground floor of the company building.

For answer explanations to these practice questions, go to curvebreakerstestprep.com/decoding-the-digital-sat

SUMMARY OF STRATEGIES

READING

The table below lists a summary of the Reading strategies by category. Key things to focus on:

1. **Highlight:** Key words or phrases
2. **Summarize:** Try to summarize text and write it down
3. **Predict:** Know the direction you want to go before looking at the answer choices
4. **POE:** Eliminate answer choices that don't match your direction or contain too strong or extreme language

QUESTION CATEGORY	STRATEGY
Vocabulary Word Choice	Write In Your Own Word
Main Idea	Read and Predict
Support or Weaken Claim	Summarize the Claim
Relevant Information From Notes	Focus on the Goal
Text interpretation	Summarize and Predict; POE
Dual Passage Comparison	Summarize and POE
Transition Words	Write In Your Own Word

GRAMMAR

The table below lists a summary of the Grammar strategies by category. Key things to focus on:

1. **Vertical Line Test:** Use the Vertical Line test for answer choices with Full or Half-Stop punctuation.
2. **3 Reasons to Use a Comma:**
    a. List
    b. Before/After non-essential
    c. Intro
3. **Be consistent:** Subjects need to agree with verbs; pronouns need to agree with nouns; tenses need to remain the same.

QUESTION CATEGORY	STRATEGY
Punctuation; Full-Stop and Half-Stop	Vertical Line Test
Punctuation; Comma Usage	Know the 3 Main Reasons
Punctuation: Apostrophes	Put Apostrophe After Thing Doing the Possessing
Punctuation: End of Sentence	Know the 3 Main Reasons
Agreement; Subject/Verb	Be Consistent and Trim the Fat
Agreement: Pronouns	Be Consistent with Subject
Misplaced Modifiers	Draw the Arrow

MATH

QUESTION CATEGORY	STRATEGY
Plug In for the Variable	Find the Target Value
Plug in the Answer	Start with B and Label Columns
Basic Algebra	Insert the variable
Slope Intercept Form of a Line	Write out the Formulas
Proportions	Write out Top and Bottom Units
Functions	Think of f(x) as y
Systems of Equations	Substitute, Stack, or Graph
Inequalities	Flip the Sign
Quadratics	Know the Basic Equations
Graphs	Select Quickest Option
Percents	Translate Text to Math
Exponents/Radicals	MADSPM
Mean/Median/Mode/Range	Use Average Pie for Mean
Probability	Success/Total
Represents Situation	Bite-size and POE
Geometry	Draw/Label/Complete Formulas/Carve
Trigonometry	SOHCAHTOA
Statistics and Survey Design	Large and Random Sample Sizes are Best

DESMOS CALCULATOR GUIDE

While you are allowed to bring your own calculator for the digital exam just as you would for the paper exam, the digital exam will now contain a built-in graphing calculator for you to use through the Desmos interface. This calculator is similar to the regular TI-84 calculator that you are used to in class, but there are some important differences.

Algebraic Math

Maximizing Your Performance

When tackling the algebraic challenges of the SAT, the Desmos calculator emerges as a powerful ally, mirroring the familiar functionalities of the classic TI-84 calculator. As you navigate through the exam, you'll find that inputting calculations into Desmos is a straightforward process: simply type your expression on the left side of the screen, keeping the order of operations firmly in mind. The answer will conveniently appear directly below your input.

Efficiency at Your Fingertips

One of the standout features of the Desmos calculator is its ability to enhance your workflow through the copy-paste function, allowing you to reuse previous calculations. Additionally, the expansive screen real estate means that you can view a comprehensive history of your past calculations without the need to scroll, allowing you to reference previous work.

Navigating Desmos: A Quick Guide

See below for how to execute common calculator functions, tailored specifically for the SAT algebra section, covering basic arithmetic operations to more advanced functions such as square roots, exponents, and trigonometric calculations.

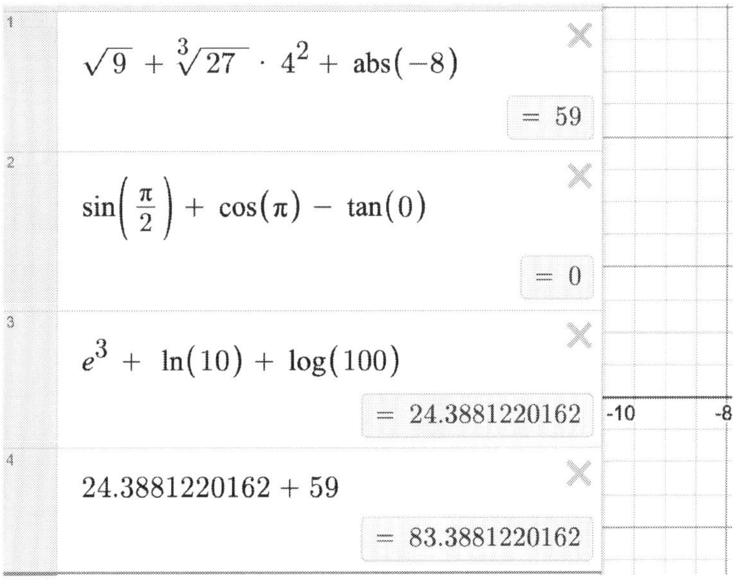

1
$\sqrt{9} + \sqrt[3]{27} \cdot 4^2 + \text{abs}(-8)$
$= 59$
2
$\sin\left(\frac{\pi}{2}\right) + \cos(\pi) - \tan(0)$
$= 0$
3
$e^3 + \ln(10) + \log(100)$
$= 24.3881220162$
4
$24.3881220162 + 59$
$= 83.3881220162$
-10
-8

Graphing

Graphing Mastery

Embarking on the graphing section of the SAT, you'll find that the Desmos calculator offers an innovative approach, distinct from traditional graphing calculators. Desmos provides an expansive, infinite graphing canvas, ensuring that you are never confined by screen limitations. This feature is particularly advantageous for visualizing the behavior of functions across a wide range of values. Zooming in and out is achieved with a simple scroll of your mouse or touchpad, allowing for precise examination or a broader overview as needed.

Inputting graphing equations is seamlessly integrated into the Desmos interface. You can enter equations for graphing in the same area where you perform algebraic calculations, starting with $y =$ or another dependent variable. The Desmos calculator immediately generates a vivid, color-coded graph on the right side of the screen, providing a clear visual representation within the infinite 2-D graphing space. This color-coding is especially helpful when dealing with multiple functions, as it allows for quick and easy differentiation between graphs.

The Desmos calculator revolutionizes the way you find key features of graphs. Unlike traditional calculators, which may require a series of button presses and menu navigations, Desmos enables you to interact directly with the graph using your mouse or touchscreen. Simply click on or hover over key points on the graph to reveal their coordinates, intersection points and roots, and other important information. Additionally, Desmos assists in locating and understanding the maximum or minimum points of a graph, crucial for analyzing the behavior of various functions.

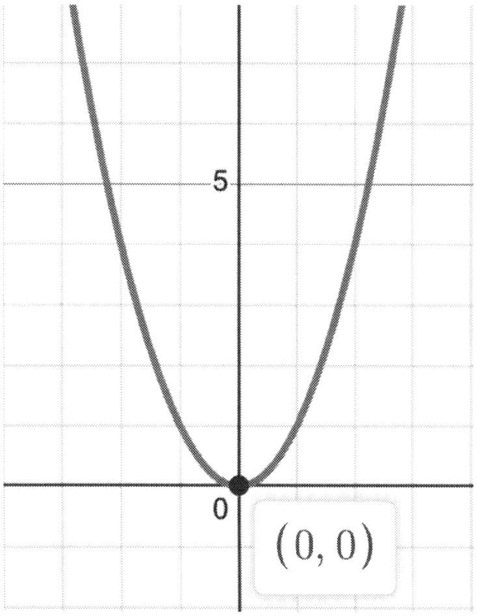

⇐ Same Graph ⇒

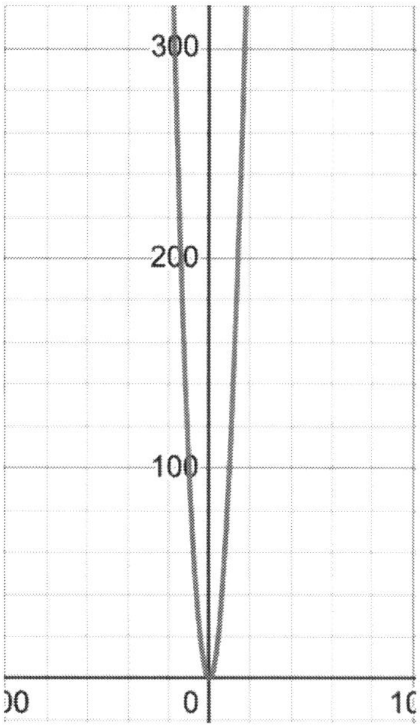

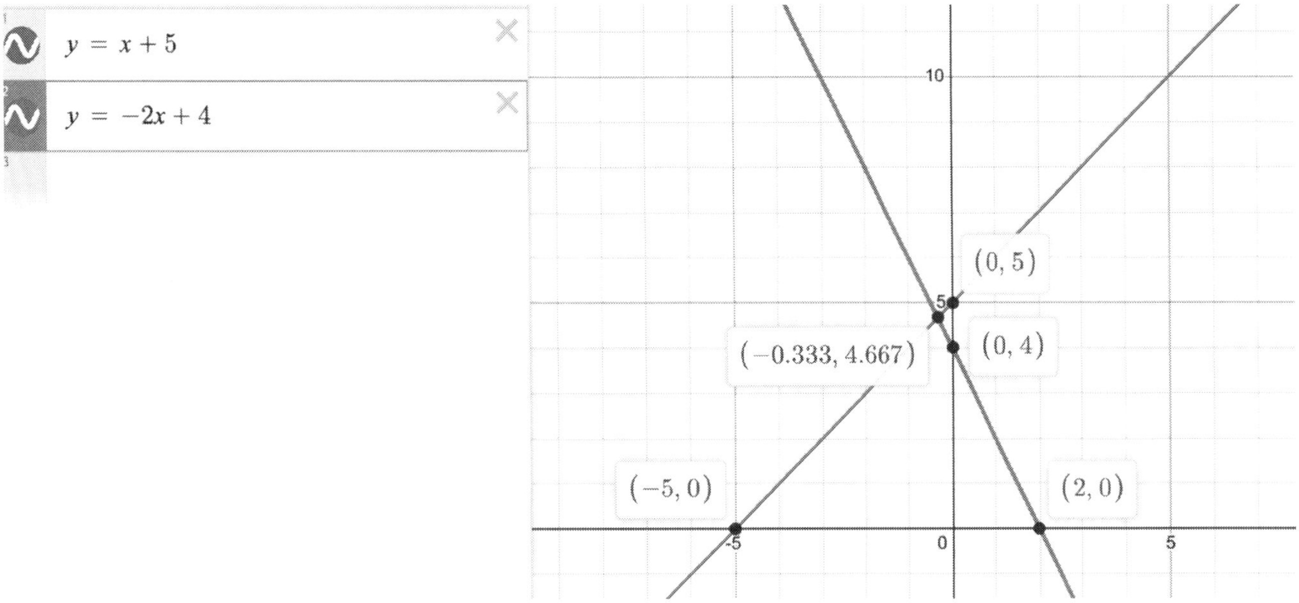

* Here I can see all important points on the graphs like intersections and intercepts

Function	How to Get
Square Root	Type **sqrt** then whatever you want inside it then the right arrow key to get out from under the radical
Cube Root	Type **cbrt** then whatever you want inside it then the right arrow key to get out from under the radical
Exponent	Use **Shift + 6** to get into the exponent and use the right arrow key to get out of the exponent
Sine	Type **Sin** then input what you want the sine of making sure to use parenthesis
Cosine	Type **Cos** then input what you want the cosine of making sure to use parenthesis
Tangent	Type **Tan** then input what you want the tangent of making sure to use parenthesis
e	Just type out **e** regularly and using proper order of operations, Desmos will recognize it as the constant number 2.718
Log / Ln	Just like the trig functions type **Log or Ln** followed by what you are looking for in parentheses
Pi	Just type out **pi** and it will turn into π
Absolute Value	Type **abs** and put what you want in parentheses to get the absolute value function

Some Example Question Uses

1. What is 20% of 340 ?

A) 30
B) 20
C) 34
D) 68

2. The function h is defined by $h(x) = x^2 + 4$. For which **Solution**
Type 20% as a number which means moving the decimal over 2 places to get .2. Then multiply this number by 340 and you will get answer D) 68.

h value of x is $h(x) = 20$?

A) 2
B) 3
C) 4
D) 5

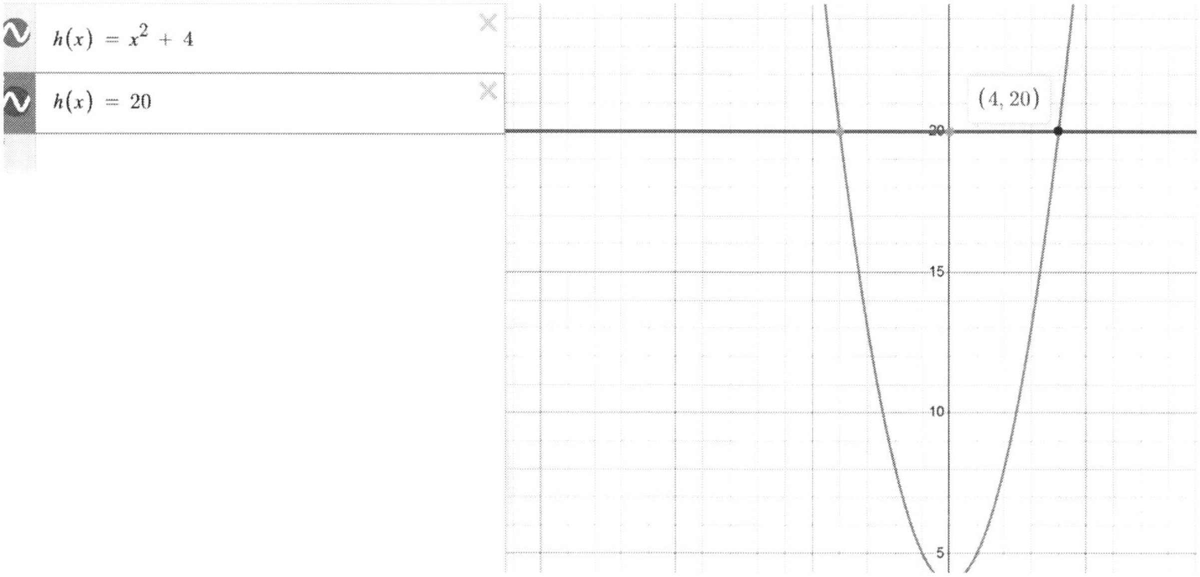

Solution

First plot the graph $h(x)$ in DESMOS then plot the line we want the function to equal. Then hover over the intersection to see where the two lines intersect and see what the x value is which in this case is C) 4.

3. The function f is defined by the equation $f(x) = 5x - 6$. What is the value of $f(x)$ when $x = 5$?

A) 19
B) 21
C) 25
D) 30

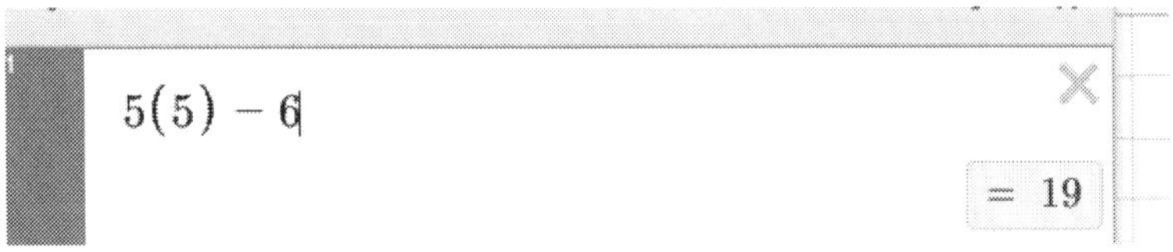

Solution

Since we know what we want x to equal and we have the function, we can just plug 5 into our function for x and figure out what the corresponding $f(x)$ value should be, which is A) 19.

$$y = -2x$$
$$5x + y = 21$$

4. The solution to the given system for equations is (x,y). What is the value of $2x$?

A) 7
B) -14
C) 14
D) 21

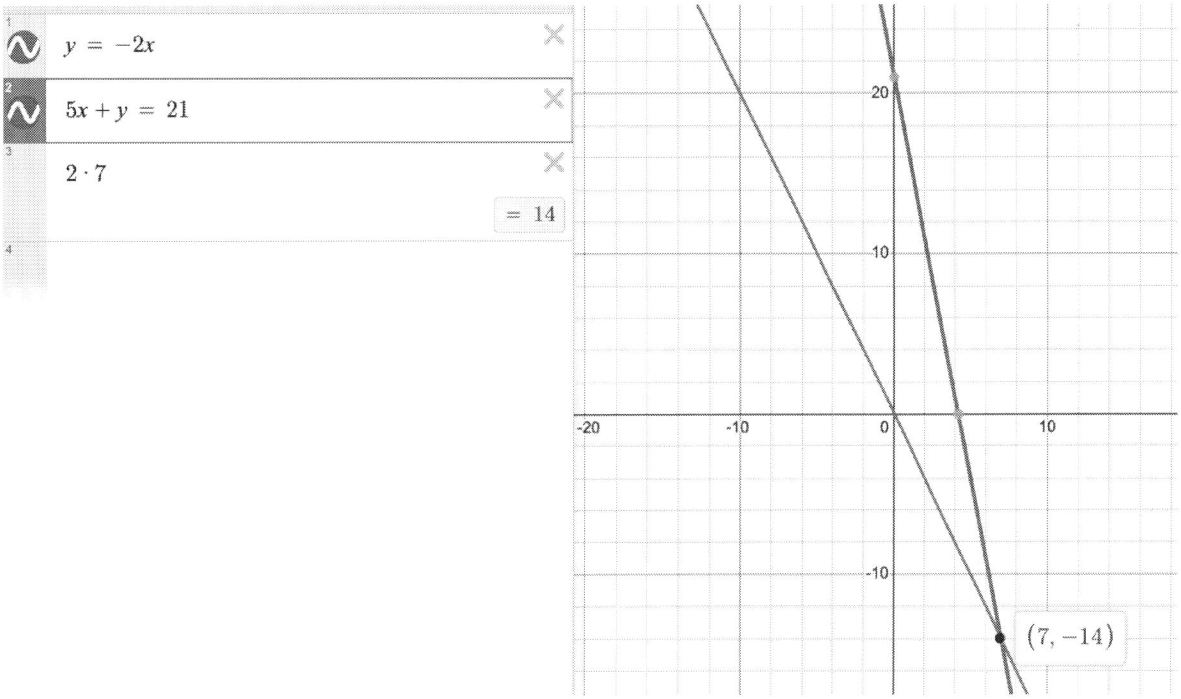

Solution

First plot the graphs in DESMOS then hover over the intersection to see where the two lines intersect and see what the x value of the intersection is which in this case is 7. Then since they ask for $2x$, we can multiply this value of 7 times 2 to get a final answer of C) 14.

$c^2 + 8c - 20$

5. What is one solution to the given equation

A) 2
B) 4
C) 8
D) 20

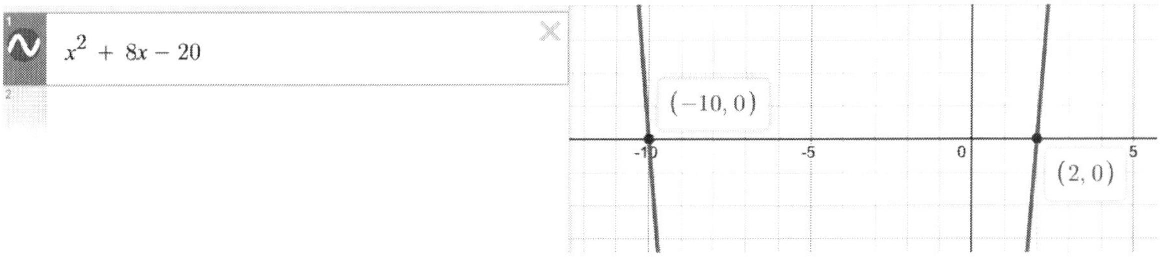

Solution

First plot the graph in DESMOS and look at the x-axis because that is where the roots/zeros/solutions will be. The variable itself does not matter so even though the question uses c, we will use x when we plug into DESMOS. Hover over these points to reveal both solutions and then look at the answer choices to see if there are any that match these points with the correct x values. The answer is A) 2.

6. Bacteria are growing in a liquid growth medium. There were 200 cells per milliliter during an initial observation. The number of cells per milliliter doubles every 5 hours. How many cells per milliliter will there be 20 hours after the initial observation?

A) 200
B) 800
C) 1000
D) 3200

Solution

Since this is an exponential function, we can plot this in DESMOS using our traditional equation for an exponential. We know 200 is the initial value, since it doubles the rate inside the parenthesis is 2 and we know that $t = 20$ which should go into our exponent. We then see that the answer is D) 3200.

7. A circle in the xy-plane has a diameter with endpoints (4, 2) and (4, 14). An equation of this circle is $(x-2)^2+(y-9)^2=r^2$, where r is a positive constant. What is the value of r?

A) 4
B) 5
C) 6
D) 7

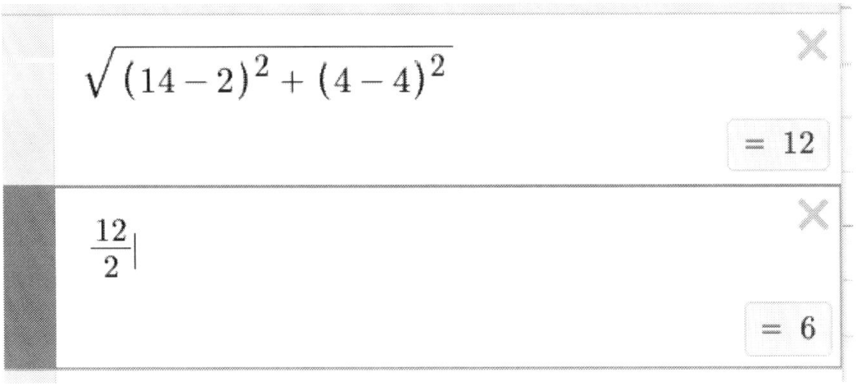

Solution

The first thing that we do is use the distance equation to find the length between the endpoints of the circle which we know will be the diameter. Once we find this, we know that the diameter is just twice the radius, so we need to divide this value (12) by 2 to get the radius C) 6.

8. In the xy-plane, the graph of the equation $y = x^2 - 10x - 121$ intersects the line $y = c$ at exactly one point. What is the value of c?

A) -100
B) -121
C) -140
D) -146

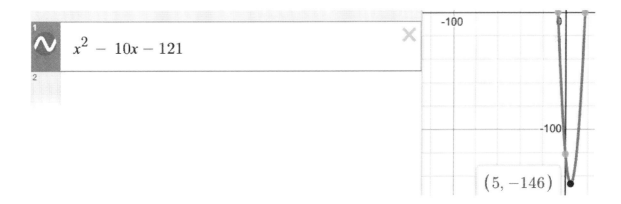

Solution

Plot this equation is DESMOS and then we know that the only time a parabola will hit a horizontal line once is at the vertex so we need to find that point. Hover over the vertex point and find the y-value associated with it and then we know that this value is the line that will only hit the parabola once, which is d) (-146).

9. The function g is defined by $g(x) = \frac{1}{5}x - 7$. What is the y-intercept of the graph $y = f(x)$ in the xy-plane?

A) -7
B) -3
C) $\frac{1}{5}$
D) 4

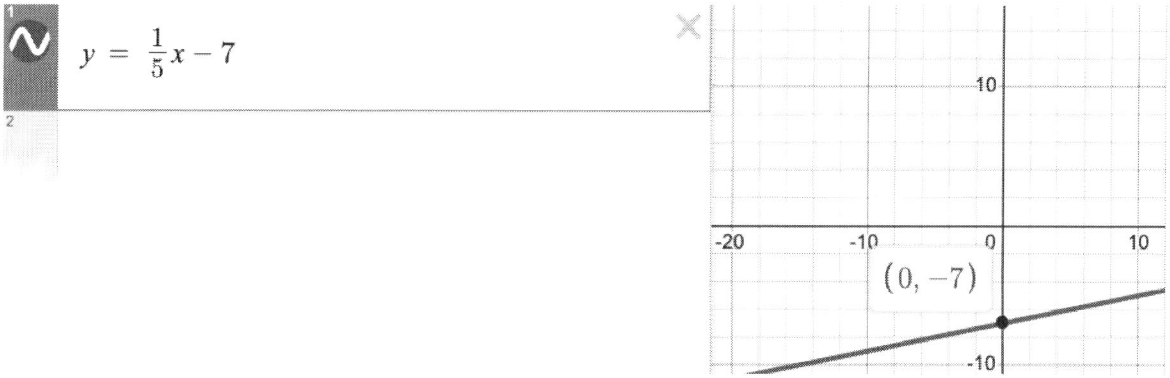

Solution

First plot the graph in DESMOS and since we are looking for the y-intercept we know that this is the value when $x = 0$. So we go down to the graph at this point to figure out what the corresponding y-value is. In this case it is answer C) -7.

$$x + 6 = 12$$
$$(x + 3)^2 = y$$

10. What ordered pair (x,y) is a solution to the given system of equations?

A) (3,36)
B) (4,49)
C) (0,0)
D) (6,81)

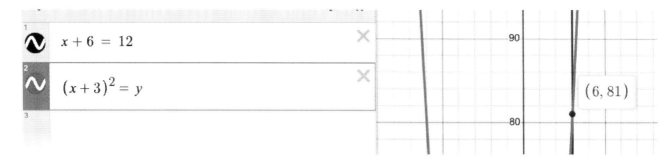

Solution

So we can plot both of these graphs just as they are in DESMOS and we are looking for the solution which is also known as the intersection point. We can highlight over this point and see the ordered pair that is the solution for this set of equations.

11. The function p is defined by $p(n) = 4n^3$. What is the value of n when $p(n) = 108$?

A) 2
B) 3
C) 4
D) 5

Solution

So first plot the graph $p(n)$ in DESMOS and then plot the value that we want to hit which is 108. Then we want to hover over the intersection point because this will give us the value of n where this happens, which is B) 3.

$$f(x) - x^2 + 32$$

12. What is the minimum value of the given function?

A) 0
B) 20
C) 28
D) 32

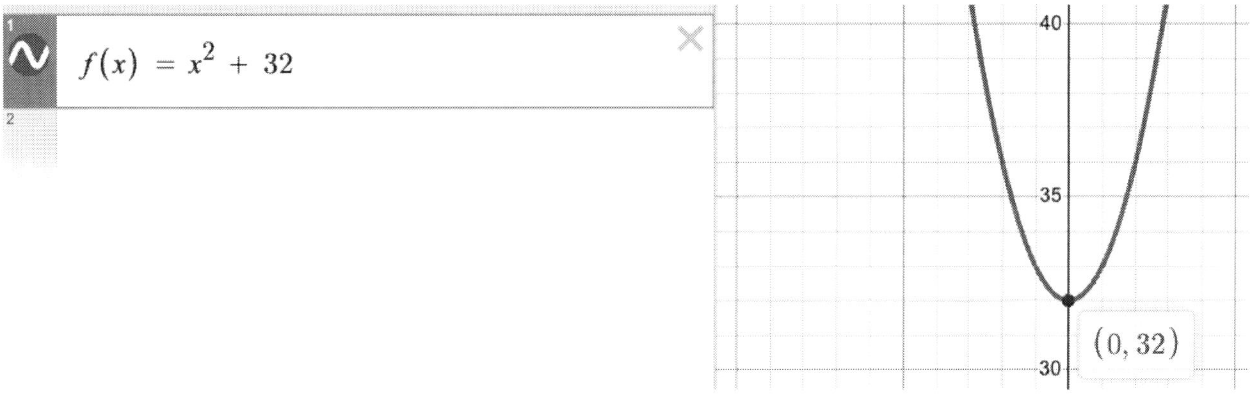

Solution

We know that the minimum value of a parabola occurs at the vertex so we are going to plot this graph to find the coordinates of the vertex. Plot this graph in DESMOS and then hover over the vertex to find the points of the vertex and see what the y-value is because that is what corresponds to the minimum value. The answer is D) 32.

3, 5, 7, 9, 3, 2, 23, 43, 7, 2

13. What is the mean of the following data?

A) 7.5
B) 8.3
C) 10.4
D) 12.2

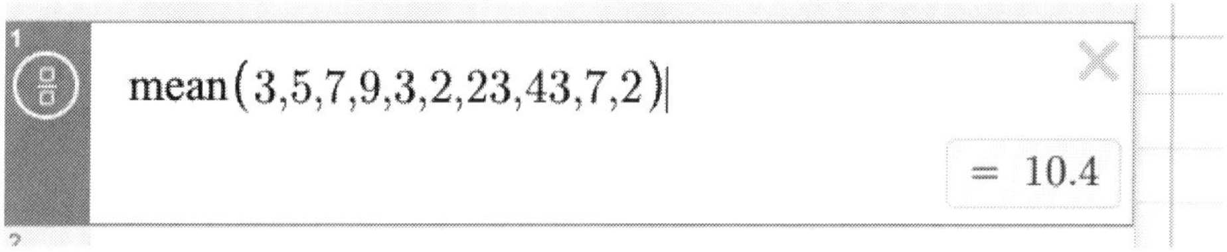

Solution

So here we can use the mean function that DESMOS has. First type mean then add a parentheses. Then add in all of the values each separated by a comma and then close the parenthesis. This function will then automatically give you the mean of the numbers. The answer is C) 10.4

14. Cory is planning a party. It costs Cory a one time fee of $25 to rent the venue and $8.25 per attendee. Cory has a budget of $150. What is the greatest number of attendees possible without exceeding the budget?

A) 12
B) 13
C) 14
D) 15

Solution

So first subtract the 25 dollars from the original 150. Then take the answer of that (125) and divide that by the amount it costs each person to attend. In this case since we cannot have a decimal amount of a person, we must round down to get an answer of 15, which is choice D.

15. If $|3x-3|=81$, what is the positive value of $x-2$?

A) 20
B) 26
C) 28
D) 81

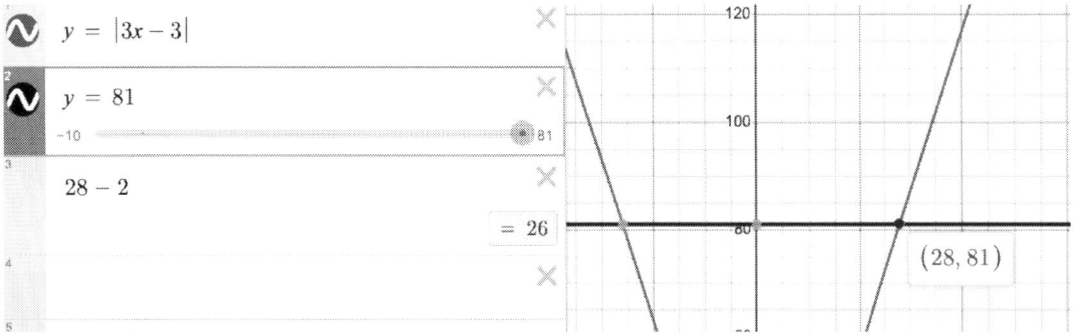

Solution

First graph the function and the value of 81 on DESMOS. Now look for the positive intersection point and hover over it to figure out the x value where this intersection happens on the positive side. Now since we want this value minus 2 we can plug that equation in below to solve for our answer, which is B) 26.

16. A cube has an edge length of 48 inches. A solid sphere with a radius of 24 inches is inside the cube, such that the sphere touches the center of each face of the cube. To the nearest cubic inch, what is the volume of the space in the cube not taken up by the sphere?

A) 516,087
B) 520,087
C) 525,243
D) 526,686

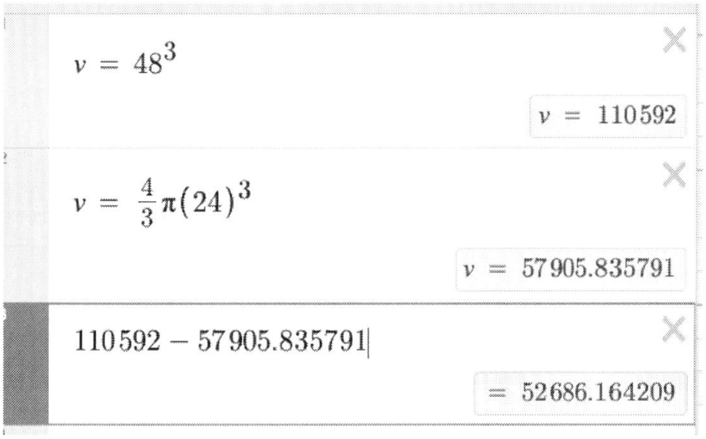

Solution

So first plug into the volume of a cube formula and then do the same thing for the volume of a sphere formula right below it. Use the numbers they give you for the components of the volumes and then subtract these two numbers to see what remaining volume is in the cube and not the sphere. The answer is choice D.

$y > -x + 3$
$y \leq 2x + 5$

17. Which graph represents the solution to the system of inequalities?

a)

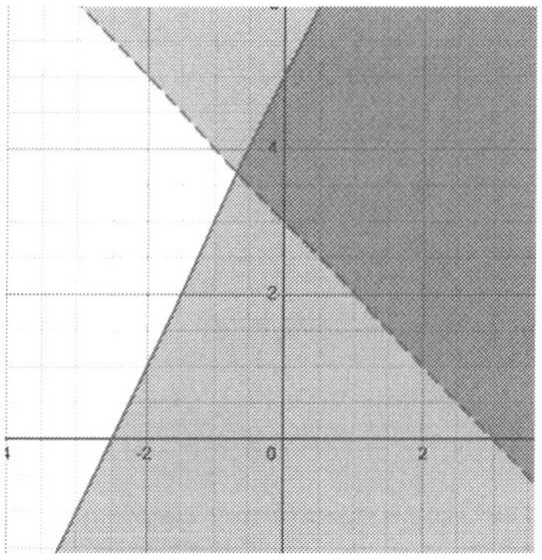

b)

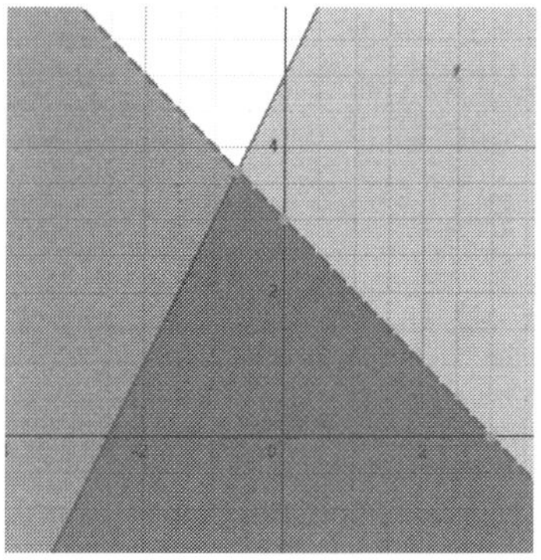

c)

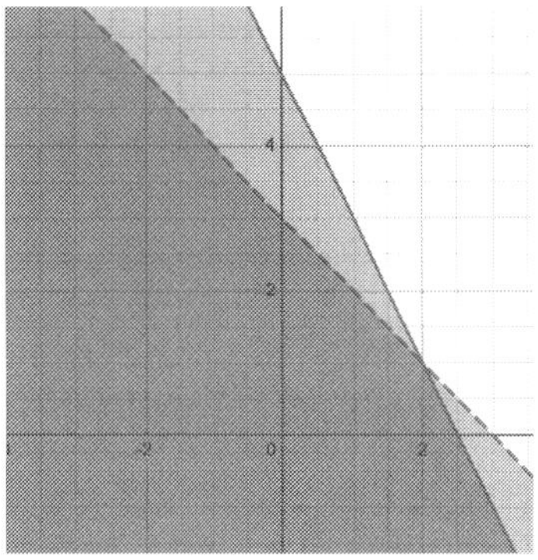

d)

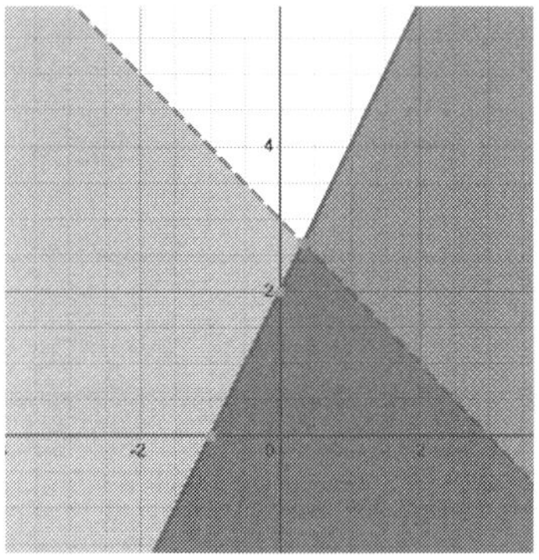

Solution

When we plug the equations into DESMOS it is important to note that the signs are different and represent dotted and solid lines respectively. When we plot the system we look at the choices and see that our graph matches choice A.

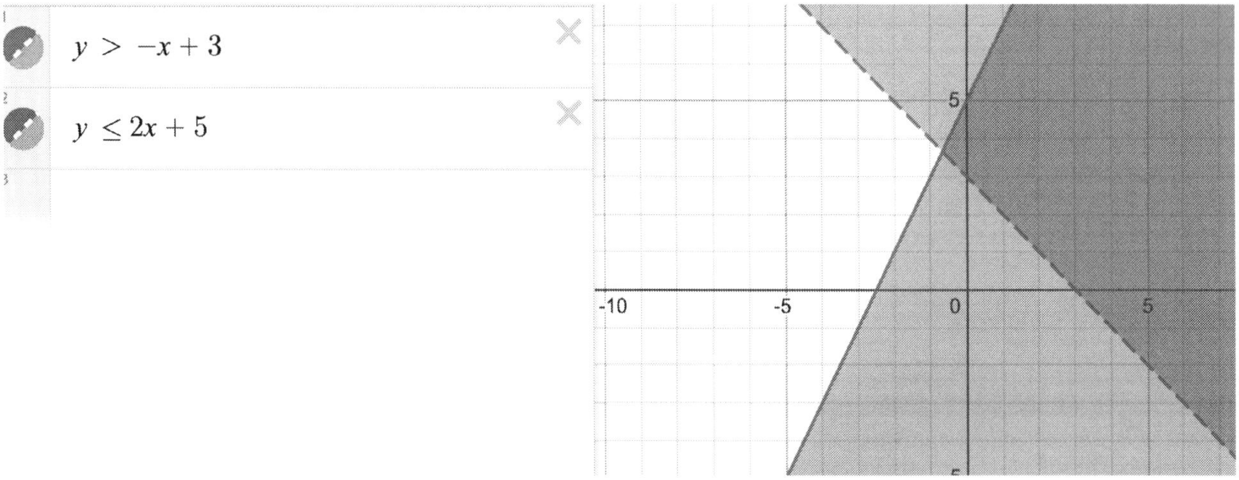

CALCULATOR TIPS AND TRICKS

PERMITTED CALCULATORS ON THE SAT

Most students use some type of TI-83 or TI-84, which is allowed by the College Board on the SAT exam. Curvebreakers recommends the TI-84 Plus CE. For more information about using calculators on the SAT, read Curvebreakers' detailed blog posts online at curvebreakerstestprep.com/blog.

PROHIBITED DEVICES

Unless students have an accommodation approved by the College Board, they can't access these items during the test or breaks:

- Phones smartwatches, fitness trackers, or other wearable technology
- Audio players, Bluetooth devices (like wireless earbuds/headphones), or any other electronic devices (except your testing device)
- Detachable privacy screens
- External keyboards for use with laptops or Chromebooks (keyboards for iPads are allowed)
- Stylus for iPad
- Any cameras, recording device, or timer
- Notes, books, or any other reference materials
- Compasses, rulers, protractors, or cutting devices
- Headphones, earbuds, or earplugs
- Unacceptable calculators that have computer-style (QWERTY) keyboards, use paper tape, make noise, or use a power cord

HOW TO USE A GRAPHING CALCULATOR

Inputting A Fraction

1) Press "alpha"
2) Press "y="
3) Press "enter" to select "1: n/d"

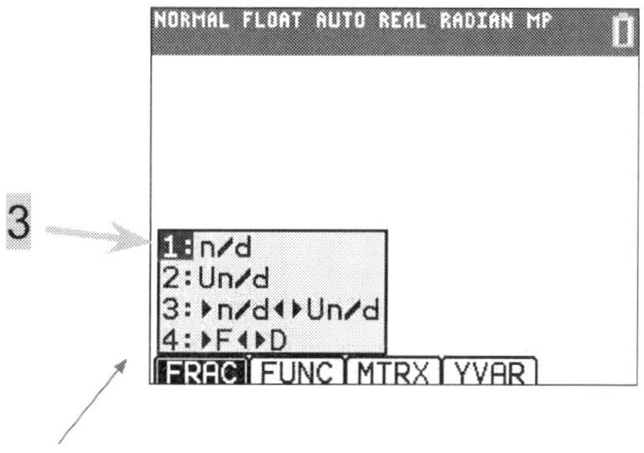

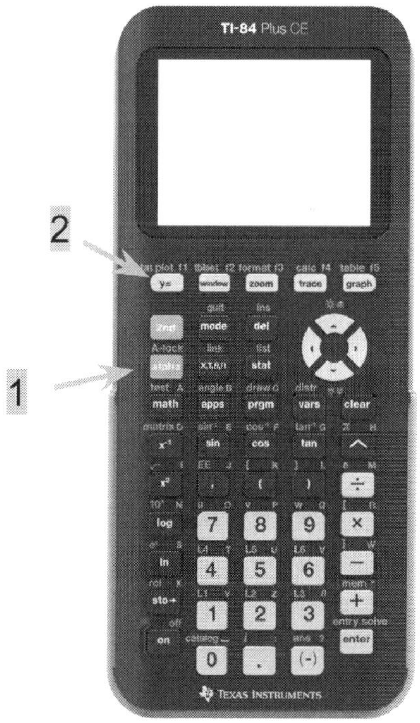

NOTE: There are several other functions you'll see in this list.

- "2: Un/d" will allow you to input a mixed number
- "3: ▸ n/d ◂ ▸Un/d" will change a fraction into a mixed number

To get a decimal in fraction form:

1) Press "math"
2) Press "enter" to select "1: ▶ Frac"
3) Press "enter"

*To get from fraction form into decimal, repeat the procedure, but select "2: ▶ Dec"

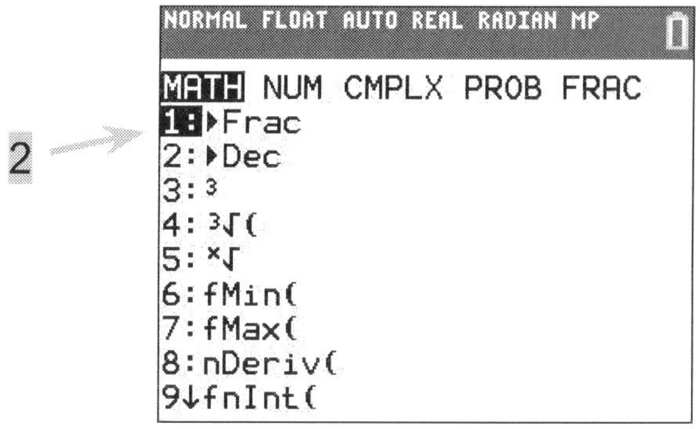

Calculating A Remainder:

1) Press "math"
2) Scroll right to "num"
3) Scroll down to "0: remainder("
4) Press "enter"
5) Input your dividend (what you're dividing)
6) Input a comma
7) Input your divisor (what you're dividing by)
8) Close parentheses and press "enter"

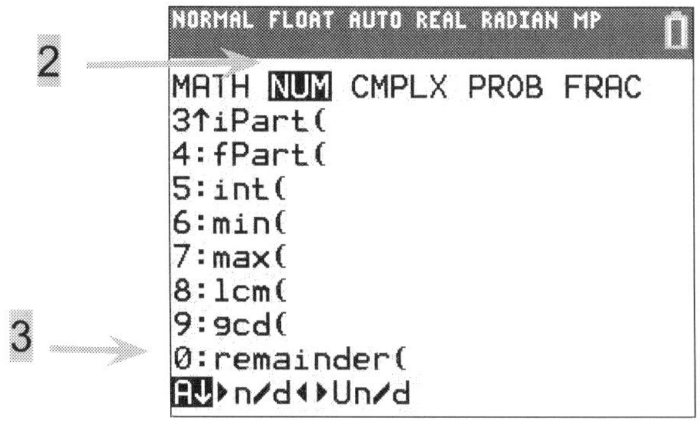

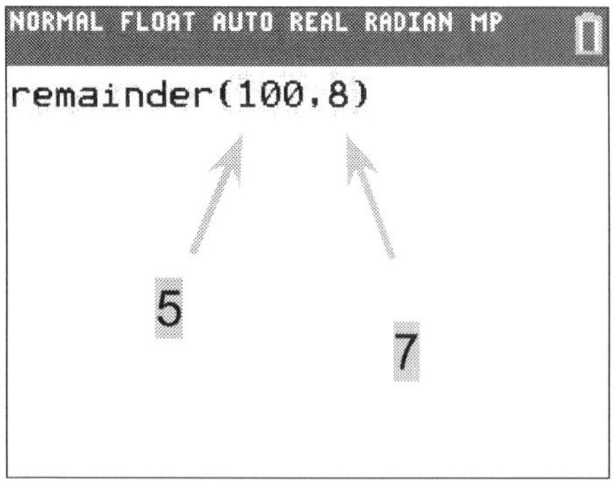

NOTE: There are several other functions you'll see in this list that can be calculated with the same steps.

- 8: lcm(" will calculate a least common multiple
- 9: gcd(" will calculate a greatest common divisor

*Place commas between your terms.

Logarithm with a Base not equal to 10:

1) Press “math”
2) Scroll down to “A: LogBASE(”
3) Press “enter”
4) Input base and what you are calculating the logarithm of

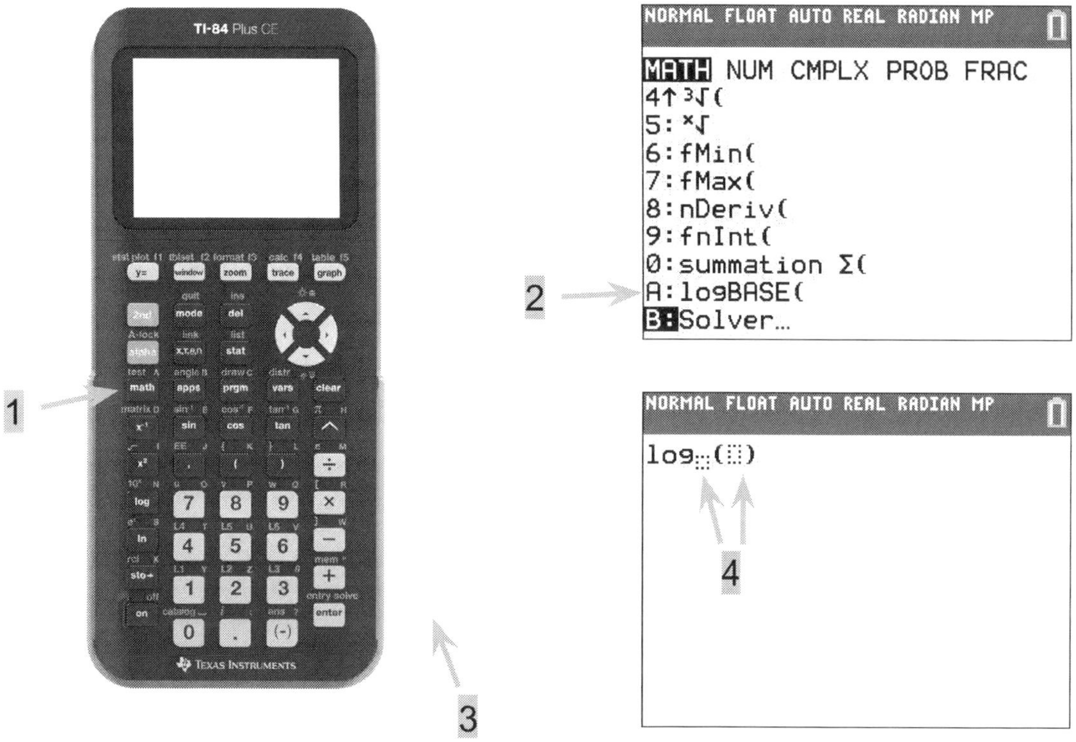

Scientific Notation

1) Press “mode”
2) Scroll down to second row and select “SCI”
3) Quit (Press 2nd and then “mode” to quit)

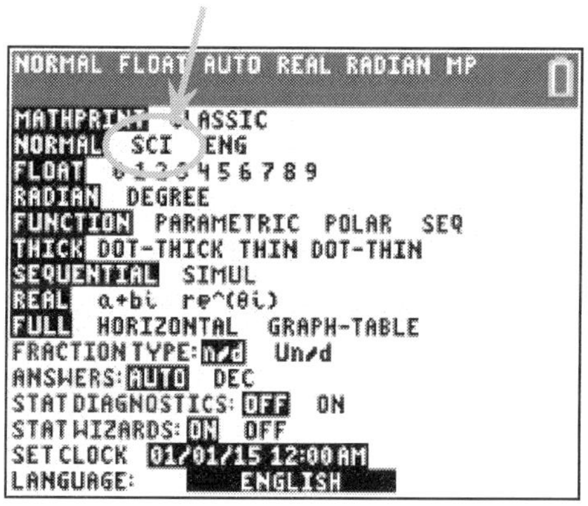

To find a zero (solution or root) by graphing:

1) Press "y="
2) Input function into Y1=
3) Press "graph" (the graph will appear in your window; if it does not, try zooming out by pressing "zoom" and scrolling down to "3: zoom out")
4) Press "2ND" and then "trace"
5) Scroll down to "2: zero" and press "enter"
6) Move the cursor to a spot on the curve to the LEFT of the zero. Push "enter"
7) Move the cursor to a spot on the curve to the RIGHT of the zero. Push "enter"
8) Push "enter" a third time
9) The x and y coordinates will appear at the bottom of the screen

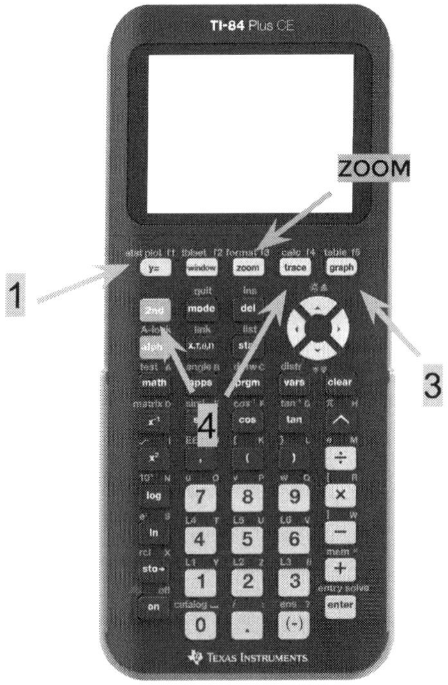

NOTE: You can find a maximum or minimum with the same procedure. In step 5, select:

- "3: minimum" to trace a minimum
- "4: maximum" to trace a maximum

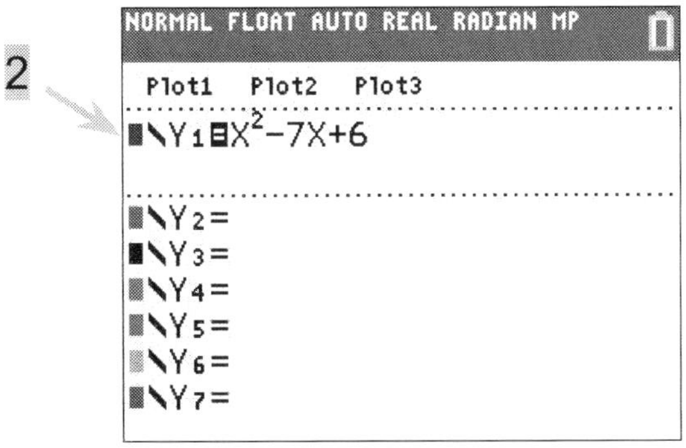

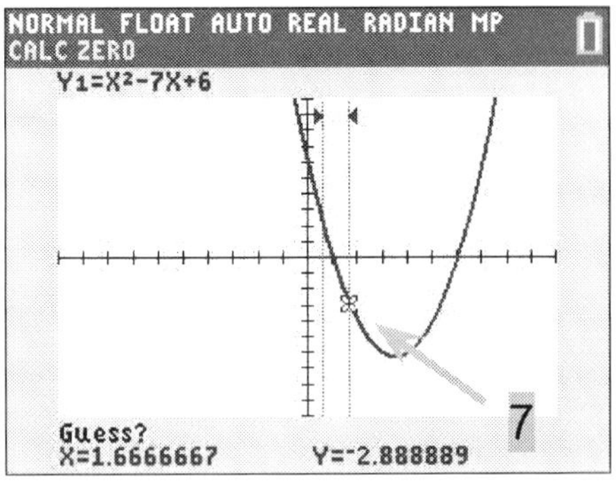

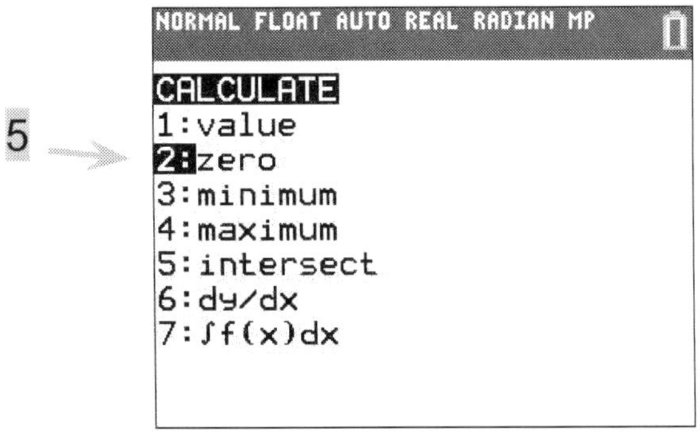

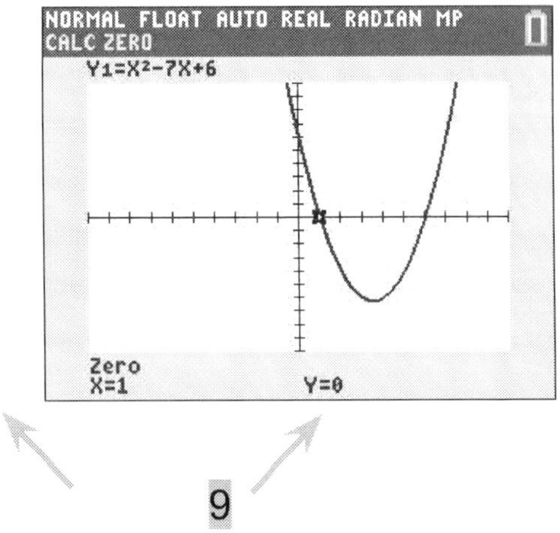

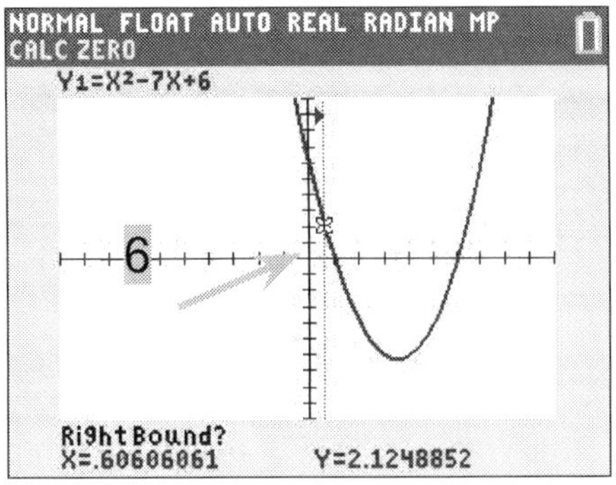

To find a point of intersection:

1) Press “y=”
2) Input first function into Y1=
3) Input second function into Y2=
4) Press “graph” (both graphs will appear in your window; if they do not, try zooming out by pressing “zoom” and scrolling down to “3: zoom out”)
5) Press “2ND” and then “trace”
6) Scroll down to “5: intersect” and press “enter”
7) Move the cursor to a spot near the intersection on the FIRST curve. Push “enter”
8) Move the cursor to a spot near the intersection on the SECOND curve. Push “enter”
9) Push “enter” a third time
10) The x and y coordinates will appear at the bottom of the screen

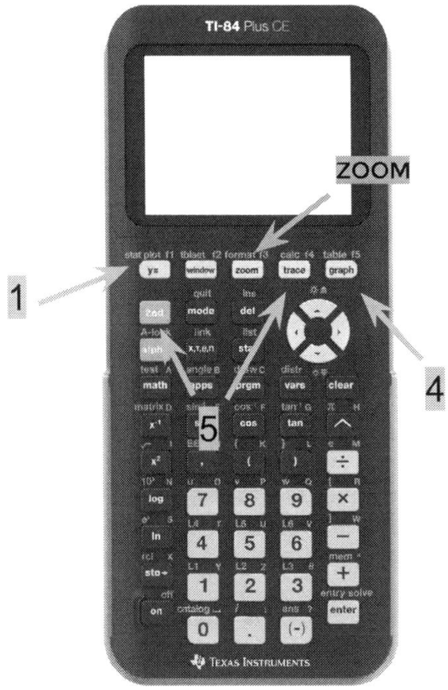

NOTE: This is a great way to solve equations that are difficult to solve by hand.

- Put one side of the equation into Y1=
- Put the other side of the equation into Y2=
- Trace the intersection

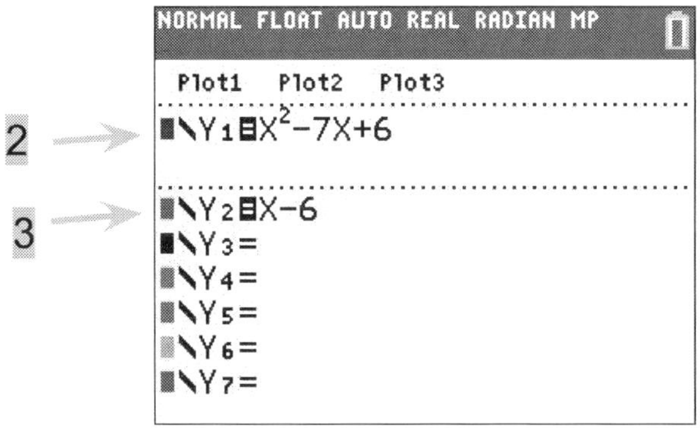

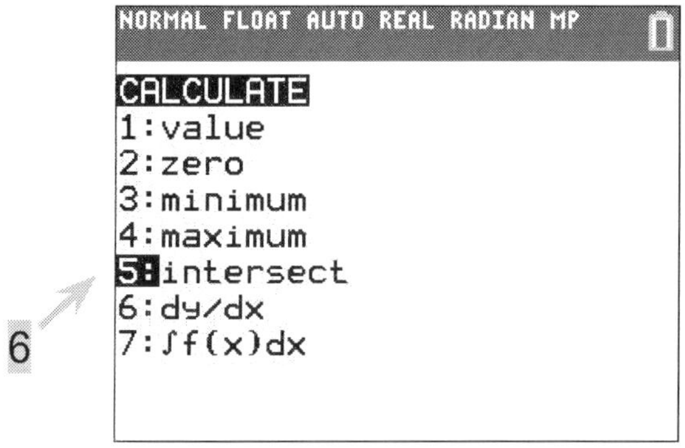

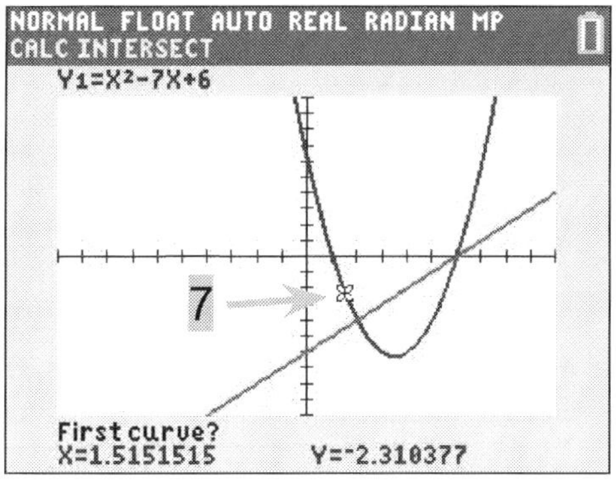

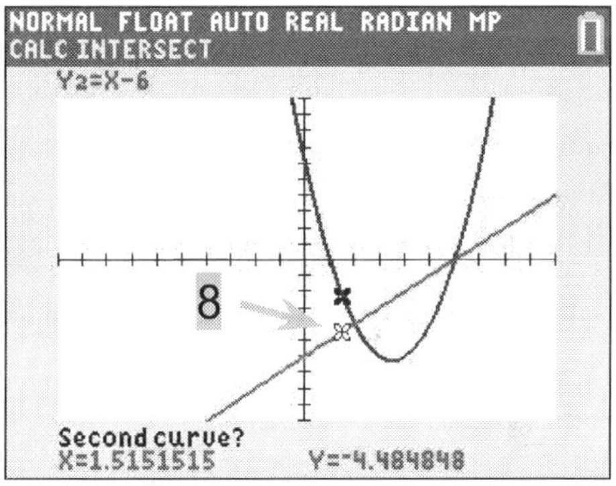

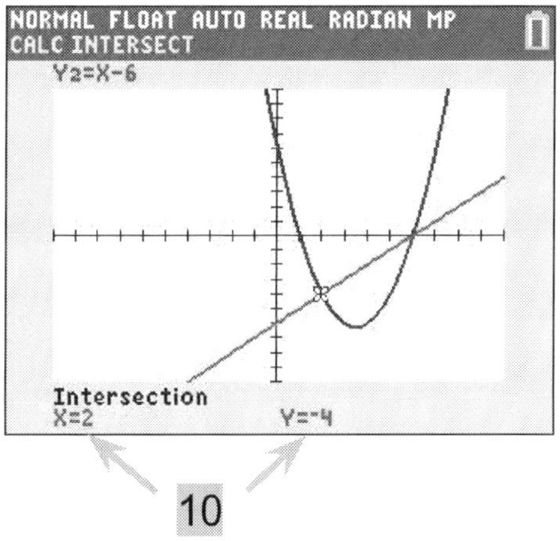

NOTE: A great way to test for **equivalency** (without needing to do the algebra) is to use the graphing component. Put one expression into Y1 and the other expression into Y2 and graph them both. If the functions are truly equivalent, they will have the same graphs.

They will also have the same table values. Viewing the table might be quicker than letting the calculator graph the entire functions. To locate a table:

1) Press “2nd”
2) Press “graph”

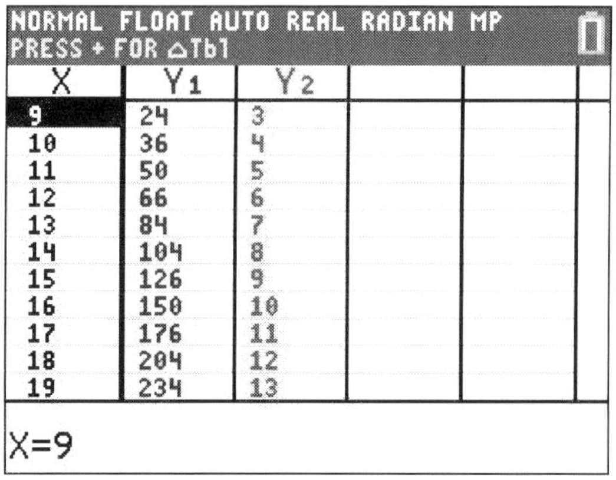

NORMAL FLOAT AUTO REAL RADIAN MP
PRESS + FOR △Tbl

X	Y1	Y2
9	24	3
10	36	4
11	50	5
12	66	6
13	84	7
14	104	8
15	126	9
16	150	10
17	176	11
18	204	12
19	234	13

X=9

NOTE: The physical graphs, trace functions, and table values can help you determine several features about a function without needing to perform any operations by hand. You can simply *observe* them. These features include:

1) Y- Intercepts and X- Intercepts (zeros)
2) Maximums & Minimums
3) Points of Intersection
4) Points of Discontinuity
5) Asymptotes
6) Limits
7) Equivalencies to other functions

To determine the factors of a number:

1) Press “y=”
2) Input that number divided by x into Y1
3) Press “2ND” and then “graph” to bring you to the table
4) Any x-y pairs that are whole numbers are factors of that initial value

2

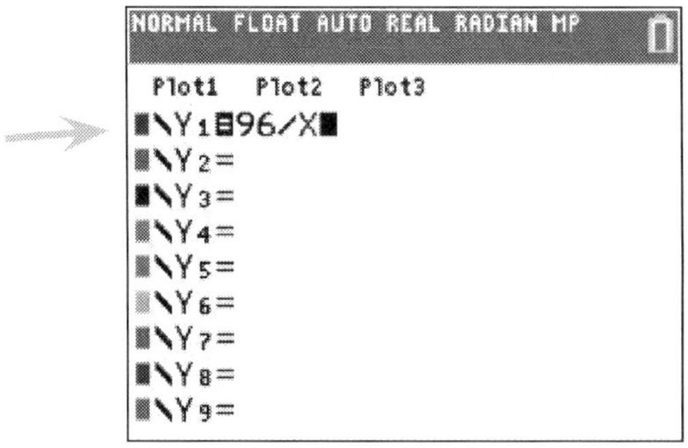

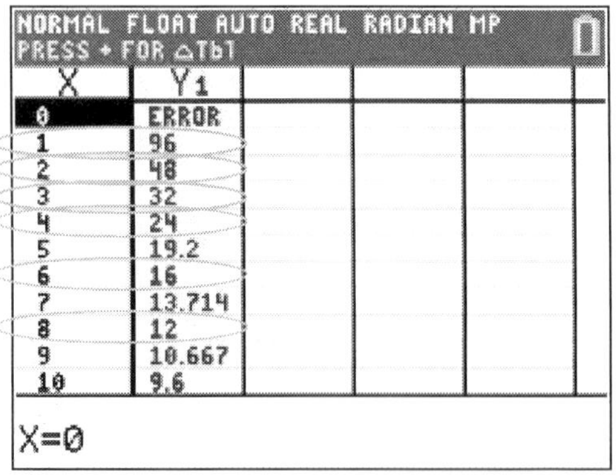

NORMAL FLOAT AUTO REAL RADIAN MP
PRESS + FOR △Tbl

X	Y1
0	ERROR
1	96
2	48
3	32
4	24
5	19.2
6	16
7	13.714
8	12
9	10.667
10	9.6

X=0

To find mean, median, and standard deviation for a data set.

1) Press “stat” and select “edit”
2) If it is a single list with no frequency, add the values into list 1 (L1)
3) Press “stat” and scroll right to “CALC” menu
4) Select “1-Var Stats”
5) Make sure “Freqlist” is blank and then push “enter” 3 times

    x = mean (average)
    σx = standard deviation
    med = median

6) If the list ***does*** have a frequency, enter the frequency of each term into list 2 (L2) and continue with steps 3 and 4
7) Scroll down to “FreqList” and input (L2) by pressing “2nd” and the number “2”
8) Press “enter” twice

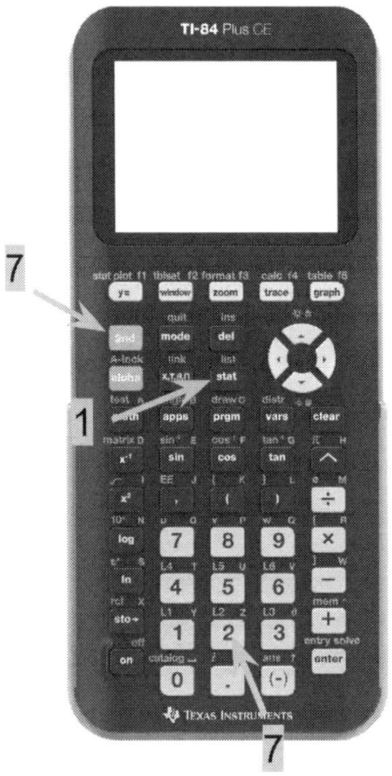

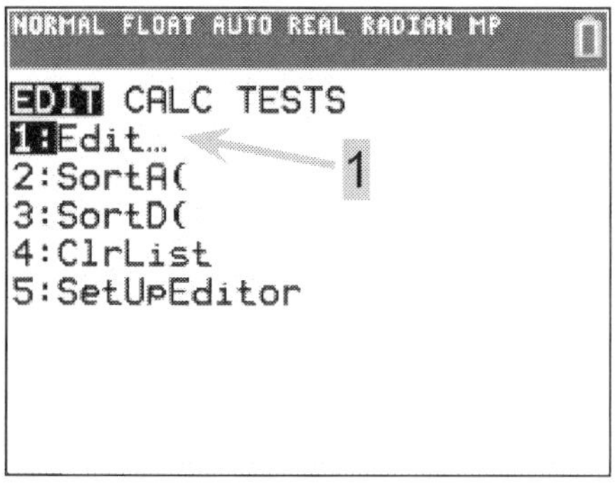

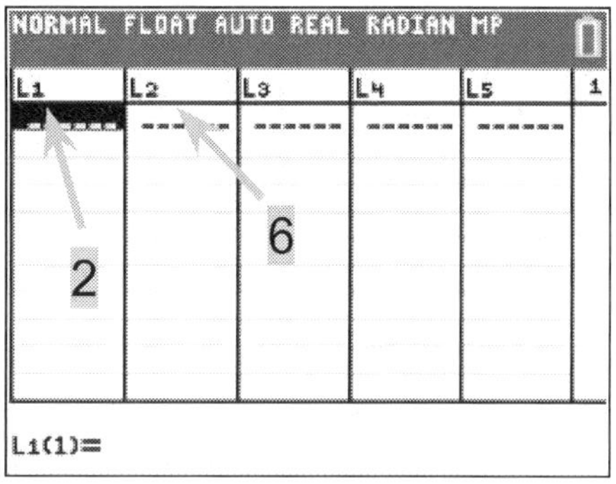

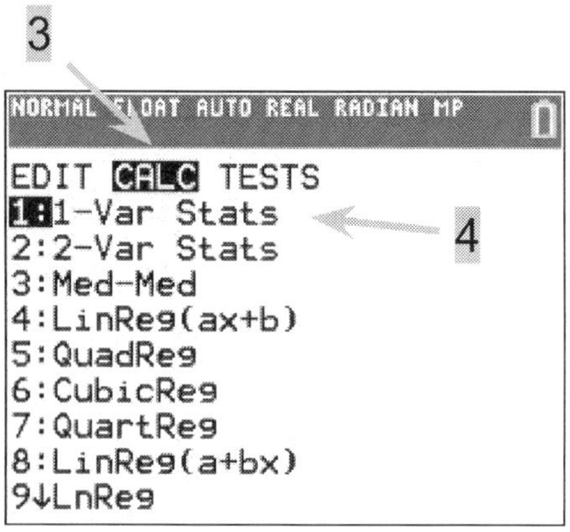

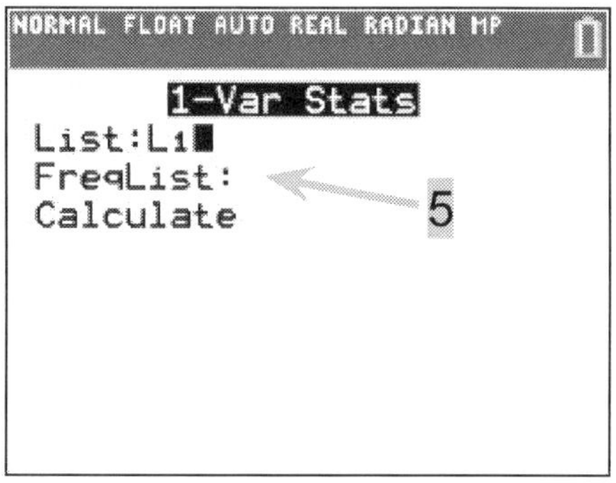

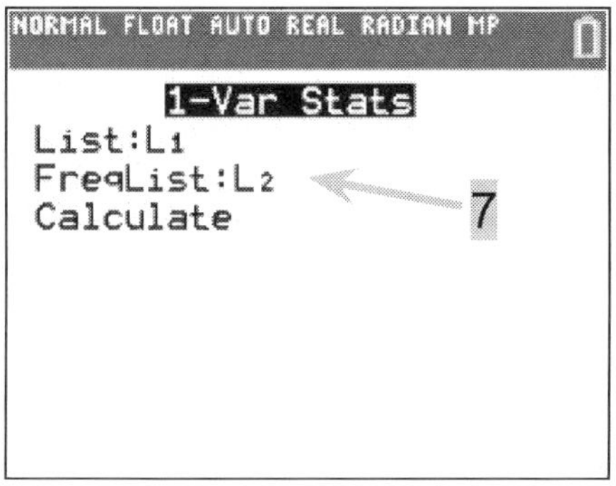

What you will see:

Scroll down to see more information (like the median)

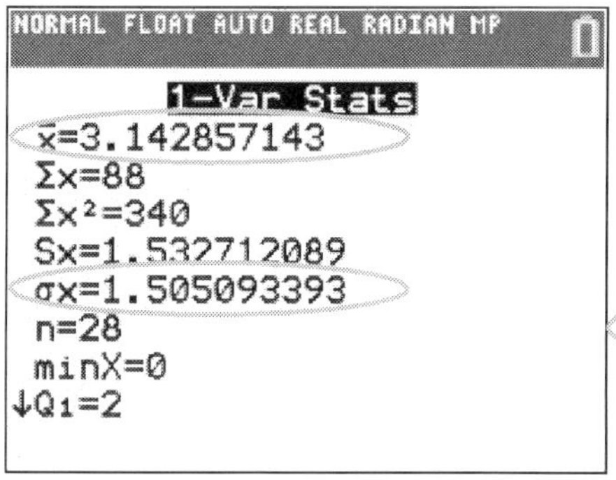

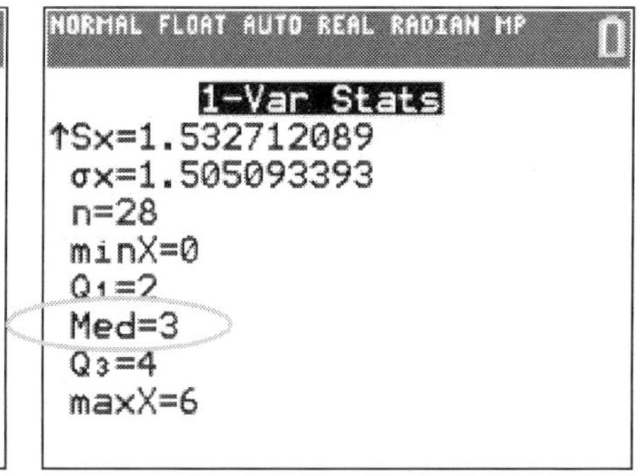

Practice Test 1

You are about to begin a full-length Practice Test. The test has four modules. The time allotted for each module is marked at the beginning of the module. Work on one module at a time. Use a timer to keep track of the time limits for every module.

Try to take the Practice Test under real test conditions. Find a quiet place to work, and set aside enough time to complete the test without being disturbed. At the end of the test, check your answers by referring to the Answer Key and fill in your raw score in the scorecard below. Also, note down the time taken by you for completing each module.

Pay particular attention to the questions that were answered incorrectly. Read the answer explanations and understand how to solve them.

My Score Card (Raw Score)

	Reading and Writing		Math	
	Module 1	Module 2	Module 1	Module 2
Out of	27	27	22	22
My Score	________	________	________	________
Time Taken	________	________	________	________

TEST BEGINS ON THE NEXT PAGE

Reading and Writing Test

27 QUESTIONS | 32 MINUTES

DIRECTIONS

The questions in this section address a number of important reading and writing skills. Each question includes one or more passages, which may include a table or graph. Read each passage and question carefully, and then choose the best answer to the question based on the passage(s). All questions in this section are multiple–choice with four answer choices. Each question has a single best answer.

1

Allowing goats to graze an area is one potential solution for removing unwanted weeds in terrain that is too rocky and remote to allow for cutting or herbicide spraying. Goats significantly reduce the incidence of the unwanted plants, but must be quickly removed to prevent them from eating everything else as well: goats lack ______.

Which choice completes the text with the most logical and precise word or phrase?

A) bias

B) prejudice

C) discrimination

D) bigotry

2

Anyone interested in a career in business needs superior communications skills. Not only are they essential to convey ideas to colleagues and explain plans clearly to ensure that work is completed effectively in a timely manner, but also they are needed to make proposals ______ to clients and potential investors.

Which choice completes the text with the most logical and precise word or phrase?

A) charismatic

B) irresistible

C) attractive

D) fascinating

CONTINUE

3

Explaining the coexistence of various plant and butterfly species is ______ to truly understand the region's biodiversity and the forces that sustain or reduce it. Such an understanding will help ecologists devise an appropriate plan that maximizes the limited funding available for conservation and that still allows for future development of the area.

Which choice completes the text with the most logical and precise word or phrase?

A) critical

B) perilous

C) condemning

D) analytical

4

The Hagia Sophia, built between 532 and 537 in Istanbul under the orders of the Roman Emperor Justinian I, has been alternately used for different religious purposes since that time. The cultural and historical value of the building and its contents are ______, as a wealth of splendid and unique details has been added over the centuries since its construction.

Which choice completes the text with the most logical and precise word or phrase?

A) congenial

B) incalculable

C) cumbersome

D) voluminous

5

By analyzing more than one million surface ocean observations from the Drake Passage, the researchers detected subtle differences between the CO_2 trends in the surface ocean and the atmosphere that suggest a strengthening of the carbon sink that is most pronounced during winter. Although the researchers aren't sure of the exact mechanism driving these changes, it's likely related to winter mixing with deep waters that have not had contact with the atmosphere for several hundred years. These results contrast with previous findings that showed that the Southern Ocean's CO_2 sink had been stagnant or weakening from the early 1990s to the early 2000s. "Given the importance of the Southern Ocean to the global oceans' role in absorbing atmospheric CO_2, these studies suggest that we must continue to expand our measurements in this part of the world despite the challenging environment," says Colm Sweeney, lead investigator on the Drake Passage study.

Which choice best states the main purpose of the text?

A) To emphasize the difficulty of collecting accurate data from the Southern Ocean

B) To illustrate the problems with amassing an adequate database on the Southern Ocean

C) To place the results of the Drake Passage study in the wider context of other studies

D) To highlight the need to correct the problem of CO_2 absorption before it is too late

6

The following text is from Oscar Wilde's 1888 short story "The Selfish Giant."

> Every afternoon, as they were coming from school, the children used to go and play in the Giant's garden. <u>It was a large lovely garden, with soft green grass.</u> Here and there over the grass stood beautiful flowers like stars, and there were twelve peach-trees that in the spring-time broke out into delicate blossoms of pink and pearl, and in the autumn bore rich fruit. The birds sat on the trees and sang so sweetly that the children used to stop their games in order to listen to them.

Which choice best states the function of the underlined sentence in the text as a whole?

A) It sets up the description of location presented in the sentences that follow.

B) It establishes a sense of contrast with the description in the previous sentence.

C) It elaborates on the previous sentence's description of the characters.

D) It introduces an ominous undercurrent to the sentences that follow.

7

An antibody-based drug is one candidate for a more effective, longer lasting overdose treatment. To explore this possibility, a team at Scripps Research Institute led by Kim D. Janda first treated mice with a vaccine that stimulated the animals to produce a slew of different antibodies against fentanyl, some of which helped protect the mice from overdoses. In the new work, the team recovered antibodies from the mice, purified them, and screened them for their ability to bind fentanyl. The team evaluated six of these antibodies against nine fentanyl analogs commonly confiscated by law enforcement. One antibody, 6A4, demonstrated the best fentanyl-binding affinity and had a six-day half-life in mice.

Which choice best explains why the author most likely included the information that the drugs were "commonly confiscated by law enforcement"?

A) To explain how the researchers obtained drugs for experimentation

B) To indicate that the research would apply to overdoses in authentic cases

C) To eliminate the argument that the trials were improperly conducted

D) To establish why special permits were needed to experiment with the drugs

8

Text 1

The views of most individuals are limited to their own happiness; and the workmen whom I beheld so busy in the arsenal of Venice saw nothing but what was good in the labor for which they received... We must have the telescope of philosophy to make us perceive distant ills; further, we know that there are individuals of our species to whom the immediate misery of others is nothing in comparison with their own advantage—for we know that in every age there have been found men very willing to perform the office of executioner.

Text 2

... it is by no means a utopian undertaking to unite the whole world of nations in such a federation ... Let <u>men but understand themselves, and the mechanism of their emotions by which they are brought into this perennial catastrophe, and they will be ready enough to take gigantic measures to prevent it.</u>

Which statement made by the author of passage 1 would support the underlined concluding argument made by the author of passage 2?

A) "We must have the telescope of philosophy to perceive distant ills."

B) "The views of most individuals are limited to their own happiness"

C) "there are individuals of our species to whom the immediate misery of others is nothing in comparison with their own advantage"

D) "in every age there have been found men very willing to perform the office of executioner"

CONTINUE

9

The following text is adapted from Herman Melville's 1851 novel, *Moby Dick; or The Whale.*

> Call me Ishmael. Some years ago—never mind how long precisely—having little or no money in my purse, and nothing particular to interest me on shore, I thought I would sail about a little and see the watery part of the world. It is a way I have of driving off the spleen and regulating the circulation. Whenever I find myself growing grim about the mouth; whenever it is a damp, drizzly November in my soul; whenever I find myself involuntarily bringing up the rear of every funeral I meet—then, I account it high time to get to sea as soon as I can. If they but knew it, almost all men in their degree, some time or other, cherish very nearly the same feelings towards the ocean with me.

Which choice best summarizes the text?

A) A ship captain describes the reasons for embarking on his career.

B) A sailor reminisces about the impetus for setting out on a voyage.

C) A merchant sailor develops an argument about his poor salary.

D) An impoverished man explains how he degenerated to his current condition.

10

The common solution of building more roads may not have the desired effect of reducing rush-hour traffic. For example, the Katy Freeway project in Houston cost millions of dollars and the upshot was that congestion got worse, with travel times increased by 55% during the evening rush hour and by a third in the mornings. The reason for that is something called "induced demand," a term introduced in the 1960s by economists. It relates to the phenomenon that if more of a good is produced, more is consumed. In the same way, if more roads are provided, more people are encouraged to drive.

According to the text, what is induced demand?

A) An idea that contradicts a widespread belief that congestion is the result of road building

B) A phenomenon that is rarely taken into account when road systems are being planned

C) A theory that is understood by city planners and has affected their traditional solutions to traffic congestion

D) A concept that can be mitigated by educating consumers about the potential effects

11

Published in 1794 by William Blake, "The Tyger" is a classic poem from a larger collection titled Songs of Experience. The poem uses the imagery of fire to delve into the question of who might have created such a dangerous creature: _____

Which quotation from "The Tyger" most effectively illustrates the claim?

A) "In what distant deeps or skies, / Burnt the fire of thine eyes?"

B) "In what furnace was thy brain? /What the anvil? what dread grasp / Dare its deadly terrors clasp?"

C) "When the stars threw down their spears, / And water'd heaven with their tears, / Did he smile his work to see?

D) "Did he who made the Lamb make thee?"

12

The following text is adapted from Mother Jones's speech to coal miners picketing in Charlestown, West Virginia, on August 15, 1912.

> They wouldn't keep their dog where they keep you fellows. You know that. They have a good place for their dogs and a slave to take care of them. The mine owners' wives will take the dogs up, and say, "I love you, dea–h." My friends, the day for petting dogs is gone; the day for raising children to a nobler manhood and better womanhood is here! You have suffered; I know you have suffered. I was with you nearly three years in this State. I went to jail. I went to the federal courts, but I never took any back water!

In the text, Mother Jones anticipates and addresses which counterargument about her credibility?

A) She is not qualified to speak for the miners because she is not a miner herself.

B) Her involvement could harm the miners' cause because she had been in jail.

C) She does not have adequate contacts in the government to enforce her demands.

D) She has been more caring of pets in the past than she has of human workers.

CONTINUE

13

Chili Peppers Exposed to Salt Stress

NaCl concen-tration (mM)	Average days to first flower	Average days to first fruit	Average number of fruits
0	23.66	48	6
30	23.66	52	3
60	31.66	66	2
90	39.66	0	0
120	40.33	0	0

This study about salt in the soil of growing chili plants indicated that increasing NaCl concentrations significantly delayed flowering and fruit ripening and significantly reduced the fruits' number, size, fresh mass and vitamins B6, B12 and C concentrations, but increased capsaicinoid concentration and consequently the fruit's tangy flavor. For example, plants ______. Thus, salt stress reduced the fruit yields and deteriorated fruit nutritional quality by reducing vitamin concentrations. Further study is necessary to check the implication of capsaicinoid synthetase activity in the increase of the capsaicinoid concentration under salt stress in our local chili cultivar fruits.

Which choice most effectively uses data from the table to complete the example?

A) subjected to high NaCl concentrations were highest in capsaicinoid.

B) subjected to high NaCl concentrations had lower nutritional value.

C) with a NaCl concentration of 90 mM took 16 extra days to flower beyond ones with no salt.

D) with a NaCl concentration of 30 mM averaged 52 chili fruits on the plant.

14

A study led by Sarah Mann aimed to provide a fuller picture of the vegan diet in which no animal products are eaten, encompassing the health of the vegan diet as well as related ethical beliefs by studying scientific and popular literature in tandem. Furthermore, the study aimed to provide an insider's perspective of the vegan diet as a means of combating stereotypes and making the diet more relatable/understandable to those who are not vegan. The research was conducted in two parts – literature review and interview study. The interviews included questions targeting personal history, related health beliefs, factors influencing the decision to become vegan, and diet.

Based on the text, why did Mann include personal interviews in her study?

A) She assumed she would find a conflict between interviews and scientific studies.

B) She expected to resolve an outstanding debate about the health benefits of veganism.

C) She decided that most of the current literature was biased against the subject of veganism.

D) She hoped to better understand the viewpoint of people who opted to become vegan.

CONTINUE

15

Scientists studying at a site called Hegra in modern Jordan found the tomb of a woman called Hinat. Her name was identified in an inscription at the entrance which claims the tomb was bought by herself and belonging to her and her descendants. Archaeologists have found the remains of over 80 people buried inside, though none of them are identified. The tomb also contains many well-preserved artifacts that offer insight into the Nabataean culture that flourished in the region about 2,000 years ago.

Based on the passage, what is most likely true about Hinat?

A) She was a royal Nabataean personage.

B) She had her own tomb because she never married.

C) She is buried with many of her ancestors.

D) She was one of the 80 people buried in the tomb.

16

It is inevitable that a world-wide event such as the Olympics has been canceled multiple times since its introduction in 1896. One notable example is when London called _____ the 1944 Summer Olympics due to World War II, as were the Winter Olympics scheduled to be held in Cortina d'Ampezzo, Italy.

Which choice completes the text so that it conforms to the conventions of Standard English?

A) on

B) up

C) off

D) around

17

Yuval Noah Harari is an Israeli historian who regularly discussed global issues with world leaders. Considered one of the foremost thinkers of his time, his current interest is delving into difficult questions combining biology and history, such as asking whether people _____ happier since the Stone Age to the present.

Which choice completes the text so that it conforms to the conventions of Standard English?

A) become

B) are becoming

C) have become

D) will have become

CONTINUE

18

Energy access and gender are deeply entwined components of the global development agenda. The transformative effect on women of access to affordable, reliable, and sustainable modern energy _____ well established by countless research studies.

Which choice completes the text so that it conforms to the conventions of Standard English?

A) are

B) were

C) has been

D) have been

19

Many theories have been proposed for how life originated on Earth, and attention has recently been directed towards hydrothermal vents, _____ occur deep underwater where continental plates diverge. In 2019, scientists from University College London conducted an experiment simulating the concentrated gasses and minerals and created protocells, or the building blocks for living molecules.

Which choice completes the text so that it conforms to the conventions of Standard English?

A) which

B) they

C) that

D) these

20

Attending the cinema allows for the exercise of personal preferences and the human need for distinction. In a nutshell, cinema attendance can be a personally expressive experience, good _____ therapeutic at the same time.

Which choice completes the text so that it conforms to the conventions of Standard English?

A) fun, and,

B) fun, and

C) fun; and

D) fun—and

21

In a 2022 paper written by Kyle Rupp and _____ the researchers explore the complex mechanisms behind the automatic ability that most people have to recognize features of the human voice, even to the point of distinguishing subtleties of emotion and intention.

Which choice completes the text so that it conforms to the conventions of Standard English?

A) associates

B) associates,

C) associates—

D) associates:

22

Even within a single musical tradition, there may be fine distinctions based on the character and color of the voice. ______ a lyric soprano has a light, refined tone and a dramatic soprano has a powerful, emotional tone.

Which choice completes the text so that it conforms to the conventions of Standard English?

A) For example among operatic voices

B) For example, among operatic voices:

C) For example: among operatic voices,

D) For example, among operatic voices,

23

The energy industry has long met demand by varying the rate at which it produces fuel. Controlling the output of an oil-fired power plant is much like changing the speed of a car—press the accelerator and more gas flows to the engine. ______ the wind cannot be turned up or down. Smart software is one solution to make wind farms more efficient and responsive.

Which choice completes the text with the most logical transition?

A) Nevertheless,

B) Despite this,

C) Furthermore,

D) However,

24

Social work can take a toll, but it is deeply rewarding when you can see a positive change in someone else's life. There are many different career paths in social work. ______ there are some administrative roles, most all social workers deal directly with clients. So regardless of the field you choose, you are most likely to interact with people on a regular basis.

Which choice completes the text with the most logical transition?

A) However,

B) While

C) Nevertheless

D) Therefore,

25

The Paleo diet includes meat, fruit, and vegetables in an attempt to recreate the eating patterns of prehistoric hunter-gatherers. Although it is a popular way to lose weight in the short term, there is no long-term credible research confirming its efficacy. ______ many scientists point out that the diet is misguided because wild grains were consumed well before the advent of farming.

Which choice completes the text with the most logical transition?

A) Subsequently,

B) Nevertheless,

C) Moreover,

D) Therefore,

CONTINUE

26

The London and Northwestern Railway War Memorial is a First World War memorial outside Euston Station in London, England. The memorial was designed by Reginald Wynn Owen and _____ employees of the London and Northwestern Railway (LNWR) who were killed in the First World War.

Which word most logically completes the text?

A) commemorates

B) idolizes

C) celebrates

D) overlooks

27

In May, 1992, the Ministry of Forestry in Vietnam and the World Wildlife Federation jointly conducted a survey and came across an astounding discovery: the first new large mammal species identified in half a century. Called a saola, <u>both the males and females have horns.</u> Almost nothing is known of their behavior, though they are classified as critically endangered.

The writer wants to change the underlined portion to emphasize the rarity of the saola. Which choice most effectively achieves that goal?

A) The first indication of a new species was when scientists discovered a skull in a hunter's home.

B) There are currently none in captivity and they live in mountains in Vietnam and Laos.

C) Since the initial sighting, they have only been positively identified on four occasions.

D) They have the fanciful common name of "Asian unicorns," though they have two horns.

No Test Material On This Page

Reading Test

27 QUESTIONS | 32 MINUTES

DIRECTIONS

The questions in this section address a number of important reading and writing skills. Each question includes one or more passages, which may include a table or graph. Read each passage and question carefully, and then choose the best answer to the question based on the passage(s). All questions in this section are multiple–choice with four answer choices. Each question has a single best answer.

1

Any country, city, or rural village could be, in fact, its own unique tourism magnet. The tourism business, though, is <u>broader</u> than just the destination. Considerations need to be made for transportation, hotels and guest accommodations, and services that link the various components of a trip, such as guide services in national parks or city bus tours.

As used in the text, what does the word "broader" most nearly mean?

A) more pronounced

B) more general

C) more spacious

D) more extensive

2

The following text is from Jane Austen's 1811 novel, "Sense and Sensibility."

> Many were the tears shed by them in their last adieus to a place so much beloved. "And you, ye well-known trees," said Marianne, "but you will continue the same, unconscious of the pleasure or the regret you occasion, and <u>insensible</u> of any change in those who walk under your shade! But who will remain to enjoy you?"

As used in the text, what does the word "insensible" most nearly mean?

A) comatose

B) negligible

C) unaware

D) insentient

CONTINUE

3

The following text is adapted from F. Scott Fitzgerald's 1922 novel, *The Beautiful and the Damned.*

> Now Adam J. Patch left his father's farm in Tarrytown early in sixty-one to join a New York cavalry regiment. He came home from the war a major, charged into Wall Street, and amid much fuss, fume, applause, and ill will he gathered to himself some seventy-five million dollars.

As used in the text, what does the word "fume" most nearly mean?

A) exhaust

B) stench

C) pollution

D) ire

4

Sometimes, behaviors have underlying reasons that are not initially apparent, as shown through a classic experiment by Walter Mischel. During the 1960s, Mischel placed a marshmallow piece in front of 600 children aged 4–6. About a third were willing to wait 15 minutes to get a whole marshmallow, and those children got higher SAT scores years later. However, Mischel's theory that willpower contributed to future success was somewhat arbitrary. A later experiment conducted by Tyler Watts and associates included a broader analysis of ethnicity and social status and determined that economic background most closely predicted the demonstrated behavior.

Which choice best states the main purpose of the text?

A) It presents the study by Tyler Watts to show that most behavioral psychology experiments are flawed.

B) It argues that experiments regarding behavior should be performed multiple times in order to determine true correlations.

C) It explains a significant problem in the current understanding of willpower in young children.

D) It discusses the study by Walter Mischel to show that there may be alternate explanations in an apparently obvious situation.

CONTINUE

5

The following text is adapted from Abraham Lincoln's last public address, given April 11, 1865.

> Some twelve thousand voters in the heretofore slave-state of Louisiana have sworn allegiance to the Union, assumed to be the rightful political power of the State, held elections, organized a State government, adopted a free-state constitution, and empowered the Legislature to confer the elective franchise upon the colored man. Now, if we reject, and spurn them, we do our utmost to disorganize and disperse them. We in effect say to the white men, "You are worthless, or worse--we will neither help you, nor be helped by you." To the blacks we say, "This cup of liberty which these, your old masters, hold to your lips, we will dash from you, and leave you to the chances of gathering the spilled and scattered contents in some vague and undefined when, where, and how."

In the text, what does the imagery of a cup of liberty mainly serve to emphasize?

A) The generosity of the Union in giving freed slaves certain benefits

B) The advances made by the Union in protecting the rights of former slaves

C) The unconscious way in which many people accept their freedoms

D) The precarious nature of the freedoms granted to former slaves in Louisiana

6

The median annual wage for urban and regional planners was $73,050 in May 2018. The median wage is the wage at which half the workers in an occupation earned more than that amount and half earned less. The lowest 10 percent earned less than $45,180, and the highest 10 percent earned more than $114,170. Employment of urban and regional planners is projected to grow 11 percent from 2018 to 2028, much faster than the average for all occupations. Demographic, transportation, and environmental changes will drive employment growth for planners. Within cities, urban planners will be needed to develop revitalization projects and address issues associated with population growth, environmental degradation, the movement of people and goods, and resource scarcity.

Which choice best states the function of the underlined sentence in the text as whole?

A) To define a term provided in the passage

B) To point out that the median wage is an insufficient measurement

C) To suggest a possible reason for the wide range in salaries

D) To provide support for the claim that employment is predicted to grow

7

Text 1

Depression is an illness of brain circuitry and chemistry that causes and is caused by changes in mood, thinking, and behavior. Behavioral activation is a type of talk therapy that helps patients free themselves from negative mood spirals by identifying a connection between actions and emotions, and gradually add small and enjoyable actions back into their lives. The process decreases avoidance, bolsters peer connection, and improves engagement in activities. This non-intrusive solution takes time, but is much healthier than covering the problem with medications.

Text 2

Studies have shown that a single ketamine infusion can often rapidly relieve depressive symptoms within hours in people who have not responded to conventional antidepressants, which typically take weeks or months to work. However, widespread use of ketamine for treatment-resistant depression has raised concerns about side effects, including feelings of floating, queasiness, visual distortions, and numbness. These conditions occurred in at least half of the participants of one study, but none persisted for more than four hours. To overcome these problems, ongoing research is necessary to develop a more practical rapid-acting antidepressant that works in the brain similarly to ketamine.

Based on the texts, how would the author of Text 1 most likely view the conclusion drawn by the author in the final sentence of Text 2?

A) Agreement, because she knows most depression treatments are insufficient

B) Reservation, because she promotes less invasive ways to address depression

C) Confusion, because she feels that the drug does not need any modification

D) Disapproval, because she contends that drug therapies are unacceptable

CONTINUE

8

The following text is adapted from Jefferson Keel's 2011 statement, "The Indian Reorganization Act—75 Years Later."

> Our predecessors had a shared vision. Indian reservations should be places where the old ways are maintained, our languages are spoken, and our children learn our traditions and pass them on. They are places where there are fish in the stream and game in the field, and food grows wild; places where our people can live and be Indian. At the same time, this vision includes modern life, economic development to sustain our people; safety and respectful relationships with our neighbors; and the blessings of education, health care and modern technology. This vision was shared by the U.S. Congress in 1934 when it passed the Indian Reorganization Act. With the IRA, Congress renewed its trust responsibility to protect and restore our tribal homelands and the Indian way of life.

What is the main idea of the text?

A) The Indian Reorganization Act is a policy in keeping with the view of the earlier Indian people themselves.

B) The Indian Reorganization Act was written by Indian predecessors in order to preserve traditional culture.

C) The Indian Reorganization Act was created in the effort to deny Native Americans the basic rights they wished for.

D) The Indian Reorganization Act has been successful in helping Native American cultures to thrive since it was enacted.

9

The following text is adapted from Fyodor Dostoevsky's 1848 short story collection, "White Nights and Other Stories."

> I came back to the town very late, and it had struck ten as I was going towards my lodgings. My way lay along the canal embankment, where at that hour you never meet a soul. It is true that I live in a very remote part of the town. I walked along singing, for when I am happy I am always humming to myself like every happy man who has no friend or acquaintance with whom to share his joy. Suddenly I had a most unexpected adventure.

According to the text, what is the reason the narrator is walking along the embankment late at night?

A) He wanted to avoid meeting other people.

B) He was escaping the pressures of the city.

C) He was returning to his quarters.

D) He sought more excitement in his life.

CONTINUE

10

As for tidal devices, the environmental impacts are considered comparably small. Wave devices will represent a much lower collision risk compared to offshore wind devices but they could create a risk of underwater collisions for diving birds. In general, environmental impacts will very much depend on the size of installation and the location selected. Potential positive effects such as the creation of roosting sites and habitat enhancement for marine birds might occur as well. The majority of the studies recommend that commercial-scale installations of ocean energy technology should be accompanied by research studies on local environmental impacts.

According to the text, which of the following will most determine how much a tidal system alters the environment?

A) The placement in the ocean

B) The number of moving parts

C) The number of research studies about it

D) The total energy it generates

11

Over the past 30 years, scientists have discovered many dinosaurs from the group known as Carcharodontosauridae, but a lack of complete fossils led to many assumptions about their structure and movement. However, a recent find in Argentina of a species named *Meraxes gigas* gives new insights. Standing 11 meters (36 feet) and weighing 4 tons, the carnivore probably appeared very much like the unrelated *Tyrannosaurus rex.* This conclusion is partly based on the discovery of an almost intact arm bone that is extremely short like those of *T. rex.*

Which finding, if true, would most strongly support the scientists' conclusion?

A) *M. gigas* and *T. rex* were discovered to have lived in time periods separated by about 20 million years.

B) The skull bones from the *M. gigas* fossil are oversized in proportion to the body, as are those of *T. rex* fossils.

C) The average size of an adult *T. rex* varied greatly, between 5 tons and almost 7 tons.

D) Remains from both *T. rex* and M. gigas show that they both were carnivores which preyed on mostly herbivorous dinosaurs.

CONTINUE

12

Biodiversity: Trees in Southern Ontario
(percentage of total trees)

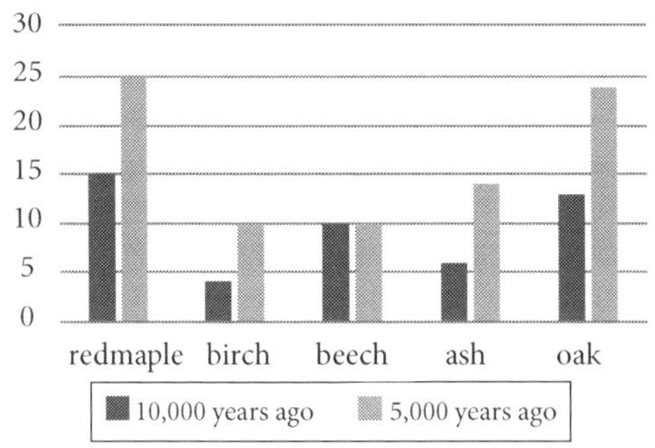

In 2003, a team of researchers studied ancient forest diversity through analyzing pollen samples in a lakebed. "What we are seeing is huge variability within tree populations over time," said scientist James Clark. For example,_____ He explained that this variability means they overlap in ways that determine which species are going to thrive and which are going to go extinct. He also proposed that the variability might itself represent a stabilizing mechanism. Clark emphasized, however, that even though the role of stabilizing mechanisms remains unknown, the results from the studies offer cautionary lessons.

Which choice most effectively uses data from the table to complete the example?

A) the percent of red maple increased by 10 percent over the time period studied.

B) the populations of beech remained stable over the time period in the study.

C) there were always fewer birch trees than ash trees in the time period studied.

D) the percentage of oak trees decreased by approximately 10 percent over the study period.

13

A seller who makes a claim about how much money a person can earn opening a franchise must provide a document that says in big type: EARNINGS CLAIM STATEMENT REQUIRED BY LAW. This document has to include many statistics including the specifics of the claim; the start and end date those earnings were achieved; the number and percentage of people who got those results or better, and any information about those people that may differ from you – for example, the part of the country where they live. Since the Rule gives the right to see written proof for the seller's earnings claims, savvy buyers exercise that right and study those materials carefully.

Which statement best identifies one of the author's implicit claims about the Earnings Claim Statement Required by Law?

A) Demographic factors may affect a franchise's earnings.

B) The earnings claims must be updated every month.

C) Most sellers do not provide the statement willingly.

D) The document is required with any building purchase.

CONTINUE

14

A serious financial investment is needed to bring Sub–Saharan Africa up to par with the global marketplace. Africa has huge potential for growth in its tourism market, but heavy tourism traffic might have a negative impact on the environment, cultural stereotypes could be exploited, and the disparity between wealthy tourists and service workers earning a modest wage may lend itself to divisions and social friction. Tourism demands higher levels of security and public health at all levels. Money spent on tourism development is money not spent on schools or clinics. On the other hand, without tourism income, there are no jobs.

One conclusion that can be drawn about the negative impact of tourism in Africa is that

A) jobs created may not provide adequate employment for all community members.

B) most of the income from tourism will not benefit the local communities at all.

C) an increase in tourism would result in a loss of local culture and traditions.

D) individuals who work in the industry may become resentful of visitors.

15

You must respect copyright laws when composing music. When you sample _____ artist's music without obtaining permission, you're infringing on the copyright to that work, no matter how big or how small a portion of it you actually use.

Which choice completes the text so that it conforms to the conventions of Standard English?

A) another

B) other

C) every

D) others

16

Although many people feel that the court system is too complicated and takes too long to bring a criminal to justice, it is an essential part of a democratic government. Imagine a world in which a _____ guilty person is condemned to death without a trial or any method of recourse.

Which choice completes the text so that it conforms to the conventions of Standard English?

A) presumed

B) presumption

C) presumably

D) presumptive

CONTINUE

17

Known best for his famous *Lord of the Rings* trilogy, author J.R.R. Tolkien also completed a translation of the epic poem "Beowulf" in 1926. His son found the manuscript and had it published in 2014, 40 years after _____ death.

Which choice completes the text so that it conforms to the conventions of Standard English?

A) his

B) Tolkiens

C) Tolkiens'

D) Tolkien's

18

Recently, astronomers discovered two new rocky planets approximately the size of Earth. Smaller than our Sun, _____ making the two planets orbiting it potentially close enough to study their atmospheres in detail. Since the cooler of the two is estimated to be 543 degrees Fahrenheit (284 degrees Celsius), there is little chance of life as we know it, though.

Which choice completes the text so that it conforms to the conventions of Standard English?

A) there are only 33 light years between the red dwarf star HD260655 and our Solar System,

B) only 33 light years separate the red dwarf star HD260655 from our Solar System,

C) our Solar System is only 33 light years away from the red dwarf star HD260655,

D) the red dwarf star HD260655 is only 33 light years away from our solar system,

CONTINUE

19

In 1967, Kenyan writer Ngugi wa Thiong'o worked as a lecturer in the department of English at the University of ______ "A Grain of Wheat in July" in the same year. He became instrumental in a movement that advanced African literature.

Which choice completes the text so that it conforms to the conventions of Standard English?

A) Nairobi and published

B) Nairobi, and published

C) Nairobi and published,

D) Nairobi, and published,

20

People often join martial arts such as karate, judo, and taekwondo in order to increase their amount of weekly exercise in an interesting way. Those who participate for extended periods, though, typically cite the development of personal qualities—particularly ______ the reason they continue.

Which choice completes the text so that it conforms to the conventions of Standard English?

A) self-control—

B) self-control—as

C) self-control—which is

D) self-control— they say is

21

Rainwater harvesting is the collection of run-off from a structure or other impervious surface in order to store it for later use. Rainwater collection systems can be as simple ______ rain in a rain barrel or as elaborate as harvesting rainwater into large cisterns to supply your entire household demand.

Which choice completes the text so that it conforms to the conventions of Standard English?

A) as: collecting

B) as, collecting

C) as—collecting

D) as collecting

22

The delicate art of Kamāl ud-Dīn Behzād, who was born circa 1455, is often considered the apogee of Islamic miniature paintings. Director of a workshop in the Herat Academy, Behzād had great influence, and his work was copied extensively both ______ his lifetime.

Which choice completes the text so that it conforms to the conventions of Standard English?

A) during, and after

B) during and after,

C) during—and after

D) during and after

CONTINUE

23

Most people have heard of search and rescue dogs, which assist the police and other responders in finding victims of crimes or natural disasters. There are two work methods that the dogs follow.. Trailing dogs follow the specific scent of one person along the path that the person took. _____ air-scent dogs sniff the general vicinity until they find any individual in the search region.

Which choice completes the text with the most logical transition?

A) Because of this,

B) By contrast,

C) Therefore,

D) Moreover,

24

It may seem that all mosquitoes hate the human race, but in reality, only the females require blood to obtain a specific protein needed to produce eggs. Males do not drink blood. _____ even if they wanted to, they do not have the mouthparts to pierce skin. It turns out that mosquitoes get most of their energy from plant nectar and fruit.

Which choice completes the text with the most logical transition?

A) Therefore,

B) Finally,

C) In fact,

D) Namely,

25

The effects of climate change are noticeable now: average temperatures are increasing, storms are more severe, and droughts are more common. In order to protect our planet and life as we know it, we _____ make changes to our daily routines as quickly as possible. If everyone works together, even small alterations such as eating more vegetables or taking public transportation can make a large difference in the long run.

The writer wants to emphasize the necessity of protecting the planet. Which choice most effectively achieves this goal?

A) can

B) will

C) might

D) must

26

As technology evolves apace and more of us work part-time, the trend of skill sets becoming obsolete is _____. For instance, LinkedIn co-founder Reid Hoffman believes that careers are now simply "tours of duty," prompting companies to design organizations that assume people will only stay a few years.

The writer wants to highlight the speed of transition. Which choice best achieves that goal?

A) accelerating in a faster and faster way

B) only accelerating

C) increasingly accelerating

D) accelerating more quickly as time goes by

CONTINUE

27

While researching a topic, a student has taken the following notes:

- Cher is a famous musician and performer born in 1946.
- She was known for regularly changing her appearance and musical styles.
- In the 1970s, she starred in a TV series that ran for 3 years.
- She collaborated with her husband on her first pop/rock hit, "I Got You Babe" (1965).
- Her 1979 disco dance song "Take Me Home" brought her fame after a hiatus.

The student wants to emphasize a point using the two songs. Which choice most effectively uses relevant information from the notes to accomplish this goal?

A) "I Got You Babe" was performed in 1965 and "Take Me Home" was performed in 1979.

B) Cher changed styles regularly, using pop/rock for "I Got You Babe" and disco for "Take Me Home."

C) In the 1970s, Cher performed in a television series as well as sang "Take Me Home."

D) Cher both collaborated with her husband and performed a disco dance song.

STOP

CONTINUE

No Test Material On This Page

No Test Material On This Page

Math

22 QUESTIONS | 35 MINUTES

DIRECTIONS

The questions in this section address a number of important math skills. Use of a calculator is permitted for all questions.

NOTES

Unless otherwise indicated: • All variables and expressions represent real numbers. • Figures provided are drawn to scale. • All figures lie in a plane. • The domain of a given function is the set of all real numbers x for which $f(x)$ is a real number.

REFERENCE

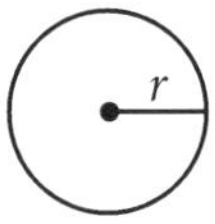

$A = \pi r^2$
$C = 2\pi r$

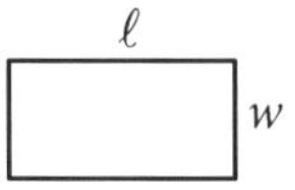

$A = \ell w$

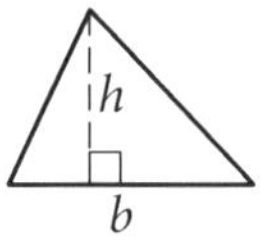

$A = \frac{1}{2}bh$

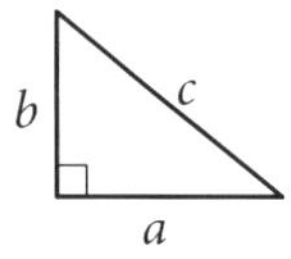

$c^2 = a^2 + b^2$

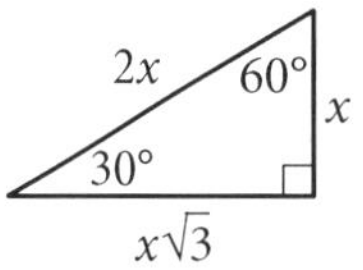

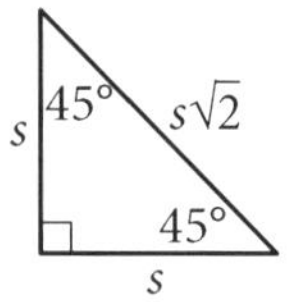

Special Right Triangles

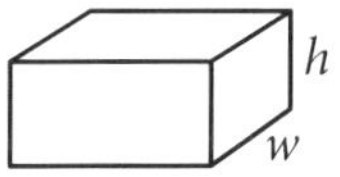

$V = \ell wh$

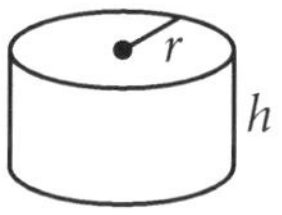

$V = \pi r^2 h$

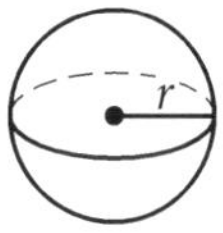

$V = \frac{4}{3}\pi r^3$

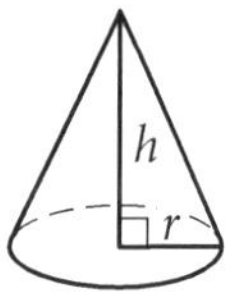

$V = \frac{1}{3}\pi r^2 h$

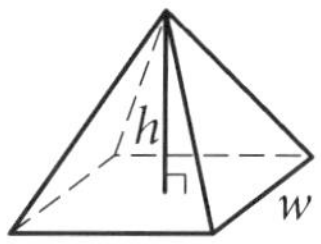

$V = \frac{1}{3}\ell wh$

The number of degrees of arc in a circle is 360.

The number of radians of arc in a circle is 2π.

The sum of the measures in degrees of the angles of a triangle is 180.

For **multiple-choice questions,** solve each problem, choose the correct answer from the choices provided, and then circle your answer in this book. Circle only one answer for each question. If you change your mind, completely erase the circle. You will not get credit for questions with more than one answer circled, or for questions with no answers circled.

For **student-produced response questions,** solve each problem and write your answer next to or under the question in the test book as described below.

- Once you've written your answer, circle it clearly. You will not receive credit for anything written outside the circle, or for any questions with more than one circled answer.
- If you find more than one correct answer, write and circle only one answer.
- Your answer can be up to 5 characters for a positive answer and up to 6 characters (including the negative sign) for a negative answer, but no more.
- If your answer is a fraction that is too long (over 5 characters for positive, 6 characters for negative), write the decimal equivalent.
- If your answer is a decimal that is too long (over 5 characters for positive, 6 characters for negative), truncate it or round at the fourth digit.
- If your answer is a mixed number (such as 3.!. 2), write it as an improper fraction (7/2) or its decimal equivalent (3.5).
- Don't include symbols such as a percent sign, comma, or dollar sign in your circled answer.

CONTINUE

1

If $4x+16=24$, what is the value of $x+4$?

A) 8

B) 6

C) 2

D) 4

2

Cocopine high school conducts annual surveys at its school to find out the number of teachers and students by gender. The results of the survey showed that there were 35 teachers and 245 students in the school.

	Students	Teacher
Male	131	
Female		16

Using the table above, if a person is chosen at random, what is the probability that the person is a male teacher?

A) $\frac{19}{280}$

B) $\frac{19}{150}$

C) $\frac{19}{35}$

D) $\frac{19}{131}$

3

If a is a solution to this equation below and $a>0$, what is the value of a?

$$|2x-3|=11$$

4

Line k is a line perpendicular to line m. Given that the equation for line m is $5y=4x+15$, which of the following could be the equation for line k?

A) $y=\frac{4}{5}x-12$

B) $y=\frac{5}{4}x+6$

C) $y=-\frac{5}{4}x-2$

D) $y=\frac{5}{4}x+10$

5

What is the center of the circle, given that its equation is $x^2+y^2-6x+4y=36$?

A) (−3, 2)

B) (2, −3)

C) (3, −2)

D) (−2, 3)

6

If $(8^x)^x \times 4^{2x}$ is equivalent to $\left(\frac{2^{ax}}{2^{-b}}\right)^x$, what is the value of a?

7

If (x, y) is a solution to the following system of inequalities, which of the following could be (x, y)?

$$-6x+3<y$$
$$y<x+6$$

A) (−2, −4)

B) (4, 7)

C) (−2, 1)

D) (−2, −4)

8

If $f(x)=2(x-3)^2+8$ is transformed to $g(x)=2(x-5)^2+5$, which of the following describes the transformation?

A) The x coordinate moves to the right 2 units and the y coordinate moves 3 units down.

B) The x coordinate moves to the left 2 units and the y coordinate moves 3 units down.

C) The x coordinate moves to the right 2 units and the y coordinate moves 3 units up.

D) The x coordinate moves to the left 2 units and the y coordinate moves 3 units up.

9

Which of the following equation best represents the graph below?

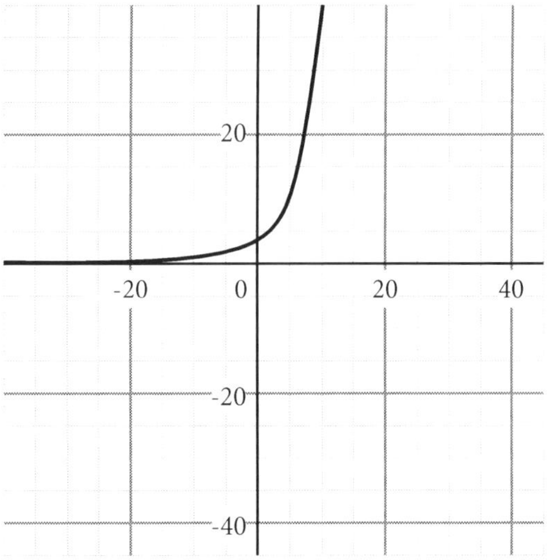

A) $y=5(0.7)^x$

B) $y=5(1.3)^x$

C) $y=3(0.7)^x$

D) $y=3(1.3)^x$

CONTINUE

10

If triangle PQR (not shown) is similar to triangle DEF shown below and DE = 2PQ, what is the value of sin R?

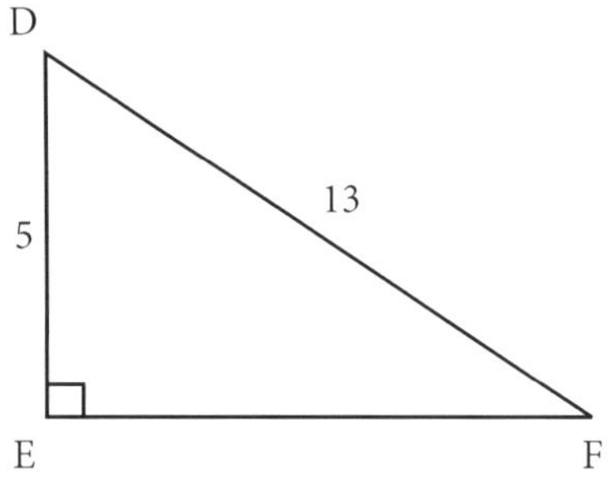

11

The average SAT score of 7 students in a class is 1,320. If a student with an SAT score of 1,460 joins the class, what will be the new average SAT score (rounded off to the nearest 10)?

A) 1,390

B) 1,340

C) 1,300

D) 1,460

12

A researcher studies bacteria in a pond and models a function that shows how the bacteria populate in the pond. Let t be the number of days since the bacteria began to populate the pond. Which of the following is the best interpretation of $(3)^{\frac{t}{14}}$ in the equation: $p(t) = 2{,}034(3)^{\frac{t}{14}}$?

A) The number of bacteria at the beginning of the study

B) The number of bacteria triples every two weeks

C) The number of bacteria increases by 3 every two weeks

D) The number of bacteria in the pond after two weeks

13

What is the value of p, if the equation below has no solutions?

$$5(x+3)-3(2-x) = px+7$$

14

How many solutions does the following system of equations have?

$$3x - 4y = 16$$

$$-6x = -8y + 32$$

A) One solution

B) Two solutions

C) Infinitely many solutions

D) No solution

15

What is the length of the minor arc AB, given that the diameter of the circle is 12 cm and the measure of the angle of sector AOB is 72°?

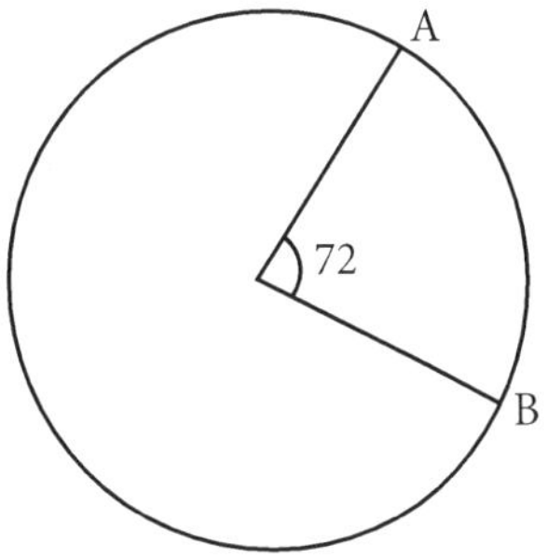

A) 2.4π

B) 28.8π

C) 12π

D) $\frac{\pi}{6}$

16

The expression $y = -2(x+3)^2 + 6$ is equivalent to $ax^2 + bx + c$, where $a < 0$ and $b < 0$. What is the value of c?

17

If the coordinates of the midpoint of line segment AB are (8, 10) and the coordinates of point A are (6, 11), which of the following would represent the coordinates of point B?

A) (7, 10.5)

B) (2, 0.5)

C) (10, 9)

D) (7, 11)

18

How many solutions does the equation $|x+3| = 0$ have?

A) 1

B) 2

C) 0

D) There is not enough information to answer the question.

CONTINUE

19

What is the value of $|f(2)|$ where $f(x) = x^2 - 20x + 9$?

A) 27

B) −27

C) 53

D) 35

20

The price of oil increased by 20% at the beginning of May. Some policies were then put in place which reduced the price of oil by 14% two weeks after the initial increase. What is the overall percentage increase or decrease in the oil?

21

A circle is inscribed in a square. If the length of one side of the square is $4\sqrt{2}$ and the area of the circle is $p\pi$, what is the value of p?

A) 32

B) 16

C) 8

D) 64

22

Which of the following is not a solution to the inequality below?

$$-3x + 6 \leq 2 - x$$

A) 2

B) 0

C) 3

D) 4

No Test Material On This Page

Math

22 QUESTIONS | 35 MINUTES

DIRECTIONS

The questions in this section address a number of important math skills. Use of a calculator is permitted for all questions.

NOTES

Unless otherwise indicated: • All variables and expressions represent real numbers. • Figures provided are drawn to scale. • All figures lie in a plane. • The domain of a given function is the set of all real numbers x for which $f(x)$ is a real number.

REFERENCE

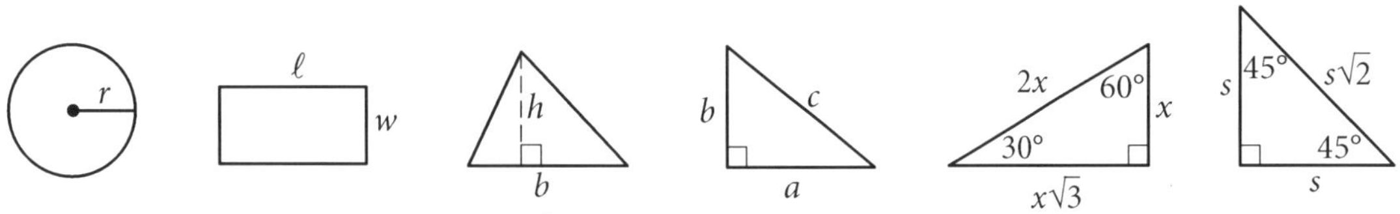

$A = \pi r^2$ $C = 2\pi r$ | $A = \ell w$ | $A = \frac{1}{2}bh$ | $c^2 = a^2 + b^2$ | Special Right Triangles

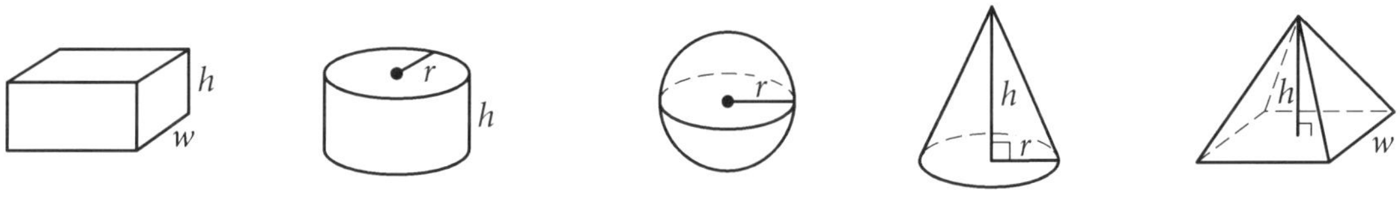

$V = \ell wh$ | $V = \pi r^2 h$ | $V = \frac{4}{3}\pi r^3$ | $V = \frac{1}{3}\pi r^2 h$ | $V = \frac{1}{3}\ell wh$

The number of degrees of arc in a circle is 360.

The number of radians of arc in a circle is 2π.

The sum of the measures in degrees of the angles of a triangle is 180.

For **multiple-choice questions,** solve each problem, choose the correct answer from the choices provided, and then circle your answer in this book. Circle only one answer for each question. If you change your mind, completely erase the circle. You will not get credit for questions with more than one answer circled, or for questions with no answers circled.

For **student-produced response questions,** solve each problem and write your answer next to or under the question in the test book as described below.

- Once you've written your answer, circle it clearly. You will not receive credit for anything written outside the circle, or for any questions with more than one circled answer.
- If you find more than one correct answer, write and circle only one answer.
- Your answer can be up to 5 characters for a positive answer and up to 6 characters (including the negative sign) for a negative answer, but no more.
- If your answer is a fraction that is too long (over 5 characters for positive, 6 characters for negative), write the decimal equivalent.
- If your answer is a decimal that is too long (over 5 characters for positive, 6 characters for negative), truncate it or round at the fourth digit.
- If your answer is a mixed number (such as 3.!. 2), write it as an improper fraction (7/2) or its decimal equivalent (3.5).
- Don't include symbols such as a percent sign, comma, or dollar sign in your circled answer.

CONTINUE

1

If m and n are solutions to the equation $f(x) = 3x^2 + 9x - 27$, what is the value of $m + n$?

A) 3

B) -9

C) -3

D) 9

2

Which of the following is equivalent to $3x^2y + 5x - (3x^2y^2 - 2x^2y)$?

A) $6x^2y - 3x^2y^2 + 5x$

B) $x^2y - 3x^2y^2 + 5x$

C) $6x^2y - 2x^2y^2 + 5x$

D) $-3x^2y^2 + 5x^2y + 5x$

3

What is the least integer value of y that satisfies the inequality below?

$$-2y + 2 < 6$$

4

How many solutions does the following system of equations have?

$$y = 2x - 5$$

$$y = 2x^2 - 18x + 45$$

A) 1

B) 2

C) 0

D) Infinite

5

If $3x - y = 11$ and $2x - 2y = 2$, what is the value of $x + y$?

A) 9

B) 5

C) 3

D) 13

6

If $\sin 32° = 0.551$, what is the value of $\cos 58°$?

7

If 1 *foot* = 12 *inches*, what is the area of the triangle (not drawn to scale) below in ft^2?

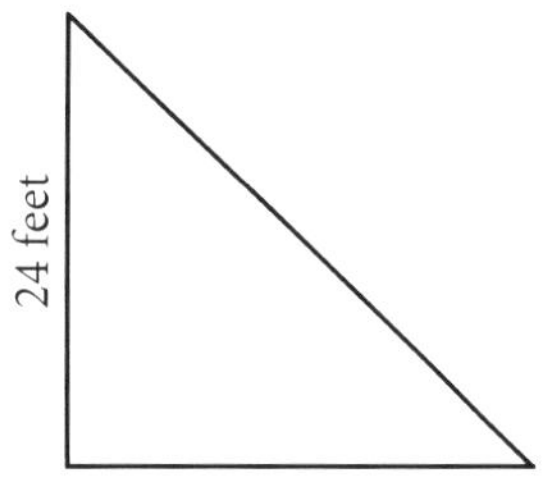

A) 120

B) 20

C) 1,440

D) 10

8

For all values of $x > 0$, which of the following is equivalent to the following equation $\frac{-5}{x} - \frac{x}{x-4}$?

A) -6

B) $\frac{x^2 + -20}{4}$

C) $\frac{-x^2 - 5x + 20}{x^2 - 4x}$

D) $\frac{-9 - x}{x - 4}$

9

Which of the following equations best represents the equation of the following graph?

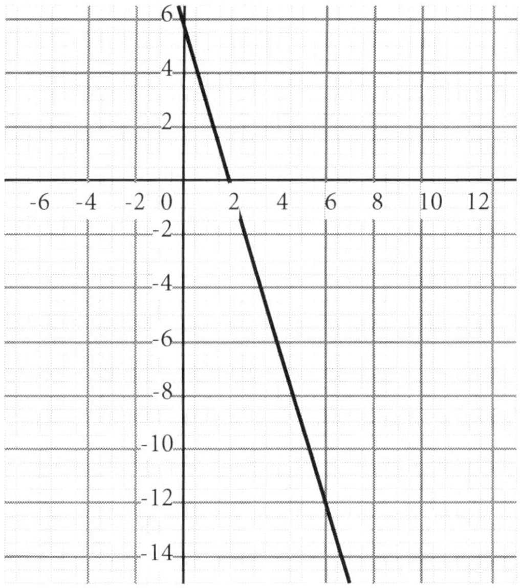

A) $3y - 9x = 18$

B) $3y + 9x = 18$

C) $6y - 12x = 36$

D) $5y + 20x = 30$

10

What is the y–intercept for the equation below?

$$y - 7 = 3^x - 5$$

CONTINUE

11

For what value of x does the function $h(x)=\dfrac{3x-5}{x^2-2x-15}$ become undefined if $x<0$?

A) 5

B) −5

C) −3

D) −4

12

If $f(3)=-1$ and $f(4)=-3$, what is the *x–intercept* for the line represented by the function $f(x)$?

A) 2.5

B) 5

C) −2

D) $\frac{2}{5}$

13

If $f(x+3)=5x-17$, what is the value of $f(2)$?

14

Amber travels from her home to the mall in $1\frac{1}{2}$ *hours*. She completes her errands in one hour

and she then travels back home in $2\frac{1}{2}$ *hours*.

If the distance from the mall to her home is x miles, find the average speed of her trip in terms of x.

A) $\frac{x}{4}$

B) $\frac{x}{2}$

C) $\frac{2x}{5}$

D) $2x$

15

Given that the length of a rectangle is 3 *meters* more than its width, what is the perimeter of the rectangle given that the area is 28 *square meters*?

A) 11

B) 22

C) 14

D) 32

16

A study conducted by a school's medical board found that 23 out of the 48 students surveyed practice sanitary routines such as washing their hands before meals. If there are 2,280 students in the school, approximately how many students in the school do not practice sanitary routines (rounded up to the nearest whole number)?

17

Which of the following is the equation of $g(x) = 2x$ when it's moved 1 unit to the left and 1 unit up?

A) $y = 2x - 1$

B) $y = 2x + 1$

C) $y = 2x + 5$

D) $y = 2x + 3$

18

What is the *x coordinate* of the vertex for the parabola represented by the equation $y = 2x^2 + 8x + 12$?

A) 6

B) –4

C) 2

D) –2

19

If $\frac{x^2 - 6x + 10}{x + 2} = A + \frac{B}{x + 2}$, what is the value of B?

20

If triangle ABC is a right triangle and B is 90° and the longest side of the triangle is 61 and the shortest side is 11, what is the length of the third side of the triangle?

A) 40

B) 60

C) 62

D) 59

CONTINUE

21

The psychology department of a school conducted a study on 20 random students in a third grade class of 58 students. 20 of the students were then offered a supplement. The study found that 15 of these students did better in their end–term exams compared to those who did not take the supplements. Which of the following statements can best be concluded from the above study?

A) Students who take supplements do better on exams.

B) Students who do not take supplements do not do well on their exams.

C) Supplements improve students' performance in their exams.

D) No conclusion can be drawn about the cause–and–effect relationship between test taking and supplement taking.

22

If $x+3y=9$ and $2x+2y=14$, what is the value of $y-x$?

A) –5

B) 5

C) 1

D) 6

STOP

No Test Material On This Page

Answer Key

Reading and Writing

Module 1

Questions	Correct	Mark your correct answers
1.	C	
2.	C	
3.	A	
4.	B	
5.	C	
6.	A	
7.	B	
8.	A	
9.	B	
10.	B	
11.	B	
12.	A	
13.	C	
14.	D	
15.	D	
16.	C	
17.	C	
18.	C	
19.	A	
20.	B	
21.	B	
22.	D	
23.	D	
24.	B	
25.	C	
26.	A	
27.	C	

Module 2

Questions	Correct	Mark your correct answers
1.	D	
2.	C	
3.	D	
4.	D	
5.	D	
6.	A	
7.	B	
8.	A	
9.	C	
10.	A	
11.	B	
12.	A	
13.	A	
14.	D	
15.	A	
16.	C	
17.	D	
18.	D	
19.	A	
20.	B	
21.	D	
22.	D	
23.	B	
24.	C	
25.	D	
26.	B	
27.	B	

Math

Module 1

Questions	Correct	Mark your correct answers
1.	B	
2.	A	
3.	7	
4.	C	
5.	C	
6.	3	
7.	B	
8.	A	
9.	D	
10.	$\frac{5}{13}$ or 0.384 or 0.385	
11.	B	
12.	B	
13.	8	
14.	D	
15.	A	
16.	−12	
17.	C	
18.	A	
19.	A	
20.	3.2	
21.	C	
22.	B	

Module 2

Questions	Correct	Mark your correct answers
1.	C	
2.	D	
3.	−1	
4.	A	
5.	A	
6.	0.551	
7.	D	
8.	C	
9.	B	
10.	3	
11.	C	
12.	A	
13.	−22	
14.	B	
15.	B	
16.	1,188	
17.	D	
18.	D	
19.	26	
20.	B	
21.	D	
22.	A	

1. **Level:** Easy | **Domain:** CRAFT AND STRUCTURE
Skill/Knowledge: Words in Context

Key Explanation: Choice C is the best answer because the underlined word is what goats "lack" or "do not have." The first half of the sentence indicates that the goats will eat "everything else" as well as "unwanted weeds." In other words, the goat does not care what it eats. **Choice C** refers to "judgment," or "refinement" about what it chooses, so fits the context of eating anything.

Distractor Explanation: Choices A and **B** are incorrect because they refer to unfairness or partiality towards one thing. However, the goats are not deliberately trying to treat one plant poorly; they eat all without preferences. **Choice D** is incorrect because it refers to an obstinate and unchanging belief about the superiority of one's group over others, but the goats do not feel they are superior to others.

2. **Level:** Easy | **Domain:** CRAFT AND STRUCTURE
Skill/Knowledge: Words in Context

Key Explanation: Choice C is the best answer because the underlined word describes how clients and investors view the proposal that the person with a career in business makes. **Choice C** refers to something that is desirable. The resulting sentence, therefore, indicates that the businessperson helps make the plan desirable to others.

Distractor Explanation: None of the other choices adequately shows how the clients and investors need to view the proposals. **Choice A** refers to a personal quality that inspires others. It does not refer to something inanimate like a proposal. **Choice B** refers to something that is impossible to avoid the effect of. The clients and investors, though, are not forced to accept the proposal. **Choice D** refers to something that is extremely interesting so that it is impossible to stop paying attention to it. Although a proposal might be fascinating, the key is to make it desirable enough that others buy into it.

3. **Level:** Hard | **Domain:** CRAFT AND STRUCTURE
Skill/Knowledge: Words in Context

Key Explanation: Choice A is the best answer because "critical" is the author's view of what "explaining such coexistence" is. The sentence continues to say that the explanation is needed to "truly understand the region's biodiversity." **Choice A** refers to something absolutely necessary, so fits the context in saying that explaining coexistence is necessary to understand biodiversity and therefore developing an appropriate plan for managing the area.

Distractor Explanation: None of the other choices accurately describes how essential "explaining such coexistence" really is. **Choice B** means "dangerous." **Choice C** refers to expressing criticism and disapproval. **Choice D** refers to using logic and reasoning.

4. **Level:** Medium | **Domain:** CRAFT AND STRUCTURE
Skill/Knowledge: Words in Context

Key Explanation: Choice B is the best answer because the blank portion needs to be a word that describes the "cultural and historical value of the building and its contents," which are described as being full of "splendid and unique details" from over the past 1,500 years. **Choice C** refers to something that is too great to mathematically determine or count. It fits the context that the building's value is so great it cannot be replaced by any money.

Distractor Explanations: None of the other choices adequately describe the precious nature of the "value of the building and its contents." **Choice A** refers to a place or thing that is pleasant and agreeable, not an intangible thing such as "value." **Choices C** and **D** refer to something that is physically large or bulky, not something intangible.

5. **Level:** Hard | **Domain:** CRAFT AND STRUCTURE
Skill/Knowledge: Text Structure and Purpose

Key Explanation: Choice C is the best answer because the main point of the paragraph is that "these results contrast with previous findings" and emphasize that more studies are needed, indicating that the Drake Passage study did not provide all the answers. Therefore, the paragraph shows how the results of the Drake Passage study fits into "the wider context" or "bigger picture" of other studies.

Distractor Explanation: Choice A is incorrect because the paragraph does not suggest that any of the data gathered so far is "inaccurate" or "not correct." Therefore, the paragraph is not being used to show how difficult it is to get correct data. **Choice B** is incorrect because the paragraph does not "illustrate" or "explain" why it is hard to "amass" or "gather" enough data. The paragraph mentions that the conditions are "challenging," but does not give any detail about why. **Choice D** is incorrect because, though the paragraph says that CO_2 absorption is important, it does not talk about "correcting" or "fixing" the problem. It only says that there needs to be more research done to understand the process better.

6. **Level:** Easy | **Domain:** CRAFT AND STRUCTURE
Skill/Knowledge: Text Structure and Purpose

Key Explanation: Choice A is the best answer. The underlined sentence shows that the garden was large and "lovely" or "appealing," and the following sentence gives various reasons that the garden was appealing to all the senses.

Distractor Explanation: Choice B is incorrect because there is no contrast with the previous sentence; the garden was lovely, so that provides a reason for the children to want to play there. **Choice C** is incorrect because the underlined sentence does not refer to "characters" or "people," only to place. **Choice D** is incorrect because there is no "ominous undercurrent" or "scary implication" in the description of the garden. It could be that the giant is very nice and there is no problem with the children playing there.

7. **Level:** Easy | **Domain:** CRAFT AND STRUCTURE
Skill/Knowledge: Text Structure and Purpose

Key Explanation: Choice B is the best answer because the phrase is used to describe the "fentanyl analogs" or "drugs comparable to fentanyl." The fact that they were "commonly confiscated" or "often seized" by law enforcement shows that the drugs are ones in common use, and therefore are likely to be illegal drugs that overdose patients had access to and used. If this is true, the research on the drugs is likely to "apply" or "be relevant" to "authentic cases" or "real situations" in which a patient overdoses on an illegal drug.

Distractor Explanation: Choice A is incorrect because the method of "obtaining" or "getting" the drugs is not mentioned. The researchers could have gotten the drugs from a variety of sources. **Choice C** is incorrect because the fact that the drugs were the kind seized by officers does not show that the trials were "improperly" or "incorrectly" done. **Choice D** is incorrect because there is no indication that the research required special permits to use the drugs. Therefore, the quote is not included to "establish" or "provide a reason" for a point that is not even mentioned.

8. **Level:** Easy | **Domain:** INFORMATION AND IDEAS
Skill/Knowledge: Cross-Text Connections

Key Explanation: Choice A is the best answer because when the author of passage 2 states that if "men but understand themselves . . . they will be ready enough to take gigantic measures to prevent [war]" he is expressing a belief in the ability of wisdom to overcome mankind's tendency towards warfare. This is very similar in intent and belief to the statement made by the author of passage 1 that, "We must have the telescope of philosophy to perceive distant ills." Both authors believe that the key to conquering our urge to ignore the suffering of others and make war is consideration and thoughtfulness.

Distractor Explanation: Choice B is incorrect because it has no relevance to the underlined concluding message in Text 2. The underlined section in Text 2 is expressing a belief in the ability of wisdom to overcome mankind's tendency towards warfare, whereas this choice emphasizes that people only concern themselves with opinions and beliefs that ensure their personal happiness. **Choice C** is incorrect because it doesn't include any information relating to the underlined concluding message in Text 2. The underlined section in Text 2 is expressing a belief in the ability of wisdom to overcome mankind's tendency towards warfare, whereas this choice emphasizes that there are people that would ignore the misery of others as long as they benefitted. **Choice D** is incorrect because it doesn't include any information relating to the underlined concluding message in Text 2. The underlined section in Text 2 is expressing a belief in the ability of wisdom to overcome mankind's tendency towards warfare, whereas this choice emphasizes that there are men that have no problem with the concept of killing or taking someone else's life.

9. **Level:** Medium | **Domain:** INFORMATION AND IDEAS
Skill/Knowledge: Central Ideas and Details

Key Explanation: Choice B is the best answer because "impetus" refers to a reason or motivation. The passage begins by explaining that the narrator will "take to the ship" whenever he is feeling morbid and needs a change.

Distractor Explanation: Choice A is incorrect because there is no indication that the narrator is a captain. He also does not appear to be a sailor as a steady career, but instead when he feels tired of being on land. **Choice C** is incorrect because the narrator says he had no money, and therefore felt like going sailing; there is no discussion of a sailor's salary. He could have had a large salary aboard ship but spent it all. **Choice D** is incorrect because, while the narrator indicates that he was "impoverished" with "little or no money in my purse," he does not say how he got to that condition

10. **Level:** Medium | **Domain:** INFORMATION AND IDEAS
Skill/Knowledge: Central Ideas and Details

Key Explanation: Choice B is the best answer because the passage says that "induced demand" is a phenomenon in which making more of a product will lead to more people wanting it; in this case, "if more roads are provided, more people are encouraged to drive." However, the passage says that the "common solution" is to build more roads, showing that in the average or common case of wanting to reduce traffic jams, the effect is not considered. If it were "taken into consideration" or "thought about," then planners would probably use a different solution than just building roads.

Distractor Explanation: Choice A is incorrect because, although the passage indicates that congestion continues as more roads are built, it does not say that induced demand "contradicts" or "goes against" that concept. There is also no hint that there is a "widespread belief" or "lots of people thinking" that building roads causes congestion; if so, the common solution would not be to build more. **Choice C** is incorrect because there is no hint that city planners are now incorporating the idea into their plans; if so, then there would not be situations like the example from Houston. **Choice D** is incorrect because there is no discussion in the passage about how to "mitigate" or "reduce" the effect. The effect is just defined.

11. **Level:** Medium | **Domain:** INFORMATION AND IDEAS
Skill/Knowledge: Command of Evidence (Textual)

Key Explanation: Choice B is the best answer. The claim is that "the poem uses the imagery of fire to delve into the question of who might have created such a dangerous creature." In choice B, the words "furnace" and "anvil" are "imagery" or "symbols" that evoke heat and fire; they are tools used to heat metal to the melting point and form it into a shape. **Choice B** refers to "delving" or "asking" the question of who might have created the "dangerous creature," which causes "deadly terrors: what furnace, anvil, and grasp could create a tiger? These questions are asking who would dare to forge and hold the tiger.

Distractor Explanation: Choice A is incorrect because it touches on the fire imagery in the "fire of thine eyes," but it does not refer to the question of who created such a creature. **Choice C** is incorrect because it only refers to the creator and the danger or fear caused by a tiger: tigers are scary enough that stars "throw down their spears" or "give up" and "water heaven with their tears" or "cry." **Choice C** does not use any fire imagery. **Choice D** also does not give any support to the claim that the poem uses fire imagery; it only wonders if someone who created a lamb could also create a tiger.

12. **Level:** Hard | **Domain:** INFORMATION AND IDEAS
Skill/Knowledge: Command of Evidence (Textual)

Key Explanation: Choice A is the best answer because a counterargument is an attack against the writer's main argument. The prompt is asking about a counterargument related to Mother Jones's "credibility" or "believability." Mother Jones "addresses" or "faces" the possible attack that she is not qualified to speak because she is not a miner by saying that she has undergone similar conditions that miners live in and suffer through: "I was with you nearly three years in this State. I went to jail. I went to the Federal courts."

Distractor Explanation: Choice B is incorrect because Mother Jones uses her experience in jail as a reason that she can empathize with the miners. It supports her argument of understanding hard conditions rather than weakens her ability to speak for miners. **Choice C** is incorrect because there is no discussion about how many government contacts she has, so she does not "anticipate" a counter argument on that topic. **Choice D** is incorrect because Mother Jones does not say how she treats pets; she is discussing the behavior of the wives of the mine owners.

13. **Level:** Easy | **Domain:** INFORMATION AND IDEAS
Skill/Knowledge: Command of Evidence (Quantitative)

Key Explanation: Choice C is the best answer because the figure lists "39.66" in the column of "average days to first flower" for 90nM of NaCl, and 23.66 days for 0 NaCl. Therefore, the difference is 16 days, which supports the claim that "increasing NaCl concentrations delayed significantly flowering" times.

Distractor Explanation: Choice A is incorrect because only the passage refers to capsaicinoids; the table does not. **Choice B** is incorrect because only the passage refers to vitamins and minerals. Nutritional value is impossible to determine from the table. **Choice D** is incorrect because for the "NaCl concentration of 30 mM" line, the table says 54 days until the first fruit appeared; that is not the total number of fruits.

14. **Level:** Medium | **Domain:** INFORMATION AND IDEAS
Skill/Knowledge: Inferences

Key Explanation: Choice D is the best answer because the passage says that Mann used personal interviews "to provide an insider's perspective." She was trying to get a clearer understanding of veganism from vegans themselves.

Distractor Explanation: Choice A is incorrect because there is no evidence that Mann expected to find a "conflict" or "opposing views" between the interviews and scientific research. She was trying to blend the two to get a more rounded view of the topic as a whole. **Choice B** is incorrect because the health benefits were analyzed through scientific studies found in the literature review; Mann was not trying to "resolve a debate" so much as "combat stereotypes" by sharing different views. **Choice C** is incorrect because there is no evidence that "most" or "the largest percentage" of literature is "biased against" or "opposing" veganism.

15. **Level:** Easy | **Domain:** INFORMATION AND IDEAS
Skill/Knowledge: Inferences

Key Explanation: Choice D is the best answer. Since the tomb inscriptions say that the tomb belonged to Hinat, it is a logical assumption that she was buried there.

Distractor Explanations: Choice A is incorrect. There is no evidence that Hinat was royal; if anything, the act of buying a tomb indicates that the populace did not make one for their ruler. **Choice B** is incorrect because, though she bought her own tomb, she had "descendants," which indicates that she had children. **Choice C** is incorrect because "ancestors" are the people who came before someone, so are the opposite of "descendants." There is no indication that anyone before Hinat was buried with her.

16. **Level:** Easy | **Domain:** STANDARD ENGLISH CONVENTIONS
Skill/Knowledge: Form, Structure, and Sense

Key Explanation: Choice C is the best answer. "Called off" is a phrasal verb that means "canceled."

Distractor Explanation: All of the other choices can be eliminated because they are phrasal verbs with meanings that do not fit the context of saying that the Olympics were not held. **Choice A** refers to visiting someone. **Choice B** refers to telephoning someone. **Choice D** refers to asking various people questions, often when organizing something or trying to find information.

17. **Level:** Medium | **Domain:** STANDARD ENGLISH CONVENTIONS
Skill/Knowledge: Form, Structure, and Sense

Key Explanation: Choice C is the best answer. The present perfect verb form using "has/have" is used to show that something started in the past and continues now. It fits the time context of the question that Harari poses, "from the stone age to the present."

Distractor Explanation: Choices A and **B** are incorrect because they are present tenses, so do not include the idea of change from the distant past. **Choice D** is incorrect because it refers to something which has not yet occurred in the future, so does not describe "from the stone age to the present."

18. **Level:** Easy | **Domain:** STANDARD ENGLISH CONVENTIONS
Skill/Knowledge: Form, Structure, and Sense

Key Explanation: Choice C is the best answer. The subject of the sentence is long, "the transformative effect on women of access to affordable, reliable, and sustainable modern energy." However, it can be reduced to the singular "the effect." **Choice C** is a singular verb that shows that the studies were done in the past and still continue today.

Distractor Explanation: All of the other choices can be eliminated because they are plural verbs, so cannot be used with the singular subject "the effect."

19. **Level:** Easy | **Domain:** STANDARD ENGLISH CONVENTIONS
Skill/Knowledge: Form, Structure, and Sense

Key Explanation:Choice A is the best answer. "Which" is a relative pronoun used after a comma to add more description to the noun that precedes the comma. In this case, "occur deep underwater where continental plates diverge" adds more information about the "hydrothermal vents."

Distractor Explanation: Choices B and **D** are incorrect because "they" and "these" are pronouns that are used in place of a noun at the start of a sentence. They create independent clauses that can stand on their own, so the resulting sentence is a comma splice. **Choice C** is incorrect because when "that" is used as the start of a relative clause after a noun, it is not preceded by a comma.

20. **Level:** Medium | **Domain:** STANDARD ENGLISH CONVENTIONS
Skill/Knowledge: Boundaries

Key Explanation: Choice B is the best answer. When three or more items are included in a list joined by "and," the items are followed by commas, but the "and" is not.

Distractor Explanation: Choice A is incorrect because there should be no comma after "and." **Choices C** and **D** are incorrect because both semicolons and a single dash should be preceded by a complete idea, but the two items before the punctuation would need to be joined by "and" for the idea to be complete.

21. **Level:** Easy | **Domain:** STANDARD ENGLISH CONVENTIONS
Skill/Knowledge: Boundaries

Key Explanation: Choice B is the best answer. "In a 2022 paper written by Kyle Rupp and associates" modifies the main clause, "the researchers explore..." by giving the context of when and where the sentence occurs. Such a modifier at the start of the sentence should be divided from the main clause with a comma.

Distractor Explanation:Choice A is incorrect because with no punctuation, the reader does not know where the main clause begins**. Choices C** and **D** are incorrect because a single dash or a colon should follow an independent clause, but the first person has no active verb ("written" modifies the noun "paper.")

22. **Level:** Easy | **Domain:** STANDARD ENGLISH CONVENTIONS
Skill/Knowledge: Boundaries

Key Explanation: Choice D is the best answer. The main clause starts, "a lyric soprano has...." The other words at the start of the sentence modify the main clause, so need to be divided with commas. "For example" is one separate idea that qualifies that the sentence is an illustration of the previous claim. "Among operatic voices" restricts the discussion to voices that are used in the opera.

Distractor Explanation: Choice A is incorrect because it has no punctuation separating the different elements of the sentence from each other, so it is hard for the reader to determine how the ideas relate to each other. **Choices B** and **C** are incorrect because a colon should follow a complete clause, but the preceding portion has no verb.

23. **Level:** Medium | **Domain:** EXPRESSION OF IDEAS
Skill/Knowledge: Transitions

Key Explanation: Choice D is the best answer. "The wind cannot be turned up or down" is a contrast with the previous discussion, which explains that oil–powered plants can control output like adjusting the flow of gas to a car. **Choice D** is used to indicate that the following information is different from what has preceded, so it effectively warns the reader of the contrast to come.

Distractor Explanation: Choices A and **B** are incorrect because they show that even though one thing happens, another also happens. They do not establish that the discussion is highlighting a difference between two things which might happen even if the other did not. **Choice C** is incorrect because it is used to add more information along the same idea to the preceding argument, not change to a contrasting thought.

24. **Level:** Easy **Domain:** EXPRESSION OF IDEAS
Skill/Knowledge: Transitions

Key Explanation: Choice B is the best answer. There is a contrast in the sentence between "some administrative roles" and the rest of people who do social work. **Choice B** is used at the start of a dependent clause to show a contrast between the clause it introduces and the main clause of the sentence.

Distractor Explanation: All of the other choices can be eliminated because they do not make the clause that they introduce dependent on a main clause; the clause can still stand on its own as a sentence. As a result, the sentence is left with two main clauses joined by a comma, a type of run–on sentence called a comma splice.

25. **Level:** Easy | **Domain:** EXPRESSION OF IDEAS
Skill/Knowledge: Transitions

Key Explanation: Choice C is the best answer. The passage is structured with the first sentence defining the diet and the second sentence giving a reason to doubt that it is effective, a reason not to follow it. The final sentence gives another reason to question whether the diet should be used. **Choice C** is used to introduce an additional argument for the same topic, so fits the context well.

Distractor Explanation: The other choices can be eliminated because they are not used to add more detail on the same topic. **Choice A** is used for a time series, but there is no indication that the lack of research was followed in time by scientists being concerned. **Choice B** is used to stress that the previous point may be true, but that the following, opposing argument is more reasonable. Therefore, it does not fit the context of two concordant ideas. **Choice D** is used to introduce a logical conclusion based on what information is already given, not to bring up new ideas.

26. **Level:** Medium | **Domain:** INFORMATION AND IDEAS
Skill/Knowledge: Inference

Key Explanation: Choice A is correct because to commemorate something means to remember the event and by doing so, to honor it. Here, the memorial commemorates the employees of LMWR killed in the First World War.

Distractor Explanations: Choice B is incorrect because to idolize is to respect or admire someone extensively. Here, the memorial has been built to remember martyrs and not only to show respect. **Choice C** is incorrect because "celebrate" is not a word used to describe the purpose of a memorial. **Choice D** is incorrect because the memorial has been built for the fallen LNWR employees and hence, cannot overlook or ignore them.

27. **Level:** Medium | **Domain:** EXPRESSION OF IDEAS
Skill/Knowledge: Rhetorical Synthesis

Key Explanation: Choice C is the best answer. The author wants to emphasize "rarity" or the fact that there are very few of the saola. The idea that they have been seen only four times in thirty years indicates that they are hard to find. In other words, there are probably not many because presumably scientists have been wanting to look for and study them.

Distractor Explanation:Choice A is incorrect because it does not emphasize the "rarity" or "unusual nature" of the animal. It is possible that many hunters have such skulls in their homes and the scientists only recently realized some were unusual. **Choice B** is incorrect because it could just mean saola are hard to raise in captivity. There could be a huge number living in the mountains in that region. **Choice D** is incorrect because it does not say anything about how common the saola are; it only describes their name

1. **Level:** Medium | **Domain:** CRAFT AND STRUCTURE
Skill/Knowledge: Words in Context

Key Explanation: Choice D is the best answer because "broader" is a comparative adjective that shows the difference between the tourism business and the destination. The paragraph shows that the tourism business contains many different aspects than just the sites: it also includes "transportation, hotels and guest accommodations, and services that link the various components of a trip." Choice D refers to something that covers a wide range of topics or deals with many elements of something, so accurately shows that tourism deals with many more elements than just the destination.

Distractor Explanation: None of the other choices effectively establishes the relationship between the tourism business and the destination. **Choice A** refers to something that is more noticeable or clear. **Choice B** refers to something that is not detailed or only covers the main points. **Choice C** refers to something that is wide in physical space.

2. **Level:** Medium | **Domain:** CRAFT AND STRUCTURE
Skill/Knowledge: Words in Context

Key Explanation: Choice C is the best answer because "insensible" is a verb that shows what the trees do to the "any change in those who walk" under them. **Choice C** means "not notice," so it correctly shows that the trees do not notice that different people are present.

Distractor Explanation: Choice A refers to an unconscious state, especially when someone is sick or injured. Therefore, it does not apply to trees that do not notice anything. **Choice B** means "trivial" or "unimportant," so does not describe what the trees do to a change in the people under them. **Choice D** is incorrect because it refers to a lack of thinking or perception of the environment around something. Although trees do not think, Marianne is talking to them as if they were animate creatures that might perceive things if they wanted to.

3. **Level:** Hard | **Domain:** CRAFT AND STRUCTURE
Skill/Knowledge: Words in Context

Key Explanation: Choice D is the best answer because "fume" refers to one of the things relating to the way that Adam amassed millions of dollars in Wall Street. The other things are "fuss" or "commotion," "applause" or "praise," and "ill will" or "hard feelings." **Choice D** refers to anger that is often related to a conflict, so aptly shows that he was very aggressive or hurt others as he "charged in" and made money.

Distractor Explanation: None of the other choices fits the list of emotional qualities reflecting what happened to Adam on Wall Street. **Choice A** refers to waste gasses, **Choice B** to an unpleasant smell, and **Choice C** to waste products.

4. **Level:** Medium | **Domain:** CRAFT AND STRUCTURE
Skill/Knowledge: Text Structure and Purpose

Key Explanation: Choice D is the best answer. The topic sentence points out that "sometimes behaviors have underlying reasons that are not initially apparent," and then gives Mischel's experiment as an example. The differing results of Watt's experiment show that a fuller analysis might reveal previously unconsidered explanations for a behavior such as deciding to wait to eat a marshmallow.

Distractor Explanation: Choice A is incorrect because, while Watt's experiment revealed a flaw in Mischel's experiment, there is no indication that "most" experiments are flawed. **Choice B** is incorrect because the passage does not say that all experiments should be performed more than once; it only gives an example of a situation where a second experiment revealed more information about a topic. **Choice C** is incorrect because the passage does not say there is a "significant problem" in the way we understand willpower now; the passage points out that a previous problem in understanding was rectified.

5. **Level:** Medium | **Domain:** CRAFT AND STRUCTURE
Skill/Knowledge: Text Structure and Purpose

Key Explanation: Choice D is the best answer because the cup of liberty is something that "your old masters" hold for the slaves. The imagery shows that the cup can be "dash[ed] from you" so that it is unclear when the "scattered contents" or "freedoms" will be given back. In other words, the imagery emphasizes the "precarious" or "unstable" nature of the freedoms. It is very easy to throw aside or break the gains that have been made.

Distractor Explanation: Choice A is incorrect because Lincoln is not saying that the Union is "generous" or "willing to give a lot." He is saying that a poor decision will remove everything that has been given so far. **Choice B** is incorrect because the cup of liberty is what "your old masters," who are slave-owners in Louisiana, hold for slaves. The cup of liberty is not the advances of the Union, only of Louisiana. **Choice C** is incorrect because the imagery does not include the reaction of people accepting the cup; it says the cup is easy to break.

6. **Level:** Easy | **Domain:** CRAFT AND STRUCTURE
Skill/Knowledge: Text Structure and Purpose

Key Explanation: Choice A is the best answer because the definition explains what a median wage is. This definition clarifies that not all planners earned the median figure of $73,050. It also explains why a total of 20% of the planners earned less than $45,180 or more than $114,170. If the reader did not know the definition of median wage, then the reason for the wide range in salaries might not make much sense.

Distractor Explanation: Choice B is incorrect because the author does not imply that the median wage is "insufficient" or "not good enough." The median wage does not give all the necessary details to know the range of salaries, but offers a valid middle point to use as a point of reference. The definition shows how the data can be used to better understand the salary that could be earned as a planner. **Choice C** is incorrect because there is no "reason" or "cause" given to explain why planners earn different amounts of money. **Choice D** is incorrect because there is no link between salary earned and number of jobs. Therefore, a definition of how the salary in the passage was calculated does not support or prove that there will be more jobs in the future.

7. **Level:** Medium | **Domain:** CRAFT AND STRUCTURE
Skill/Knowledge: Cross–Text Connections

Key Explanation: Choice B is the best answer because the conclusion of Text 2 is that researchers need to develop a new drug to treat depression.

The author of Text 1 would probably respond with "reservation" or "some doubt" because she promotes behavioral activation, a non-invasive method that does not use any medications at all, to retrain the brain into positive patterns. She probably would encourage avoiding invasive methods like introducing drugs into the body if possible.

Distractor Explanation: Choice A is incorrect because the author of Text 1 indicates that behavioral activation is successful. She does not discuss any other method of treatment, so it is impossible to tell if she would say that "most" treatments do not work. **Choice C** is incorrect because the author of Text 1 does not refer to drug performance at all. **Choice D** is incorrect because there is not enough information to tell whether the author of Text 1 "contends" or "argues" that drugs are "unacceptable" or "not allowable." She may agree that drug therapies should be attempted when other methods fail.

8. **Level:** Medium | **Domain:** INFORMATION AND IDEAS
Skill/Knowledge: Central Ideas and Details

Key Explanation: Choice A is the best answer because Keel describes the "vision" or "dream" of the Indian's "predecessors" or "earlier people," then states that "This vision was shared by the U.S. Congress in 1934 when it passed…the Indian Reorganization Act." In other words, Keel feels that the vision was "shared" or "in keeping"—both mean "the same"—with each other.

Distractor Explanation: Choice B is incorrect because Keel indicates that the IRA was written by the government, not by the predecessors, even though the goals were the same. **Choice C** is incorrect because the policy matched the desires of the Indians to "protect and restore our tribal homelands and the Indian way of life." The policy did not "deny" or "remove" rights from the Indians. **Choice D** is incorrect because there is no indication of how well the policy has upheld its goals.

9. **Level:** Easy | **Domain:** INFORMATION AND IDEAS
Skill/Knowledge: Central Ideas and Details

Key Explanation: Choice C is the best answer because the passage says that the narrator's "way lay along the canal embankment," which shows that he was on the embankment because it was the "route" or "way" he needed to go. The first line says the reason he was taking that route was, "I was going towards my lodgings." "Quarters" and "lodgings" both refer to the place where one lives, so he was headed towards his quarters.

Distractor Explanation: None of the other choices are supported by evidence from the passage. **Choice A** is incorrect because, although the embankment was usually deserted, "at that hour you never meet a soul," there is no proof that he was trying to avoid other people. **Choice B** is incorrect because he went on his walk to escape the pressures of the city, but the embankment was on his return trip as he was going home to his lodgings. **Choice D** is incorrect because the embankment was usually deserted, so that is not a place that he would have looked for excitement or adventure.

10. **Level:** Medium | **Domain:** INFORMATION AND IDEAS
Skill/Knowledge: Central Ideas and Details

Key Explanation: Choice A is the best answer because "placement" refers to "location." The passage directly states that "environmental impacts will very much depend on… the location selected"

Distractor Explanation: None of the other choices are supported by evidence from the passage. **Choice B** is incorrect because, although the passage does say that moving parts can kill wildlife, it does not say that is the most important factor when determining environmental change. **Choice C** is incorrect because the studies revealed how the system affects the environment, but do not change the effects. There is no discussion at all of **Choice D,** the total energy generated.

11. **Level:** Hard | **Domain:** INFORMATION AND IDEAS
Skill/Knowledge: Command of Evidence (Textual)

Key Explanation: Choice B is the best answer. The scientists' conclusion is that "the carnivore probably appeared very much like the unrelated *Tyrannosaurus rex.*" **Choice B** gives a detail about the "appearance" or "how it looks" that show that there is a similarity: both species had a head that was "oversized" or "very large" when compared to the rest of the body. Therefore, they both looked like they had big heads.

Distractor Explanation: Choice A is incorrect because a long separation of time could mean that the dinosaurs had evolved in different ways and looked very different. **Choice C** is incorrect because it shows a way that the dinosaurs looked different rather than a way that they are similar. Both dinosaurs were large, but *T. rex* would have, in general, been much larger. **Choice D** is incorrect because it only shows a similarity in diet. It is possible that two carnivores have very different physical characteristics or appearances while still eating the same food.

12. **Level:** Easy | **Domain:** INFORMATION AND IDEAS
Skill/Knowledge: Command of Evidence (Quantitative)

Key Explanation: Choice A is the best answer because the claim is that there "is huge variability within tree populations over time." In other words, Clark is stressing how much of a change there is. **Choice A** accurately uses information from the graph to explain that one species increased greatly, thus supporting the claim.

Distractor Explanation: Choice B is incorrect because it shows stability rather than variability or change. **Choice C** is incorrect because it is extremely vague and does not show change within the species' composition. It only shows that there is more of one species than another, and those percentages could have remained constant. **Choice D** is incorrect because it incorrectly says there was a "decrease" rather than an "increase" in the number of oak trees. There were more 5,000 years ago…which is a more recent time than 10,000 years ago.

13. **Level:** Medium | **Domain:** INFORMATION AND IDEAS
Skill/Knowledge: Inferences

Key Explanation: Choice A is the best answer because the fact that "any information about those people that may differ from you – for example, the part of the country where they live" must be included implies that the information is essential for interpreting the data. Since the data is related to earnings claims and the percentage of people who actually reached the earnings, then it can be reasonably inferred that differences in environment affects the earnings. Since "demographic factors" are differences between parts of the population, those are important to estimate if one person will earn the same amount as other investors.

Distractor Explanation: Choice B is not supported by the passage. The earnings claims must include the dates that earnings were achieved, but there is no evidence regarding how often the document is "updated" or "rewritten." It is possible that the same document could be used for many years. **Choice C** is incorrect because, while some sellers may be happy to provide evidence about their claims, there is no indication that "most" do not want to give the document to the buyer. **Choice D** is incorrect because the paragraph says that any sellers of a franchise must provide the document, not every building for sale.

14. **Level:** Medium | **Domain:** INFORMATION AND IDEAS
Skill/Knowledge: Inferences

Key Explanation: Choice D is the best answer because the passage says that one problem of tourism is that there could be "divisions and social friction," meaning conflicts, as a result of the "disparity" or "difference" between tourists and the workers who get lower pay. In other words, the local workers could become "resentful" or "dissatisfied" because of the difference in wages.

Distractor Explanation: None of the other choices are supported by evidence from the passage. **Choice A** is incorrect because there is no indication about which members of the community are employed. **Choice B** is incorrect because, while some regions might not benefit immediately from tourism because development money is spent on "schools or clinics," the passage implies that tourism is a good choice for Africa because it creates jobs. **Choice C** is incorrect because there is no discussion of replacing local cultures and traditions with new ones; if anything, "cultural stereotypes will be exploited" implies that some cultural details will be preserved to share with tourists.

15. **Level:** Easy | **Domain:** STANDARD ENGLISH CONVENTIONS
Skill/Knowledge: Form, Structure, and Sense

Key Explanation: Choice A is the best answer. It is a singular word which refers to "one more," which in the context refers to "one artist other than yourself." It fits the idea of sampling music from someone who is not yourself.

Distractor Explanation: Choice B is incorrect because, while it can be used to refer to different artists that are not yourself, it needs a plural noun, "artists" as there is no "the" in front of it. **Choice C** is used to describe all other artists, but the context is referring to taking work from one, as seen in the singular "copyright to that work." **Choice D** is incorrect because it is used as an object on its own, not with another noun like "artist."

16. **Level:** Medium | **Domain:** STANDARD ENGLISH CONVENTIONS
Skill/Knowledge: Form, Structure, and Sense

Key Explanation: Choice C is the best answer. The underline modifies the following word, "guilty," which is an adjective describing "person." **Choice C** is an adverb, so is properly used with an adjective.

Distractor Explanation: Choices A and **D** are

incorrect because they are adjectives, so should not be used to describe another adjective. They are used when referring to nouns. **Choice B** is a noun, so should not be used to modify another part of speech.

17. **Level:** Medium | **Domain:** STANDARD ENGLISH CONVENTIONS
Skill/Knowledge: Form, Structure, and Sense

Key Explanation: Choice D is the best answer. An apostrophe and s are used to show possession for one person; in this case, the death of J.R.R. Tolkien.

Distractor Explanation: Choice A is incorrect because it is too ambiguous; it could refer to either Tolkien or his son. **Choice B** is incorrect because an s forms a plural noun, but does not indicate possession. **Choice C** is used to show the possession of more than one person, but the context implies that Tolkien died and his son was still alive to publish the manuscript.

18. **Level:** Medium | **Domain:** STANDARD ENGLISH CONVENTIONS
Skill/Knowledge: Form, Structure, and Sense

Key Explanation: Choice D is the best answer. "Smaller than our sun" is a modifier that should be followed by the noun it refers to, in this case, "the red dwarf star HD260655."

Distractor Explanation: All of the other choices are incorrect because the modifier at the start of the sentence illogically describes the incorrect noun. In **Choice A**, "smaller than our Sun" refers to the generic "there." In **Choice B**, it refers to "only 33 light years," and in **Choice C** it refers to "our solar system."

19. **Level:** Easy | **Domain:** STANDARD ENGLISH CONVENTIONS
Skill/Knowledge: Boundaries

Key Explanation: Choice A is the best answer. In this text, "and" joins two verb phrases, "worked…" and "published…." Two verbs should not be divided by commas if they share the same subject; in this case, "Kenyan writer Ngugi wa Thiong'o" does both actions. There should also not be a comma between the verb "published" and its object, "A Grain of Wheat in July."

Distractor Explanation: Choices B and **D** are incorrect because there should be no comma after "Nairobi" because the "and" joins two verbs with the same subject. **Choices C** and **D** are incorrect because there should be no comma after "published." A comma is needed between a verb and a quote only when the quoted information is a complete sentence, not when the marks are indicating the title of a book.

20. **Level:** Easy | **Domain:** STANDARD ENGLISH CONVENTIONS
Skill/Knowledge: Boundaries

Key Explanation: Choice B is the best answer. When additional information is included in a sentence using two dashes, then the main part of the sentence should remain grammatically correct. By removing the aside, it is easier to determine that the proper sentence structure uses the idiom "cite XX as YY." **Choice B** completes this structure.

Distractor Explanation: All of the other choices are incorrect because they create a grammatically incorrect main clause. **Choice A** places two nouns in a row without any particle or preposition showing how they relate to each other. **Choices C** and **D** add an additional subject (which or they) and verb.

21. **Level:** Easy | **Domain:** STANDARD ENGLISH CONVENTIONS
Skill/Knowledge: Boundaries

Key Explanation: Choice D is the best answer. The idiom "as XX as YY" should have no punctuation dividing the elements from each other; they are part of the same idea.

Distractor Explanation: All of the other choices can be eliminated because they divide the standard idiom "as XX as YY" with punctuation. **Choices A** and **C** are incorrect because a colon and a single dash in a sentence should follow a complete clause, but the idea in front of the punctuation is incomplete. **Choice B** is incorrect because commas are used to divide separate ideas from the main clause.

22. **Level:** Easy | **Domain:** STANDARD ENGLISH CONVENTIONS
Skill/Knowledge: Boundaries

Key Explanation: Choice D is the best answer. "Both" refers to the two ideas "during his lifetime" and "after his lifetime." No punctuation should separate the parts of an idea joined by "both," especially as the shared idea of "lifetime" is included at the end.

Distractor Explanation: All of the other choices include unnecessary punctuation. **Choice A** makes the preposition "during" stand on its own without a noun to clarify it; there needs to be something specifying "during what." **Choice B** divides "his lifetime" from the two prepositions that refer to it. is incorrect because a single dash should follow a complete sentence, but "during" is dangling.

23. **Level:** Easy| **Domain:** EXPRESSION OF IDEAS
Skill/Knowledge: Transitions

Key Explanation: Choice B is the best answer because the passage is discussing two kinds of dogs that track people in different ways. **Choice B** sets up the idea that the following information is going to be very different from what precedes, so it effectively shows that the two dogs work under two methods that are distinct.

Distractor Explanation: Choices A and **C** are incorrect because they are used to show the result of an argument. However, the fact that air-scent dogs sniff an area is not the result of the discussion that trailing dogs follow a specific scent. **Choice D** is used to introduce more information on the same topic, so erroneously makes the reader think the discussion will continue with more details about trailing dogs.

24. **Level:** Easy | **Domain:** EXPRESSION OF IDEAS
Skill/Knowledge: Transitions

Key Explanation: Choice C is the best answer. **Choice C** is used to provide emphasis for a preceding claim by adding details that support that claim. **Choice C** therefore fits the context of adding the detail that males are physically not capable of drinking blood to the more general preceding claim that they do not drink blood.

Distractor Explanation: Choice A is used to show a logical conclusion of an argument that is being developed, but the fact that males do not have a special mouth is not necessarily the logical result of not drinking blood; it is more of a cause. It is possible for the males to have the special mouth but not use it. **Choice B** is used to summarize items in a list or conclude a section in a passage, but in this case, there is an additional idea which follows: mosquitos get energy from plants. **Choice D** is incorrect because it is used to add the specific example that illustrates a claim. However, the passage implies that there are more reasons for not drinking blood than the mouth shape. Rather, the reason is that they don't need the protein.

25. **Level:** Easy | **Domain:** EXPRESSION OF IDEAS
Skill/Knowledge: Rhetorical Synthesis

Key Explanation: : **Choice D** is the best answer. The writer wants a strong word that shows a strong need to do something, and **Choice D** emphasizes the idea of obligation or necessity.

Distractor Explanation: Choice A is incorrect because it only shows that something is possible, not that it is necessary to do. **Choice B** indicates that there is no doubt that the act will occur in the future, as opposed to stressing the fact that it needs to be done. **Choice C** is much milder than **Choice D,** giving the indication that making changes is a possibility or option, but not imperative.

26. **Level:** Medium | **Domain:** EXPRESSION OF IDEAS
Skill/Knowledge: Rhetorical Synthesis

Key Explanation: Choice B is the best answer. "Accelerating" includes the idea of getting increasingly fast or greater over time, so no additional words are needed.

Distractor Explanation: All of the other choices can be eliminated as redundant. They include words with the same meaning as "accelerating," distracting the reader from the point of the sentence.

27. **Level:** Hard | **Domain:** EXPRESSION OF IDEAS
Skill/Knowledge: Rhetorical Synthesis

Key Explanation: Choice B is the best answer. The student emphasizes the second bullet that Cher explored different styles by highlighting the point that the two songs are of different styles.

Distractor Explanation: None of the other choices highlights a common feature. **Choice A** only says that the songs were performed at different times. **Choice C** refers to a song and a television series, but there is no unifying theme about why those are notable. **Choice D** also refers to two unrelated facts: the reader does not know how or why they are significant.

1. **Level:** Easy | **Domain:** ALGEBRA
Skill/Knowledge: Linear equations in one variable
Testing point: Solving equations with one variable

Key Explanation: Choice B is correct. This question can be solved in two ways. The most efficient way to solve the equation is to factor out the 4 from the left side of the equation yielding $4(x+4)=24$. Dividing both sides of the equation by 4 yields $(x+4)=\frac{24}{4}$, which equates to $(x+4)=6$, which is **Choice B.**

The second way to solve this equation is to subtract 16 from both sides of the equation. The result is $4x+16-16=24-16$ which in turn translates to $4x=8$. Dividing both sides of the equation by 4 gets $x=2$. However, the question asks for the value of $x+4$, and not x, which will then be 2 + 4, or 6.

Distractor Explanation: Choice A is incorrect as this is the value of $4x$ when 16 is subtracted from both sides of the equation. **Choice C** is incorrect as this is the value of x. **Choice D** is incorrect as this answer may be the result of a conceptual error or miscalculation.

2. **Level:** Medium | **Domain:** PROBLEM-SOLVING AND DATA ANALYSIS
Skill/Knowledge: Probability and conditional probability | **Testing point:** Conditional probability

Key Explanation: Choice A is correct. Given that there are 35 teachers in the school, according to the table, there are 16 female teachers. Thus, the number of male teachers in the school is 35 – 16 = 19. The number of people in the school is found by adding the number of teachers to the number of students as follows: 245 + 35 = 280. Therefore, of the 280 people in the school, 19 are male teachers and the probability of selecting a male teacher is $\frac{19}{280}$.

Distractor Explanation: Choice B is incorrect since it is the probability of choosing a teacher given that he is already male. **Choice C** is incorrect, since it's the probability of choosing a male given that he is already a teacher. **Choice D** is incorrect as it is conceptually incorrect because it mixes students and teachers.

3. **Level:** Easy | **Domain:** ADVANCED MATH
Skill/Knowledge: Nonlinear equations in one variable and systems of equations in two variables
Testing point: Solving absolute value equations

Key Explanation: Absolute value equations usually have two solutions. The first step would be to remove the parentheses and set up two linear equations as follows:

$2x - 3 = 11$ and $2x - 3 = -11$

To solve for x in the first equation, add 3 to both sides of the equation as follows:

$2x - 3 + 3 = 11 + 3$

$2x = 14$

$x = 7$

To find the second solution solve for x in the second equation by adding 3 to both sides of the equation as follows:

$2x - 3 + 3 = -11 + 3$

$2x = -8$

$x = -4$

Thus, the positive solution for x is 7.

4. **Level:** Easy | **Domain:** ALGEBRA
Skill/Knowledge: Linear functions | **Testing point:** Perpendicular lines

Key Explanation: Choice C is correct. Perpendicular lines meet at 90–degree angles and have opposite sign reciprocal slopes. Putting the given equation into slope–intercept form $y = mx + b$ by dividing all terms by 5, yields $y = \frac{4}{5}y + 3$. The m in the slope–intercept form of the equation represents the slope of the line. Therefore, the slope of the line is $\frac{4}{5}$ and the opposite reciprocal slope is $\frac{-5}{4}$, which is the slope of the perpendicular line.This makes **Choice C** the only correct answer.

Distractor Explanation: Choice A is incorrect as the line would be parallel to m rather than perpendicular as the lines have the same slope. **Choices B** and **D** are incorrect as they are the negative of the perpendicular slope.

5. **Level:** Medium | **Domain:** GEOMETRY AND TRIGONOMETRY
Skill/Knowledge: Circles | **Testing point:** Standard form of the equation of a circle and completing the square

Key Explanation: Choice C is correct. To find the center of the circle, first transform the equation to its standard form $(x-h)^2 + (y-k)^2 = r^2$, where (h, k) is the center of the circle and r is its radius. To get the equation in standard form, complete the square. To do this, first, rearrange the terms in the equation to have all the x's and y's near each other as follows: $x^2 - 6x + y^2 + 4y = 36$. The standard form of a quadratic equation is $ax^2 + bx + c$ Next, working with just $x^2 - 6x$, with $a = 1$ and $b = -6$, add $\left(\frac{b}{2}\right)^2$ or $\left(\frac{-6}{2}\right)^2$ to both sides of the equation to get $x^2 - 6x + 9 + y^2 + 4y = 36 + 9$. Next, working with just $y^2 + 4y$, with $a = 1$ and $b = 4$, add $\left(\frac{b}{2}\right)^2$ or $\left(\frac{4}{2}\right)^2$ to both sides of the equation to get $x^2 - 6x + 9 + y^2 + 4y + 4 = 36 + 9 + 4$ or 49. Next, factoring $x^2 - 6x + 9$ yields $(x - 3)^2$, and factoring $y^2 + 4y + 4$ yields $(y+2)^2$, to get $(x-3)^2 + (y+2)^2 = 49$

Therefore, the center of the circle will be (3, –2).

Distractor Explanation: Choice A is incorrect because if the standard form of a circle equation is read incorrectly then $(-h, -k)$ would be incorrectly determined to be the center of the circle. **Choice D** is incorrect as the x and y coordinates have been reversed. **Choice B** is incorrect as this is the negative of incorrect **Choice D**.

6. **Level:** Hard | **Domain:** ADVANCED MATH
Skill/Knowledge: Equivalent expressions | **Testing point:** Exponents and matching coefficients

Key Explanation:
$(8^x)^x \times 4^{2x} = ((2^3)^x)^x \times (2^2)^{2x} = 2^{3x^2} \times 2^{4x}$

This yields 2^{3x^2+4x} using exponent rules.

$\frac{2^{ax^2}}{2^{-bx}} = 2^{ax^2+bx}$ using exponent rules.

Therefore,

$3x^2 + 4x = ax^2 + bx$

$a = 3$

7. **Level:** Medium | **Domain:** ALGEBRA
Skill/Knowledge: Linear inequalities in one or two variables | **Testing point:** Solving systems of linear inequalities

Key Explanation: Choice B is correct. The most

efficient way to solve the problem is to substitute the given answer choices into the system of inequalities and see which answer makes both inequalities valid. Plugging in **Choice A** into the first inequality yields

$-6(-2) + 3 < -4$

$12 + 3 < -4$

$15 < -4$, which is false. Plugging in **Choice B** into the first inequality yields $-6(4) + 3 < 7$

$-24 + 3 < 7$

$-21 < 7$, which is true. Next, plug **Choice B** into the second inequality which yields

$7 < 4 + 6$

$7 < 10$. This is true, making **Choice B** the correct option.

Distractor Explanation: Choice A does not work as shown above. Plugging **Choice C** into the first inequality yields

$-6(-2) + 3 < 1$

$12 + 3 < 1$

$15 < 1$, which is not true. Plugging **Choice D** into the first inequality yields

$-6(-2) + 3 < -4$

$12 + 3 < -4$

$15 < -4$, which is not true.

8. **Level:** Hard | **Domain:** ADVANCED MATH
Skill/Knowledge: Nonlinear functions | **Testing point:** Transformations of quadratic equations

Key Explanation: Choice A is correct. The vertex form of the equation of a parabola is $y = (x - h)^2 + k$, where (h, k) is the vertex of the parabola. Thus, the vertex of the $f(x)$ equation is (3, 8) and the vertex of the $g(x)$ equation is (5, 5). Therefore, the x coordinate moves to the right 2 units from $f(x)$ to $g(x)$, and the y coordinate moves down 3 units.

Distractor Explanation: Choice B is incorrect as the x coordinate is moving to the right, not the left. A student may pick this option if he or she assumes that since h has reduced by 2 units it is moving to the left. **Choice C** is incorrect because the y coordinate is moving down not up. **Choice D** is incorrect. This incorrect answer may be selected if the student transformed $g(x)$ onto $f(x)$ instead of the other way around.

9. **Level:** Easy | **Domain:** ADVANCED MATH
Skill/Knowledge: Nonlinear functions | **Testing point:** Identifying the equation of an exponential function from a graph

Key Explanation: Choice D is correct. The graph depicts an exponential growth equation, which has its standard equation $y = ab^x$, where if in an exponential equation $b > 1$, then the equation represents exponential growth. The value of a in the equation represents the initial value of the equation when $x = 0$. Using the process of elimination, choices A and C can be ruled out as their b values are less than 1 and thus represent exponential decay, not growth. **Choice A** can also be ruled out as it gives an initial value of 5 whereas the graph shows a smaller initial value. **Choice D** is correct as it is the only equation that shows that the graph is increasing exponentially and has a *y–intercept* of less than 5.

Distractor Explanation: See the process of elimination answer explanations above.

10. **Level:** Medium | **Domain:** GEOMETRY AND TRIGONOMETRY
Skill/Knowledge: Right triangles and trigonometry | **Testing point:** Similar triangles and use of SOHCAHTOA

Key Explanation: Since triangle *DEF* and triangle *PQR* are similar, angles *F* and *R* are congruent. Therefore, $\sin R = \sin F$. Therefore using *SOHCAHTOA* the *sin* of an angle is equal to the length of the opposite side to the angle divided by the length of the hypotenuse of the triangle. Thus, the *Sin* of *F* is $\frac{5}{13}$.

11. **Level:** Easy | **Domain:** PROBLEM-SOLVING AND DATA ANALYSIS
Skill/Knowledge: One-variable data: distributions and measures of center and spread | **Testing point:** Finding the mean

Key Explanation: Choice B is correct. To find the average of a set of data, divide the total sum of the values of the data by the number of items. The average of the SAT scores of the 7 students is 1,320. Therefore, the sum of their scores would be $1{,}320 \times 7 = 9{,}240$. Adding in the SAT score of the 8th student, the new sum of the SAT scores will be $9{,}240 + 1{,}460 = 10{,}700$. The new average SAT score will be $\frac{10{,}700}{8} = 1{,}337.5$, which is 1,340 rounded to the nearest tens place.

Distractor Explanation: Choice A is incorrect as this is the average of the average SAT scores of the 7 students and the score of the new student $\frac{(1{,}320 + 1{,}460)}{2}$. **Choice C** is incorrect as this is the mean score if the new higher score is subtracted from the sum of the current sum of scores and divided by 6. **Choice D** is incorrect as this answer incorrectly assumes that the new score will be the new average SAT score.

12. **Level:** Easy | **Domain:** PROBLEM-SOLVING AND DATA ANALYSIS
Skill/Knowledge: Two-variable data: models and scatterplots | **Testing point:** Exponential function interpretation

Key Explanation: Choice B is correct. The 3 in the exponential equation above represents the growth factor. It indicates a tripling of the bacteria. When $t = 14$ the growth factor in the equation becomes $3^{\frac{14}{14}}$, which is 3, and therefore at $t = 14$ days the amount of bacteria triples. There are 14 days in two weeks which makes **Choice B** the correct answer.

Distractor Explanation: The equation for an exponential model is $y = ab^x$, where a represents the initial amount of the data. **Choice A** is incorrect because $a = 2{,}034$ would represent the amount of bacteria at the beginning of the study and not the given term. **Choice C** is incorrect because it assumes that the model is linear, however, the model is exponential. **Choice D** is incorrect as this answer gives $rp(t)$ and not the given term in the equation.

13. **Level:** Easy | **Domain:** ALGEBRA
Skill/Knowledge: Linear equations in one variable
Testing point: Linear equation with no solutions

Key Explanation: The first step is to use the distributive property to expand out the terms on the left side of the equation as follows:

$5(x + 3) - 3(2 - x)$

$5x + 15 - 6 + 3x$

Combining like terms on the left side of the equation yields $8x + 9$

Therefore, for the equation below to have no solutions, the lines represented by both sides of the equation need to be parallel, and thus have the same slope and different *y-intercepts*. Since the equations are in slope–intercept form $y = mx + b$, with different *y-intercepts*, the slope of the line represented by $8x + 9$ is 8 and thus $p = 8$.

14. **Level:** Hard | **Domain:** ALGEBRA
Skill/Knowledge: Systems of two linear equations in two variables | **Testing point:** Finding the number of solutions in a system of equations

Key Explanation: Choice D is correct. To compare the equations, do math operations to get the equations in the slope–intercept form $y = mx + b$, where m is the slope of the line and b is the *y–intercept*. First, simplify the second equation by dividing out a 2 from all terms to get: $-3x = -4y + 16$. Adding $4y$ to both sides of the equation and adding $3x$ to both sides of the equation yields $4y = 3x + 16$. Dividing all terms in the equation by 4 to get it into slope–intercept form yields $y = \frac{3}{4}x + 4$. Adding $-3x$ to both sides of the first equation yields $-4y = -3x + 16$. Dividing all terms in the equation by – 4 yields $y = \frac{3}{4}x - 4$. Looking at the revised equations the lines have the same slope but different *y–intercepts*, making the lines parallel. Parallel lines do not intersect, and therefore there is no solution to the system of equations.

Distractor Explanation: Choice A is incorrect because to have one solution, the slopes of both equations should not be equal, and they are. **Choice B** is incorrect because linear systems cannot have 2 solutions. **Choice C** is incorrect because to have infinitely many solutions the equations would need to represent the same line and thus be the same (the slopes and *y–intercepts* of the two lines would be the same); they are not.

15. **Level:** Medium | **Domain:** GEOMETRY AND TRIGONOMETRY
Skill/Knowledge: Circles | **Testing point:** Finding the length of a minor arc

Key Explanation: Choice A is correct. The length of the minor arc is found by using the formula $\frac{\theta}{360}\pi d$, where theta is the measure of the central angle and d is the diameter of the circle. Therefore, the length of minor arc AB is $\frac{72}{360}\pi(12) = 2.4\pi$, which is **Choice A.**

Distractor Explanation: Choice B is incorrect as it gives the area of the minor sector AOB. **Choice C** is incorrect as it is the circumference of the whole circle. **Choice D** is incorrect as it is $\frac{12\pi}{72} = \frac{\pi}{6}$ and may be due to a calculation error.

16. **Level:** Medium | **Domain:** ADVANCED MATH
Skill/Knowledge: Equivalent expressions | **Testing point:** Matching coefficients

Key Explanation: $(x + 3)^2$ is equal to $(x+3)\times(x+3)$. Using the foiling method to multiply out the terms, yields $x^2 + 3x + 3x + 9$, or $x^2 + 6x + 9$. Using the distributive property, $-2(x^2 + 6x + 9) + 6 = -2x^2 - 12x - 18 + 6$, which is equivalent to $-2x^2 - 12x - 12 = ax^2 + bx + c$. Therefore, $c = -12$.

17. **Level:** Easy | **Domain:** GEOMETRY AND TRIGONOMETRY
Skill/Knowledge: Lines, angles, and triangles | **Testing point:** Midpoint between two points on a line

Key Explanation: Choice C is correct. To find the midpoint between two points on a line (x_1, y_1)

and (x_2, y_2), use the midpoint coordinates formula $\left(\frac{x_1+x_2}{2}, \frac{y_1+y_2}{2}\right)$

Therefore the coordinates of the midpoint of line segment AB can be found from the following equations: $\frac{6+x_2}{2}=8$ and $\frac{11+y_2}{2}=10$. Using cross products, solve $x_2 + 6 = 16$, or $x_2=10$, and $y_2 + 11 = 20$, or $y_2 =9$. Therefore, the coordinates of point B are $(10, 9)$.

Distractor Explanation: Choice A is incorrect and is found when the midpoint formula is used incorrectly with $(8, 10)$ and $(6, 11)$ as the points. **Choice B** is incorrect and is found by subtracting in the midpoint formula instead of adding. **Choice D** is incorrect and may be arrived at through a conceptual error.

18. **Level:** Easy | **Domain:** ADVANCED MATH
Skill/Knowledge: Nonlinear functions | **Testing point:** Finding the number of solutions to an absolute value equation

Key Explanation: Choice A is correct. Since the absolute value is equal to zero, the only value that makes the absolute value equation equal to zero is $x = -3$. Thus, there is only one solution.

Distractor Explanation: Choice B is incorrect as to have two solutions the absolute value must be equal to a positive number. Zero is not a positive number. **Choice C** is incorrect because for an absolute value to have 0 solutions, it must be equal to a negative number and zero is not a negative number. **Choice D** is incorrect as there is enough information to answer the question.

19. **Level:** Easy | **Domain:** ADVANCED MATH
Skill/Knowledge: Nonlinear functions | **Testing point:** Absolute value and value of a function

Key Explanation: Choice A is correct. To find $f(2)$, substitute 2 for all values of x in the equation as follows:

$(2)^2 - 20(2) + 9 = -27$.

To find $|f(2)|$ take the absolute value of -27 which is 27, or **Choice A**.

Distractor Explanation: Choice B is incorrect as the question requires the absolute value of the function value and not the function value itself. **Choices C** and **D** are incorrect and can be arrived at through miscalculations.

20. **Level:** Easy | **Domain:** PROBLEM-SOLVING AND DATA ANALYSIS
Skill/Knowledge: Percentages | **Testing point:** Percentage increase and decrease

Key Explanation: Assume that the initial price of the oil was x. The price of oil after the 20% increase would be $1.2x$. This price is then decreased by 14%. Thus, 86% of the oil price remains and thus $0.86 \times 1.2x = 1.032x$. This shows that after the two changes, the price of oil has increased overall by 3.2%.

21. **Level:** Easy | **Domain:** GEOMETRY AND TRIGONOMETRY
Skill/Knowledge: Circles | **Testing point:** Area of a circle inscribed in a square

Key Explanation: Choice C is correct. The length of a side of the square is equal to the diameter of the circle. The area of a circle can be found using the formula πr^2, where r is the radius of the circle.

The radius of a circle is half of its diameter, so the radius of the circle is $\frac{4\sqrt{2}}{2}$ or $2\sqrt{2}$. Therefore, the area of the circle is $\left(2\sqrt{2}\right)^2 \times \pi$ or 8π.

Therefore, $p = 8$.

Distractor Explanation: Choice A is incorrect. This is the value of the area of the square and not the circle. **Choice B** is incorrect. This is the value of two times the diameter of the circle. **Choice D** is incorrect. This is the value of the area of the circle if the radius is equal to 8.

22. **Level:** Medium | **Domain:** ALGEBRA
Skill/Knowledge: Linear inequalities in one or two variables | **Testing point:** Solving a linear inequality

Key Explanation: Choice B is correct. To solve, first add x to both sides of the equation to get: $-2x + 6 \leq 2$. Next, subtract 6 from both sides of the equation to get:
$-2x \leq -4$ Finally, divide both sides by -2 which flips the inequality sign yielding $x \geq 2x$ is, therefore, greater than or equal to 2. Only Choice B is not in the domain of the equation.

Distractor Explanation: Choices A, **C**, and **D** are incorrect. These answer choices are solutions to the inequality and answer the opposite of what the question is asking.

1. **Level:** Easy | **Domain:** ADVANCED MATH
Skill/Knowledge: Nonlinear functions | **Testing point:** Sum of the solutions

Key Explanation: Choice C is correct. The equation represents a quadratic in the form $ax^2 + bx + c$, where a=3, b=9, and c=−27. The sum of the solutions to a quadratic equation is given by the formula $\left(\frac{-b}{a}\right)$,Therefore, the sum of the solutions of the quadratic equation would be $\left(\frac{-9}{3}\right)$, or −3.

Distractor Explanation: Choice A is incorrect as it is $\left(\frac{b}{a}\right)$, not $-\left(\frac{b}{a}\right)$. **Choice B** is incorrect because it is the product of the solutions to the quadratic equation and not the sum of them. The product of the solutions of a quadratic equation is given by the formula $\left(\frac{c}{a}\right)$, which is $\left(\frac{-27}{3}\right)$ or −9. **Choice D** is incorrect as it is the negative of the product of the solutions.

2. **Level:** Easy | **Domain:** ADVANCED MATH
Skill/Knowledge: Equivalent expressions | **Testing point:** Combining like terms

Key Explanation: Choice D is correct. First, distribute the negative to the terms in the parentheses as follows:
$3x^2y + 5x - 3x^2y^2 + 2x^2y$. Combining like terms yields $5x^2y + 5x - 3x^2y^2$ which is **Choice D** when the terms are arranged in standard form.

Distractor Explanation: Choices A and **C** are incorrect due to miscalculation or lack of concept knowledge. **Choice B** is incorrect. The sign changes of the terms in the parentheses when the negative sign is distributed to these terms and the parenthesis is removed.

3. **Level:** Medium | **Domain:** ALGEBRA
Skill/Knowledge: Linear inequalities in one or two variables | **Testing point:** Solving for a linear inequality

Key Explanation: To solve the inequality, first subtract 2 from both sides to get: $-2y + 2 - 2 < 6 - 2$

Next, divide both sides by −2 to get: $y > -2$
Note that multiplying or dividing by a negative number in an inequality flips the inequality sign. −1 is the least possible integer value of y which satisfies the inequality $y > -2$.

4. **Level:** Easy | **Domain:** ADVANCED MATH
Skill/Knowledge: Nonlinear equations in one variable and systems of equations in two variables
Testing point: Discriminant and solving for linear and quadratic equations

Key Explanation: Choice A is correct. Using the substitution method, substitute the first equation for y in the second equation yielding $2x - 5 = 2x^2 - 18x + 45$.

Next, subtract the $2x$ from both sides to get $-5 = 2x^2 - 20x + 45$. Add 5 to both sides of the equation to get $0 = 2x^2 - 18x + 50$. The discriminant of a quadratic equation is $b^2 - 4ac$, when the quadratic equation is in the form $ax^2 + bx + c$. In the quadratic equation $a = 2$, $b = -20$, and $c = 50$. The value of the discriminant determines the number of solutions for a quadratic equation. Therefore, plugging in the values of a, b, and c into the discriminant, yields $(-20)^2 - 4(2)(50)$ which yields $400 - 400 = 0$
Therefore, the system will have one solution as the discriminant = 0.

Distractor Explanation: Choices A and **C** are incorrect, most likely due to a miscalculation.

Choice D is incorrect. Quadratic equations can't have an infinite number of solutions.

5. **Level:** Easy | **Domain:** ALGEBRA
Skill/Knowledge: Systems of two linear equations in two variables | **Testing point:** Solving linear systems using elimination or substitution

Key Explanation: Choice A is correct. The most efficient way to solve the system of equations is to subtract the two equations resulting in $x + y = 9$.

The system of equations can also be solved using the elimination or substitution methods to find x and y individually and then adding the values of x and y to find the answer.

Distractor Explanation: Choice B is incorrect as it is the value of x only and not $x + y$. **Choice D** is incorrect as it is found by the sum of the two equations which instead yields $5x - 3y = 13$, which does not give the value of $x + y$. **Choice C** is incorrect as it is due to a miscalculation or a conceptual error.

6. **Level:** Easy | **Domain:** GEOMETRY AND TRIGONOMETRY
Skill/Knowledge: Right triangles and trigonometry | **Testing point:** Trigonometric identities

Key Explanation: There is a trigonometric identity which states that $\sin x = \cos (90° - x)$

Therefore, $\sin 32° = \cos 58°$ and thus $\cos 58° = 0.551$.

7. **Level:** Hard | **Domain:** GEOMETRY AND TRIGONOMETRY
Skill/Knowledge: Lines, angles, and triangles | **Testing point:** Conversion of measurements and area of triangles

Key Explanation: Choice D is correct. The area of a triangle is found by the formula $A = \frac{1}{2} \times$ base $\times$ height. Since the answer is required in *ft squared*, we will need to convert any lengths of the sides of the triangle that are in *inches* to *feet*.

Therefore, 10 *inches* can be converted to *feet* by multiplying it by $\frac{1}{12}$, which gives $\frac{10}{12}$ feet. This reduces to $\frac{5}{6}$ *ft*.

Using the area of a triangle formula, the area is $\frac{1}{2} \times \frac{5}{6} \times 24 = 10$ *ft*.

Distractor Explanation: Choice A is incorrect as this is the area of the triangle without having converted any of the side *lengths* to *feet*. **Choice B** is incorrect as even though the measurements have been converted to feet, the formula for the area used was *base* $\times$ *height* which is not the correct formula. **Choice C** is incorrect as this is the area if all the side lengths were in inches instead of *feet*.

8. **Level:** Hard | **Domain:** ADVANCED MATH
Skill/Knowledge: Equivalent expressions | **Testing point:** Subtracting fractions with variable denominators

Key Explanation: Choice C is correct. All the given answer choices have one term, and not two like the original expression. Thus, the two fractional expressions need to be combined into one fraction by getting them both over the least common denominator. The least common denominator of the two terms is $x(x - 4)$. To get both terms over the least common denominator the first term needs to be multiplied by $\frac{(x-4)}{(x-4)}$ and the second term needs to be multiplied by $\frac{x}{x}$, yielding

$$\frac{-5(x-4)}{x(x-4)} = \frac{x(x)}{x(x-4)}$$

Since the denominators of the fractions are equal, the numerators can be combined over a single fraction as follows:

$$\frac{-5(x-4)-x(x)}{x(x-4)} = \frac{-5x+20-x^2}{x^2-4x},$$

which is **Choice C**.

Distractor Explanation: Choice A is incorrect as the question asked to simplify the terms and not solve for anything. **Choices B** and **D** are incorrect and may be due to a conceptual error or miscalculation.

9. **Level:** Easy | **Domain:** ALGEBRA
Skill/Knowledge: Linear equations in two variables | **Testing point:** Identifying linear equations from graphs

Key Explanation: Choice B is correct. The slope-intercept equation of a line is $y = mx + b$, where m is the slope and b is the *y-intercept* of the equation. The slope m of a line can be found using the equation $m = \frac{(y_2 - y_1)}{(x_2 - x_1)}$, where (x_1, y_1) and (x_2, y_2) represent any two points on the line.

Pick two points on the line that are easy to find on the graph. The x and y intercepts of the line are two good points to use. Using points (2, 0) and (0, 6), the slope of the line can be found by plugging these points into the slope formula, yielding $\frac{(6-0)}{(0-2)}$, or $\frac{6}{-2} = -3$. The *y-intercept* of the line is 6. Therefore $y = -3x + 6$. All of the answer choices are written in an offset of the standard equation of a line $ax + by = c$. Adding $3x$ to both sides of the slope-intercept form of the equation gives the standard equation of the line as $3x + y = 6$. Multiplying all terms of the equation by 3 to better match the form of the answer choices yields $9x + 3y = 18$, which matches **Choice B**.

Distractor Explanation: Choice A is incorrect as this equation represents a line with a positive slope. From the graph the slope of the line is negative. **Choice C** is incorrect because the slope of the line is −3 and not 2. **Choice D** is incorrect because the slope of the line is −3 and not −4 .

10. **Level:** Easy | **Domain:** ADVANCED MATH
Skill/Knowledge: Nonlinear functions | **Testing point:** Finding *y-intercept*

Key Explanation: The *y-intercept* occurs where $x = 0$, $y - 7 = 3^0 - 5$. Anything to the power of zero $= 1$, so $y - 7 = 1 - 5$. Adding 7 to both sides of the equation to solve for y yields $y - 7 + 7 = 1 - 5 + 7$, $y = 3$.

11. **Level:** Medium | **Domain:** ADVANCED MATH
Skill/Knowledge: Nonlinear functions | **Testing point:** Finding the value that makes a function undefined

Key Explanation: Choice C is correct. A function is undefined when the denominator is equal to 0. To find what values of x make this occur, solve the equation $x^2-2x-15 = 0$ for x. Use the grouping method of factoring to determine what two numbers multiply to −15 but add up to −2. The two numbers would be −5 and 3. Thus, the middle term of the quadratic equation can be written as $-5x + 3x$, instead of $-2x$ as follows: $2-5x+3x-15=0$. Grouping the terms and factoring out the greatest common factor of each group, yields $x(x - 5)+3(x - 5) = 0$. $(x+3)(x-5) = 0$, $x = -3$, and $x = 5$. Only the solution to the quadratic equation $x=-3$ meets the question condition that x be less than zero. Thus, C is the correct answer.

Distractor Explanation: Choice A is incorrect since this is the positive x value of the solution and the value needs to be less than zero. **Choice B** is incorrect as it gives the negative value 5, which could be the result of factoring incorrectly. **Choice D** is incorrect. It may be due to a miscalculation.

12. **Level:** Medium | **Domain:** ALGEBRA
Skill/Knowledge: Linear functions | **Testing point:** Finding the *x–intercept* given two points

Key Explanation: Choice A is correct. $f(3) = -1$ and $f(4) = -3$ represent the x and y values of two points on a line. The points are (3, –1) and (4, –3). To find the x–intercept of the line represented, the equation of the line first needs to be determined. The slope–intercept form of the equation of the line, $y = mx + b$ is easiest to use. In this equation, m represents the slope of the line and b its *y–intercept*. The slope of a line can be found using the slope formula $m = \frac{(y_2 - y_1)}{(x_2 - x_1)}$. Plugging in the two points into the slope formula yields

$m = \frac{-3-(-1)}{4-3} = -2$.

Therefore the equation of the line is $y = -2x + b$.

To find b, plug either point into the equation and solve for b. Using the point (3, –1) yields

$-1 = -2(3) + b$, $-1 = -6 + b$, $b = 5$.

Therefore the equation of the line is $y = -2x + 5$. The *x–intercept* of a line occurs where $y = 0$. Plugging in zero for y into the equation and solving for x gives the following *x–intercept*:

$0 = -2x + 5$, $2x = 5$, $x = 2.5$ *or* $\frac{5}{2}$.

Distractor Explanation: Choice B is incorrect as this is the *y–intercept*. **Choice C** is incorrect as this is the slope of the line. **Choice D** is incorrect and is the result of a miscalculation in solving for the *x–intercept*.

13. **Level:** Hard | **Domain:** ALGEBRA
Skill/Knowledge: Linear functions | **Testing point:** Transformations and Solving for function values

Key Explanation: The function $f(x + 3)$ is moved to the left by 3 units, therefore we should also move the x value in $f(x)$ to the left by 3 units to get $2 - 3$ or $f(-1)$

Therefore $f(-1)$ is found by substituting –1 into the equation for x as follows:
$5(-1) - 17 = -22$.

14. **Level:** Hard | **Domain:** PROBLEM–SOLVING AND DATA ANALYSIS
Skill/Knowledge: Ratios, rates, proportional relationships, and units | **Testing point:** Calculating average speed with unknown variable

Key Explanation: Choice B is correct. Average speed is calculated by taking the total distance traveled divided by the total time to travel that distance.

The total distance traveled would be $x + x = 2x$

The total time taken would be 2.5 *hrs* + 1.5 *hrs* = 4 *hrs*

Therefore, the average. speed = $\frac{2x}{4} = \frac{x}{2}$

Distractor Explanation: Choice A is incorrect as it does not account for the fact that there is a return trip. **Choice C** is incorrect as it incorrectly accounts for the time it took Amber to do her errands. **Choice D** is incorrect as it may be due to a conceptual error or the student incorrectly found the total distance traveled.

15. **Level:** Easy | **Domain:** GEOMETRY AND TRIGONOMETRY
Skill/Knowledge: Area and volume | **Testing point:** Perimeter of a rectangle

Key Explanation: Choice B is correct. If the width of the rectangle is *w*, the length would be $w+3$. The area of a rectangle can be found by multiplying the width of the rectangle by its length.

Therefore the area of the rectangle would be $w(w+3)=28$. Using the distributive property, the equation can be expanded out to:

$$w^2+3w=28$$

$$w^2+3w-28=0$$

Factoring the equation yields $(w+7)(w-4)=0$

Setting both factors of the equation equal to 0 results in $w=-7$ and $w=4$. Since the width of a rectangle cannot be negative, –7 is not a valid width for the rectangle. Therefore the width of the rectangle would be 4 and the length would be $4+3$ or 7. The perimeter of a rectangle is found by the formula $P=2(l+w)$. Plugging in the determined values for *w* and *l* yields

$2(7+4)=22$ or **Choice B**.

Distractor Explanation: Choice A is incorrect as this value is the sum of the length and the width and not two times the sum. **Choice C** is incorrect as this is half the area. **Choice D** is incorrect and may be due to conceptual error.

16. **Level:** Easy | **Domain:** PROBLEM-SOLVING AND DATA ANALYSIS
Skill/Knowledge: Inference from sample statistics and margin of error | **Testing point:** Inference from sample statistics

Key Explanation: The students surveyed who do not practice sanitary routines are (48 – 23) = 25. It can therefore be extrapolated that $\frac{25}{48}$ of all the students in the school donot practice sanitary routines. Therefore $\left(\frac{25}{48}\right)\times 2{,}280$ or 1,187.5 students. This rounds up to 1,188 students.

17. **Level:** Medium | **Domain:** ALGEBRA
Skill/Knowledge: Linear functions | **Testing point:** Linear transformations

Key Explanation: Choice D is correct. To move one unit up, 1 is added to the equation. To move 1 unit to the left, 1 is added to the *x* term in the equation as follows

$y = 2\ (x + 1) + 1$

$y = 2x + 2 + 1$

$y = 2x + 3$

Distractor Explanation: Choice A is incorrect as this is moving the line to the right 1 unit and up by 1 unit. **Choice B** is incorrect as this is moving the line only up by one unit and not moving it to the left. **Choice C** is incorrect as this answer may be due to a conceptual issue.

18. **Level:** Medium | **Domain:** ADVANCED MATH
Skill/Knowledge: Nonlinear equation in one variable and systems of equations in two variables
Testing point: Finding the vertex of a parabola

Key Explanation: Choice D is correct. The standard form of a parabola is represented by the equation $y = ax^2 + bx + c$. In the equation given, $a = 2$, $b = 8$, and $c = 12$. The *x* coordinate of the vertex is found using the formula $\left(\frac{-b}{2a}\right)$. Thus, $\left(\frac{-8}{2(2)}\right)=-2$

Distractor Explanation: Choice A is incorrect as this is the product of the solutions to the quadratic equation. **Choice B** is incorrect as this is the sum of the solutions to the quadratic equation. **Choice C** is incorrect and is found by incorrectly using $\left(\frac{b}{a}\right)$.

19. **Level:** Easy | **Domain:** ADVANCED MATH
Skill/Knowledge: Equivalent expressions | **Testing point:** Long division and remainder theorem

Key Explanation: B is the remainder when $x^2 - 6x + 10$ is divided by $x + 2$. When the divisor is equated to 0, we find $x = -2$, we can then find the remainder by substitute -2 in place of x $\left(-2^2 - 6(-2) + 10\right)$ which yields 26, this is the value of B.

20. **Level:** Easy | **Domain:** GEOMETRY AND TRIGONOMETRY
Skill/Knowledge: Lines, angles, and triangles | **Testing point:** The pythagorean theorem

Key Explanation: Choice B is correct. The Pythagorean theorem states that the sum of the squares of the lengths of the sides of a right triangle is equal to the square of the length of the hypotenuse of the triangle, or $a^2 + b^2 = c$. Plugging in 11 for a and 61 for c yields $11^2 + b^2 = 61^2$

$b^2 = 61^2 - 11^2$

$b^2 = 3{,}721 - 121$

$b^2 = 3{,}600$

Therefore, $b = 60$.

Distractor Explanation: Choices A and **D** are incorrect and may be due to conceptual or calculation errors. **Choice C** is incorrect and can be found by adding $61^2 + 11^2$ and finding the square root instead of subtracting the two numbers.

21. **Level:** Easy | **Domain:** PROBLEM-SOLVING AND DATA ANALYSIS
Skill/Knowledge: Evaluating statistical claims: observational studies, and experiments | **Testing point:** Observational experiments

Key Explanation: Choice D is correct. This statement is true because it is not certain that taking supplements would directly equate to an improvement in student performance. It is not known if all other variables were kept constant. Therefore, a direct cause-and-effect relationship cannot be determined. Also, the sample size is too small to generalize to a larger population.

Distractor Explanation: Choices A, **B**, and **C** are incorrect. These statements are false and imply that there is a relationship between student performance and taking supplements.

22. **Level:** Easy | **Domain:** ALGEBRA
Skill/Knowledge: Systems of two linear equations in two variables | **Testing point:** Solving for system of linear equations

Key Explanation: Choice A is correct. The most efficient way to answer this question is to not solve the system of equations for x and y individually, but rather to subtract the second equation from the first, yielding $-x + y = -5$. Therefore $y - x = -5$.

Distractor Explanation: Choice B is incorrect. This is the negative value of option A and is due to a calculation mistake. **Choice C** is incorrect. This is the value of y. **Choice D** is incorrect. This is the value of x.

Practice Test 2

You are about to begin a full-length Practice Test. The test has four modules. The time allotted for each module is marked at the beginning of the module. Work on one module at a time. Use a timer to keep track of the time limits for every module.

Try to take the Practice Test under real test conditions. Find a quiet place to work, and set aside enough time to complete the test without being disturbed. At the end of the test, check your answers by referring to the Answer Key and fill in your raw score in the scorecard below. Also, note down the time taken by you for completing each module.

Pay particular attention to the questions that were answered incorrectly. Read the answer explanations and understand how to solve them.

My Score Card (Raw Score)

	Reading and Writing		Math	
	Module 1	Module 2	Module 1	Module 2
Out of	27	27	22	22
My Score	________	________	________	________
Time Taken	________	________	________	________

TEST BEGINS ON THE NEXT PAGE

Reading and Writing Test

27 QUESTIONS | 32 MINUTES

DIRECTIONS

The questions in this section address a number of important reading and writing skills. Each question includes one or more passages, which may include a table or graph. Read each passage and question carefully, and then choose the best answer to the question based on the passage(s). All questions in this section are multiple-choice with four answer choices. Each question has a single best answer.

1

Hyraxes are small, furry, herbivorous mammals with short tails that live primarily in Africa; one species is also found in the Middle East. These little animals spend time in trees or rocky outcrops. They _____ resemble guinea pigs, but in reality, are much more closely related to sea cows and elephants.

Which choice completes the text with the most logical and precise word or phrase?

A) logically

B) customarily

C) superficially

D) universally

2

The following text is adapted from a publication by Jefferson Keel's 2011 publication, "The Indian Reorganization Act—75 Years Later: Renewing our Commitment to Restore Tribal Homelands and Promote Self-determination."

> Today, the Indian Reorganization Act (IRA) is as necessary as it was in 1934. The purposes of the IRA were frustrated first by World War II and then by the termination era. Work did not begin again until the 1970s with the self-determination policy, and since then, Indian tribes are building economies from the ground up.

As used in the text, what does the word "frustrated" most nearly mean?

A) annoyed

B) unfulfilled

C) dissatisfied

D) thwarted

3

The following text is adapted from Mother Jones's speech to coal miners in West Virginia in 1912

> The guards of the mining companies beat, abuse, maim, and hold up citizens without process of law; deny freedom of speech, a provision guaranteed by the Constitution; deny the citizens the right to assemble in a peaceable manner for the purpose of discussing questions in which they are concerned.

As used in the text, what does the word "provision" most nearly mean?

A) allocation

B) arrangement

C) contingency

D) requirement

4

The following text is from Frances Hodgson Burnett's 1905 novel "A Little Princess."

> If Sara had been older or less punctilious about being quite polite to people, she could have explained herself in a very few words. But, as it was, she felt a flush rising on her cheeks. Miss Minchin was a very severe and imposing person, and she seemed so absolutely sure that Sara knew nothing whatever of French, that she felt as if it would be almost rude to correct her. The truth was that Sara could not remember the time when she had not seemed to know French.

Which choice best states the function of the underlined sentence in the text as a whole?

A) It gives a description of the physical appearance of one of the characters.

B) It establishes why one of the characters was not comfortable in the situation.

C) It reinforces an emotional state alluded to in the previous sentence.

D) It introduces the interaction between two characters in the following sentences.

CONTINUE

5

The following text is adapted from Herman Melville's 1851 novel, "Moby Dick; or The Whale."

> Now, when I say that I am in the habit of going to sea...I never go as a passenger; nor, though I am something of a salt, do I ever go to sea as a Commodore, or a Captain, or a Cook. I abandon the glory and distinction of such offices to those who like them. No, when I go to sea, I go as a simple sailor, right before the mast, plumb down into the forecastle, aloft there to the royal mast-head. True, they rather order me about some, and make me jump from spar to spar, like a grasshopper in a May meadow. And at first, this sort of thing is unpleasant enough. But this wears off in time.

The narrator brings up the analogy of a grasshopper to anticipate which of the following arguments?

A) A regular crew member does not receive enough compensation.

B) The duties of a simple sailor are sufficient to occupy that person's time.

C) The narrator should try to work his way up to a position as an officer.

D) It is important to obey orders from a superior officer aboard a ship.

6

The following text is adapted from F. Scott Fitzgerald's 1922 novel, "The Beautiful and the Damned."

> At fifty-seven years old Adam Patch determined, after a severe attack of sclerosis, to consecrate the remainder of his life to the moral regeneration of the world. He became a reformer among reformers. He levelled a varied assortment of uppercuts and body-blows at liquor, literature, vice, art, patent medicines, and Sunday theatres. From an armchair in the office of his Tarrytown estate he directed against the enormous hypothetical enemy, unrighteousness, a campaign which went on through fifteen years, during which he displayed himself a rabid monomaniac, an unqualified nuisance, and an intolerable bore. The year in which this story opens found him wearying; <u>1861 was creeping up slowly on 1895;</u> his thoughts ran a great deal on the Civil War, somewhat on his dead wife and son, almost infinitesimally on his grandson Anthony.

Which choice best states the function of the underlined portion in the text as a whole?

A) It indicates that Adam Patch was living in the past rather than the present.

B) It provides a reason Adam Patch did not reflect often on the deaths of his wife and son.

C) It offers the reason that Adam Patch dedicated most of his time to campaigning against vices.

D) It clarifies the previous claim that Adam Patch was an intolerable bore.

CONTINUE

7

The following text is adapted from Tien Nguyen's 2019 publication, "Antibodies Reverse Synthetic Opioid Overdoses in Mice."

> Medical professionals have only one treatment option, a drug called naloxone, against acute opioid overdoses, which is a growing problem that in 2017 killed more than 47,000 people in the US. The fast-acting treatment, sold as Narcan, races towards the brain where it blocks opioid receptors, denying the drugs access to them. But naloxone breaks down after about an hour, which allows a relapse into overdose unless the drug is re-administered. Naloxone's short lifetime also makes it less effective against powerful synthetic opioids like fentanyl and carfentanil, which are 100- and 10,000-fold stronger than morphine, respectively.

Which choice best explains why naloxone is not completely desirable as a solution for patients who have overdosed on opiates?

A) Naloxone is only able to protect a patient for a limited period.

B) Naloxone is more expensive than other available treatment options.

C) Naloxone offers no results for overdoses of many opiate drugs.

D) Naloxone has harmful side effects which can injure the patient.

8

Why does the sky turn red at sunrise and sunset? The reason is Rayleigh Scattering, which is actually the same effect that you see in a rainbow when light hits rain. Light travels in waves, with red waves being the longest visible light and blue being the shortest. The shorter the wave, the easier it scatters into different directions. During the day, the Sun shines directly down on the atmosphere, so all wavelengths enter and the sky looks blue to a viewer. However, when the Sun gets lower on the horizon, the light is traveling through a much larger distance of the atmosphere to reach the same place on the Earth's surface. At that angle, many of the shorter blue waves get scattered into outer space, and only the longer, red waves, which travel in a straighter line before being scattered, reach the viewer.

Why does the author mention a rainbow in the text?

A) To explain where waves of light originate

B) To offer an example that the reader might recognize

C) To present an exception to a general rule

D) To show why blue waves scatter more easily than red waves

CONTINUE

9

The following text is adapted from Fyodor Dostoevsky's 1848 collection of stories, "*White Nights and Other Stories.*"

> Leaning on the canal railing stood a woman with her elbows on the rail, she was apparently looking with great attention at the muddy water of the canal. She was wearing a very <u>charming</u> yellow hat and a <u>jaunty</u> little black mantle. "She's a girl, and I am sure she is dark," I thought. She did not seem to hear my footsteps, and did not even stir when I passed by with bated breath and loudly throbbing heart. I was taken aback when I realized she was not just gazing at the water, but sobbing uncontrollably.

In the text, what is the main function of the words "charming" and "jaunty"?

A) They show that the girl's true age belied her outward appearance.

B) They establish that the girl was not suitably clad for the weather.

C) They identify the reason for the narrator's interest in the girl.

D) They highlight a contrast between the girl's appearance and her actions.

10

Most of the population in Sub-Saharan Africa works in subsistence agriculture to make a living and feed their typically large families. In recent decades, there has been enormous rural-to-urban migration to the major cities, which are extremely overcrowded. At the center of the main business districts are modern high-rise business offices well connected to the global economy, but outside are slums with no services and miserable, unsanitary conditions. The informal sector of the economy—that which is not regulated, controlled, or taxed—has become the primary system of doing business. The lack of government regulation prevents taxes from being assessed or collected, which, in turn, diminishes support for public services or infrastructure.

Based on information from the text, which of the following would best illustrate a transaction that occurs in the informal sector of the Sub-Saharan economy?

A) A farmer trades several chickens for enough wood to build a house for his newly-married son.

B) An international corporation from Denmark invests money in erecting a new school in a rural area.

C) A governor uses tax money to build a bridge, but hires a construction company owned by a good friend.

D) A young man from a rural area moves to a large city because he wants to find a better job.

CONTINUE

11

The US Cities with the Greatest Percentage of Residents who Commute by Bicycle

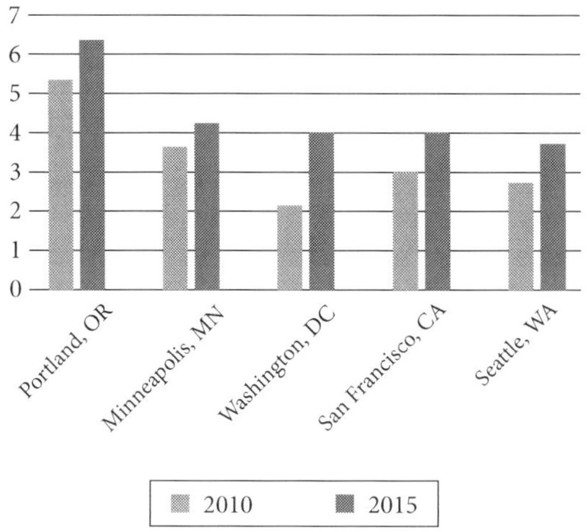

Based on data from the US Census Bureau

Why do people ride bicycles to work? Weather is not everything, as there is an annual average of 156 days of rain in the top commuting city, Portland, Oregon. Making cycling safer by adding protected bike lanes can increase ridership. Another option is making bikes more accessible, such as was done in the District of Columbia, which added 400 bike share depots since 2010. The success of such programs is evident: ______

Which choice most effectively uses data from the graph to complete the example?

A) Ridership in Washington, DC, increased from just over 2 percent in 2010 to 4 percent in 2015.

B) Washington, DC, used to have lower ridership than any other of the top five cities for bicycle commuters in 2010.

C) Portland, Oregon, now boasts over 6 percent of commuters who ride bikes and Washington, DC, has increased to 4 percent.

D) Washington, DC now has more bicycle commuters than San Francisco, California or Seattle, Washington.

CONTINUE

12

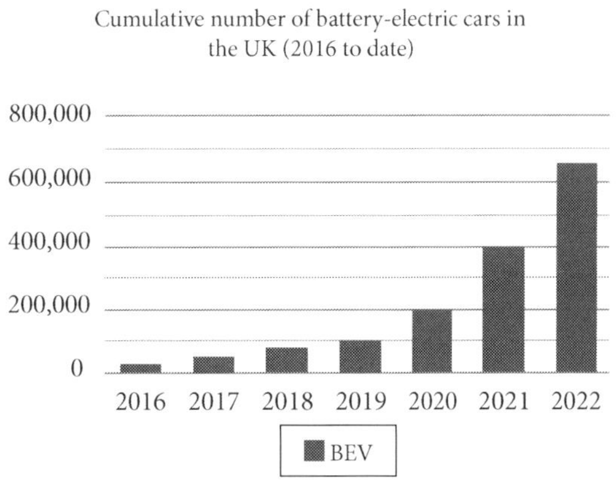

Source: SMMT, December 2002

According to a study released by The Society of Motor Manufacturers and Traders (SMMT), the number of electric cars registered in the United Kingdom has increased dramatically over the years, showing increasing customer preference for battery-electric cars over traditional cars. However, this customer preference for battery-electric cars has not increased uniformly over the years. For instance, ______________

Which choice most effectively uses data from the graph to complete the text?

A) between 2016 to 2019, less than 200,000 battery-electric cars were registered in the UK

B) in 2020, less than 300,000 battery-electric cars were registered in the UK

C) by 2022, almost 700,000 electric cars had been registered

D) while the number of registered electric cars rose by 200,00 between the years 2020 and 2021, there was a spike of almost 300,000 additional cars registered in 2022

13

A new species of salamander, *Tylototriton phukhaensis,* was named in 2020. The defining feature is a distinct head ridge, though it also has head horns and a stripe down its back. A molecular examination shows that it is closely related to two of the four other *Tylototriton* species found in Thailand. First identified from a 20-year-old photograph in a travel magazine, biologists speculated whether the species still existed in the wild, but ______

Which choice most logically completes the text?

A) had to base their assessments on the *Tylototriton* species that were more readily available to them.

B) were able to locate living specimens that could provide enough information for a positive identification.

C) spent years vainly scouring the tropical rainforests before determining that it was probably indeed extinct.

D) finally concluded that the photograph might have been inaccurate or was possibly even created as a hoax.

CONTINUE

14

Menkes disease is lethal and there is no known cure, so most patients die within the first decade of their lives, most before the age of 3. Because it is so rare, few pharmaceutical companies are investing in research related to the disease. Through the NIH Undiagnosed Diseases program, we evaluated a patient who presented clinically with abnormal hair and cognitive dysfunction. The hair abnormalities observed in our patient resemble those found in Menkes syndrome, but sequence analysis of the ATP7A gene and relevant biochemical testing showed that ATP7A wasn't involved in causing our patient's clinical features.

Which statement regarding Menkes disease can be most reasonably inferred from the passage?

A) Pharmaceutical companies are irresponsible in their attitude towards the disease.

B) Patients are usually not aware that they have the disease until its advanced stages.

C) There are not enough patients to make the development of a cure financially viable.

D) Giving a patient adequate ATP7A supplements can help reduce the effect of the disease.

15

There's nothing like homemade red Thai chili paste to enliven a meal. Most cooks opt for store-bought substitutes, however, because traditionally it takes over 30 minutes of grinding ingredients such as chili pepper, lemongrass, cilantro, _____ in a mortar and pestle.

Which choice completes the text so that it conforms to the conventions of Standard English?

A) shallots and, lime

B) shallots, and lime

C) shallots, and lime,

D) shallots, and, lime

CONTINUE

16

William Shakespeare is often misquoted, but at other times, phrases are used in a context very different from what they were intended to be. While "now is the winter of our _____ frequently used to mean a horrible time, it actually signals a time of change for the better in the drama "Richard III."

Which choice completes the text so that it conforms to the conventions of Standard English?

A) discontent." It is

B) discontent," is

C) discontent", is

D) discontent" is

17

Algeria marks its 53rd year of independence this _____ bitter struggle for freedom in the late 1950s and early 1960s became a central focus of the global movement against colonialism. It also influenced the evolving forms of oppression and resistance in apartheid South Africa.

Which choice completes the text so that it conforms to the conventions of Standard English?

A) month, the

B) month—the

C) month: the

D) month. The

18

The Earth's core is _____ a very valuable source of energy, but scientists have only begun to determine how to harness its extreme heat, which may be 10,800 degrees Fahrenheit—about the same temperature as the surface of the Sun.

Which choice completes the text so that it conforms to the conventions of Standard English?

A) potent

B) potency

C) potential

D) potentially

CONTINUE

19

The second smallest country by area in the world after Vatican City, Monaco is a mere 2.1 square kilometers. Most famous for the Monte Carlo Casino, ______. In fact, Monaco is a pioneer in marine conservation with one of the first protected marine areas in the world.

Which choice completes the text so that it conforms to the conventions of Standard English?

A) there is also an oceanographic museum in the country which is world-class.

B) the country also is home to a world-class oceanographic museum.

C) a world-class oceanographic museum is also in the country.

D) a museum of oceanography which is world-class is also in the country.

20

Given the number of incidents involving handguns in the past several years, politicians are considering new legislation to regulate the sale and possession of various firearms. Some critics claim that rather than increase the number of laws, police should make more effort to come ______ offenders.

Which choice completes the text so that it conforms to the conventions of Standard English?

A) out of

B) up with

C) down on

D) down with

21

Environmentalists have been trying a variety of solutions to remove plastic waste from the ocean. This serious problem will not be resolved easily, though, because the removal of waste from the ocean is a much slower process ______ the introduction of new plastic pollution.

Which choice completes the text so that it conforms to the conventions of Standard English?

A) as

B) then

C) than

D) to

22

Those who paid attention to the music industry started to notice the decades-long trend of Billboard-topping tracks that directly incorporated inspiration from their predecessors in the form of sampling. ______ Drake sampled Ms. Lauryn Hill, who sampled Wu Tang Clan, who sampled Gladys Knight and the Pips.

Which choice completes the text with the most logical transition?

A) Ultimately,

B) In addition,

C) Furthermore,

D) For example,

CONTINUE

23

Since it was completed in 1911, the Stoclet House in Belgium has been among the finest examples of the Vienna Secession of the Art Nouveau style. The integrity of the exterior architecture and garden remains almost untouched, and the interior has undergone few changes. Even much of the furniture is original. _____ the house fulfills the architectural criteria necessary for a UNESCO World Heritage site, which it became in 2009.

Which choice completes the text with the most logical transition?

A) Subsequently,

B) Otherwise,

C) Therefore,

D) However,

24

Messier 47 is a well-known star cluster that contains mostly massive, hot blue stars. It was first identified in 1654 by an Italian astronomer named Giovanni Hodierna. Charles Messier, without knowledge of Hodierna's discovery, independently cataloged the cluster about a hundred years later. _____ he wrote down erroneous coordinates, so the Messier 47 remained lost until its presence was confirmed by T.F. Morris in 1957.

Which choice completes the text with the most logical transition?

A) Finally,

B) Ironically,

C) Specifically,

D) Accordingly,

CONTINUE

25

While researching a topic, a student has taken the following notes:

1. The African grey hornbill (Lophoceros nasutus) is a member of the Hornbill family of mainly tropical near-passerine birds found in the Old World.
2. It is a widespread and common resident breeder in much of sub-Saharan Africa and the southwest of the Arabian Peninsula.
3. The African grey hornbill has escaped or been deliberately released into Florida, USA, but there is no evidence that the population is breeding and may only persist due to continuing releases or escapes.
4. At 45–51 cm (18–20 in) in length, the African grey hornbill is a large bird, although it is one of the smaller hornbills.
5. The African grey hornbill is widespread over much of sub-Saharan Africa. It prefers open woodland and savannah.

The student wants to emphasize that it is unlikely that the African grey hornbill will rapidly multiply in Florida. Which choice most effectively uses relevant information from the notes to accomplish this goal?

A) The African grey hornbill is a smaller hornbill and is easier to hunt down

B) It seems likely that the presence of the African grey hornbill is due to a deliberate release or escape, with no proof of breeding

C) The African grey hornbill is only commonly found in sub-Saharan Africa where the climate is highly unlike Florida

D) It is a tropical bird that is only widespread in open woodland and savannah areas

26

"Predictive analytics" is a term that is often used with big data. In essence, the term refers to the use of historical data and statistical techniques such as machine learning to make predictions about the future. <u>An example is how Netflix knows what you want to watch before you do, making suggestions based on your past viewing habits.</u> It is important to note that data doesn't just refer to rows and columns in a spreadsheet, but also to more complex files such as videos, images, and sensor data.

The writer is considering deleting the underlined sentence. Should the writer make this change?

A) Yes, because it disrupts the flow of logic in the paragraph.

B) Yes, because the example would be better placed at the start of the paragraph.

C) No, because it provides a necessary transition to new information.

D) No, because it provides a concrete example to help the reader better understand a concept.

CONTINUE

27

Pierre Omidyar became one of the richest men in the world as the founder of eBay. He has invested large amounts of his fortune in antitrust cases against big tech companies. He says that big tech companies are overly powerful and are a danger to democracy.

Which choice most effectively combines the underlined sentences?

A) that he says are

B) against big tech companies, which he says are

C) against big tech companies because big tech companies are, he says,

D) antitrust cases, which are cases against what in his opinion are big tech companies that are

No Test Material On This Page

Reading Test

27 QUESTIONS | 32 MINUTES

DIRECTIONS

The questions in this section address a number of important reading and writing skills. Each question includes one or more passages, which may include a table or graph. Read each passage and question carefully, and then choose the best answer to the question based on the passage(s). All questions in this section are multiple-choice with four answer choices. Each question has a single best answer.

1

Tourism is a growing sector of the global economy. Travel and tourism jobs are increasing worldwide, but Africa as a whole attracts less than 5 percent of total world tourists. However, Sub-Saharan Africa has a strong supply-side potential to attract tourists. Beach resorts alone create a large ______. The coastal waters of the Indian Ocean boast some of the finest beaches in the world, with plenty of opportunities for water sports.

Which choice completes the text with the most logical and precise word or phrase?

A) haul

B) persuasion

C) draw

D) connection

2

Noted for his contributions to understanding seventeenth-century art in the Netherlands, John Montias had a formal education in cultural economics. His studies of art auction sales from the period led to breakthroughs in the understanding of the ______ painter Johannes Vermeer.

Which choice completes the text with the most logical and precise word or phrase?

A) conspicuous

B) eminent

C) radiant

D) absolute

CONTINUE

3

The following text is from The Best Plays of the Old Dramatists by Havelock Ellis.

> "The earliest known edition of The Tragical History of Doctor Faustus is that of 1604; there is a second edition with date of 1609, agreeing in almost every particular with the first; a third edition with new scenes and many alterations, was published in 1616...
>
> It is very doubtful if any of the additions to the edition of 1616 are by Marlowe; Mr. Bullen thinks that some of them are. They are often ingenious, and sometimes, they are improvements. They appear to be written by a clever and <u>facile</u> imitator of Marlowe's style."

As used in the text, what does the word "facile" most nearly mean?

A) accomplished

B) successful

C) effortless

D) superficial

4

Horses have been demonstrated to possess complex thought processes that involve associations, memories, and recognition of emotions in other species. For example, in one experiment, horses were shown photographs of human faces that were angry or happy. <u>The people in the photographs were all strangers to the horses.</u> Several hours later, the actual person entered the field and stood near the horse with a neutral expression. In every case, the horses avoided approaching the people whose photographs had displayed anger.

What is the purpose of the underlined sentence in the overall structure of the text?

A) It explains how the subjects were selected for the experiment.

B) It points out that horses have a limited range of human contacts.

C) It highlights the importance of expression in communication.

D) It shows the researchers eliminated one possible weakness in the study.

CONTINUE

5

While life is a special kind of complex chemistry, the elements involved are nothing special: carbon, hydrogen, oxygen and so on are among the most abundant elements in the universe. Complex organic chemistry is surprisingly common. Amino acids, just like those that make up every protein in our bodies, have been found in the tails of comets. There are other organic compounds in Martian soil. And 6,500 light years away a giant cloud of space alcohol floats among the stars. Habitable planets seem to be common too. The first planet beyond our Solar System was discovered in 1995. Since then astronomers have catalogued thousands.

What technique does the author of the text use to build the argument?

A) Personal anecdotes

B) Comprehensible analogies

C) Unsubstantiated theories

D) Summaries of findings

6

Text 1

Chromosomes were unknown in 1834 when Gregor Mendel proposed his classic concept of heredity. In the late 1880s, scientists finally could stain cell structures with the clarity to see chromosomes. Walter Sutton and Theodor Boveri, in 1902 and 1903 respectively, independently published papers suggesting that genes were located in specific places on the chromosomes, which came in matched pairs except for the male Y chromosome.

Text 2

Thomas Hunt Morgan criticized the Sutton–Boveri chromosome theory of inheritance. However, he noticed some unusual trends while conducting experiments on fruit flies. A few males had white rather than red eyes, so he bred them and observed the results. He determined that white was a recessive mutation which did not appear in any first-generation females, though it might resurface in subsequent generations. After careful documentation, he published his conclusion that eye color genes were located on the X chromosome.

Based on the texts after his experiments, how would Thomas Hunt Morgan (Text 2) most likely describe the view Sutton and Boveri presented in Text 1?

A) It is largely correct, but it required some adjustment concerning minor details.

B) It is not compelling because he had definitive data contradicting the theory.

C) It may seem plausible, but it is not supported by scientific findings.

D) It probably holds true despite his initial skepticism of it.

7

Giant anteaters are neotropical mammals that, as their name suggests, consume ants, termites, and grubs, though they do occasionally eat fruit. Their habitat ranges from Central to South America in swamps, forests, and grasslands where their favored prey is common. The solitary foragers have specialized tongues so they can consume thousands of ants in a few minutes after breaking open a nest, and they quickly abandon the site when soldier ants emerge to protect the colony.

Which choice best states the main idea of the text?

A) Giant anteaters live alone in neotropical areas that have not been disturbed by humans.

B) There are fewer opportunities for giant anteaters to eat since soldier ants are more vigilant.

C) Giant anteaters have adapted so that they are able to gather sufficient food.

D) Despite the danger of soldier ants, giant anteaters prefer to eat ants over other food sources.

CONTINUE

8

Scientist James Clark and graduate student Jason McLachlan of Duke University published findings from a study analyzing tree pollen extracted from ancient lake sediments in the journal Nature. According to Clark, the purpose of their study was to address a central scientific problem in explaining the diversity of tree species in a forest. "In the mathematical models ecologists use to describe how different species compete for resources such as light, moisture and nutrients, it can be difficult to get species to coexist," he said. "In models, slight advantages allow one species to 'out-compete' the other, leading to extinction, that is, loss of biodiversity. And so, ecologists have put a lot of effort into trying to understand the differences among species that would allow one species to coexist with another species."

According to the text, what is the primary purpose of analyzing tree pollen extracted from ancient lake sediments?

A) To explore the ramifications of a mathematical model

B) To isolate factors that allow a phenomenon to happen

C) To identify the causes of an unusual incident

D) To isolate the flaws in a common theory

9

Robin Williams (1951–2014) has often been considered one of the best American comedians of all time. Famous for creating engaging characters at the spur of the moment, Williams began his career as a stand-up comic and moved on to win many prestigious awards for his roles in motion pictures. Everyone who knew him described him as full of natural talent and energy: ______

Which quotation most effectively illustrates the claim?

A) "Williams helped us grow up." (Alyssa Rosenberg)

B) "He gave his...talent freely and generously to those who needed it most—from our troops stationed abroad to the marginalized on our own streets." (Barack Obama)

C) "The world is forever a little darker, less colorful and less full of laughter in his absence." (Zelda Williams)

D) "He came in like a hurricane...there goes my chance in show business." (David Letterman)

10

Figure 1: Deaths from Drug Overdoses in the United States by Year

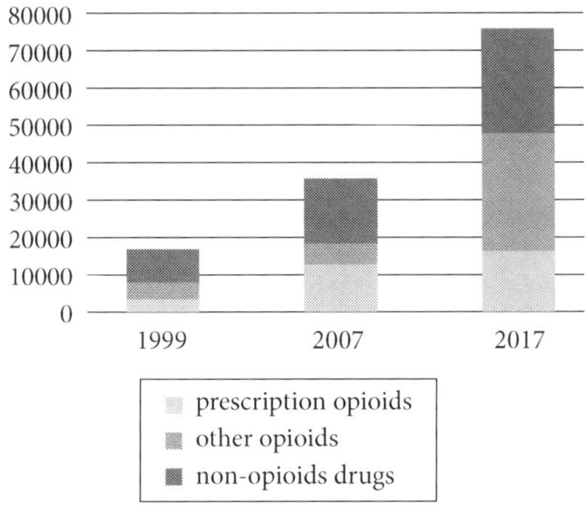

Data from National Institute on Drug Abuse, 2019.

In a potential advance in treating opioid overdose, researchers have developed long-lasting monoclonal antibodies that selectively bind potent synthetic opioids and reverse their effects in mice. The researchers propose that the antibodies could one day be administered as a stand-alone treatment or as part of a more effective combination treatment against opioid overdoses. This is extremely important, given that in 2017 alone, there were approximately ____.

Which choice most effectively uses data from the graph to complete the example?

A) 18,000 deaths caused by any drug overdoses

B) 38,000 deaths caused by any type of opiate drug overdose

C) 48,000 deaths caused by drug overdoses on any opiate

D) 75,000 deaths caused by prescription opiate drug overdoses

CONTINUE

11

Population change in the EU Member States during 2019 *(per 1,000 residents)*

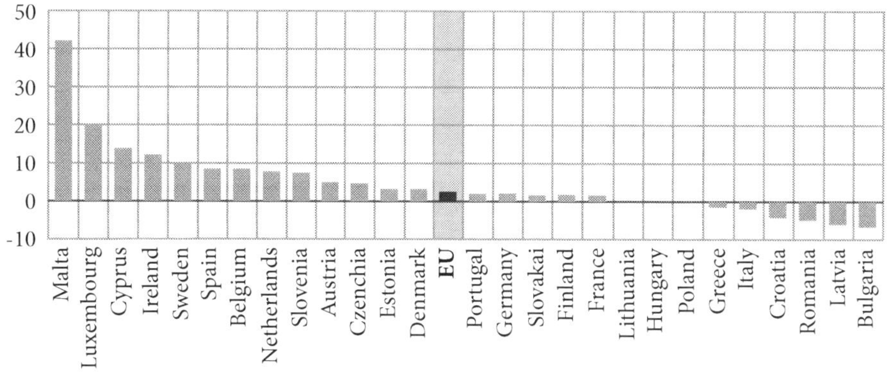

During 2019, there was an increase in population in eighteen member states. By far the highest population increase was recorded in Malta, followed by Luxembourg, Cyprus, Ireland, and Sweden. Conversely, ______

Which choice most effectively uses data from the graph to complete the text?

A) the largest population decreases were recorded in Bulgaria, Latvia, Romania, Croatia, and Italy

B) Italy recorded a negative population growth

C) only a few countries recorded an increase in population

D) 4.7 million deaths were registered in the EU in 2019

12

Studies have shown that a single, subanesthetic-dose (a lower dose than would cause anesthesia) ketamine infusion can often rapidly relieve depressive symptoms within hours in people who have not responded to conventional antidepressants, which typically take weeks or months to work. However, widespread off-label use of intravenous subanesthetic-dose ketamine for treatment-resistant depression has raised concerns about side effects, especially given its history as a drug of abuse. "The most common short-term side effect was feeling strange or loopy," said Acevedo-Diaz, of the Section on the Neurobiology and Treatment of Mood Disorders, part of the NIMH Intramural Research Program (IRP) in Bethesda, Maryland.

According to the text, what is the major concern of doctors about using ketamine to control depression for long periods of time?

A) It may not be effective when used repeatedly.

B) It has serious side effects in conjunction with other drugs.

C) Patients could become addicted to the drug.

D) Patients who take the drug sometimes relapse.

13

Robert Henri (1865-1929) was an American painter and teacher who disliked the conservative restrictions placed on the highly-polished art by artists affiliated with the National Academy of Design. With several colleagues, he introduced a new style that depicted the seedy underside of urban life in a bold, realistic fashion. Critics dubbed the artists with the title of "Ashcan School" because they drew sketches in the streets of New York and depicted dirty snow, laundry hanging out to dry, and other scenes of everyday life.

Based on the text, what is most likely true about artists affiliated with the National Academy of Design?

A) They used a bold, realistic style for their paintings.

B) They did not live or work in New York City.

C) They avoided subjects that were undignified.

D) They preferred to draw scenes related to summertime.

CONTINUE

14

Waterfalls come in many shapes. One classic form is the punchbowl, such as at Eagle Falls in Oregon. In such a ______ water flows down a narrow chute into a wide pool at the bottom. It is easy to swim in the tranquil waters at the base.

Which choice completes the text so that it conforms to the conventions of Standard English?

A) waterfall

B) waterfall,

C) waterfall:

D) waterfall;

15

Scott Evans is a golf ball diver. In other words, he dives into the water hazards placed on golf courses to collect and recycle the balls which accidentally landed there. His job may sound fun, but it is not ______ spends hours in murky water and can get trapped by unseen obstacles.

Which choice completes the text so that it conforms to the conventions of Standard English?

A) easy, he

B) easy; because he

C) easy. Since he

D) easy. He

16

Northern New Zealand is home to some of the oldest forests on Earth. Forests filled with kauri, the Maori name for the *Agathis australis* tree, ______ back to the Jurassic period over 135 million years ago.

Which choice completes the text so that it conforms to the conventions of Standard English?

A) date

B) dating

C) they date

D) those forests date

17

While training departments try to give us what we need to stay ahead in the competitive market, research ______ that they are also falling behind: employees rate their Learning & Development departments lower than almost any other product in the consumer landscape.

Which choice completes the text so that it conforms to the conventions of Standard English?

A) are showing

B) will show

C) showed

D) shows

18

Elizabeth Catlett, ______ artwork is Modernist with African and Mexican influences, was a leading figure in portraying images related to race, gender, and class as it was experienced by Black Americans in the twentieth century.

Which choice completes the text so that it conforms to the conventions of Standard English?

A) her

B) who

C) whose

D) which

19

The German pianist Clara Schumann (1819–1896) is considered one of the finest performers of the Romantic period. Her career spanned over sixty years, much of which was spent traveling around Europe. In addition to giving concert performances, ______ composed many works for the piano.

Which choice completes the text so that it conforms to the conventions of Standard English?

A) she

B) her

C) hers

D) she's

20

Many organizations are turning to a policy called "job sharing" in an effort to retain good employees. Dividing one full-time job between two employees ______ a company to recruit talented workers who do not have the time or inclination to work 40 hours every week.

Which choice completes the text so that it conforms to the conventions of Standard English?

A) allow

B) allows

C) allowing

D) to allow

21

The collection of rainwater is known by many names throughout the world. ______ from rainwater collection to rainwater harvesting to rainwater catchment. Rainwater harvesting is a viable technology in an urban setting, as all that is needed to take advantage of this resource is to capture the free water falling onto a roof and direct it to a storage tank.

Which choice completes the text so that it conforms to the conventions of Standard English?

A) They ranges

B) Their range

C) These range

D) The names ranges

CONTINUE

22

Dandelions are usually considered to be useless weeds. ______ they can be used in many recipes, as the leaves are edible and perfect for salads. Mature flowers are bitter, but young buds are sweet and taste slightly like honey.

Which choice completes the text with the most logical transition?

A) Therefore,

B) Nevertheless,

C) In particular,

D) Moreover,

23

Guernica, a painting in oil on canvas, is one of Pablo Picasso's masterpieces and arguably one of the most influential anti-war paintings of all time. Though Picasso typically painted in private, he allowed influential visitors into his studio to observe the progress in order to promote awareness of the Spanish Civil War. ______ the completed painting was exhibited around the world to raise funds for war relief efforts.

Which choice completes the text with the most logical transition?

A) In addition,

B) By contrast,

C) Consequently,

D) For instance,

24

Ethiopian Prime Minister Abiy Ahmed was awarded the 2019 Nobel Peace Prize for his efforts to end the ongoing stalemate between Ethiopia and Eritrea. At the beginning of his tenure, he was lauded for progressive decisions. ______ he was accused of restricting the freedom of the press and detaining innocent people who held opposing views.

Which choice completes the text with the most logical transition?

A) Additionally,

B) Accordingly,

C) Subsequently,

D) Consequently,

25

______ there's something inherently appealing about entrepreneurs and the stories of why and how they do what they do. People are attracted to social entrepreneurs like Nobel Peace Prize laureate Muhammad Yunus for many of the same reasons they find business leaders like Steve Jobs so compelling—these people come up with ideas that dramatically improve people's lives.

At this point, the writer wants to show the depth of appeal. Which choice most effectively achieves the writer's goal?

A) On the most basic level,

B) At a basic and fundamental level,

C) At a level and depth that is fundamental,

D) On levels which are fundamental and basic,

CONTINUE

26

While researching a topic, a student has taken the following notes:

1. Ludovico Maria Enrico Einaudi is an Italian pianist and composer who trained at the Conservatorio Verdi in Milan.
2. He has composed the scores for a number of films and television productions and has won several awards for his compositions.
3. Einaudi is most known for being the most-streamed classical artist of all time with his music reaching over 1 million streams daily, and 2 billion streams in total.
4. His latest album Seven Days Walking: Day One has become the fastest-streamed classical album of all time since its release on 15 March 2019. The project is a series of digital albums released monthly over seven consecutive months.
5. Day One interweaves piano and string and focuses on several main themes that will recur in different forms on subsequent albums.

The student wants to emphasize Einaudi's most well-known achievement. Which choice most effectively uses relevant information from the notes to accomplish this goal?

A) Among his many achievements, composer Ludovico Maria Enrico Einaudi trained at the Conservatorio Verdi in Milan and has won multiple awards

B) He has composed for multiple films and television shows

C) Einaudi is known as the most-streamed classical artist of all time, with 2 billion streams in total

D) Einaudi has come up with highly innovative projects, including combining recurring notes of piano and string in different albums

27

The term "ghost kitchen" may make you think of a haunted house. In reality, it is just a physical space to prepare food that will be eaten elsewhere. The number of ghost kitchens is actually ______, since multiple brands or restaurants can share a low-rent space to make meals sold on delivery food apps.

The writer wants to emphasize how fast the number is increasing. Which choice completes the text and achieves the writer's goal?

A) multiplying

B) inflating

C) skyrocketing

D) getting bigger

STOP

No Test Material On This Page

Math

22 QUESTIONS | 35 MINUTES

DIRECTIONS

The questions in this section address a number of important math skills. Use of a calculator is permitted for all questions.

NOTES

Unless otherwise indicated: • All variables and expressions represent real numbers. • Figures provided are drawn to scale. • All figures lie in a plane. • The domain of a given function is the set of all real numbers *x* for which *f*(*x*) is a real number.

REFERENCE

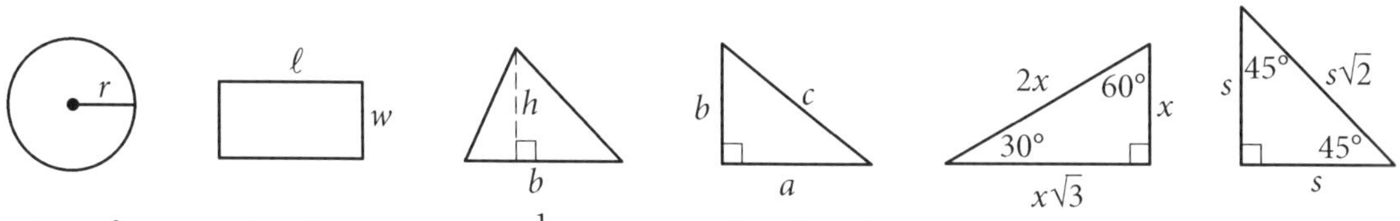

$A = \pi r^2$ $C = 2\pi r$ $A = \ell w$ $A = \frac{1}{2}bh$ $c^2 = a^2 + b^2$ Special Right Triangles

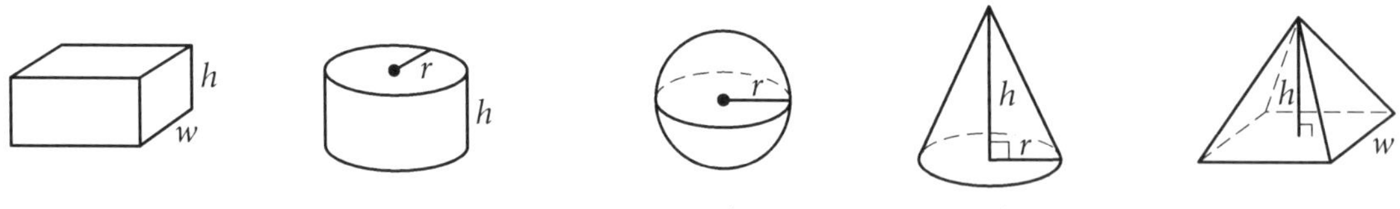

$V = \ell wh$ $V = \pi r^2 h$ $V = \frac{4}{3}\pi r^3$ $V = \frac{1}{3}\pi r^2 h$ $V = \frac{1}{3}\ell wh$

The number of degrees of arc in a circle is 360.

The number of radians of arc in a circle is 2π.

The sum of the measures in degrees of the angles of a triangle is 180.

For **multiple-choice questions,** solve each problem, choose the correct answer from the choices provided, and then circle your answer in this book. Circle only one answer for each question. If you change your mind, completely erase the circle. You will not get credit for questions with more than one answer circled, or for questions with no answers circled.

For **student-produced response questions,** solve each problem and write your answer next to or under the question in the test book as described below.

- Once you've written your answer, circle it clearly. You will not receive credit for anything written outside the circle, or for any questions with more than one circled answer.
- If you find more than one correct answer, write and circle only one answer.
- Your answer can be up to 5 characters for a positive answer and up to 6 characters (including the negative sign) for a negative answer, but no more.
- If your answer is a fraction that is too long (over 5 characters for positive, 6 characters for negative), write the decimal equivalent.
- If your answer is a decimal that is too long (over 5 characters for positive, 6 characters for negative), truncate it or round at the fourth digit.
- If your answer is a mixed number (such as 3.!. 2), write it as an improper fraction (7/2) or its decimal equivalent (3.5).
- Don't include symbols such as a percent sign, comma, or dollar sign in your circled answer.

CONTINUE

1

Ash has a walking and cycling routine. For every minute she walks, she burns 20 calories. And for every minute she cycles, she burns 35 calories. If she burns 340 calories on a particular day after walking for x minutes and cycling for y minutes, which of the following equations best represents her routine?

A) $340 - 20x = 35y$

B) $35y - 20x = 340$

C) $340 - 20y = 35x$

D) $35x - 20y = 340$

2

The graph below shows velocity (*y–axis*) plotted against time (*x–axis*). For how many data points is the actual value higher than the predicted values on the line of best fit?

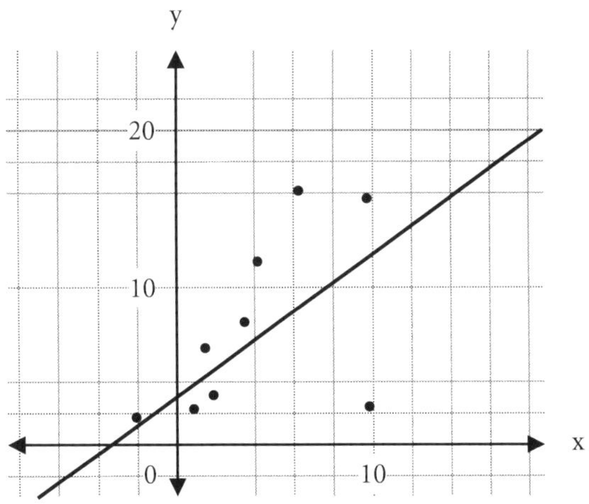

A) 9

B) 6

C) 3

D) 2

3

x	$f(x)$
–2	30
0	12
3	0
5	2

Which of the following is a factor of $f(x)$?

A) $(x+2)$

B) $(x-3)$

C) x

D) $(x-5)$

4

What is the value of s for the following system of equations?

$$(t-5)+2(s-3)=8$$

$$2(t-5)-3(s-3)=-19$$

5

How many solutions does the equation below have?

$$3(x-2)-2(x-1)=-x+2(x+2)-8$$

A) 0

B) 1

C) 2

D) Infinitely many

6

Which of the following is equivalent to $2g^{\frac{4}{5}}g^{\frac{2}{5}}$?

A) $\sqrt[5]{2g^6}$

B) $\sqrt[5]{32g^6}$

C) $2\sqrt[6]{g^5}$

D) $\sqrt[6]{2g^5}$

7

A researcher found the mean mass of all cheetahs in a park. He found that the mean mass of all cheetahs in the park is between 120 *lbs* and 182 *lbs*. What is the value of the margin of error for the mean mass of the cheetahs in the park?

8

What is the value of $f(6)$, if $f(2x) = 9x - 7$?

A) 20

B) 47

C) 101

D) 11

CONTINUE

9

A teacher takes note of the shoe sizes for 21 students in his class and creates the table below. Which of the following statements is true about the data below?

Shoe size	Frequency
1	3
2	4
3	4
4	7
5	2
6	1

A) The mean is greater than the median

B) The mean is the same as the median

C) The median is greater than the mean

D) There isn't enough information to answer the question.

10

What is the value of a in the given equation $27^x \div 81^{-x} = 3^{ax}$?

11

If the value of the sum of interior angles of the hexagon is $b\pi$, what is the value of b?

A) 0.25

B) 1

C) 4

D) 2

12

What is the value when 80 is increased by 200%?

A) 200

B) 160

C) 240

D) 280

13

If $1+\frac{a\sqrt{2}}{2}$ is a solution to the equation $2x^2-4x-7=0$, what is the possible value of a?

14

A real estate company kept a track of the number of houses it sold in October. Its team came up with the model $h(t) = 262 - 8t$, and t represents the number of days. Which of the following best represents 262?

A) The number of houses at the end of October

B) The number of houses at the beginning of October

C) The number of houses sold per day in October

D) The number of houses sold in the first 8 days of October.

15

ABC is a right–angled triangle, where B is 90° and angle C is 30°. If AC = 32, what is the area of triangle ABC.

A) $128\sqrt{3}$

B) $128\sqrt{2}$

C) $16\sqrt{3}$

D) $16\sqrt{2}$

16

If $(5xy+3)-(6xy-2xy^2+2) = axy^2+bxy+c$, what is the value of $a + b$?

17

What is the product of the roots for the equation $3x^2+6x-24=0$?

A) 3

B) −8

C) 2

D) −2

18

Which of the following best represents the equation of the graph below?

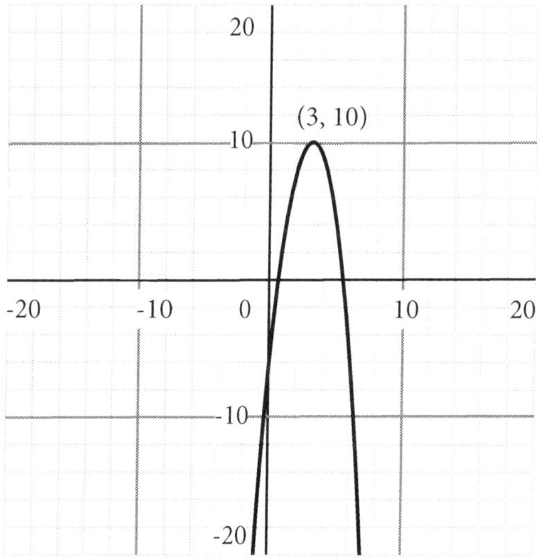

A) $y = 2(x+3)^2+10$

B) $y = -2(x-3)^2+10$

C) $y = 2(x-3)^2+10$

D) $y = -2(x+3)^2+10$

CONTINUE

19

If $-3(-2 + 2x) = ax + b$, what is the value of ab?

20

What is the possible value of $f(x)$ when $x = 0$?

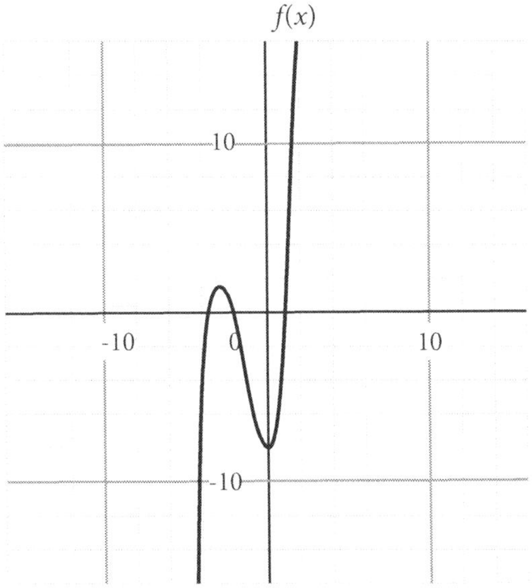

A) 8

B) −8

C) 4

D) −4

21

If $\frac{3}{4}(x-5)=27$, what is the value of $x - 5$?

A) 41

B) 36

C) $\frac{81}{4}$

D) 31

22

Which of the following coordinates would be true for the following system of inequalities?

$$y > -2x - 1$$

$$3y < x + 9$$

A) (−2, 1)

B) (1, 4)

C) (3 , 1)

D) (−3, 3)

No Test Material On This Page

Math

22 QUESTIONS | 35 MINUTES

DIRECTIONS

The questions in this section address a number of important math skills. Use of a calculator is permitted for all questions.

NOTES

Unless otherwise indicated: • All variables and expressions represent real numbers. • Figures provided are drawn to scale. • All figures lie in a plane. • The domain of a given function is the set of all real numbers *x* for which *f*(*x*) is a real number.

REFERENCE

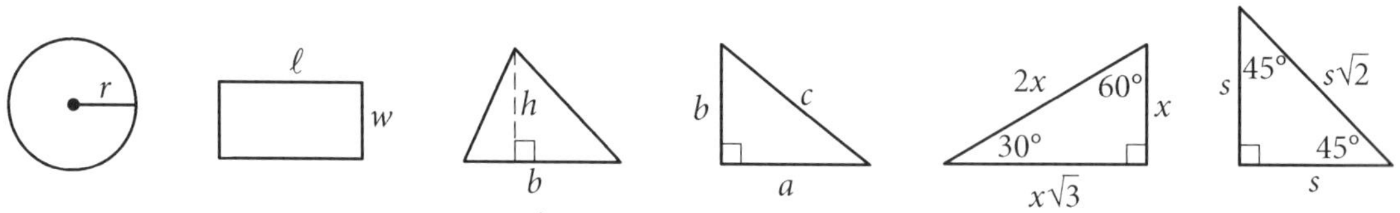

$A = \pi r^2$
$C = 2\pi r$

$A = \ell w$

$A = \frac{1}{2}bh$

$c^2 = a^2 + b^2$

Special Right Triangles

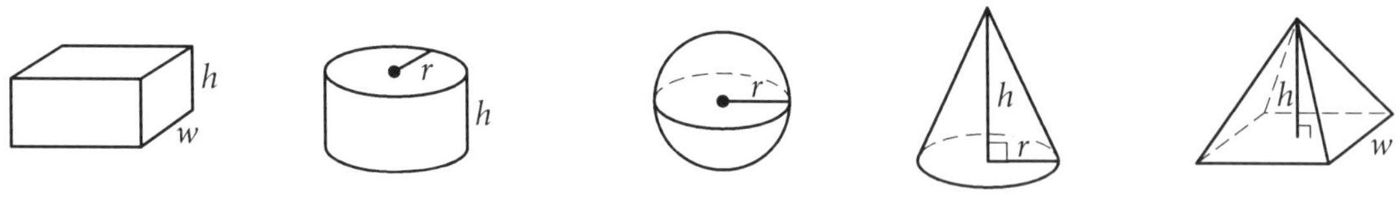

$V = \ell wh$

$V = \pi r^2 h$

$V = \frac{4}{3}\pi r^3$

$V = \frac{1}{3}\pi r^2 h$

$V = \frac{1}{3}\ell wh$

The number of degrees of arc in a circle is 360.

The number of radians of arc in a circle is 2π.

The sum of the measures in degrees of the angles of a triangle is 180.

For **multiple-choice questions,** solve each problem, choose the correct answer from the choices provided, and then circle your answer in this book. Circle only one answer for each question. If you change your mind, completely erase the circle. You will not get credit for questions with more than one answer circled, or for questions with no answers circled.

For **student-produced response questions,** solve each problem and write your answer next to or under the question in the test book as described below.

- Once you've written your answer, circle it clearly. You will not receive credit for anything written outside the circle, or for any questions with more than one circled answer.
- If you find more than one correct answer, write and circle only one answer.
- Your answer can be up to 5 characters for a positive answer and up to 6 characters (including the negative sign) for a negative answer, but no more.
- If your answer is a fraction that is too long (over 5 characters for positive, 6 characters for negative), write the decimal equivalent.
- If your answer is a decimal that is too long (over 5 characters for positive, 6 characters for negative), truncate it or round at the fourth digit.
- If your answer is a mixed number (such as 3.!. 2), write it as an improper fraction (7/2) or its decimal equivalent (3.5).
- Don't include symbols such as a percent sign, comma, or dollar sign in your circled answer.

CONTINUE

1

If p and q are solutions to the equation below, which of the following best represents $p+q$?

$$|3x - 1| = 2$$

A) $\frac{1}{3}$

B) 1

C) $\frac{2}{3}$

D) $-\frac{1}{3}$

2

Which of the following coordinates lie on the circle whose equation is $(x-3)^2 + y^2 + 8y = 84$?

A) (1, 7)

B) (−2, 5)

C) (−3,4)

D) (3, −6)

3

If *sin* $C = 0.986$ and *cos* $63 = 0.986$, what is the value of C?

4

If $\frac{2-2i}{3+4i}$ is equal to $a+bi$. What is the value of a?

A) $\frac{-2}{25}$

B) $\frac{-14}{25}$

C) $\frac{2}{3}$

D) $\frac{-1}{2}$

5

Which of the following can be the value of x for the system of equations below?

$$y = 2x^2 - 9x + 7$$

$$y = 2x - 2$$

A) $\frac{11}{2}$

B) −1

C) $\frac{9}{2}$

D) $\frac{7}{2}$

6

What is the positive solution to the following equation?

$$3|3x-2| - |6x-4| = 7$$

7

Which of the following represents a *line l* (not shown) which is perpendicular to the *line m* (shown below)?

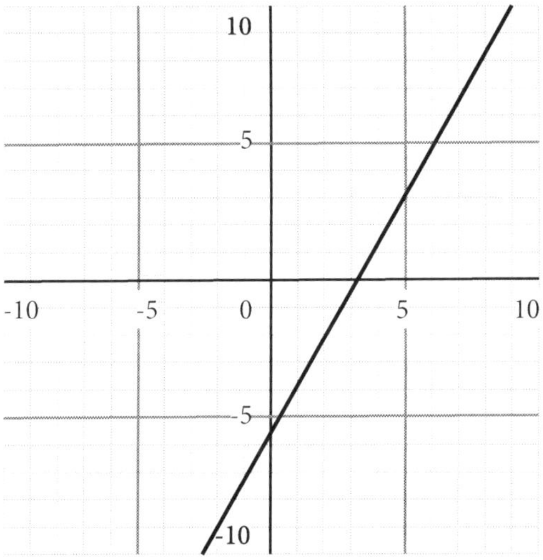

A) $3y = 5x - 15$

B) $5y = 3x + 15$

C) $5y = -3x + 15$

D) $3y = 5x + 10$

8

What is the circumference of the circle whose equation is $x^2 + 6x + y^2 - 4y = 51$

A) 64π

B) 8π

C) 14.28π

D) 16π

9

In the triangle ABC (not drawn to scale) shown below, $\angle ABC = 2x - 2$ and $\angle BAC = x + 3$.
If $\angle ACD = 118°$, what is the value of x?

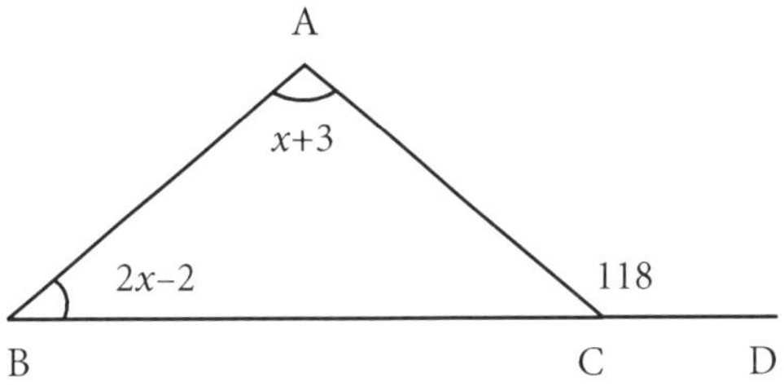

10

It takes 4 carpenters to build a bed in 3 days, how many carpenters will it take to build the bed in 2 days?

A) 12

B) 6

C) 8

D) 24

CONTINUE

11

Which of the following is equivalent to $(5xy+3x)(x-2y)$?

A) $5x^2y-6xy$

B) $5x^2y+3x^2+10xy^2-6xy$

C) $5x^2y+3x^2-10xy^2-6xy$

D) $-5x^2y^2+3x^2-6xy$

12

What is the value of y, if $7x - 4y = 1$ and $5x + 2y = 8$?

13

Which of the following is NOT a solution to the following equation?

$$-2x \leq 8-x$$

A) −8

B) −10

C) 2

D) −7

14

If an unfair coin is tossed 20 times, and it lands on heads 14 times. What would be the probability of it landing on heads the 21st time?

A) 0.5

B) 0.20

C) 0.3

D) 0.7

15

What is the value of $x - y$ if $3y - 2x = 16$ and $5x + y = -6$?

A) 6

B) 4

C) −2

D) −6

16

A student conducted research on how many fish there are in a pond after m months and came up with the model, $f(x) = 1{,}200(1.03)^m$.

He wanted to have the time on the model in d days instead, as shown below

(assuming 1 month has 30 days)

$$f(x) = 1{,}200(1.03)^{ad}$$

What is the value of a?

CONTINUE

17

If the radius of a circular cylinder is 6, what is the volume of the cylinder if the height is twice its radius?

A) 432π

B) 864π

C) 216π

D) 108π

18

What is the value of the angle EOD, if the angle DRE is 35°?

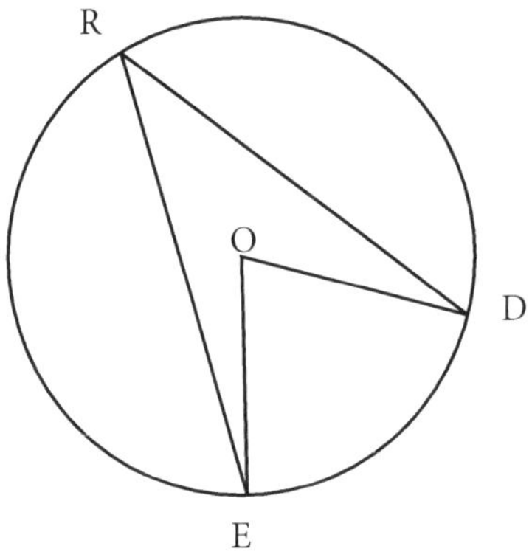

A) 70°

B) 35°

C) 60°

D) 55°

19

Which of the following is equivalent to

$$\frac{4x^2-3}{2x+\sqrt{3}}?$$

A) $2x-\sqrt{3}$

B) $2x+\sqrt{3}$

C) $2x-3$

D) $2x+3$

20

If the system of equations below has infinite solutions, what is the value of b?

$$9x-14y=-3$$
$$ax-by=6$$

21

If $3x+5y=ax-4x-by$, what is the value of a?

A) 3

B) 1

C) -5

D) 7

CONTINUE

22

Which of the following values is a solution to inequality?

$$3x + 2 < -5(x + 6)$$

A) 4

B) 3

C) -4

D) -5

STOP

No Test Material On This Page

Answer Key

Reading and Writing

Module 1

Questions	Correct	Mark your correct answers
1.	C	
2.	D	
3.	D	
4.	C	
5.	D	
6.	A	
7.	A	
8.	B	
9.	D	
10.	A	
11.	A	
12.	D	
13.	B	
14.	C	
15.	B	
16.	D	
17.	D	
18.	D	
19.	B	
20.	C	
21.	C	
22.	D	
23.	C	
24.	B	
25.	B	
26.	D	
27.	B	

Module 2

Questions	Correct	Mark your correct answers
1.	C	
2.	B	
3.	D	
4.	D	
5.	D	
6.	D	
7.	C	
8.	B	
9.	D	
10.	C	
11.	A	
12.	C	
13.	C	
14.	B	
15.	D	
16.	A	
17.	D	
18.	C	
19.	A	
20.	B	
21.	C	
22.	B	
23.	A	
24.	C	
25.	A	
26.	C	
27.	C	

Math

Module 1

Questions	Correct	Mark your correct answers
1.	A	
2.	B	
3.	B	
4.	8	
5.	D	
6.	B	
7.	31	
8.	A	
9.	A	
10.	7	
11.	C	
12.	C	
13.	3	
14.	B	
15.	A	
16.	1	
17.	B	
18.	B	
19.	−36	
20.	D	
21.	B	
22.	C	

Module 2

Questions	Correct	Mark your correct answers
1.	C	
2.	C	
3.	27°	
4.	A	
5.	C	
6.	3	
7.	C	
8.	D	
9.	39	
10.	B	
11.	C	
12.	$\frac{3}{2}$ or 1.5	
13.	B	
14.	D	
15.	D	
16.	$\frac{1}{30}$ or 0.0333	
17.	A	
18.	A	
19.	A	
20.	−28	
21.	D	
22.	D	

1. **Level:** Medium | **Domain:** CRAFT AND STRUCTURE
Skill/Knowledge: Words in Context

Key Explanation: Choice C is the best answer because the blank portion shows how hyraxes resemble guinea pigs. **Choice C** refers to something that is only on the outside or surface, so fits the context of saying that the hyrax and guinea pig look similar, but they are not really related.

Distractor Explanations: None of the other choices accurately explain how hyraxes resemble guinea pigs. **Choice A** refers to something that makes sense through reasoning, but one would reason that if the hyrax is related to an elephant, then it should look more like one. **Choice B** refers to something that happens by habit or tradition, but appearance is not based on habit. **Choice D** refers to something that happens in all cases or everywhere, so does not establish that some people see a general similarity.

2. **Level:** Medium | **Domain:** CRAFT AND STRUCTURE
Skill/Knowledge: Words in Context

Key Explanation: Choice D is the best answer because "frustrated" refers to what World War II and the termination era did to the purposes of the IRA. Choice D means "blocked" or "prevented," which fits the context of showing that events prevented the goals of the IRA from being completely fulfilled; that is why it is still needed today.

Distractor Explanation: Choices A and C can be eliminated because they are emotional responses, but "the purposes of the IRA" are inanimate and cannot experience emotions. **Choice A** means "irritated" and **Choice D** means "not happy with something." **Choice B** is incorrect because "fulfilling" refers to something doing the act of making another thing happen. However, it does not fit the context because World War II and the termination era were not things that could "fulfill" or make the IRA's goals happen. They were obstacles that stopped other things from fulfilling the purposes of the IRA.

3. **Level:** Hard | **Domain:** CRAFT AND STRUCTURE
Skill/Knowledge: Words in Context

Key Explanation: Choice D is the best answer because "provision" is something that is guaranteed by the Constitution, freedom of speech. **Choice D** refers to something that is necessary or must happen, so it fits the context of saying that freedom of speech is a right or need to be guaranteed by the highest law of the country.

Distractor Explanation: None of the other choices adequately shows what is guaranteed by the Constitution. **Choice A** refers to the process of sharing something. **Choice B** refers to plans or preparations, but does not include the idea that they must occur. **Choice C** is a future event that might occur but cannot be accurately predicted.

4. **Level:** Medium | **Domain:** CRAFT AND STRUCTURE
Skill/Knowledge: Text Structure and Purpose

Key Explanation: Choice C is the best answer. The underlined sentence says that Sara flushed, which typically happens in anger or embarrassment. In this context, she appears embarrassed because she is not old or experienced enough—and was too "punctilious" or "careful"—to explain how she felt in a few words. The fact that she flushes highlights her sense of awkwardness and embarrassment.

Distractor Explanation: Choice A is incorrect because the sentence only says that Sara flushed. It does not explain what she looked like; she could be tall, short, dark-haired or blonde, dressed nicely, etc. **Choice B** is incorrect because the underlined sentence only establishes that Sara blushes. It does not give a reason why; the following sentences show she could speak French but was reluctant to tell Miss Minchin so. **Choice D** is incorrect because there is no interaction between characters in the following sentences. The underlined portion is expanded upon with a reason for blushing, not actions.

5. **Level:** Hard | **Domain:** CRAFT AND STRUCTURE
Skill/Knowledge: Text Structure and Purpose

Key Explanation: Choice D is the best answer because the narrator describes his actions on the boat, "jumping from spar to spar" as similar to the jumping of a grasshopper. This work is because "they rather order me about some"; presumably "they" are the officers that are not "simple sailors." He says that it is true that he has to hop around obeying orders, but says that "at first, this sort of thing is unpleasant enough" but that "this wears off in time." Therefore, the analogy "anticipates" or "defends against" the argument that such work is "distasteful" or "unpleasant" because he says he is used to the role.

Distractor Explanation: Choice A is incorrect because "compensations" refers to payment, but the text does not contain references to money. **Choice B** is incorrect because the question is asking for an argument that the grasshopper analogy is used to disprove. Since the grasshopper analogy is that sailors are hopping around, or busy, the argument being disproved should be the opposite, that sailors are not busy. **Choice C** is incorrect because the analogy of the grasshopper does not show that it is necessary or not to obey orders; the narrator merely says he does and that it is distasteful at first but he gets used to it.

6. **Level:** Hard | **Domain:** CRAFT AND STRUCTURE
Skill/Knowledge: Text Structure and Purpose

Key Explanation: Choice A is the best answer because the phrase implies that Adam Patch still felt he was living in 1861, whereas really years had passed the times were changing. The phrase gives a reason for him to "weary" and become tired... he had been so wrapped up in reforms, but his causes were not current or relevant any more. His thoughts were still focused on events such as the Civil War rather than on everyday life or his grandson.

Distractor Explanation: Choice B is incorrect because the passage implies that Adam focused on things that interested him. The fact that the wife and son died in the past is not the reason that he thinks about them infrequently; he doesn't really care about them as much as he does about things that happened earlier, like the Civil War. **Choice C** is incorrect because the fact that the times changed was the reason that his campaign against vices started to fade. The changing times is not why he started to fight against vice. **Choice D** is incorrect because someone can be interesting even if the times change. The reason that Adam was a bore was his actions during that time.

7. **Level:** Easy | **Domain:** INFORMATION AND IDEAS
Skill/Knowledge: Central Ideas and Details

Key Explanation: Choice A is the best answer because the text says that naloxone breaks down quickly, "after about an hour." This is "not completely desirable" or "unwanted" because it means that the drug needs to be carefully administered and the progress of the patient watched or the patient could "relapse" or "return to the original condition."

Distractor Explanation: Choice B is incorrect because there is no discussion of price in the text. **Choice C** is incorrect because the passage does not say that naloxone has "no results" for some drugs. It only claims that it is less effective, meaning it has results that are not as strong, for "powerful synthetic opioids like fentanyl and carfentanil." **Choice D** is incorrect because there is no evidence of side effects related to naloxone. The only negative effect implied is that it needs to be readministered because it wears off quickly.

8. **Level:** Easy | **Domain:** INFORMATION AND IDEAS
Skill/Knowledge: Central Ideas and Details

Key Explanation: Choice B is the best answer. The text is summarizing a potentially confusing effect that involves bending light waves. The reader has presumably seen a rainbow, however, so that image might help the reader visualize light bending when it hits the atmosphere as being similar to light bending when it hits rain.

Distractor Explanations: Choice A is incorrect because "originate" means "begin," but light does not begin in a rainbow. **Choice C** is incorrect because the example of the rainbow shows the rule or effect of Rayleigh Scattering, it is not an "exception" or "not part of" the rule. **Choice D** is incorrect because the idea of a rainbow does not tell the reader "why" or "the reason" blue scatters more easily; a rainbow just offers an image which shows that colors separate in different ways when they hit something like rain or the atmosphere.

9. **Level:** Hard | **Domain:** INFORMATION AND IDEAS
Skill/Knowledge: Central Ideas and Details

Key Explanation: Choice D is the best answer because the words "charming" and "jaunty" are often associated with cute, fun things. They imply that the yellow hat and black mantle were sweet or endearing things that a happy young girl might wear, for example, to a party. However, the girl is crying on a canal railing, so her cheerful clothes form a "contrast" or "opposite" impression.

Distractor Explanation: Choice A is incorrect because the passage indicates that the girl is relatively young; the narrator starts by calling her a "woman" and shifts to "girl" after he gets a closer look. Clothes described as "charming" and "jaunty" are suitable for a younger person, so do not "belie" or "contradict" that she is young. **Choice B** is not supported by the passage because there is no description of the temperature or that her clothing was inappropriate; for example, she was not shivering because she was too cold. **Choice C** is incorrect because the narrator noticed the woman's action of leaning on a railing before noting her appearance. Her clothing is described as he takes a closer look.

10. **Level:** Medium | **Domain:** INFORMATION AND IDEAS
Skill/Knowledge: Command of Evidence (Textual)

Key Explanation: Choice A is the best answer because the passage defines the informal sector of the economy as "that which is not regulated, controlled, or taxed." Therefore, a situation where goods are bartered between people would count as "informal" because there is no money changing hands and no taxes paid on the exchange.

Distractor Explanation: Choice A is incorrect because the projects sponsored by a foreign investor would most likely need to go through an approval process and the school would need to pass at least a basic inspection. **Choice A** would include regulations and controls, so would be considered formal. **Choice C** is incorrect because, while it might not be completely honest, there would still need to be nominal proof about how much tax money was spent and what it was used for. **Choice D** is weak because there is no evidence in the example to elaborate on the young man's situation. For example, he could have filed all the correct paperwork, moved into a new apartment, and been paying income taxes from his new salary.

11. **Level:** Medium | **Domain:** INFORMATION AND IDEAS
Skill/Knowledge: Command of Evidence (Textual)

Key Explanation: Choice A is the best answer. The claim is that "such programs" are successful. There are two programs listed, making cycling safer and making bikes accessible. There are no specific examples of increasing safety, but the passage describes the details making bikes accessible by adding bike share depots in DC. **Choice A** shows that the program in DC, which started in 2010, probably has strong results, as ridership increased by over a percent in the five years after that policy was started.

Distractor Explanation: Choice B is incorrect because it only says that DC had low ridership, but there is no indication of change. The reader does not know that the ridership increased after the program started. **Choice C** is incorrect because it focuses on Portland, but there is no indication that Portland did anything to make cycling safer or more accessible. **Choice C** also refers to DC, but the percentage of commuters is lower than that of Portland, so it could appear that the program was not very successful. **Choice D** is incorrect because the reader does not know whether the program helped make the number of commuters in DC greater. It is possible that all along, there have been more commuters than the other cities. It is even possible that ridership in DC decreased after the program started.

12. **Level:** Medium | **Domain:** INFORMATION AND IDEAS
Skill/Knowledge: Command of Evidence (Quantitative)

Key Explanation: Choice D is correct because it shows an example of the inconsistent growth between the years 2020 to 2022. The previous sentence in the text talks about how the customer preference for electric cars has not increased uniformly. Choice D further illustrates this idea.

Distractor Explanation: All the other choices are incorrect because the text must be completed with an example that illustrates the uneven rise in customer preference for battery-electric cars. **Choices A** and **B** both only state the number of electric cars registered between 2016-2019 and 2020, respectively. **Choice C** is incorrect because it does not offer a comparison that shows an uneven increase.

13. **Level:** Medium | **Domain:** INFORMATION AND IDEAS
Skill/Knowledge: Inference

Key Explanation: Choice B is the best answer. The third sentence refers to "a molecular examination" which established genetic relationships with other species. Therefore, the biologists must have had molecules from actual salamanders to work with. In other words, they must have found at least one specimen in the wild to compare with the four Thai *Tylototriton* species.

Distractor Explanation: All of the other choices are incorrect because a molecular examination only of the species that were available, not using *T. phukhaensis*, would not be able to determine the molecular characteristics of *T. phukhaensis* well enough to know what species are related or not. The other choices all give scenarios in which the scientists did not find examples of the new species for comparison.

14. **Level:** Easy | **Domain:** INFORMATION AND IDEAS
Skill/Knowledge: Inference

Key Explanation: Choice C is the best answer because the text establishes that the disease does not have many patients: "Menkes is a rare X-linked disease." As a direct result of that rarity, "few pharmaceutical companies are investing in research related to the disease." In other words, the companies are not "investing" or "putting money" into research because it is rare. The logical implication is that the companies will not get enough profits back from their investment; the process of creating a cure is "not financially viable" or "will lose money."

Distractor Explanation: Choice A is incorrect because the text does not condemn the decision of the pharmaceutical companies. The tone is neutral and stating the fact that companies have not done research on Menkes disease, rather than saying that the company should invest money even though they will not be able to recoup their losses. **Choice B** is incorrect because the text does not discuss the stages of the disease or when the disease can be diagnosed. It is possible that the disease could be diagnosed from right after birth or even through prenatal testing before any symptoms have appeared. **Choice D** is incorrect because, while the text indicates that the disease is linked to the ATP7A gene, it says there is no cure and there is no mention of supplements.

15. **Level:** Medium | **Domain:** STANDARD ENGLISH CONVENTIONS
Skill/Knowledge: Boundaries

Key Explanation: Choice B is the best answer. The proper structure for joining a list of over two nouns with "and" is to place a comma after each of the nouns that precedes "and." In this case, there should be a comma after "chili pepper," "lemongrass," "cilantro," and "shallots." No other punctuation is needed because "such as…lime" restricts the type of "ingredients" to specific ones that are ground together.

Distractor Explanation: Choices A and **D** are incorrect because there should be no comma after "and" in a list. The comma after "shallots" is sometimes omitted, but would only be acceptable if there were no other commas in the underlined portion. **Choice C** is incorrect because there should be no comma after "lime." The following portion is necessary to the understanding of the main sentence, so should not be separated with any punctuation.

16. **Level:** Medium | **Domain:** STANDARD ENGLISH CONVENTIONS
Skill/Knowledge: Boundaries

Key Explanation: Choice D is the best answer. When a phrase is used as part of a sentence, the punctuation aside from the quotation marks should adhere to usual structures. In this case, the quotation is part of a clause subordinated by the conjunction "while." Replacing the quotation with XX, it is easier to see that the quote is the subject and "is used" is the verb, so no punctuation should divide the underlined portion: "While XX is frequently used…"

Distractor Explanation: Choice A is incorrect because the portion before the period is not a complete sentence because there is no active verb. **Choices B** and **D** are incorrect because no comma should divide the subject from the verb in a clause; the placement inside or outside the quote mark is irrelevant in this context.

17. **Level:** Easy | **Domain:** STANDARD ENGLISH CONVENTIONS
Skill/Knowledge: Boundaries

Key Explanation: Choice D is the best answer. There are two independent clauses that can stand on their own as sentences on either side of the underlined portion. Therefore, they should be divided into two separate sentences with a period.

Distractor Explanation: Choice A is incorrect because it is a comma splice between two independent clauses. **Choices B** and **C** can be eliminated because a single dash or colon can follow an independent clause, but the following portion needs to explain or add more detail to the previous sentence. In this case, the following portion changes to a different topic, from the 53rd year of independence to the struggle for freedom.

18. **Level:** Easy | **Domain:** STANDARD ENGLISH CONVENTIONS
Skill/Knowledge: Form, Structure, and Sense

Key Explanation: Choice D is the best answer. The underlined portion refers to "is," showing that the claim has a possibility but not certainty of being true. **Choice D** is an adverb, which can be used to modify a verb.

Distractor Explanation: All of the other choices can be eliminated because they do not modify a verb. **Choices A** and **C** are adjectives, which modify nouns. **Choice B** is a noun.

19. **Level:** Medium | **Domain:** STANDARD ENGLISH CONVENTIONS
Skill/Knowledge: Form, Structure, and Sense

Key Explanation: Choice B is the best answer. "Most famous for the Monte Carlo Casino" is a modifier which needs to refer to the following noun. In this case, the modifier describes "the country" and shows what the country is most famous for.

Distractor Explanation: All of the other choices can be eliminated because the modifier "Most famous for the Monte Carlo Casino" refers to something other than the country. In **Choice A**, the modifier is followed by the generic "there." In addition, "which is world-class" appears to refer to the preceding noun, "the country" rather than the "oceanographic museum." In **Choices C** and **D**, the modifier refers to the museum; the placement of "world-class" does not affect the answer choice.

20. **Level:** Medium | **Domain:** STANDARD ENGLISH CONVENTIONS
Skill/Knowledge: Form, Structure, and Sense

Key Explanation: Choice C is the best answer. "To come down on" is a phrasal verb which means "to deal severely with," so fits the context of saying that if police are severe on offenders, there is no need to make more laws.

Distractor Explanation: All of the other choices are incorrect because they are phrasal verbs with meanings that do not fit the context of explaining what police should do to the offenders. **Choice A** refers to leaving a place. **Choice B** refers to creating something. **Choice D** refers to catching an illness.

21. **Level:** Medium | **Domain:** STANDARD ENGLISH CONVENTIONS
Skill/Knowledge: Form, Structure, and Sense

Key Explanation: Choice C is the best answer. "Much XX-er than" is a standard idiom of comparison, which in this case shows that the speed of pollution entering the ocean is faster than the speed of pollution being removed from the ocean.

Distractor Explanation: All of the other choices can be eliminated because they do not complete the idiom "much XX-er than" using a standard word.

22. **Level:** Easy | **Domain:** EXPRESSION OF IDEAS
Skill/Knowledge: Transitions

Key Explanation: Choice D is the best answer because it is used to introduce an "example" or "illustration" that supports a claim. The part preceding the underline is a claim that people noticed that sampling occurred. The following portion is a specific illustration of that claim, a list of people who sampled each other's music.

Distractor Explanation: None of the other choices adequately shows the relationship between the preceding and following sentences. **Choice A** refers to the final statement in a list or the result of an action. **Choices B** and **C** are used to provide different ideas that support the same claim rather than an example of the preceding claim.

23. **Level:** Easy | **Domain:** EXPRESSION OF IDEAS
Skill/Knowledge: Transitions

Key Explanation: Choice C is the best answer because it is used to introduce the conclusion of an argument. In this case, the text explains why the Stoclet House is important, and the conclusion is that the house qualifies to be a UNESCO World Heritage site.

Distractor Explanation: Choice A is incorrect because it is used to introduce something that comes later in a series, but the qualification to be a World Heritage site does not come after the building is created as a classic in its style and in good condition, it is because the building is in good condition. **Choice B** is incorrect because it shows something that would happen in a different situation, but in this case, the qualification and the described situation both occurred. **Choice D** is used to show a contrast or change in ideas, not continue a logical train of thought.

24. **Level:** Medium | **Domain:** EXPRESSION OF IDEAS
Skill/Knowledge: Transitions

Key Explanation: Choice B is the best answer because it refers to something that is wryly humorous because it was in error or had something other than the intended result. **Choice B** fits the context of saying that Messier named the cluster but lost it due to writing "erroneous" or "wrong" information about it.

Distractor Explanation: Choice A is incorrect because it is used to introduce the last item in a list or discussion, but the text continues the story with what happens several hundred years later. **Choice C** is incorrect because it signifies that the following is an example or clarification of the previous claim, but making an error is not an example of cataloging stars. **Choice D** is used to show that the following is done in a way appropriate for the circumstances, so does not fit the context of making an error.

25. **Level:** Medium | **Domain:** EXPRESSION OF IDEAS
Skill/Knowledge: Rhetorical Synthesis

Key Explanation: Choice B is the best answer. The notes mention that "there is no evidence that the population is breeding" and that the small population of the African grey hornbill in Florida "may only persist due to continuing releases or escapes."

Distractor Explanation: Choice A is incorrect because it does not explain why the bird will not rapidly multiply in Florida. **Choice C** is incorrect because the notes offer no comparison between the climate in sub-Saharan Africa and Florida. **Choice D** is incorrect because the notes do not mention that the African grey hornbill is only widespread in open woodland and savannah areas. Instead, it mentions that "it prefers open woodland and savannah."

26. **Level:** Medium | **Domain:** EXPRESSION OF IDEAS
Skill/Knowledge: Rhetorical Synthesis

Key Explanation: Choice D is the best answer. The underlined sentence is a specific, probably familiar example of how historical data, in this case, viewing habits, can be used to make predictions or suggestions. The sentence gives the reader an easy point of reference to understand the abstract concept of predictive analysis.

Distractor Explanation: Choices A and **B** are incorrect because the underlined sentence should remain in the text. It does not disrupt the logic and would not be better earlier in the paragraph, as it comes after the abstract idea is described. **Choice C** is incorrect because the example is not necessarily related to the following sentence; it elaborates on the previous one.

27. **Level:** Medium | **Domain:** EXPRESSION OF IDEAS
Skill/Knowledge: Rhetorical Synthesis

Key Explanation: Choice B is the best answer. "Which is" subordinates the second sentence so it modifies the previous noun, "big tech companies," while at the same time eliminating repeated words.

Distractor Explanation: Choice A is incorrect because it changes the meaning from big tech companies being overly powerful and a danger to antitrust cases being overly powerful and a danger. **Choice C** is incorrect because it retains the unnecessary repetition of "big tech companies" and complicates the sentence structure with "he says" set aside by commas. **Choice D** is incorrect because it repeats "cases" and adds an element of meaning that is not in the original sentences: "in his opinion" makes the big tech companies ones that he decides are big tech.

1. **Level:** Medium | **Domain:** CRAFT AND STRUCTURE
Skill/Knowledge: Words in Context

Key Explanation: Choice C is the best answer because in the sentence, the underlined word is what beach resorts create. Choice C refers to the trait of being attractive and interesting enough to entice people to come. It fits the context of saying that even if there were no other tourist destinations, beach resorts are very attractive and interesting to tourists.

Distractor Explanation: Choice A is incorrect because it refers to a large number of items collected by someone, but the beach resorts do not have a lot of things that they bought or amassed. **Choice B** refers to the act of convincing someone to do something. However, the beaches do not try to make people come; they are just interesting enough that people want to visit. **Choice D** relates to a link or attachment rather than something that pulls from afar

2. **Level:** Easy | **Domain:** CRAFT AND STRUCTURE
Skill/Knowledge: Words in Context

Key Explanation: Choice B is the best answer. The blank needs an adjective that describes the painter named Johannes Vermeer. "Eminent" refers to someone or something famous in a given field. In this context, it shows that the painter Johannes Vermeer is well-known in the field of art.

Distractor Explanation: None of the other choices create a logical sentence. **Choice A** refers to something that is easy to see. Vermeer is from the seventeenth century, so although his art is famous, he is no longer visible. **Choice C** refers to something glowing or shining, which does not accurately describe a person. **Choice D** refers to something complete or not modified, so it does not effectively describe a person.

3. **Level:** Hard | **Domain:** CRAFT AND STRUCTURE
Skill/Knowledge: Words in Context

Key Explanation: Choice D is the correct option. The author says that of the additions to the 1616 edition, many are clever but only sometimes are they improvements. Therefore, as used in the last sentence of the passage, "facile" refers to a superficial or shallow imitation of Marlowe's style of writing.

Distractor Explanation: Choice A is incorrect because the sentence does not talk about the accomplishments of the imitator. In fact, the previous sentence points to how only some of the additions are improvements. Choices B and C are incorrect because there is no evidence to point out that all the additions to the 1616 edition are successful or effortless.

4. **Level:** Medium | **Domain:** CRAFT AND STRUCTURE
Skill/Knowledge: Text Structure and Purpose

Key Explanation: Choice D is the best answer because the underlined sentence explains that the photographs were of strangers. That detail can eliminate the weakness that the horses already knew the people and were reacting according to their experiences rather than that they were identifying an emotion from a picture of a face.

Distractor Explanations: Choice A is incorrect because the sentence does not say how the "subjects" or "people in the experiment" were "selected" or "chosen." For example, they could have answered an advertisement or they could have been students in a class. **Choice B** is incorrect because the sentence does not say how many people the horses know; they could know many people. **Choice C** is incorrect because the entire text shows that expression is important for interspecies communication, but the underlined sentence does not stress that point

5. **Level:** Hard | **Domain:** CRAFT AND STRUCTURE
Skill/Knowledge: Text Structure and Purpose

Key Explanation: Choice D is the best answer because the author gives many scientific reasons that life may exist, but does not describe the research that went into determining the "findings" or "results." For example, he says, "Amino acids, just like those that make up every protein in our bodies, have been found in the tails of comets," giving the findings of experiments on comets but not explaining how the amino acids were found. The same is true for his discussion of organic compounds in Martian soil, a giant cloud of space alcohol, and the discovery of thousands of habitable planets.

Distractor Explanation: Choice A is incorrect because "personal anecdotes" are stories from the author's experience, but the author does not discuss any details from his life. **Choice B** is incorrect because there are no "analogies" or "comparisons used to teach" in the text. **Choice C** is incorrect because "unsubstantiated" means that there is no evidence to support the theories. However, the facts that the author brings up, such as the presence of organic compounds in Martian soil, is presumably based on research and supported by facts that are not discussed in the passage.

6. **Level:** Medium | **Domain:** CRAFT AND STRUCTURE
Skill/Knowledge: Cross-Text Connections

Key Explanation: Choice D is the best answer. The Sutton-Boveri theory is "that genes were located in specific places on the chromosomes." The passage says that Morgan "criticized the theory" at first or was "initially skeptical," but "after careful documentation," determined that certain genes are located on the X chromosome, showing that he had changed his mind and thought that there were indeed at least some genes in specific places on chromosomes.

Distractor Explanation: Choice A is incorrect because there is no indication that details needed to be adjusted for the theory to be correct. **Choice B** is incorrect because Morgan found "definitive" or "convincing" data that supported, not "contradicted" or "went against" the theory. **Choice C** is incorrect because Morgan derived scientific findings that supported the theory, even though he originally thought it was not "plausible" or "realistic."

7. **Level:** Medium | **Domain:** INFORMATION AND IDEAS
Skill/Knowledge: Central Ideas and Details

Key Explanation: Choice C is the best answer. Giant anteaters have physically adapted by evolving "specialized tongues" that help them eat. They have also adapted behaviorally by living in an area where "their favored prey is common" and by learning to abandon the nest when soldier ants arrive.

Distractor Explanation: Choice A is incorrect because there is no indication that giant anteaters do not live in areas disturbed by humans; they could still live in swamps, forests, and grasslands around people. **Choice B** is incorrect because the passage does not say that ants are "more vigilant" or that there are "fewer opportunities." The passage only says that the ants are "vigilant" in protecting. **Choice D** is incorrect because the passage does not specify which food the anteaters prefer. It is possible that they might like grubs better, but they have fewer chances to eat them.

8. **Level:** Medium | **Domain:** INFORMATION AND IDEAS
Skill/Knowledge: Central Ideas and Details

Key Explanation: Choice B is the best answer because the text states that "the purpose of their study was to address a central scientific problem in explaining the diversity of tree species in a forest." In other words, the purpose was to "isolate factors" or "determine elements" that permit the "phenomenon" or "situation" of coexisting tree species to occur.

Distractor Explanation: Choice A is incorrect because "ramifications" are "consequences." The study does not establish the consequences of the models; it is trying to explain why in reality there are coexisting species, whereas mathematical models have not solved that question. **Choice C** is incorrect because an "incident" refers to a specific event or occurrence, not an ongoing process. The researchers are trying to find a general explanation that holds valid for more than one specific event. **Choice D** is incorrect because the study does not point to "flaws" or "errors" in proposed theories. It is trying to find an answer to a question that was unexplainable at the time.

9. **Level:** Hard | **Domain:** INFORMATION AND IDEAS
Skill/Knowledge: Command of Evidence (Textual)

Key Explanation: Choice D is the best answer. The claim is that Williams was "full of natural talent and energy." **Choice D** gives the idea of energy through a comparison with a hurricane, a powerful weather phenomenon. The fact that the speaker was worried about his own chances in show business alludes to the idea that Williams was so talented that no one else had a chance.

Distractor Explanation: The other choices can be eliminated because they do not encompass both ideas of talent and energy. **Choice A** is incorrect because it only states that Williams was kind or helpful. **Choice B** shows that he was talented, but not that he was energetic. **Choice C** also implies that he was talented and less exciting when he was around, but does not convey the idea of energy.

10. **Level:** Easy | **Domain:** INFORMATION AND IDEAS
Skill/Knowledge: Command of Evidence (Textual)

Key Explanation: Choice C is the best answer because "any opiate" would include both users of prescription opiates and users of non-prescription opiates. In Figure 1, any opiate refers to the combination of the bottom and middle sections of the column. The right-hand column for 2017 has a combined amount of about 48,000 deaths, since the second section of the bar reaches to just under the 50,000 line.

Distractor Explanation: Choice A is incorrect because there were 18,000 deaths by "any" or "all combined" drug overdoses in 1999, not

2017. In 2017, there were 18,000 deaths caused by prescription opiates, the bottom section, but not all drugs combined; the latter is over 70,000. **Choice B** is incorrect because "any type of opiate" would refer to both prescription and non-prescription, the bottom two sections of the columns. However, none of the columns have those two sections total 38,000. **Choice D** is incorrect because 75,000 is the approximate total number of deaths in 2017, not the total for prescription opiates, which is just the bottom section of the column.

11. **Level:** Medium | **Domain:** INFORMATION AND IDEAS
Skill/Knowledge: Command of Evidence (Quantitative)

Key Explanation: Choice A is the best choice. The previous sentence in the text talks about the countries that recorded the highest growth in population. The sentence to be completed begins with "conversely". Thus, an opposite example must be provided which mentions the countries with a decrease in population.

Distractor Explanation: Choice B is incorrect because it only mentions one country. Since the previous sentence in the text mentions the top 5 countries that recorded a population increase, the ideal choice would be an example that mentions the top 5 countries with a population decrease. **Choice C** is incorrect because it does not provide an example that it is the opposite of the previous sentence. **Choice D** is incorrect because the text does not mention anything about the number of deaths registered.

12. **Level:** Easy | **Domain:** INFORMATION AND IDEAS
Skill/Knowledge: Inference

Key Explanation: Choice C is the best answer because the text says, "widespread off-label use of intravenous subanesthetic-dose ketamine for treatment-resistant depression has raised concerns about side effects, especially given its history as a drug of abuse." "Especially" indicates that the main concern is that ketamine is associated with drug abuse or addiction problems.

Distractor Explanation: None of the other choices are supported by evidence from the passage. **Choice A** is incorrect because there is no discussion of it becoming less effective. **Choice B** is incorrect because, while there is a concern of side effects, there is no mention of the effects "in conjunction with" or "at the same time as" using other drugs. **Choice D** is incorrect because a "relapse" is a return to a former condition. There is no discussion in the passage about whether the patients become depressed again or not.

13. **Level:** Easy| **Domain:** INFORMATION AND IDEAS
Skill/Knowledge: Inferences

Key Explanation: Choice C is the best answer because Henri produced work that was "a new style" than that of the National Academy of Design, which he "disliked." The passage says that his style had "depicted the seedy underside of urban life," meaning he painted things that were not considered fashionable or proper; they were "undignified" or "not majestic." Therefore, it is likely that the Academy artists "avoided" or "did not draw" such things.

Distractor Explanations: Choice A is incorrect because the text says Henri used a "bold, realistic style" and that the Academy artists used a "highly–polished" style. Since Henri was trying to create a new way of painting, the two styles probably have little overlap. **Choice B** is incorrect because the text does not say that the artists were not in New York; it only implies that they did not draw sketches in the streets. **Choice D** is incorrect because "dirty snow" is only one example of Henri's art. It is possible that the artists drew winter scenes, but they avoided the dirt and squalor in their pictures.

14. **Level:** Easy | **Domain:** STANDARD ENGLISH CONVENTIONS
Skill/Knowledge: Boundaries

Key Explanation: Choice B is the best answer. "In such a waterfall" is a prepositional phrase that indicates a situation. Phrases should be divided from the main clause in a sentence by a comma.

Distractor Explanation: Choice A is incorrect because without any punctuation, it is unclear where the prepositional phrase ends and the main clause begins. **Choices C** and **D** are incorrect because colons and semicolons should follow a complete independent clause, but the preceding portion cannot stand on its own as a sentence.

15. **Level:** Easy | **Domain:** STANDARD ENGLISH CONVENTIONS
Skill/Knowledge: Boundaries

Key Explanation: Choice D is the best answer. There are two ideas with subjects and verbs, so they can be divided into separate sentences.

Distractor Explanation: Choice A is incorrect because it is a comma splice between two independent clauses. **Choice B** is incorrect because "because" subordinates the following information. A semicolon should not be followed by a subordinate clause, only an independent clause. **Choice C** is incorrect because "since" creates a subordinate clause which cannot stand on its own as a sentence.

16. **Level:** Easy | **Domain:** STANDARD ENGLISH CONVENTIONS
Skill/Knowledge: Boundaries

Key Explanation: Choice A is the best answer. The portion between the italics, "the Maori... tree," modifies "kauri." To better see the structure of the main clause, remove the portion between the italics. It is then clear that the subject "Forests filled with kauri" needs to be followed by a verb, in this case, the phrasal verb "date back."

Distractor Explanation: Choice B is incorrect because it leaves the main clause without an active verb—"dating back..." is subordinated, but there is no complete clause before it. **Choices C** and **D** are incorrect because they include an extra noun. Two nouns should not be used in a row within a clause without subordinating one of them.

17. **Level:** Easy | **Domain:** STANDARD ENGLISH CONVENTIONS
Skill/Knowledge: Form, Structure, and Sense

Key Explanation: Choice D is the best answer. Research results are presented in the present tense as "universal truths."

Distractor Explanation: All of the other choices can be eliminated because they do not use the standard form for showing currently accepted research results. **Choice A** is a progressive tense, though "research" can be used in the plural. **Choice B** is a future tense. **Choice C** is the past tense, which is only acceptable if the results have subsequently been proven erroneous.

18. **Level:** Easy | **Domain:** STANDARD ENGLISH CONVENTIONS
Skill/Knowledge: Form, Structure, and Sense

Key Explanation: Choice C is the best answer. The section between the commas, "______ artwork...influences" is a clause that modifies the previous noun, Elizabeth Catlett. **Choice C** is used to show that the subject of the clause belongs to the preceding noun. Therefore, it effectively shows that the subject "artwork" belongs to "Catlett."

Distractor Explanation: Choice A is incorrect because "her" creates an independent clause rather than a relative clause that modifies the previous word. **Choices B** and **D** are incorrect because they act as the subject of clause, adding more information about the preceding noun; they cannot be followed directly with another subject, "artwork."

19. **Level:** Easy | **Domain:** STANDARD ENGLISH CONVENTIONS
Skill/Knowledge: Form, Structure, and Sense

Key Explanation: Choice A is the best answer. The underlined portion needs to be a subject that is followed by the verb "composed."

Distractor Explanation: Choice B is incorrect because it indicates possession and needs to be followed by a noun. **Choice C** is incorrect because it is an object rather than a subject. **Choice D** is incorrect because it shows possession and needs to be followed by a noun. Alternatively, it could be a contraction for "she is," which does fit the past-tense context or the verb "composed."

20. **Level:** Easy | **Domain:** STANDARD ENGLISH CONVENTIONS
Skill/Knowledge: Form, Structure, and Sense

Key Explanation: Choice B is the best answer. The underlined portion is the main verb of the sentence. The entire preceding portion, "dividing one full-time job between two employees," is the subject. Though it may appear plural, the subject can be simplified to "dividing." When a verb ending in "-ing" is used as a subject, it is considered singular, and **Choice B** is a singular verb.

Distractor Explanation: Choice A is incorrect because it is plural, so does not agree with the singular "dividing." **Choices C** and **D** can be eliminated because they do not create a complete sentence; the underlined portion should be an active verb form.

21. **Level:** Medium | **Domain:** STANDARD ENGLISH CONVENTIONS
Skill/Knowledge: Form, Structure, and Sense

Key Explanation: Choice C is the best answer. "They" is plural, so correctly refers to the plural noun "many names" from the previous sentence. "Range" is plural, so it agrees with the plural noun.

Distractor Explanation: Choices A and **D** can be eliminated because "ranges" is singular, so does not agree with the plural noun. **Choice B** is incorrect because it is a noun rather than a noun and verb. As a result, the sentence is a fragment with no active verb.

22. **Level:** Medium | **Domain:** EXPRESSION OF IDEAS
Skill/Knowledge: Transitions

Key Explanation: Choice B is the best answer because it is used to show a contrast or change in topic. It fits the context of saying that dandelions are viewed as weeds, but in reality, they can be eaten many ways.

Distractor Explanation: None of the other choices are used to indicate that there is a contrast of ideas. **Choice A** is incorrect because it is used to introduce the logical conclusion of an argument, but the idea that dandelions are edible is not a logical reason to view them as weeds. **Choice C** is used to add a specific detail that clarifies the previous claim. **Choice D** is used to add more reasons in support of the previous claim.

23. **Level:** Easy | **Domain:** EXPRESSION OF IDEAS
Skill/Knowledge: Transitions

Key Explanation: Choice A is the best answer because it is used to add another detail to develop a discussion. In this context, **Choice A** adds what happened to the finished painting after the discussion of what Picasso did while making the painting.

Distractor Explanation: Choice B is incorrect because it is used to introduce an opposing or conflicting idea, but the final sentence continues the theme of the painting being influential for the cause against war. **Choice C** is incorrect because it shows the logical result of a series of actions. Though the final sentence expands on the idea of the anti-war protests, it is not necessarily given that after showing people the painting, Picasso would exhibit the painting to raise funds. **Choice D** is incorrect because it is used to add an example of a previous claim, but the following sentence discusses a time sequence rather than giving more detail about the visitors who entered his studio.

24. **Level:** Medium | **Domain:** EXPRESSION OF IDEAS
Skill/Knowledge: Transitions

Key Explanation: Choice C is the best answer. The passage is structured with the first two sentences explaining the good that Ahmed did. The portion following the underline has a different tone from receiving the Nobel Prize. **Choice C** is used to show something that happened at a later time, so fits the context of saying that first he was praised but later he was accused of certain problems.

Distractor Explanation: Choice A is incorrect because it is used to add more information on the same topic, so it does not effectively show that the praise changed to concern over Ahmed's actions. **Choice B** is incorrect because it means that the following is fitting or appropriate given the preceding information, but in this case, being accused of bad things is not appropriate for a winner of a Nobel Prize. **Choice D** is incorrect because it is used to introduce the logical result of the preceding argument, but the following is not a logical result of winning a peace prize.

25. **Level:** Hard | **Domain:** EXPRESSION OF IDEAS
Skill/Knowledge: Rhetorical Synthesis

Key Explanation: Choice A is the best answer. It concisely shows that the level of the appeal is "basic" or very deep and essential.

Distractor Explanation: All of the other choices can be eliminated as redundant; the extra words distract from the intended meaning. In **Choices B** and **D**, "basic" and "fundamental" are synonyms. In **Choice C**, "level" and "depth" have the same meaning in the context.

26. **Level:** Medium | **Domain:** EXPRESSION OF IDEAS
Skill/Knowledge: Rhetorical Synthesis

Key Explanation: Choice C is the best answer. The notes mention that is he most known for being the most-streamed classical artist of all time.

Distractor Explanation: Choice A is incorrect because this is not his most significant achievement. **Choice B** is also incorrect as the notes do not mention this as being his most significant achievement. **Choice D** is incorrect because the statement only describes his music projects and not a significant achievement.

27. **Level:** Medium | **Domain:** EXPRESSION OF IDEAS
Skill/Knowledge: Rhetorical Synthesis

Key Explanation: Choice C is the best answer. It implies a very fast rate, so indicates that the number of ghost kitchens is increasing extremely fast.

Distractor Explanation: Choices A and **D** are incorrect because they only indicate an increase; they do not include any hint that the rate is fast. **Choice B** is incorrect because it includes undertones of getting too big too fast, implying that the number may decrease soon, such as when the economy inflates and then collapses.

1. **Level:** Easy | **Domain:** ALGEBRA
Skill/Knowledge: Linear equations in two variables | **Testing point:** Converting English to Algebra to create a two variable equation

Key Explanation: Choice A is correct. She burns 20 calories when she walks every minute. Therefore, she burned $20x$ calories after x minutes. She also burns 35 calories every minute she cycles and therefore burns $35y$ calories after y minutes. The equation would therefore be $20x + 35y = 340$. Subtracting $20x$ from both sides of this equation yields
$35y = 340 - 20x$.

Distractor Explanation: Choice B is incorrect because it states that the difference between the calories burned from cycling and burned from walking is equal to 340. **Choice C** and **Choice D** are incorrect. The rate of 20 calories per minute can only be multiplied by x minutes of walking. And the rate of 35 calories per minute can only be multiplied by y minutes of cycling.

2. **Level:** Easy | **Domain:** PROBLEM-SOLVING AND DATA ANALYSIS
Skill/Knowledge: Two-variable data: models and scatterplots | **Testing point:** Identifying points on a scatter plot

Key Explanation: Choice B is the correct answer because the number of dots that have a higher value than the line of best fit are the dots above the line i.e 6.

Distractor Explanation: Choice A is incorrect as this is the number of dots on the graph. **Choice C** is incorrect as this is the number of dots below the line of best fit. **Choice D** is incorrect; it may be a conceptual error or lack of understanding of the question.

3. **Level:** Easy | **Domain:** ADVANCED MATH
Skill/Knowledge: Nonlinear functions | **Testing point:** Using the remainder theorem

Key Explanation: Choice B is correct. The remainder theorem states that if $f(x)$ is divided by $x-a$, the remainder would be $f(a)$. Therefore when $f(a) = 0$, then $x-a$ is a factor of the function $f(x)$. In this case, $f(3)= 0$, therefore $x-3$ is a factor of the equation $f(x)$.

Distractor Explanation: Choices A, **C**, and **D** are incorrect. Based on the table, dividing $(x+2)$, x, or $(x-5)$ from $f(x)$ will not yield a remainder of 0.

4. **Level:** Easy | **Domain:** ALGEBRA
Skill/Knowledge: System of two linear equations in two variables. | **Testing point:** Solving for one variable in a system of linear equations

Key Explanation: Simplify the first equation by using the distributive property which yields $t - 5 + 2s - 6 = 8$. Adding 5 and 6 to both sides of the equation yields $t + 2s = 19$. Simplify the second equation by using the distributive property which yields $2t - 10 - 3s + 9 = -19$. Adding 10 and subtracting 9 from both sides of the equation yields $2t - 3s = -18$. To find the value of s, use the elimination method and multiply -2 by the first equation. This yields $-2t -4s = -38$. Then, add the two equations which yield $-7s = -56$. Dividing -7 from both sides of the equation yields $s = 8$.

5. **Level:** Easy | **Domain:** ALGEBRA
Skill/Knowledge: Linear equations in one variable
Testing point: Solving linear equations in one variable

Key Explanation: Choice D is correct. Simplify the equation by using distributive property, which yields
$3x - 6 - 2x + 2 = -x + 2x + 4 - 8$.
Combining like terms yields $x - 4 = x - 4$. This

shows that the equation is the same on both sides. So, any value of x makes the equation true. Therefore, the equation has infinitely many solutions.

Distractor Explanation: Choice A is incorrect because to have no solutions, solving the equation will result in a false statement. **Choice B** is incorrect because to have one solution, solving the equation will yield x equal to a number. **Choice C** is incorrect because linear equations do not have 2 solutions.

6. **Level:** Hard | **Domain:** ADVANCED MATH
   Skill/Knowledge: Equivalent expressions | **Testing point:** Converting between exponents and radicals

   Key Explanation: Choice B is correct. To simplify the variable with different exponents, add the exponents of $g^{\frac{4}{5}}$ and $g^{\frac{2}{5}}$ which yields $g^{\frac{6}{5}}$. Making 2 have the same exponent as g yields $32^{\frac{1}{5}}.g^{\frac{6}{5}}$.

   Putting them inside the radical sign yields $\sqrt[5]{32g^6}$

   Distractor Explanation: Choice A is incorrect because the 2 did not have any exponent and thus should have been left outside the root or converted to the fifth. **Choice C** and **Choice D** are incorrect and may result from interchanging the numerator and denominator of the exponent.

7. **Level:** Medium | **Domain:** PROBLEM-SOLVING AND DATA ANALYSIS
   Skill/Knowledge: Inference from sample statistics and margin of error | **Testing point:** Finding the margin of error

   Key Explanation: To find the margin of error, first find the midpoint of the sample mean mass. This yields $\frac{120+182}{2}=151$. The margin of error would be the difference between the midpoint and either of the sample mean masses. Subtracting 151 from 182 yields 31.

8. **Level:** Hard | **Domain:** ALGEBRA
   Skill/Knowledge: Linear functions | **Testing point:** Solving a linear function

   Key Explanation: Choice A is correct. To find $f(6)$, first find the value of x which will be plugged into the equation $f(2x)$. Equating $2x$ to 6 and solving for x yields $x = 3$. Plugging 3 to $9x-7$ yields 20. Therefore, $f(6) = 20$.

   Distractor Explanation: Choice B is incorrect and may result from plugging 6 directly into the equation. **Choice C** is incorrect and may result from substituting x with $2x$ and plugging 6 into the equation. **Choice D** is incorrect and may result from plugging 2 directly into the equation.

9. **Level:** Medium | **Domain:** PROBLEM-SOLVING AND DATA ANALYSIS
   Skill/Knowledge: One-variable data: distributions and measures of center and spread | **Testing point:** Finding the mean and median

   Key Explanation: Choice A is correct because. The median of the above data set of 21 students will be the $\frac{21+1}{2}$, which is the 11th shoe size, which is then represented by 3. The mean shoe size can then be calculated by adding the products of the shoe size and their corresponding frequency and dividing the sum by the total number of students. This yields a sum of 67. Dividing the sum by 21 yields a mean of 3.19. Therefore, the mean will be larger than the median.

Distractor Explanation: Choice B and **C** are incorrect as they are both false statements. **Choice D** is incorrect because there is sufficient information to answer the question.

10. **Level:** Medium | **Domain:** ADVANCED MATH
Skill/Knowledge: Equivalent expressions | **Testing point:** Using exponent rules

Key Explanation: To solve for a, first make the bases equal. Converting 27^x to a base 3 yields 3^{3x}. Converting 81^{-x} to a base 3 yields $(3^4)^{-x}$ or 3^{-4x}. The equation will now become $3^{3x} \div 3^{-4x} = 3^{ax}$. On the right side of the equation, the bases are divided, which means that the exponents must be subtracted. Subtracting the exponents yields $3^{(3x-(-4x))} = 3^{ax}$ or simply $3^{7x} = 3^{ax}$. Equating the exponents yields $7x = ax$. Dividing both sides of the equation by x yields $7 = a$.

11. **Level:** Hard | **Domain:** GEOMETRY AND TRIGONOMETRY
Skill/Knowledge: Lines, angles, and triangles | **Testing point:** Finding the sum of the Interior angles of a polygon

Key Explanation: Choice C is correct. The sum of interior angles in a polygon is represented by $180°(n-2)$. A hexagon has 6 sides and therefore the sum of interior angles in the hexagon will be $180(6-2) = 720°$. 720 degrees in radian form will be $\frac{720}{180} = 4\pi$. Therefore $b = 4$.

Distractor Explanation: Choice A is incorrect and may result in calculating $\frac{180}{720}$. **Choice B** is incorrect and may result in calculating $\frac{720}{720}$. **Choice D** is incorrect and may result in calculating $\frac{720}{360}$.

12. **Level:** Easy | **Domain:** PROBLEM-SOLVING AND DATA ANALYSIS
Skill/Knowledge: Percentages | **Testing point:** Finding the percentage increase

Key Explanation: Choice C is correct. If 80 is increased by 200%, that means that the new value will be 300% of 80 which is 240. An alternative solution is to find 200% of 80 and add it to 80 which yields 240.

Distractor Explanation: Choice A is incorrect because it is the percentage. **Choice B** is incorrect because it is the increase without adding the original. **Choice D** is incorrect because it is the sum of 80 and 200.

13. **Level:** Easy | **Domain:** ADVANCED MATH
Skill/Knowledge: Nonlinear functions | **Testing point:** Using the quadratic formula

Key Explanation: To solve for the quadratic equation, use the quadratic formula $\frac{-b \pm \sqrt{b^2 - 4ac}}{2a}$, where $a = 2$, $b = -4$ and $c = -7$. Substituting the values to the formula yields $\frac{-(-4) \pm \sqrt{(-4)^2 - 4(2)(-7)}}{2(2)}$. Simplifying this yields $\frac{4 \pm \sqrt{72}}{4}$ or $1 \pm \frac{\sqrt{72}}{4}$. Simplifying $\sqrt{72}$ yields $6\sqrt{2}$. Therefore, the expression becomes $1 \pm \frac{6\sqrt{2}}{4}$ or $1 \pm \frac{3\sqrt{2}}{2}$. Since the expression is now in the same format as $1 \pm \frac{a\sqrt{2}}{2}$, then $a = 3$.

14. **Level:** Easy | **Domain:** ALGEBRA
Skill/Knowledge: Linear functions | **Testing point:** Interpretation of terms in a linear function

Key Explanation: Choice B is correct. This is because 262 is the *y-intercept* of the model and represents the number of houses on day 0, which is the beginning of October.

Distractor Explanation: Choice A is incorrect because the number of houses at the end of October is represented by $h(x)$. **Choice C** is incorrect as the number of houses sold per day would be 8. **Choice D** is incorrect as the number of houses sold on the first day of October is represented when $x = 8$.

15. **Level:** Medium | **Domain:** GEOMETRY AND TRIGONOMETRY
Skill/Knowledge: Right triangles and trigonometry | **Testing point:** Working with special triangles

Key Explanation: Choice A is correct. A 90 – 60 – 30 triangle has a hypotenuse of $2x$, a shorter leg of x, and a longer leg of $x\sqrt{3}$. The area of this triangle can then be found by the formula $\frac{1}{2} \times base \times height$. Substituting the base and the height yields $\frac{1}{2} \times x \times x\sqrt{3}$ or $\frac{x^2\sqrt{3}}{2}$. The given side AC is the hypotenuse of the triangle. So, 32 = $2x$ which yields $x = 16$. Substituting 16 to the formula yields $\frac{16^2\sqrt{3}}{2}$ or $128\sqrt{3}$.

Distractor Explanation: Choice B and **Choice D** are incorrect and may result from using $\sqrt{2}$ instead of $\sqrt{3}$. **Choice C** is incorrect because this is one of the sides of the triangle.

16. **Level:** Easy | **Domain:** ADVANCED MATH
Skill/Knowledge: Equivalent expressions | **Testing point:** Matching coefficients

Key Explanation: Using distributive property on the left side of the equation yields $5xy + 3 - 6xy + 2xy^2 - 2 = axy^2 + bxy + c$. Combining like terms yields $2xy^2 - xy + 1 = axy^2 + bxy + c$. Comparing the coefficients on both sides of the equation, yields $a = 2$, $b = -1$, and $c = 1$ Therefore, $a + b = 1$.

17. **Level:** Easy | **Domain:** ADVANCED MATH
Skill/Knowledge: Nonlinear equations in one variable and systems of equations in two variables
Testing point: Finding the product of the roots of a quadratic equation

Key Explanation: Choice B is correct. In a quadratic equation ($ax^2 + bx + c = 0$), the product of the roots can be found by $\frac{c}{a}$, Using the given equation, $c = -24$ and $a = 3$. Thus, the product of the roots will be $\frac{-24}{3}$ or -8.

Distractor Explanation: Choice A is incorrect as this is the value of a. **Choice C** is incorrect and may result from calculating $\frac{b}{a}$. **Choice D** is incorrect and may result from calculating the sum of the roots which is $\left(\frac{-b}{a}\right)$.

18. **Level:** Medium | **Domain:** ADVANCED MATH
Skill/Knowledge: Nonlinear functions | **Testing point:** Using the vertex form of a quadratics equation

Key Explanation: Choice B is correct. The general equation of a parabola is given by $y = a(x - h)^2$

+ k, where (h, k) denotes the coordinate of the vertex. In this case, $h = 3$ and $k = 10$. Thus, the equation becomes $y = a(x-3)^2 + 10$. The sign of a denotes the orientation of the parabola. If a is positive, the parabola opens upward. If a is negative, the parabola opens downward. In this case, the parabola opens downward so the value of a must be negative. Therefore, the equation of the parabola is $y = -2(x - 3)^2 + 10$.

Distractor Explanation: Choice A and **Choice C** are incorrect since their a is positive which would suggest that the graph opens upwards however the graph opens downwards. **Choice D** is incorrect and may result from using (–3, 10) as the vertex instead of (3, 10).

19. **Level:** Easy | **Domain:** ALGEBRA
Skill/Knowledge: Linear equations in one variable
Testing point: Matching coefficients

Key Explanation: Using the distributive property, the equation becomes $6 - 6x = ax + b$ or $-6x + 6 = ax + b$. Comparing the coefficient and the constant on both sides of the equation yields $a = -6$ and $b = 6$. Therefore, the product of a and b is –36.

20. **Level:** Easy | **Domain:** ADVANCED MATH
Skill/Knowledge: Nonlinear functions

Key Explanation: Choice B is correct.
When $x = 0, f(x) = -8$ at the coordinate (0, –8).

21. **Level:** Medium | **Domain:** ALGEBRA
Skill/Knowledge: Linear equations in one variable
Testing point: Finding the value of x in a linear equation

Key Explanation: Choice B is correct. To find the value of x, multiply both sides of the equation by $\frac{4}{3}$.
This yields $(x-5) = 27 \times \frac{4}{3}$ or simply $(x - 5) = 36$.

Distractor Explanation: Choice A is incorrect and may result from calculating the value of x.

Choice C is incorrect and may result from multiplying $\frac{3}{4}$ to both sides of the equation instead of $\frac{4}{3}$.

Choice D is incorrect and may result from conceptual or calculation errors.

22. **Level:** Hard | **Domain:** ALGEBRA
Skill/Knowledge: Linear inequalities in one or two variables | **Testing point:** Finding solution to a system of linear inequalities

Key Explanation: Choice C is correct. To solve such questions, the best method would be to substitute the points to the inequalities and check if the statements are true or false.
Substituting (3, 1) to the first inequality yields $1 > -2(3) - 1$ or $1 > -7$, which is true.
Substituting (3, 1) to the second inequality

yields $3(1) < 3 + 9$ or $3 < 12$, which is also true. Therefore, the coordinate (3, 1) lies inside the intersection of the two inequalities.

Distractor Explanation: Choice A is incorrect. Substituting (–2, 1) to both inequalities will result in one false statement.
Choice B is incorrect. Substituting (1, 4) to both inequalities will result in one false statement.
Choice D is incorrect. Substituting (–3, 3) to both inequalities will result in false statements.

1. **Level:** Easy | **Domain:** ADVANCED MATH
Skill/Knowledge: Nonlinear equations in one variable and system of equations in two variables | **Testing point:** Solving absolute value equations

Key Explanation: Choice C is correct. To calculate the two solutions (p & q), equate the contents of the absolute value symbol to both the positive and negative values of the number on the other side of the equation. To obtain the first solution (p), solve for x in the equation $3x - 1 = 2$. Adding 1 to both sides of the equation yields $3x = 3$. Dividing 3 from both sides of the equation yields $x = 1$. Thus, $p = 1$. To obtain the second solution (q), solve for x in the equation $3x - 1 = -2$. Adding 1 to both sides of the equation yields $3x = -1$. Dividing 3 from both sides of the equation yields $x = -\frac{1}{3}$. Thus, $q = -\frac{1}{3}$. Adding 1 and $-\frac{1}{3}$ yields $\frac{2}{3}$. Therefore, $p + q = \frac{2}{3}$.

Distractor Explanation: Choice A is incorrect and may result from multiplying the second solution (q) by −1. **Choice B** and **Choice D** are incorrect as these are the two solutions to the equation.

2. **Level:** Medium | **Domain:** GEOMETRY AND TRIGONOMETRY
Skill/Knowledge: Circles | **Testing point:** Using equation of a circle

Key Explanation: Choice C is correct. To solve this question, plug each point into the equation of the circle. A coordinate that lies on the circle means that the equation will be equal on both ends. Plugging the point (−3, 4), the equation becomes $(-3 - 3)^2 + 4^2 + 8(4) = 84$. Simplifying the equation, this yields $84 = 84$.
Therefore, point (−3, 4) lies on the circle.

Distractor Explanation: Choice A is incorrect. Plugging the point (1, 7) into the equation yields $109 = 84$. Therefore, it lies outside the circle. **Choice B** is incorrect. Plugging the point (−2, 5) into the equation yields $90 = 84$. Therefore, it lies outside the circle. **Choice D** is incorrect. Plugging the point (3, −6) into the equation yields $-12 = 84$. Therefore, it does not lie on the circle.

3. **Level:** Easy | **Domain:** GEOMETRY AND TRIGONOMETRY
Skill/Knowledge: Right triangles and trigonometry | **Testing point:** Using trigonometry identities

Key Explanation: $\sin x = \cos(90 - x)$. So, if $\sin C$ and $\cos 63$ are equal, then the angles would add up to 90°. Therefore, $63° + C = 90°$. Subtracting 63° from both sides of the equation yields $C = 27°$.

4. **Level:** Hard | **Domain:** ADVANCED MATH
Skill/Knowledge: Equivalent expressions | **Testing point:** Working with complex numbers

Key Explanation: Choice A is correct. Rationalize the denominator of $\frac{2-2i}{3+4i}$ by multiplying the fraction by the denominator's conjugate which is $\frac{3-4i}{3-4i}$. This yields $\frac{6-6i-8i+8i^2}{9-16i^2}$. Substituting −1 to i^2 yields $-\frac{2}{25}-\frac{14}{25}i$. Matching the coefficients yields $a = -\frac{2}{25}$ and $b = -\frac{14}{25}$.

Distractor Explanations: Choice B is incorrect as this would be the value of b. **Choice C** and **Choice D** are incorrect and may result from miscalculation or conceptual errors.

5. **Level:** Medium | **Domain:** ADVANCED MATH
Skill/Knowledge: Nonlinear equations in one variable and systems of equations in two variables
Testing point: Solving system of linear and quadratic equations

Key Explanation: Choice C is correct. To solve for x, we can equate the two equations.
This yields $2x - 2 = 2x^2 - 9x + 7$.
Subtracting $2x$ and adding 2 to both sides of the equation yields $2x^2 - 9x + 7 - 2x + 2 = 0$.
Combining like terms yields $2x^2 - 11x + 9 = 0$. To solve the quadratic equation use either the factor method or the quadratic formula. Using the factor method, get the two factors of $18x^2$ whose sum is $-11x$.
The two factors are $-2x$ and $-9x$ which makes the equation $2x^2 - 2x - 9x + 9 = 0$.
Grouping the first two terms together and the last two terms together yields $(2x^2 - 2x) - (9x - 9) = 0$
Factoring out the greatest common factor yields $2x(x - 1) - 9(x - 1) = 0$.
Factoring out the common binomial yields $(x - 1)(2x - 9) = 0$. Equating both factors to 0 yields the two solutions, which are $x = 1$ and $x = \frac{9}{2}$ or 4.5

Distractor Explanation: Choice A is incorrect and may result from adding the two solutions. **Choice B** is incorrect as it is the negative of one of the solutions. **Choice D** is incorrect and may result from getting the difference between the solutions.

6. **Level:** Hard | **Domain:** ADVANCED MATH
Skill/Knowledge: Nonlinear equations in one variable and systems of equations in two variables
Testing point: Solving absolute equation

Key Explanation: To obtain the solutions, first simplify the equation by factorization. Factoring out 2 from $|6x - 4|$ yields $2|3x - 2|$. Factoring out $|3x - 2|$ from $3|3x - 2| - 2|3x - 2| = 7$ yields $(3 - 2)|3x - 2| = 7$ or $|3x - 2| = 7$. Then, equate the contents of the absolute value symbol to both the positive and negative values of the number on the other side of the equation. To obtain the first solution, solve for x in the equation $3x - 2 = 7$. Adding 2 to both sides of the equation yields $3x = 9$. Dividing 3 from both sides of the equation yields $x = 3$. To obtain the second solution, solve for x in the equation $3x - 2 = -7$. Adding 2 to both sides of the equation yields $3x = -5$. Dividing 3 from both sides of the equation yields $x = \frac{-5}{3}$.

Therefore, the positive solution to the equation is 3.

7. **Level:** Easy | **Domain:** ALGEBRA
Skill/Knowledge: Linear functions | **Testing point:** Creating equations from graphs

Key Explanation: Choice C is correct.
Calculating the slope of the given line using the points $(-5, 0)$ and $(3, 0)$ yields $\frac{5}{3}$. A slope of a line perpendicular to this will be the negative reciprocal of the slope of the given line.
Therefore, a line perpendicular to this should have a slope of $\left(\frac{-3}{5}\right)$.
To get the slope of a line from the equation, convert the equation to slope-intercept form.
Dividing both sides of the equation by 5, **Choice C** becomes $y = -\left(\frac{3}{5}\right)x + 3$.
Since the coefficient of x is $-\left(\frac{3}{5}\right)$, then this line is perpendicular to the given line.

Distractor Explanation: Choice A is incorrect as this is the equation of the line in the graph.

Choice B is incorrect as this is the equation of a line that has a slope of $\frac{3}{5}$. **Choice D** is incorrect as this is the equation of a line that has a slope of $\frac{5}{3}$ making it parallel to the given line.

8. **Level:** Easy | **Domain:** GEOMETRY AND TRIGONOMETRY
Skill/Knowledge: Circles | **Testing point:** Finding the circumference of a circle given it's equation

Key Explanation: Choice D is correct. To find the circumference of a circle, first, find the radius of the circle or the diameter. Rewrite the given equation into the standard form for the equation of a circle, by completing the squares. This yields $x^2 + 6x + 9 + y^2 - 4y + 4 = 51 + 9 + 4$. Simplifying the equation yields $(x + 3)^2 + (y - 2)^2 = 64$. Since the equation is now in standard form, then $r^2 = 64$. Solving for r yields 8 as the radius. Using the formula of the circumference which is $2\pi r$ yields 16π.

Distractor Explanation: Choice A is incorrect and may result from solving for the area of the circle instead of the circumference. **Choice B** is incorrect and may result from using πr instead of $2\pi r$ to solve for the circumference. **Choice C** is incorrect and may result from using $\sqrt{51}$ as the radius of the circle.

9. **Level:** Medium | **Domain:** GEOMETRY AND TRIGONOMETRY
Skill/Knowledge: Lines, angles and triangles | **Testing point:** Using the exterior angle theorem

Key Explanation: According to the Exterior Angle Theorem, the exterior angle of a triangle is equal to the sum of the opposite and non-adjacent interior angles.

Therefore, $\angle$ ABC + $\angle$ BAC = $\angle$ ACD.
The equation will now become $2x - 2 + x + 3 = 118$.
Combining like terms yields $3x + 1 = 118$.
Subtracting 1 from both sides of the equation yields $3x = 117$.
Dividing 3 from both sides of the equation yields $x = 39$.

10. **Level:** Easy | **Domain:** PROBLEM-SOLVING AND DATA ANALYSIS
Skill/Knowledge: Ratio, rates, proportional relationships, and units | **Testing point:** Creating and solving rate equation

Key Explanation: Choice B is correct. The question presents an inverse proportion problem where the number of carpenters (x) is inversely proportional to the number of days it requires to build a bed (y). Using the formula $xy = k$ and the given data $x = 4$ and $y = 3$ yields 12 as the value of k. Thus, the inverse proportion equation becomes $xy= 12$. To solve for the corresponding number of carpenters, substitute 2 with y which then yields $2x = 12$. Solving for x yields 6 as the number of carpenters needed to build the bed in 2 days.

Distractor Explanation: Choice A is incorrect as this represents the value of the constant k. **Choice C** is incorrect as this is the product of four carpenters and 2 days. **Choice D** is incorrect as this is a miscalculation or conceptual error.

11. **Level:** Easy | **Domain:** ADVANCED MATH
Skill/Knowledge: Equivalent expressions | **Testing point:** Using the FOILing method to multiply expressions

Key Explanation: Choice C is correct. Using distributive property yields, $5xy\,(x - 2y) + 3x\,(x - 2y)$. Simplifying the expression yields $5x^2y + 3x^2 - 10xy^2 - 6xy$.

Distractor Explanation: Choice A and **Choice D** are incorrect and may result from applying the distributive property incorrectly. **Choice B** is incorrect and may result from a miscalculation error in multiplying $5xy$ and $-2y$.

12. **Level:** Medium | **Domain:** ALGEBRA
Skill/Knowledge: Systems of two linear equations in two variables | **Testing point:** Solving for a variable in a system of linear equations

Key Explanation: To solve for y, use the elimination method. Multiplying 2 to the second equation yields $10x + 4y = 16$. Adding the first and second equations yields $7x + 10x - 4y + 4y = 1 + 16$. Combining like terms yield $17x = 17$. Dividing 17 from both sides of the equation yields $x = 1$. Substituting the value of x to the first equation yields $7(1) - 4y = 1$ or $7 - 4y = 1$. Subtracting 7 from both sides of the equation yields $-4y = -6$. Dividing -4 from both sides of the equation yields $y = \frac{3}{2}$ or 1.5.

13. **Level:** Easy | **Domain:** ALGEBRA
Skill/Knowledge: Linear inequalities in one or two variables | **Testing point:** Solving for x in an inequality

Key Explanation: Choice B is correct. Adding x to both sides of the equation yields $-2x + x \leq 8 - x + x$ or $-x \leq 8$.
Dividing both sides of the equation by -1 yields $x \geq -8$. Therefore, x is greater than or equal to -8. And -10 is the only option that is less than -8.

Distractor Explanation: Choices A, C, and **D** are incorrect. These values will make the inequality true and are considered solutions.

14. **Level:** Easy | **Domain:** PROBLEM-SOLVING AND DATA ANALYSIS
Skill/Knowledge: Probability and conditional probability | **Testing point:** Finding the probability of an event

Key Explanation: Choice D is correct. The unfair coin is tossed 20 times and 14 of these land on heads making the probability of the unfair coin landing on heads $\frac{14}{20} = 0.7$. Therefore the probability of the coin landing on heads the 21st time will be 0.7.

Distractor Explanation: Choice A is incorrect as this is the probability of landing on heads on a fair coin. **Choice B** is incorrect and may result from a miscalculation or conceptual error. **Choice C** is incorrect as it gives the probability of the unfair coin landing on tails.

15. **Level:** Medium | **Domain:** ALGEBRA
Skill/Knowledge: Systems of two linear equations in two variables | **Testing point:** Solving for x and y in a system of linear equations

Key Explanation: Choice D is correct. Solve for x and y either by substitution or by elimination. Using the elimination method, multiply 3 by both sides of the second equation. This yields $(5x + y = -6)\ 3$ or $15x + 3y = -18$. Subtracting the second equation from the first equation yields $-17x = 34$. Dividing both sides of the equation by -17 yields $x = -2$. Substituting the value of x to the second equation yields $5(-2) + y = -6$. Simplifying the equation yields $y = 4$. Subtracting y from x yields $-2, -4$, or -6.

Distractor Explanation: Choice A is incorrect and may result from subtracting x from y. **Choice B** is incorrect because it is the value of y. **Choice C** is incorrect as it is the value of x.

16. **Level:** Easy | **Domain:** ADVANCED MATH
Skill/Knowledge: Nonlinear functions |
Testing point: Converting the unit on exponential functions

Key Explanation: Since the equations are still equal, then $1,200(1.03)^m = 1,200(1.03)^{ad}$. Dividing both sides of the equation by 1,200 yields $(1.03)^m = (1.03)^{ad}$. Since the bases are equal, equate the exponents which yield $m = ad$. Since 1 *month* = 30 *days*, then $1 = a(30)$. Dividing 30 from both sides of the equation yields $\frac{1}{30} = a$.

17. **Level:** Easy | **Domain:** GEOMETRY AND TRIGONOMETRY
Skill/Knowledge: Area and volume | **Testing point:** Finding the volume of a cylinder

Key Explanation: Choice A is correct. The volume of a cylinder is given by the formula $\pi r^2 h$. Using the given data, $h = 2r$. Therefore, $h = 2(6) = 12$. Therefore, the volume will be $\pi(6)^2(12) = 432\pi$.

Distractor Explanation: Choice B is incorrect and may result from interchanging the values of r and h. **Choice C** is incorrect and may result from calculating the surface area of the cylinder instead of volume. **Choice D** is incorrect and may result from conceptual or calculation errors.

18. **Level:** Easy | **Domain:** GEOMETRY AND TRIGONOMETRY
Skill/Knowledge: Circles | **Testing point:** Using circle theorems

Key Explanation: Choice A is correct. An angle subtended at any point of the circle is half the angle subtended at the center. This means that $\angle$ DOE = 2 $\angle$ DRE. Therefore, $\angle$ DOE = 2(35°) = 70°.

Distractor Explanation: Choice B is incorrect because it implies that the angles are equal. **Choice C** and **D** are incorrect and this maybe due to conceptual or calculation errors

19. **Level:** Easy | **Domain:** ADVANCED MATH
Skill/Knowledge: Equivalent expressions |
Testing point: Factoring using the difference of two squares

Key Explanation: Choice A is correct. This question can be solved using factorization.
Using the difference of squares, $x^2 - a^2$ becomes $(x + a)(x - a)$.
Transforming the numerator of $4x^2 - 3$ to the format $x^2 - a^2$ yields $(2x)^2 - (\sqrt{3})^2$. Factoring the expression yields $(2x+\sqrt{3})(2x-\sqrt{3})$.

This would result to $\frac{(2x+\sqrt{3})(2x-\sqrt{3})}{(2x+\sqrt{3})}$.

Canceling out the binomial $2x+\sqrt{3}$ from both numerator and denominator yields $2x-\sqrt{3}$.

Distractor Explanation: Choice B is incorrect and would result if the student mistook the denominator for a minus sign. **Choice C** and **Choice D** are incorrect and may result from conceptual or calculation errors.

20. **Level:** Hard | **Domain:** ALGEBRA
Skill/Knowledge : Systems of two linear equations in two variables | **Testing point:** Working with systems of equations with Infinite solutions

Key Explanation: Equations that have infinite solutions are equations that are the same line just written differently. They have the same slope and the same *y–intercept*.
In the above equation, neither are similar. To

make them similar, multiply the top equation by -2 which yields $-18x + 28y = 6$.
Comparing the coefficients of the first and second equations yields $a = -18$ and $b = -28$.

21. **Level:** Easy | **Domain:** ALGEBRA
Skill/Knowledge: Linear equations in two variables | **Testing point:** Matching coefficients

Key Explanation: Choice D is correct. To find the value of a, we have to first group like terms together.
Adding $4x$ to both sides of the equation yields $3x + 5y + 4x = ax - 4x - by + 4x$
or simply $7x + 5y = ax - by$. This makes $a = 7$ and $b = -5$

Distractor Explanation: Choice A is incorrect because this would be the value of a if the $-4x$ had been ignored
Choice B is incorrect and may result from conceptual or calculation error.
Choice C is incorrect because this would be the value of b instead.

22. **Level:** Easy | **Domain:** ALGEBRA
Skill/Knowledge: Linear inequalities in one or two variables | **Testing point:** Solving for x in an inequality

Key Explanation: Choice D is correct. Using the distributive property yields $3x + 2 < -5x - 30$. Adding $5x$ and subtracting 2 from both sides of the equation yields $3x + 5x < -30 - 2$ or $8x < -32$. Dividing 8 from both sides of the equation yields $x < -4$. Since -5 is less than -4, then it is a solution to the inequality.

Distractor Explanation: Choice A and **Choice B** are incorrect because they are both greater than -4. **Choice C** is incorrect because the value of x must be less than and not equal to -4.